29 September 1977

George Perry has written and edited several books, including *The Penguin Book of Comics* and *The Films of Alfred Hitchcock*. He was the co-author of *A Competitive Cinema*, a study of the economics of the British film industry. He is a journalist, and currently assistant editor of the Sunday Times Magazine.

George Perry

The Great British
Picture Show

From the nineties to the seventies

Paladin

Granada Publishing Limited
Published in 1975 by Paladin
Frogmore, St Albans, Herts AL2 2NF

First published in Great Britain by
Hart-Davis, MacGibbon 1974
Copyright © George Perry 1974
Made and printed in Great Britain by
Richard Clay (The Chaucer Press) Ltd
Bungay, Suffolk
Set in Monotype Ehrhardt

This book is sold subject to the condition that it
shall not, by way of trade or otherwise, be lent,
re-sold, hired out or otherwise circulated
without the publisher's prior consent in any
form of binding or cover other than that in
which it is published and without a similar
condition including this condition being imposed
on the subsequent purchaser.
This book is published at a net price and is
supplied subject to the Publishers Association
Standard Conditions of Sale registered under the
Restrictive Trade Practices Act, 1956.

Contents

Acknowledgements

The idea for a history of the British cinema came from the late Tony Richardson, shortly after he set up Paladin Books. My thanks are also due to Paul Mayersberg for his constant advice and encouragement, John Kobal for most of the stills in this book, the staff of the British Film Institute and the National Film Archive, Fred Zentner of the Cinema Bookshop whose help in tracking down rare printed matter has been invaluable, various companies whose lineage includes some of the past great trade names in the British film industry, Fox-Rank Ltd, MGM-EMI Ltd, Columbia-Warner Ltd, Cinema International Corporation Ltd and others. I must thank Ann Wallace for typing most of the manuscript and Catherine Gurr, who typed the index.

There is a bibliography of books on the British cinema on page 340. The most important are Rachel Low's compendious four-volume history, the PEP Report of 1952, Charles Oakley's *Where We Came In*, Denis Gifford's magnificent and monumental *British Film Catalogue* and Alan Wood's study *Mr Rank*, 1952 but there are many others that are of interest. It should be added that *Cinema TV Today* and its antecedent journals provided much valuable source material.

Introduction

Speak of the French cinema and immediately there springs to mind a quality as hard to define as it is to imitate. Even if the film-makers are poles apart in intention and approach, as disparate in time and style as say Feuillade and Godard, somehow we can sense the essential Frenchness of their work. That same robust uniqueness also characterizes the Italian and the Swedish cinema. Is the British cinema comparable in achievement, or must it be dismissed as merely the product of a Hollywood satellite? In other words, is the British cinema worth regarding seriously, and if it is are there recognizable threads of style relating the earliest pioneering to the films of today?

Any examination in detail of the British contribution to the motion picture reveals a disappointing diminution in its importance since the remarkable pioneering period which lasted from the last decade of the nineteenth century to around 1906. Certainly, in spite of constantly recurring crises throughout its long history, British film output has never fallen as low as that of France during the Occupation, but on a qualitative level it has trailed behind. The number of world-renowned figures produced by Britain is few, and most are actors and actresses fortunate enough in voice or physique to claim attention on either side of the Atlantic. The number of internationally regarded 'pantheon' directors is minute while creators on the level of Hitchcock and Chaplin have become almost totally identified with the American cinema. The domestic industry has never been adequate to sustain its most promising talents and the handful of internationally respected British directors, such as Victor Saville, David Lean, Carol Reed and John Schlesinger, have achieved that status as much for their work in America or for American companies as for their earlier, entirely British-based films, many of which failed to get an adequate distribution in the transatlantic market.

The granting of social respectability was unnaturally delayed for the cinema in Britain. America, with business acumen conquering narrow-minded literary and theatrical snobbism, readily embraced the new medium of films, once it had been established as a commercial reality. Even in the fevered days of the film's infancy, the American cinema was able to make an enduring artistic contribution, both in the epic masterpieces of D. W. Griffith on the one hand, and the unsurpassed level of comic vitality displayed by Keaton, Lloyd, Chaplin, Sennett and other great clowns of the silent era on the other. In France, an acceptance of experimentation and expressionism did not necessarily run counter to the traditions of the intellectual establishment and film provided a new medium for avant-garde invention, even if the early buffooneries of Méliès offered ingenious trickery and music-hall slapstick rather than high art. But Méliès was left behind by such talents as Clair, Pagnol, Vigo, Renoir, Carné and Bunuel, all somehow surmounting the usual commercial difficulties that impeded progress.

In Britain, when films arrived, the theatrical world was that of Wilde, Shaw and Pinero, and the stage play had achieved, after more than two centuries of cultural neglect in the wake of Puritanism, its highest level of respectability. Suspicious as ever of change, the British allowed the cinema to develop in a hole-in-the-corner manner with magistrates, in their constant quest for scapegoats for social evils, eagerly attaching blame for petty crime on addiction to the darkened movie halls. Despairingly the film-makers sought spurious respectability by luring their actors and directors from the theatres. Such transitions were not always happy – a screen performance could seriously impair a reputation. Much more distressing, however, was the effect on the films themselves, for many were merely photographed stage plays, boringly presented and absurdly over-acted.

Excessive theatricality was for many years a hallmark of the British film. In America not only was the cinema to discover the wide open spaces, but it was also to put a whole continent between the theatres of the east and the studios of the west. In Britain, on the other hand, the cosy scale of the country led to the grouping of the major film studios in and around the capital so that an actor could film all day and appear on the West End boards in the evening. Such moonlighting is still common today, much to the amazement of Americans, who not only recognize a distinction between stage and screen acting but also believe in a single-minded dedication to one form or the other during the run of a play or the production of a film. The actor who appears exclusively in films is far more rare in Britain than in America although the most distinguished members of the profession

– Gielgud, Scofield, Richardson – rarely desert the stage to perform on the screen. Within the British cultural establishment the theatre is still regarded as superior to the film. For years the Arts Council has quite rightly supported the theatre, but only towards the end of the 1960s was any government support forthcoming for the setting-up of regional equivalents of the National Film Theatre, and subsequent policy has not been conspicuously constructive.

On a business level it would appear that the film industry in Britain has been remarkably lucky to have survived at all. Throughout its whole seventy-five years or so it has stumbled from crisis to crisis, prey to political folly on the one hand and semi-fraudulent wheeler-dealing on the other. So often the industry has been flat on its back, awaiting rape, and then disagreeably surprised when the violation has taken place. Even in its period of greatest acclaim the effects of war and a crippling entertainments tax kept the fruits of its success tantalizingly at bay and robbed the industry of a chance to consolidate at a time when the will was there.

Can, then, a definable character be found in the British cinema? It is tempting and easy to produce a rapid generalization. The British cinema's diffidence, its punch-pulling, its polite avoidance of controversy have something in common with the national character. Passion and anger are rare; if an attack has to be made it is often with satire and irony as the chosen weapons. To some tastes the British cinema is prissy, mealy-mouthed and sycophantic. The hierarchical social structure persists in the cinema, as in other industries, with a management and shop-floor distinction, in spite of the egalitarian atmosphere of film-making. Directors tend to be recruited from the middle class and even when they speak with a radical voice the accent is that of Repton rather than Runcorn. In the post-1945 period when the first Labour Government with a working majority was pushing British society through the great transformation that produced the welfare state, the best comments the cinema could make were Asquith's *While the Sun Shines*, a farce on the wartime liberalizing of the peerage, Launder and Gilliatt's *Captain Boycott*, an insipid account of an Irish landowner in Victorian times getting his desserts, and the Boultings' *The Guinea Pig*, which was about a grammar-school boy finding his way in an ancient public school. Two of these three films were originally stage successes and all show a middle-class preoccupation with inherited institutions and values. Although this list is selective, where were the truly radical films that had a message of hope, despair or even approval? Should Powell and Pressburger's admirable and thoughtful *A Matter of Life and Death* really be regarded as an allegory of Britain under socialism, as Raymond Durgnat* has argued, and if so, was not the conceit somewhat obscure, since it eluded every major critic of the time?

Almost without exception the film-makers of the 1940s had respectable middle-class backgrounds and as often as not public-school educations. For all their left-wing sympathies, the Boultings, Anthony Asquith (son of a Liberal Prime Minister) and Carol Reed held a very remote view of the working class. If the lower orders intruded into the film they were treated whimsically as in *Passport to Pimlico*, patronizingly as in countless war films where the real action with the officers is punctuated by glimpses of comic cockney stokers below decks, or ineptly as in such adapted stage successes as *No Room at the Inn* or *Good Time Girl*. Significantly, a success of 1950 was *The Blue Lamp*, hailed as a triumph of realistic, documentary-like portrayal of common life. In fact it was a eulogistic tribute to the police, excellently written by an ex-special constable, later to spawn an unctuous, sentimentalized television series about the friendly neighbourhood copper.

Several pressures prevented films from adopting more radical social positions in that period. Foremost was the industry's fear and suspicion of involvement in controversy, part of the entrenched belief that the public went to the cinema in order to be entertained, not to think. But behind this was the repressive form of censorship imposed at that time by the British Board of Film Censors. Attacks on the establishment were not only discouraged, they were actively forbidden. It would have been equally unthinkable to make a film about police corruption or brutality or criticize any contemporary institution. It is hard in the 1970s to appreciate just how restrictive the pressures were. Social criticism, at least of things British, tended to be retrospective. Hence the flurry of historical costume pieces. It was all right to discuss the bad behaviour of the Victorians (*Captain Boycott*, *Great Expectations*, *Oliver Twist*, *Esther Waters*, *Hungry Hill* and many others). Today the climate is very different. Some of the credit is due to television, which, for all its shortcomings, provided a platform for a genuinely democratic dramatic idiom. Any episode of the eternal Salford soap opera, *Coronation Street*, displays a feeling for speech, manner and background far in advance of the average British film of twenty-five years ago. The traffic has been two-way and the realistic

* Raymond Durgnat, *A Mirror for England*, Faber, 1970.

approach of such films as *Kes* or *Poor Cow* owe much to television, not least being the training of their directors. Open discussion of once forbidden topics has led to the removal of old taboos and relaxed the restrictions on subject matter. The television impact of the original *Z-Cars* series in 1962 and dramatized documentaries such as *Cathy Come Home* has made its mark in the cinema.

But the change had begun earlier. Towards the end of the fifties, when the age of rationing had been replaced by the age of affluence and the trauma of Suez had registered in the British psyche as the final outburst of the now defunct imperialist tradition, a new mood began to seep into the cinema, urged on by the advent of the English Stage Company at the Royal Court Theatre. *Room at the Top* was a considerably over-rated film, conventional in its plot treatment and paper-thin in its characterization, but it was based on a sour, celebrated first novel by John Braine, a disgruntled Northern librarian and one of a group of young writers labelled by the press as 'angry young men'. It was regarded as the harbinger of a new approach to film-making, breaking one of the old censorship taboos by showing that the woman had actually enjoyed her orgasm (for that matter admitting that she had had one). The film coincided with the upsurge of discontent with Britain's direction, distaste for the Macmillan brand of Tory *laissez-faire* and anxiety over nuclear involvement which produced the CND and the Aldermaston marches. *Room at the Top*, with its opportunist hero screwing the establishment of his northern town and the mill-owner's daughter, provided a readily identifiable index of reaction for the suburban filmgoer. Many of the films that followed were more successful in exploiting this mood (*Saturday Night and Sunday Morning, The Loneliness of the Long-Distance Runner* and *Billy Liar*) but all had in common the reawakened hero who, far from being a nice boy, is compelled to protest against his society before its enveloping tentacles submerge his personality in sterile conformity. There is nothing specially new about this figure, for he was familiar in the French cinema years before. Indeed, it was the impetus of the *nouvelle vague*, particularly the two best-known early examples, Godard's *A Bout de Soufle* and Truffaut's *Les Quatre Cent Coups*, both of 1959, which provided the obvious prototypes for a new generation of British directors. In British films this new hero was remarkably fresh. A decade earlier even such an impassioned rebel figure as Johnny in Carol Reed's *Odd Man Out* (1947) showed leanings towards gentility in his attitudes towards the Church and the heroine.

But the modern culture hero is the figure acutely defined by Herbert Marcuse in *Eros and Civilization*: '... the trickster and (suffering) rebel against the gods, who creates culture at the price of perpetual pain. He symbolizes productiveness, the unceasing effort to master life; but, in his productivity, blessing and curse, progress and toil are inextricably entwined.'* Hence the final torment of Arthur Seaton in *Saturday Night and Sunday Morning*, hurling his last defiant stone at the housing estate to which he will be enchained for the rest of his life.

The change that British films underwent during the 1960s accorded with the general relaxation of artistic constraints in other fields – a process assumed to have been precipitated by the *Lady Chatterley* trial of 1960. The ancient office of Lord Chamberlain was abolished; this official had, since the reign of Charles II, imposed a censorship on the theatre and the absurdity of his later decisions was a frequent subject for ribald press comment. Only the cinema now retains a fully imposed machinery of censorship, and, while it is fair to say that during the period of John Trevelyan's secretaryship a considerable liberalization occurred, it is also true that in its present form the British Board of Film Censors is anachronistic and over-protective. The multiplication of cinema clubs and other methods of evading censorship has tended to promote the very voyeuristic attitudes that the Board attempted to eliminate. The comparative freedom of television, even its ability to show films originally given 'X' certificates to family audiences, is a frequent irritant.

The promise of the Woodfall school of film-making which produced *A Taste of Honey*, *Saturday Night and Sunday Morning*, *The Entertainer* and others was not sustained and the industrial and commercial obstacles are now so formidable that it is hard for certain directors with acknowledged and even envied reputations abroad to set up films in their home country. If it is hard for them, there is little hope for promising newcomers. Those who have established a bridgehead in films have tended to arrive via television, the whipping boy for most of the economic ailments that have undermined the film business. Yet for al' that, television is a training ground offering the most important of elements in a young career, an appreciative audience. While the pace, editing and ear of the cinema has been greatly influenced by the junior medium, there is an inbuilt resistance to the adoption of television techniques, and as far as technological development is concerned the

* Herbert Marcuse, *Eros and Civilization*, Routledge, 1955.

cinema is extraordinarily backward, the industry preserving an entrenched interest in the equipment and methods employed a quarter of a century ago. This particular form of conservatism is by no means alien to the American cinema as well, where there is also a tendency to permit flexibility at a price so high that it defeats the purpose. What has been proved, not just by the underground film-makers but by the persistence and tireless energy of devotees such as Kevin Brownlow, Christopher Mason and Barney Platts-Mills, is that it is possible to make films without the mammoth crews and bulky equipment insisted upon in mainstream film-making. Such truths were discerned many years ago in European countries, but Wardour Street has always liked to behave like a third-rate imitation of Sunset Boulevard. Rigidity, lack of imagination and stereotyped thinking have driven many talents out of Britain or, worse still, out of the industry altogether.

Part of the failure of the British cinema to achieve an independent stature is undoubtedly due to the accident of a shared language with the United States. American influence and domination of the distribution companies in Britain have led to the dichotomy of British production. On the one hand American companies have regarded Britain as an American out-station, a place in which to make films with considerably lower overheads than in California with an English-language market of a useful size. The results, made with stars and directors acceptable on both sides of the Atlantic, are often indistinguishable from the native American film, even if they qualify under Board of Trade definition as British. The favourable terms of Eady money did much to encourage this type of film, which at least kept studios open and technicians in work. But the financing of such films was bound to be superior to that of the completely British product, largely because the market potential in Britain is too small to produce a profit return on anything more than the most modestly budgeted production. The second factor, seemingly in contradiction, is that of quota. From the time when the quota was first applied its benefits carried a string. The 'quota quickies' of the thirties may have kept people in work, but they did little to generate enthusiasm for British films, and until the Second World War they were, with few exceptions, notorious for their shoddy and vapid values. Even with the much reduced output of recent years something of the 'quickie' atmosphere persists in the supporting feature area of suburban programmes, which so often consist of unctuous sponsored documentaries, rejected television pilots and, until recently, cheaply produced 'B' pictures, in spite of the wealth of worthwhile short features denied circuit screen-space.

Blame can certainly be attached to the system. The coalescence of exhibition power into two main groups, the favour of one being essential if the producers wish to see their money back, led to a release pattern unduly rigid in comparison with that of other countries and placed an unnaturally high onus on the qualities of caution, safety and dullness. Stories such as the initial rejection, by both circuits, of *Tom Jones*, later a record-breaking hit at the box-office, are too numerous to be laughed off. The defence by the exhibitors that they are in business to provide what people want to see sets up its own vicious circle – the public sees what it is offered, until they are too apathetic to bother any more, and another once-flourishing cinema becomes a bingo hall or a supermarket. The realization that there are ways to improve the conditions in which films are shown came very late in the day for both Rank and ABC, and the flurry of cinema reconstructions, twinnings, triplings and entertainment complexes that peeled off the drawing-boards in the late 1960s and early 1970s may not succeed in re-educating a public already lost to other diversions. That television, for all its pulpy ratings-fodder, can reach monumentally sized audiences with serious documentaries and even avant-garde continental films shunned by the exhibitors when they first became available demonstrates that, with the right conditioning, audience taste in Britain would have been far higher. What is particularly dispiriting is that ideas circulating years ago are only now beginning to be tried out, long after the crisis point has been reached.

The foregoing observations embody the reasons for the relatively disappointing level of creativity displayed by the British cinema. But it would be unfair to suggest that the story is entirely a downbeat one, or that nothing of any importance has emerged over the years. On the contrary, it is not a difficult task to name many films of high quality which could not possibly have been made by any other country, so British are they in their execution. Even when fashion and mannerisms of the day produce unintentional risability a couple of decades later, quite often the original can still convey the essence, the flavour of a period, and offer the social historian valuable research material. Such side benefits are part of the fascination and singularity of the film medium. A middle-period Humphrey Jennings documentary such as *Listen to Britain* or *Diary for Timothy* offers an insight into the thoughts of ordinary people in wartime far more effectively than many books on the subject. The atmosphere comes across so strongly that a modern viewing is something of an emotional experience in Proustian recollection; there it is, that is exactly how Trafalgar Square looked when the emergency water tanks and National Savings posters cluttered the base of Nelson's column. Again, in a film as finely conceived as Coward and Lean's *Brief Encounter* (1946) the sad, pointless, middle-class love affair, that never reached the point of genuine adultery, is absolutely of its time. Today the couple would have been in bed at the first whistle, and that would have been that, but to students of the *mores* of an earlier generation it offers a fascinating insight into the collective psychology of its day. Those films which made a special virtue of exploring some aspect of English character, particularly the relationship with other nationalities, are very rewarding: for instance, Powell and Pressburger's *Colonel Blimp* (1943), Anthony Asquith's *The Demi-Paradise* (1943) and *The Way to the Stars* (1945), Lean's *This Happy Breed* (1944), Charles Crichton's *Hue and Cry* (1947) and Victor Saville's *South Riding* (1938).

Nor has the British cinema been lacking in ambition, even though Hungarians and Americans have quite often been the catalysts. Korda for *Things to Come* (1936) imported its director from Hollywood, but was nevertheless able to offer an eccentrically British view of salvation through science that could only have originated from the idiosyncratic vision of H. G. Wells. Pascal's *Caesar and Cleopatra* (1945) was, when made, the most expensive film ever, and that fact and the coincidence of the Second World War tended to cause its worth to be undervalued, a fate that certainly did not overtake the equally ambitious *Henry V* (1944). But modesty of scale, intimacy of action and simplicity of plot have always seemed to produce the most satisfaction. On such terms did the Ealing comedies succeed and the British thrillers of Alfred Hitchcock. Even prestigious works such as Lean's *Great Expectations* (1946) and *Oliver Twist* (1948) benefit from a low-key style constantly involving the spectator with the protagonists. An intimate, cosy style is still favoured. As recently as the brief reign of Bryan Forbes when he was in charge of production at Elstree it was interesting to observe that the two most successful of the first half-dozen films had this diminished scale. Either one of them could have been made twenty or more years earlier. One was a charmingly photographed, episodic, classic children's story set in Edwardian Yorkshire against a background of old steam locomotives chuffing through green scenery, *The Railway Children*, and the other was an equally anodyne excursion into the juvenile literature world, *The Tales of Beatrix Potter*, a masked ballet which had Sir Frederick Ashton leaping up and down disguised as Mrs Tiggywinkle. Satisfyingly large audiences followed, offering Wardour Street evidence that blandness and innocuous good taste have the knack of being more profitable than the shocks and unpredictability of a more spontaneous and gutsy film approach. On such foundations the British film has, after a fashion, flourished, but a good name in that area of cinema is better than none at all.

1 The Beginning

No one man was solely responsible for the birth of cinematography. The principle of persistence of vision, on which moving pictures are based, was already known early in the nineteenth century, and in 1824 P. M. Roget presented a paper to the Royal Society which gave a detailed exposition of its effects. Somehow men in several countries were simultaneously moving towards an invention which was to transform the process of communication and provide it with the first new dimension since the earliest practical printing presses of the fourteenth century. Many of the initial pioneers were working with basic principles which are still applicable to film today, although at the time they failed to appreciate their importance; others managed to produce moving pictures of some sort by methods which proved to be technological dead ends, incapable of further development. Still others saw their discoveries pirated and their reputations left unheralded.

Britain was represented at the very gestation of the cinema. Even before the true motion picture had been evolved there were men such as William George Horner (1786–1837), who invented the Zoetrope, a series of pictures mounted inside a drum. When it was revolved these pictures, viewed through slots, merged into one and appeared to move. Another major figure in the cinema's pre-history was Eadweard Muybridge, an Englishman from Kingston-upon-Thames, who in 1877, in California, rigged up a series of cameras to record the successive movements of a galloping horse. From there he moved into detailed analysis of human movements and the resulting pictures were used to illustrate books and lectures. While he was the first person to show successive phases of movement in detail he had no intention of animating the pictures using persistence of vision, and so, like many of the pioneer figures, brilliant as his achievement was he only partially solved the problem.

It took the inspiration of a German, Ottomar Anschütz, to make the connection and to devise an apparatus by which a series of pictures could be viewed in rapid succession, and it was left to a Frenchman, Etienne-Jules Marey, to devise a single camera to record movement, in place of the battery of twenty-four that Muybridge required. With it Marey shot chronophotographs, or pictures on fixed plates, at the rate of twelve a second, and somehow he managed to project them. As early as 1888 he was experimenting with celluloid film. This was a new invention originating from America and which had been successfully exploited by George Eastman, founder of the Eastman Kodak Company.

Another American, the remarkable inventive genius, Thomas Alva Edison, was looking for an improvement for his successful phonograph, a means of adding moving pictures to its lifelike recorded sounds. He entrusted the research work to an assistant, W. Laurie Dickson, at Menlo Park, to whom a great deal of the credit must be given. Dickson devised a camera – the Kinetograph – which used film, 35mm. wide, still the standard gauge of today, with four sprocket holes per frame by which the smooth advance of the film was ensured. The year was 1888. In the following months the camera was put into use and on 6 October 1889 a projection took place at Menlo Park. But Edison at that time eschewed projection as the means of showing off the new invention; instead he built a kind of peepshow machine which he called the Kinetoscope and which contained a fifty-foot loop of film which could be viewed by one person at a time. His dismissal of projection meant that his claim to be the principal inventor of cinematography is severely qualified.

Meanwhile, in England two people of interest were at work. One was a Frenchman, living in Leeds, Louis Le Prince, who in 1888 patented a sixteen-lens camera to take moving pictures and a projector by which to show them. In the following year he was working with a single-lens camera and was using a Maltese-cross type of mechanism, which was to be the basis of the perfected film camera. No man seems to have got nearer to the complete invention than Le Prince. Suddenly in 1890 he disappeared from a train travelling from Dijon to Paris, vanishing, it would seem, from the face of the earth. Nothing was ever heard of him again. The other visionary figure was a London barrister, Wordsworth Donisthorpe, who as early as 1878 had written in *Nature* suggesting the combining of the newly invented phonograph with some form of moving photography. In 1889 he made a camera with W. C. Crofts, and a piece of exposed film showing Trafalgar Square exists in the Kodak Museum. The shape of the frame is circular, but nevertheless it is a notable, if neglected, step in the process of discovery.

Far too much attention, however, has been paid to the efforts of William Friese-Greene. His tombstone at Highgate describes him as 'The Inventor of Kinematography'. This he most certainly was not and the claims that have been made on his behalf are an embarrassment to a nation usually given to undervaluing its men of genius. Friese-Greene was an enthusiastic dabbler who produced many inventions, few of which could be developed beyond the initial idea. Influenced by J. A. R. Rudge, who had brought the magic lantern to a high degree of sophistication with the Biophantascope, Friese-Greene was able to offer even further improvements. He built a camera that was capable of taking up to half a dozen pictures a second – too slow to give a complete illusion of movement. He also produced, in 1889, a camera using celluloid film, but there is no evidence that it worked. It has been claimed that he wrote to Edison giving full details of his mechanism and that the plans were unacknowledged, although Edison's Kinetoscope showed remarkable coincidences. Brian Coe in a studied reassessment of Friese-Greene in the *Photographic Journal* (March–April 1962) convincingly deflated this and many other claims made for him. Friese-Greene never made any financial success from his cinema inventions and drifted through a series of bankruptcies, eventually falling dead after delivering an incoherent speech to a meeting convened in 1921 to consider the prevailing crises in the film industry. All that was in his pockets was the price of an admission ticket. In 1951 his life story was filmed as a special industry contribution to the Festival of Britain and called *The Magic Box*. Unfortunately it was based on the misleading biography by Miss Ray Allister and this helped to perpetuate the myth that he was the main inventor of the medium.

The world's first projected film performance before a paying audience is generally believed to have taken place in the Grand Café, Boulevard des Capucines, Paris, on 28 December 1895, when Louis and Auguste Lumière exhibited a few strips with titles such as *The arrival of a train at the station*. In February 1896 they exhibited their apparatus in London at the Polytechnic Hall in Regent Street. Their mechanisms included a claw movement which drove the film through the projector gate and stopped it momentarily. Within a few weeks they had transferred to the Empire, a theatre in Leicester Square specializing in variety. There a short twenty-minute film programme would appear, sandwiched between such acts as Mademoiselle Marthe Marthy, Eccentric Comedienne, and Belloni and the Bicycling Cockatoo. The Lumière films were simple and direct presentations of often mundane sights, such as workers pouring out of a factory or a ship unloading its cargo. To audiences who had paid to see singers, comedians, jugglers and illusionists the Lumière Cinématographe was an amusing and completely novel insertion in the normal variety bill. At that time expectations for the device were limited and the management could only perceive it as an addition to live theatrical performance.

The year 1896 would seem to signify the real moment of birth for the British cinema. Another inventor of the time, Birt Acres, who although born in Richmond, Virginia, had English parents, devised a comparatively lightweight camera and used it to film the Oxford and Cambridge boat race and the Derby at Epsom in 1895, although it took somewhat longer to work out a means of projecting his pictures. He was the first person to make a motion picture record of a news event. In January 1896 he demonstrated his camera and projector to the Royal Photographic Society. Unlike other pioneers of the period, Acres was not an instinctive showman and preferred to consider the scientific possibilities of the new medium. While the initial success of the Lumière programme at the Empire caused music-hall proprietors throughout the metropolis to book Acres as a supporting attraction, interest in his activities was not sustained and he faded quickly from the scene.

It was in this same year, 1896, that another pioneer began making a major impact. If there has to be a father of the British cinema then Robert William Paul is the man. An optical instrument maker by training, with a workshop in Hatton Garden, he became the first important British film producer. He was also the first Englishman to give a public performance to a paying audience. His initial entry into the business came as a result of Edison's failure to protect his Kinetoscope in Great Britain. Paul copied it and placed fifteen of his own machines on show at Earls Court in 1895. Edison was not pleased by Paul's open piracy of his patent and refused to supply him with Kinetoscope strips for his machines when openly requested. So Paul began making his own material. His first was called simply, *Rough Sea at Dover*. In February 1896, on the same day that the Lumières were having their first showing, he projected some of his films to an audience at Finsbury Technical College. The following month he demonstrated a programme to a paying audience at Olympia. As a result of the interest that his performance aroused he was hired by the Alhambra, another variety theatre on the east side of Leicester Square where the Odeon now stands. Paul filmed the 1896 Derby and showed the result the same night, much to the delight of the Prince of Wales, whose horse Persimmon won the race. He also established a small studio on the roof of the theatre. He was to remain at the Alhambra four years, although his initial engagement was for a mere fortnight. At first, the longest of his films lasted only for a minute and a quarter (eighty feet) although some were half this length. His level of artistic invention was not high and a routine standby to fill out his fifteen-minute programme was the filmed variety turn. Many well-known vaudeville performers were induced before Paul's cameras to give sixty seconds' worth of their stage act. Surprisingly this elementary film exercise was relatively popular. Paul did, however, in 1896 produce the first narrative film to be made in Britain, that is, a film that required actors and a story. Lasting a minute, it was called *The Soldier's Courtship* and had a cast of three – a soldier, a nursemaid and an old lady who interrupts their courting. It was filmed on the Alhambra roof and was the first of many short comedies to be produced in his rooftop studio. The other main part of his output was the topical film, short news items such as ship-launchings, sporting events, royal visits. In 1899 he opened a small studio at Southgate and equipped it with special facilities to produce trick effects, including a trolley-mounted camera at a time when it was normal for cameras to be firmly anchored to one position.

The first film studios were very elementary and most fiction pictures were shot in any location that happened to be handy – waste ground, deserted streets, building sites and so on. One of the first studios in the world and probably the first in Britain was built in 1897 behind the Tivoli in the Strand by the American E. B. Koopman for the Mutoscope and Biograph Company. The chief output was directed towards the Mutoscope slot machines but the company supplied its own projectors for certain music halls and the Palace Theatre in the West End. The whole studio rotated towards the direction of the light in the manner of the famous Edison 'Black Maria' studio in the United States. Paul's studio, however, was a stage with a glass roof and sliding doors in front which could be opened up on fine days. The camera, in the open air, faced the exposed stage which was equipped with wings, traps and scenery just like a theatre stage. This was the usual type of film studio in use at this time. Many were very small. That of Cecil Hepworth, artistically the greatest of the pioneers, which he built in 1898 in his garden at Walton-on-Thames, was only ten feet by six feet.

Hepworth, the son of a well-known magic lantern lecturer, entered the industry in 1896 at the age of twenty-one. He had made and patented a hand-feed arc-lamp for use in projectors and managed to sell half a dozen of them to Robert Paul. Later he bought some old throw-out footage from Paul and ran it through an improvised projector in his basement off the Charing Cross Road. He built up a programme combining film and magic lantern slides and toured the country's lecture halls. His next step was to improve the 'flickerless' projector that Charles Urban, who was to manage Edison's interests in England, had brought from America. Urban was impressed and offered Hepworth a job at Maguire and Baucus, later the Warwick Trading Company, the Edison agents. In 1897 Hepworth published a book called *The ABC of the Cinematograph*, probably the first film handbook. The first film he made was of the Oxford and Cambridge boat race in 1898, but shortly afterwards Urban dismissed him. He then set up a developing and printing business of his own at Walton, which after a few months expanded into film production. The first film was made in 1898 and was called *Express Trains in a Railway Cutting*. It was fifty feet long and was the first of many such subjects that comprised the Hepworth catalogue.

Meanwhile a pioneer group of film-makers was emerging in Brighton. Apart from William Friese-Greene there was Esme Collings, his former partner and a portrait photographer who founded the so-called Brighton school. In 1896 Collings produced some thirty short films but little was heard of him afterwards and he failed to break into the major market. Another Brighton figure was G. A. Smith whose career was more promising. His first films were straightforward actuality shots but at a very early date he had begun experimenting with trick photography, some years ahead of others. In 1900 he ceased production on his own account and joined Warwick Trading where in collaboration with Urban he was to produce his Kinemacolour system. There was also James Williamson, a Hove chemist, who began showing films as an adjunct to his lantern lectures in 1896. He shot his first film in 1897 and began selling them in 1898. Soon he was making fifty short subjects a year. He kept his overheads low by doing nearly everything himself and using his own sons as actors; consequently he was able to make a considerable amount of money. Unfortunately there was little artistic merit in the Brighton output and it was merely a brief interlude for the rapidly developing British film industry which, in comparison with that of other countries, was not only prolific in output but also had an impressive technical lead.

In the earliest period it was customary for the film producer to sell his print outright at so much a foot to whoever wanted to put it on show. The present-day tripartite system of producer, distributor, exhibitor was still some way off. But in 1897 two itinerant showmen, Walker and Turner, began renting their film collection to their colleagues for single showings. It was the beginning of Walturdaw, a name still remembered in Wardour Street.

This arrangement spared the showmen unnecessary expense and the chore of maintaining large stocks of footage, which was on highly inflammable silver nitrate stock. Distribution was a haphazard business and the initiative for renting came from the exhibitors. But there were no exclusive rights at that time and the same film would be on sale as well as on hire. The early renters first bought their films on the open market. It was to be several years before distribution became properly organized.

Exhibition, too, had not settled down to its modern form. At first it was the music halls which included films sandwiched between regular variety acts. But although nearly every town in the country had its own vaudeville theatre, the travelling film men set up their apparatus in church halls, clubs and assembly rooms as well. Some showmen hired a hall for as long as they could get an audience. Empty shops were rented and turned into improvised 'penny gaffs' for film shows. Randall Williams claimed to be the first person to install a travelling booth at a fairground at King's Lynn in 1896 and soon no fair worth the name was without its bioscope. More often than not there would be two or three in keen competition. The usual layout consisted of a large tent fronted by two wagons, the entrance to the booth in the middle. On one side would be a stage from which a barker would harangue the crowds and a pretty girl or two offered further inducements to the potential audience. There would also be a mechanical organ and an engine to work the generator. These structures became more and more elaborate as the shows became increasingly competitive and outside stages became big enough to support whole troupes of dancers.

One of the best-known travelling showmen was Walter Haggar, who besides showing films in his fairground booth also made films of his own and circulated them to other exhibitors. One of the gimmicks employed in the fairs was the promise that local material would be included in the show, and to this end the showmen had their cameras primed and ready for cranking. Haggar later made films that had merit in their own right, such as *The Salmon Poachers*, which sold 480 prints, and *The Life of Charles Peace*. He did much to remove the fairground sideshow image from the cinema, although bioscopes were to persist at funfairs until the First World War, long after the first purpose-built picture houses had appeared.

The French cinema had reached a more rapid maturity than the British, largely due to the emergence of the director of near-genius, Georges Méliès, who as early as 1899 was using the cinema as a medium for narrative fantasy. His training was that of a magician and the cinema offered him a fresh and abundant scope for magic. Eventually it was to be his limitation, but for a time he exerted a considerable influence on British film-makers such as Paul and Smith, who although already accomplished in cinematic trickery found Méliès's work immensely stimulating. Other Frenchmen who were to become important in Britain were two businessmen, Léon Gaumont, whose company opened an office in Cecil Court in 1898, and later Charles Pathé who was to set up a production company in England. Gaumont in Britain was run by Colonel A. C. Bromhead and eventually started producing pictures as well as distributing them. By the early 1900s the number of films handled by the company in a year was over a hundred.

As the subject matter of films began to depart from the simple portrayal of movement towards something resembling a story, so the taste of audiences improved and they began to demand more for their entertainment. It was a good time for the newsreels – there had been the Boer War and the departure of innumerable troopships, to say nothing of footage from Africa itself. There had been the death of the old Queen, the first royal funeral in history to be observed by movie cameras, recording the scene for all time. There were the first car races, including the Gordon Bennett, filmed by Hepworth. There was the Coronation of Edward VII.

Meanwhile there were story films such as Williamson's *Fire*, 280 feet in length, with five scenes and part of the stock tinted red for heightened realism. In 1903 an important film came from America from the Edison Company. It was a western, *The Great Train Robbery*, directed by Edwin S. Porter. It was ten minutes long and developed a plot in several scenes, the first time that a film had been given the luxury of a proper story line. Its impact on the whole film world was powerful.

Hepworth expanded his running times. His *Alice in Wonderland* consisted of sixteen scenes carefully based on the Tenniel illustrations and reaching a length of 800 feet. In 1904 Hepworth broke with his partner, H. V. Lawley, shortly before making the most famous of his films, *Rescued by Rover*. It was the first Hepworth film to use professional actors, although the baby was a young Hepworth and the dog belonged to the director, who also played the harassed father. The professionals were the two baby-stealers. The film cost £7 13s. 9d. to make, which included half-guinea fees for the performances of the actors. It ran for seven minutes – not by any means remarkable in that respect, for Hepworth's own *Falsely Accused*, made earlier, was twice as long. What made *Rescued by Rover* different from its predecessors were its pace and the care of its editing which were quite new to the cinema. It was a great success commercially, selling a total of 395 prints. One of the peculiarities of success was that the film had to be remade, and remade again, because the original negatives wore out through repeated printing in an effort to catch up with the demand.

Hepworth's London office was in Cecil Court, off Charing Cross Road, where Warwick, Gaumont and other film companies had their offices. The little pedestrian thoroughfare became known as 'Flicker Alley', and it was the first headquarters of the film industry. The move westwards to Wardour Street came later. Today the last link with Cecil Court's part in the early history of the cinema is the presence of an employment agency specializing in film jobs.

The early days were characterized by a free-booting, buccaneering spirit – there were no established rules to obey and each film-maker was at liberty to devise his own way of doing things. There were no precedents, nor were there big organizations with specialist departments to create a procedural mystique. The early directors had to be able to write their screenplays, paint the scenery, crank the camera and even act. A large number of them had got into the business in order to cash in on what seemed to be a lucrative craze. There was no artistic ambition or desire to produce work of lasting value.

Much of the actuality material made during the first ten years has an intrinsic historical merit which divorces it from the motives operating when it was initially produced. But the story films in which made-up situations are presented are for the most part feeble and banal, even allowing for the technical immaturity of the period. That audiences could be induced to watch a programme consisting of badly acted, unimaginatively photographed and dismally constructed films alongside the work of Méliès and Hepworth, which gained wide distribution, is hard to conceive; but it was a time when the attraction of novelty still held and critical judgement was not at a premium.

Obviously, it was not a situation that would persist, and by 1906 changes in the presentation of moving pictures were beginning to take effect. The cinema was ceasing to be only a fairground entertainment to catch the passing crowd. An audience of regulars was starting up, albeit a fairly unintelligent one which would have found playgoing beyond its capacity, both financially and intellectually.

2 Dawn Comes

Hales Tours was an enterprise in Oxford Street, London, in 1906. It was a variation on the showmanship tradition in which the cinema has its roots. At sixpence a time members of the public sat in a bogus railway train which rocked and swayed, while a screen at the front of the coach offered a view of filmed scenery flashing past. This device could pull in a thousand people a day and it inspired several competitors. The idea of mounting a camera on the front of a locomotive to record a train's progress was by no means new – in fact such films had been a staple product since the beginning. But at last an attempt had been made to relate the presentation to the subject matter and to break out from the music hall, lantern lecture and fairground format.

It was the start of a rash of converted shops, roller rinks and other buildings into film theatres. Penny gaffs sprouted all over the country, doing little to enhance the reputation of the cinema, since many of them were dirty and flea-ridden and the standards of projection often appalling. Colonel Bromhead of Gaumont had opened one seating 100 people, the Daily Bioscope in Bishopsgate, as early as 1904, although it did not remain in business very long. In America the Bijou theatre was already becoming a feature of exhibition, but Britain, probably because of the stronger fairground interests, was slower to follow. It is difficult to say for certain which was the first exclusive film theatre in this country, but Miss Rachel Low advances the claim of the Balham Empire, which was offering a two-hour programme in the middle of 1907. Nevertheless, as the same time the fairground shows were at their peak, Hull Fair for instance having no less than eight bioscopes in operation simultaneously. The Bijou type of theatre, seating about 300 people on padded seats, with a pianist, or sometimes two or three musicians providing an accompaniment, began to make its appearance from about 1908 onwards. The new gentility, with its

29

scented atmosphere, potted ferns and fluted columns, was a deliberate attempt to elevate the social status of film shows which had been given a tarnished reputation by the sleazy penny gaffs.

It was at about this time that the film circuit was born. In 1908 there were three exhibiting companies with £110,000 capital. Two years later there were 295 with £3,035,951 capital. One of the first in the field was Electric Theatres, which at the end of 1908 had five theatres running a continuous seventy-five minute programme and charging an admission of threepence per head. Provincial Cinematograph Theatres was an important early circuit, founded in 1909 with the intention of operating a film theatre in every town with a population of 250,000 or more. Its formation could be said to have been the birth of the Rank Organization, for many years later it was the oldest film company to be absorbed by that behemoth of the British film industry. As buildings and equipment improved so costs rose and the difference between the cheapjack penny gaffs and the new picture palaces became more apparent, particularly as the former were forced to rely on outdated and outworn programme material. Consequently by about 1910 the penny gaffs were dead, although their reputation was unfortunately to live on.

Changes occurred, too, in distribution, which was forced to become more rational. The old open-market system, whereby a film was sold outright for sixpence a foot, regardless of content, was still widely in use, although obviously archaic and fraught with peril from unscrupulous 'dumpers'. A disadvantage of the system was that it standardized the producer's return, no matter how much effort he put into the picture, an unnecessary fetter on creativeness. Rental charges were based on the selling charges, and the rental reduced on each successive hiring as the quality of the print deteriorated. The film exchange came into being as a means by which exhibitors could pool their resources and lower their costs. If a film was very popular hundreds of prints might be made and sold or rented, but the consequence would be that a given district was then saturated and there was no monopoly. The exclusive rental was still unheard of. Pricecutting and dumping went on fiercely until its climax when Pathé, responsible for one in five of every film distributed in Britain, slashed their sale prices from sixpence to fourpence a foot, forcing everyone else to do the same. Colonel Bromhead is said to have initiated the system of exclusive booking contracts whereby the highest bidder could be sure of not having the same film shown in the same area by his rival, but it was to be several years before the open-market system was to disappear completely.

Not only was the industry itself beginning to recognize the need for rationalization, it also realized that some of the self-imposed restraints would require the force of law. Consequently the first Cinematograph Films Act, which arose from a bill introduced by Herbert Gladstone, the Home Secretary of the time, was generally welcomed by the trade. It was felt that official recognition by Parliament would ease difficult relationships which were developing with certain local authorities. These had arisen through the lack of standard practice in the enforcement of existing regulations concerning safety measures, staffing and general conditions. When the Cinematograph Act became law in January 1910 it was realized, too late, that undesirable as the previous free-for-all had been there were now the beginnings of a dangerous degree of official interference in the film business.

The most controversial interpretation concerned the clause dealing with the safety of audiences in the event of fire. Instead of reading the Act to relate specifically to physical safety, certain authorities extended the ambiguous language to embrace moral responsibility for an audience's well-being, and this could mean the power to endorse or prescribe film programmes. The London County Council decided to license cinemas in the same way as music halls, and banned Sunday performances. The courts maintained this procedure in spite of arguments that it was not the purpose of the Act. One magistrate at Tower Bridge dismissed a summons against a Sunday exhibitor on the grounds that the London County Council was acting *ultra vires* in their interpretation of the new regulations. The LCC appealed and managed to get the judgement reversed. There was a climate of opinion in the country that the film industry was reprehensible, and responsible for the decline in moral standards. Pontifications from magistrates when delinquents blamed the cinema for providing the cue for their misdeeds expressed the growing public concern. Crude and gruesome posters outside cinemas exacerbated the feelings of an outraged section, but the showman's insistence on profaning Sunday with money-making was probably the last straw. Britain was sufficiently close to the age of Victoria to be still thoroughly imbued with sabbatarian virtues and the more important issues of safety, at a time when reels of highly inflammable film used to spill out around the projectionist's feet and when appalling deaths frequently occurred throughout the world as a result of fire, were relegated to the background as controversy raged over the local authorities' right to prevent Sunday opening. As far as the trade was concerned Sunday was a night of good takings. The solution was an absurd compromise – that Sunday opening would be permitted, provided that the takings be given to charity. Some exhibitors accepted this odd and penal condition, and kept their cinemas open. But the authorities found that although it was easy to pass the law, its enforcement was a very different matter.

The other major trade problem of the late Edwardian period was the relationship between the producers and the exhibitors, with the distributors now emerging as uneasy middlemen. The producers blamed renters and exhibitors for showing films for too long, thus killing the market for new products. The film-makers wanted films to be withdrawn after a certain period, but because they had in most cases relinquished all rights by selling the prints on the open market it was difficult for them to have any say in what subsequently happened. Boycotts and other measures were used as sanctions with little success. It was during this period of militancy that industrial organizations sprang into existence – the Kinematograph Film Makers' Association in 1907, the Association of Film Renters in 1910 and the Cinematograph Exhibitors' Association in 1912. The projectionists, too, formed a union, after being refused membership of the Variety Artists Federation in 1907. This was the National Association of Cinematograph Operators (initially the Bioscope Operators' Association) and it sought a minimum wage and certificates of proficiency. However, it was difficult to get more than a handful of the operators all over the country to join. Efforts were made to write into the Cinematograph Act clauses which would enforce a minimum standard of skill for projectionists, and a licensing system for them, so that incompetence and mishandling of films could be rooted out. It was unsuccessful and for several years afterwards indifferent projection standards were a further hazard to the general acceptance of the cinema as an artistic medium.

British film production was already lagging behind that of France and Italy in Europe, and America, largely as a result of the premature retirement, lack of interest or disillusionment of many of the pioneers who had earlier given the industry a lead over its rivals. In 1910 Pathé dominated the market and gave France a share of 36 per cent of all the films released in Britain. America came next with 28 per cent, then Italy with 17 per cent. Britain was responsible for only 15 per cent. What was even more depressing about the British contribution was that the films themselves were not markedly better than those of a few years earlier, whereas the American products, for instance, were constantly improving. The British industry tended to be complacent and unambitious, and spent far too much time in local squabbles instead of developing overseas markets. The Americans had a massive home market and were thus able to inject greater profits into their film output. Britain, on the other hand, desperately needed extensive overseas outlets if it hoped to rival American standards. That such markets were not forthcoming is a matter of regret, for already, more than sixty years ago, a pattern of decline and crisis had been established, a theme that recurs with frequency throughout the entire life of the British cinema. It is a widely held belief that Britain maintained a dominant position until the First World War, then relinquished the lead to the Americans who were not otherwise engaged. Such thinking is a chauvinistic fallacy; the truth is that the battle was lost before 1910.

In America a patents war had raged from the very beginning when Edison first registered his Kinetoscope. Its climax came in 1908 when ten major companies came together and formed the Motion Picture Patents Company with the avowed purpose of monopolizing the industry. Pathé and Méliès in France were also included, although Britain was excluded. Independent producers had either to pay a licence fee or work clandestinely. In 1910 the Patents Company formed the General Film Company which was to be the sole distributor of films in the United States. Foreign competition was ruthlessly put down. All film exchanges were closed except for that of William Fox, who fought the Trust. A counter-move was the formation of the International Projecting and Producing Company in 1909 to which many English producers belonged and which arranged for importation of films at half a cent a foot, the same terms offered by the Patents Trust. However, British distribution prospects in the United States were hopelessly damaged. The Patents Company was finally put out of business by a Federal Court ruling in 1915, long after its influence had been corroded by the emergence of a band of outstanding independent producers like Adolph Zukor and Carl Laemmle who formed the International Motion Picture Company (IMP).

One of the methods Laemmle used to beat the Trust was the invention of the 'star' system in 1909. Until then the performers had been anonymous even though their faces became familiar through repetition and thus built up fan followings. Anonymity meant low salaries. Laemmle gambled by billing Florence Lawrence, the hitherto un-

33

known name of the 'Imp' girl, whom he had lured from Biograph, a Trust company, where she had been known as the 'Biograph' girl. The public was delighted and the independents found a weapon with which to battle the Patents Company, by enticing away their actors and actresses. But inevitably it was to lead to drastically higher costs.

The star system appeared in Britain in 1910. It meant that not only would film performers be named but that their personalities and private lives would be exploited for publicity. It is extraordinary that the notion had not occurred to film producers earlier in view of the fact that the regular appearance of an anonymous performer could create great public interest. The first stars to be acclaimed in Britain were Americans including Florence Lawrence. But Hepworth and others started to build up their own performers. The first true English star was Gladys Sylvani who appeared in Hepworth films, the most outstanding being *Rachel's Sin* in 1911.

The Hepworth Company had, in common with most British companies in the early part of this period, suffered a decline. For a time all production activities at Walton ceased. A fire destroyed the studio in 1907 and Hepworth moved into the business of importing foreign films. It was a black day when the best of Britain's film-makers was reduced to this. Robert Paul's production record became increasingly sparse in the same period and by 1910 it ceased altogether, when he returned to his original business as an optical instrument manufacturer. G. A. Smith had also turned more and more to scientific experimentation and eventually quit the commercial world.

One of the men who did not drop out and who managed to prosper in this period was Charles Urban, an American who had emigrated a decade earlier to look after the Edison interests. He established his own company in 1903 and in 1907 amalgamated with Eclipse, a French firm he had also founded. The Charles Urban Trading Company distributed the Vitagraph output from America, and thus, with narrative films made by the French company, and travelogues and actualities produced by the English side of the business, his attack on the market was multi-pronged. One of Urban's outstanding producers was Percy Smith, one of the first men to exploit stop-motion techniques for scientific purposes. He photographed growing plants a frame at a time over a period of days so that the film, when projected at the normal speed, showed a speeded-up version of the life cycle. Urban was also a colour pioneer, being responsible for patenting G. A. Smith's two-colour process, Kinemacolour, in 1905. After Urban's impressive new premises in Wardour Street had been opened in 1908 colour films became very popular, in spite of the fact that a special projector was needed for the process. Subjects that had a touch of pageantry were filmed, the best known being the Delhi Durbar in 1910, and eventually colour was used for drama films. Unfortunately Urban attempted to establish a monopoly with his system, granting extremely restrictive licences for showing the films. Consequently there was an unsatisfied public demand and competitors stepped into the field, either using stencil processes or coming as close as they dared to actually pirating Urban's patent. His monopoly was finally ended in 1914 after a court decision went against him.

At roughly the same time W. G. Barker was earning a great reputation for showmanship and enterprise. His start in films had been through topical subjects, having been the managing director of Warwick before branching out on his own in 1909. He built a studio at Ealing and began to film some very ambitious projects. He persuaded Sir Herbert Tree and his company to appear in *Henry VIII*, paying the then astronomical fee of £1,000 to the actor knight. It was the first major film version of an established stage production in England. It lasted for an hour, an unprecedented length since the trade at the time believed that it was impossible to sustain an audience's interest with a single subject for such a period. He announced that all copies of the film would be publicly burnt six weeks after release, thus sending the price soaring. It was one of the first examples of exclusive film renting, although the method by which it was achieved was undoubtedly questionable. It did, however, focus attention on one of the disgraces of the film business, the circulation of tired prints. Barker's output tended to be enthusiastically patriotic, biased towards episodes from British history. He was alleged to have reaped a profit of £35,000 from his filmed biography of Queen Victoria, *Sixty Years a Queen*. His Ealing stock company was advertised with pride as 'all-British' although it was an uphill fight in a business now beginning to feel the impact of the world's sweetheart, Mary Pickford, and other Hollywood headliners. Barker was a grandiose but not an artistic film-maker and subtlety was not one of his virtues. But at an early date he was manipulating vast numbers of extras and bravely tackling subjects on an epic level.

The year 1911 marked the beginning of a mild renaissance. Hepworth, rising to the challenge offered by the foreign films he was distributing, decided to return to production in order to match and improve the quality. *Rachel's Sin* with Gladys Sylvani was the turning point. Hepworth was a careful film-maker, striving after technical excellence. His work was consistently characterized by tact and modesty which sometimes seemed dull compared with the flamboyance of Barker. His films also reflected a sense of national pride, but it was a reserved Englishness, calm and respectable rather than heroic and swashbuckling. He built Chrissie White and Alma Taylor into stars in a series of comedies, and he made Ivy Close, winner of a *Daily Mirror* beauty competition, an important name in the cinema. She was the mother of a baby who was to become a well-known director three decades later, Ronald Neame. Hepworth also made money by renting his rebuilt and well-equipped studios at Walton to other production companies.

Dr Ralph Tennyson Jupp, founder of Provincial Cinematograph Theatres, entered production in 1913 with a company called London Films, which had its studio in the Middlesex suburb of Twickenham. He was the first man to work out a policy of vertical integration, combining the functions of producer, distributor and exhibitor under one umbrella. The company's successful launching resulted from Jupp's very un-English willingness to seek financial and artistic support from America. Harold Shaw and George Loane Tucker were engaged as directors, both from Carl Laemmle's Imp studios. The first release was an adaptation of Sir Arthur Conan Doyle's *Rodney Stone* entitled *The House of Temperley*, a film which was highly profitable. The infusion of American talent was the subject of considerable criticism, but then, as subsequently, the survival of the British film industry was to a very great extent due to the interest that American film producers took in it. London Films maintained the high standard achieved by the first production. Unusually for this period, feature films represented their entire output.

By now the film industry had been in existence long enough for a new supply of trained craftsmen to be available for producers. The old pragmatic amateur approach to film-making was under pressure. There was now a pride in special skills. It was no longer one of the director's chores to crank the camera. The cameramen themselves were learning new ways to photograph scenes and the art of editing was becoming recognized. Similarly, styles of acting were evolving. There was a rush of stage performers after Tree had paved the way, and many other West End actors turned to films. The transition was not too happy; it was hard for an actor, trained to magnify his performance so that it could be understood in the back row of the gallery, to modify it so that it did not overwhelm the camera only a few feet from him. Sir Johnston Forbes-Robertson appeared in Hepworth's production of *Hamlet*, made for Gaumont in 1913, a reproduction of his farewell performance that same year at Drury Lane. It was an expensive film, budgeted at £10,000, and including a canvas and plaster Elsinore on the cliffs at Lulworth Cove. Hepworth described how it was necessary to substitute action for the words of the play in the silent medium of the cinema. Although the results were dull, the cult of transferring stage productions to the screen continued unabated. Several Shakespeare films were produced, each adapted from an original stage presentation.

After the theatre the great source of film material was the Victorian novel, particularly the work of Dickens which was considered very cinematic. Hepworth, in particular, turned to Dickens and began to make films of hitherto unheard of running times. *David Copperfield*, released in 1913, was 7,500 feet. There was, it seemed, a desire in the industry to have things both ways. On the one hand literary master-pieces lent a social cachet to the cinema, a fake respectability and moral uplift; and on the other, since the subjects chosen were always familiar and unadventurous, there was no risk of alienating the audience's interest. The cinema was playing it safe and turning its back on original, creative screenplays. Britain was no place for the aspiring screenwriter to learn his business – if he wanted to see his own work on the screen he had to go to America. He could try his hand at comedy, but it would have been a dismal experience for comedy before the First World War was no repository of artistic innovation. British screen humour was firmly rooted in the knockabout music-hall tradition. Similar situations recurred in film after film suggesting a desperate search for safe formulae rather than simple gag-stealing. It was France, not Britain, which produced a comic genius like Max Linder; it was Hollywood, not Britain, which took advantage of the genius of the London-born Charlie Chaplin. It was America which was prepared to give an opportunity to the Canadian, Mack Sennett, to produce his unprecedented and hilarious films which some sixty years afterwards still make the world laugh. In Britain, however, comedy was vulgar and low, ignored by the major companies and short-changed by the smaller ones. The occasional music-hall star was lured before the cameras for his turn to be filmed, and one or two, like George Robey, made proper films. But it was a barren scene.

A few years earlier Britain had produced more films than any other country. Now it was lying low in the league. The primary cause was the social attitude towards the cinema. Lack of public acceptance meant lack of finance and talent. It was a hard life, working for the films in those days, with bankruptcy an ever-present threat. The worst blow came in 1914, with the outbreak of war, when suddenly competition with America could no longer even be contemplated. It was a position common to all the European film industries.

One important development of the pre-war period in the cinema was the emergence of a properly organized censorship procedure. In order to avoid the worst consequences of local interference in films the industry set up its own self-regulating body, the British Board of Film Censors. As a result of loopholes in the Cinematograph Act of 1909 local censorship had become a distinct possibility. The Government refused to form its own censorship board, a commendably correct decision, but was sympathetic to entrusting control to the industry itself. The new Board came into being in 1913 under the presidency of G. A. Redford, a former reader of plays for the Lord Chamberlain. Under him were four film examiners whom he appointed. Their task was to view every film and report back should there be any objectionable matter. Then the offending shots would be removed. Their other main duty was to classify each film as U (suitable for universal exhibition) or A (not recommended for children). There were initially only two rules: no nudity and no representations of Christ. In time the categories of forbidden material were expanded but no code was laid down in writing, a tradition that still prevails in the BBFC. The Board liked to think that every case was decided on its merits and that a written code would inhibit producers unfairly.

The Board had to win the confidence of local authorities who were not and are still not compelled to take notice of their rulings. Some held out for a long time before giving formal recognition to the BBFC's certificates (London, in fact, not accepting the Board until 1921). In the early years the Board's work was hindered by local decisions, by persons in the trade circumventing the BBFC and getting local approval direct, and by the government's refusal to permit any form of official sanction for it. Inevitably the BBFC's role in film politics has always been fraught with ambiguities. While the system has on the whole worked well, it is only as good as the man in charge, and at some periods the Board has undeniably exercised overmuch restraint on British film-makers.

3 The Great War

For the cinema 1914 was a year of hope. Although the length of films had decreased, there was no decline in the number of films shot, and for the studios 1914 and 1915 were busy times. When older companies suspended their activities, they were replaced by new firms. In 1916, after his Kinemacolour defeat, Urban went back to America and in the following year closed down his British interests. Dr R. T. Jupp's London Films found itself in serious financial trouble in 1915 and many of the American personnel that had given the company its unique quality drifted away. So by 1916 production had virtually ceased. This state of affairs was as much the result of Jupp's ill-health and withdrawal from the business as of the war. Barker was another pre-war producer who fell on hard times, after his notable British Civil War epic *Jane Shore* in 1915, and ceased production. Hepworth, however, continued to flourish and although a subsidiary company, Turner Films, which made pictures starring the Vitagraph Girl from America, Florence Turner, under the direction of Larry Trimble, did go out of business, its principals transferred to the main Hepworth studios. One of Trimble's 1916 productions was *Far From the Madding Crowd*. But by the end of the year he and Florence Turner had returned to the United States.

A new name in the industry was G. B. Samuelson, a film renter who had handled Barker's *Sixty Years a Queen*. In 1914 he opened studios at Worton Hall, Isleworth, and persuaded George Pearson, an ex-headmaster who had found his way into films at what was then considered the mature age of thirty-six, to leave Pathé and join him. Pearson's first work for Samuelson was a six-reeler, Conan Doyle's *A Study in Scarlet*, the first of the Sherlock Holmes films. The Rockies were simulated by a location at Cheddar Gorge, and the plains of Utah by Southport Sands. Then he began *A Cinema Girl's Romance* at Worton Hall, but on the outbreak of war Samuelson ordered the hasty assembly of a fictitious newsreel, to begin three days later, and all other work was set aside. Fred Paul, formerly Pearson's Sherlock Holmes, played both the Kaiser and Kitchener. Within two weeks *The Great European Tragedy* had been shown to the trade with great success. Unfortunately it became a signal for other producers to rush out a flood of war pictures and the market was quickly saturated, with depressing results at the box-office. *A Cinema Girl's Romance* was again dropped when Pearson was ordered to make a biography of a recently deceased general, *The Life of Lord Roberts*. This time Dovedale in Derbyshire was made to serve as Afghanistan. Only then was Pearson allowed to complete the *Cinema Girl* film. Pearson was undoubtedly the most interesting new director of the period. His handling of extras was impressive and his ingenuity with sparse material remarkable. Although Samuelson was an energetic and stimulating firebrand, his artistic taste was not up to his powers of invention, which is probably why he gradually faded from film production.

After making *John Halifax, Gentleman* Pearson left Samuelson and went to Gaumont, which had opened a large £30,000 studio at Lime Grove, Shepherd's Bush, in 1915. This was a large sum to spend on a British studio although small in comparison with the average at that time in Hollywood. Pearson became Chief Film Director and Fred Paul, the actor, replaced him at Worton Hall. Gaumont had hitherto merely distributed its French product, but now it was ready to start British production in earnest. One of Pearson's most interesting assignments during the war years was to create a British rival to the French series character, Fantomas. He chose the name Ultus, from the Latin for avenger, and engaged Aurele Sydney to play the title role. The first, *Ultus – the Man from the Dead*, was favourably received and three more Ultus films followed before the series ended in 1917. Pearson also made *Sally Bishop* from a novel by Temple Thurston, with Aurele Sydney and Peggy Hyland.

A landmark, not only for America but also for the world cinema, was the release in 1915 of D. W. Griffith's monumental picture *The Birth of a Nation*. It was the first 'hard-ticket' presentation, with specially inflated admission prices. After its appearance the cinema was never the same again and its impact had a profound effect on many filmmakers, Barker's *Jane Shore*, for instance, being inspired as a British counterpart to the story of the American war between the States.

By 1917 the war in Europe had reached such proportions that the Government was forced to conscript all able-bodied men for the fighting services. The draining of manpower from the studios had a devastating effect on the film industry, and production virtually ceased. But already the public had turned against the British cinema in general, as a result of the mass of inferior films being supplied by the producers. There was little respect for original work; films had mostly been based on well-known novels or popular stage successes which were usually filmed with no attempt to 'open up' the subjects for the screen. During the latter part of the war the amount of new British product was exceeded eighteen times by foreign footage then available, most of it American. And America, where the star system had taken root with rewarding financial results, had an industry which was constantly adventurous and imaginative.

As early as 1915 it had been suggested that imported films should be taxed. In 1917 Sidney Morgan, a producer, urged that British exhibitors be forced to show a minimum quota of British material, since the better-organized American publicity, star system and block booking were detrimental to the home industry. He proposed that the quota should stand at thirty-three per cent. The exhibitors' response was to blame the producers for the sorry condition of the British cinema and to argue that the public would not be able to stomach a heavy diet of home-produced films after sampling the delights of Hollywood. It was, the exhibitors felt, a denial of choice and, of course, a potential reduction of revenue for them. Block booking was an extension of the exclusive system, a logical consequence of the disappearance of the old open-market free-for-all. The next pernicious practice was blind booking, which meant that films were pencilled in as much as a year in advance, long before they had been trade-shown, and in some cases before they had even been made. On the one hand it was argued that this approach saved the exhibitor's time, expense and work and that he knew best what his audiences wanted anyway; and, on the other, that stagnation and sterility were the inevitable results. But a good new film that suddenly appeared either threw the system out of gear, or failed to get the bookings it deserved. The renter was in many cases being superseded by direct hiring from the producer, and tough battles raged within the trade while the European armies were locked on the Western Front.

To add to its problems war conditions had imposed restrictions on the film industry. The 1915 budget levied an Import Tax on all imported goods, and in 1916 an Entertainments Tax was introduced, which included the theatre and sporting events. On the very low prices of a penny and twopence the tax amounted to an extra halfpenny but on higher priced seats it meant an increase of only ten per cent. This was a situation of marked social unfairness since cinemas in poor areas were severely hit while West End theatres scarcely felt it. Although the trade accepted that the tax was a necessary part of the war effort there were considerable protests, and minor although still unsatisfactory amendments to the tax were made in spite of the Bioscope's claim that 700 cinemas had closed as a result of it. The trade gritted its teeth and paid up, or passed the tax on in the form of higher-priced seats. This was done with as good a grace as possible because both the trade and public believed that it was all to help the war effort. Had they known that they would continue to pay the tax for many years after the Second World War the protests would have been more vociferous – governments have an unpleasant reluctance to give up a tax once they have invented it.

The Import Tax in 1915 was extended later in the war to a prohibition of film exports, not on grounds of censorship but in order that no intentional or unintentional trading with the enemy should occur. These restrictions were removed at the cessation of hostilities. But by then Britain had lost its world trade markets.

The film scene during the war was not entirely without hope. In one area there was considerable innovation and excitement, that of newsreel and documentary. At first the military authorities had been suspicious of both still and film cameramen and had offered few opportunities for them to shoot what was happening on the Western Front. But as the war progressed it was apparent that the Germans had learned the propaganda value of the cinema. The War Office relented and began inviting film producers on to the War Office Topical Committee with the intention of getting official cameramen to the front. By 1917 the Committee was producing its own newsreel, or Topical Budget, to use the contemporary title. One of the cameramen, Geoffrey Malins, later wrote a book, *How I Filmed the War*, describing his experiences in France. For the first time the film men came under fire, sharing the dangers of the fighting men. In the cinema's infancy the Boer War had only been observed at a distance, and there were many examples of deliberate faking, then accepted as a matter of course. The bulk of the 1914–18 war newsreels have been carefully preserved by the Imperial War Museum and form a remarkable historical collection, conveying more vividly than the most precise literary description the horror of the conditions in which men fought. Malins was one of the cameramen who filmed *The Battle of the Somme*, released as a full-length feature within four weeks of the action. Shots of troops being mown down by enemy fire alarmed filmgoers, but the tone of the film received official commendations, with even the King declaring that 'the public should see these pictures'. There were marked propaganda overtones, particularly where sub-titles were concerned. It was an emotional time and no effort was spared to trade on the public propensity to regard the Germans as worse than animals. *The Somme* was followed by other battle films, *St Quentin, Ancre, Arras. The Battle of Ancre* featured the first tanks going into action in September 1916. It captured the public's imagination and aroused a mass of press comment, for once favourable to the cinema.

The first chairman of the War Office Cinematograph Committee, which replaced a less effective Trade Committee, was Sir Max Aitken, later to become Lord Beaverbrook. The trade was represented by William Jury, a renter. Eventually the Committee came under the control of the Ministry of Information, with Beaverbrook at its head. There were two feature films sponsored by the Government – the first, and most important, was D. W. Griffith's *Hearts of the World*, the first instance of a major American director using British technical facilities. It produced about £13,000 for the British taxpayer. The other was *The Invasion of Britain*, a costly production by Herbert Brenon, another American director, which took so long to make that the war was over by the time it was complete, and consequently it was not publicly shown. There were, however, innumerable instances of shorts, special announcements and tags being issued by the Government. Tags were the predecessors of *Food Flashes* in the Second World War, two-minute pictures offering messages connected with the war effort, tacked on to the regular newsreel.

Ordinary commercial films with war themes continued to appear, even though the public, as in the Second World War, regarded the cinema as a means of escape from the rigours of shortages, rationing and bombing. The animated cartoon, which owed its origins to American comic strip artists like Winsor McCay and Bud Fisher, who had begun experimenting on film in the years preceding the war, began to be seen in Britain. Usually the artist's hand was visible, drawing his subjects at lightning speed with the aid of an undercranked camera. Elementary as the technique was, it provided the cinema with the work of such notable cartoonists as Harry Furniss, Lancelot Speed and Dudley Buxton. Another animation technique in these early days employed cut-out figures which were moved and photographed by stop-motion against appropriate backgrounds. These two techniques were considered fitting for war subjects, which were not otherwise regarded as suitable material for humorous treatment. The most famous cartoon series was *John Bull's Animated Sketchbook*, the work of Buxton and Anson Dyer, which appeared monthly in 1915 and 1916. The drawings of the famous war cartoonists, Bruce Bairnsfather, creator of 'Old Bill', and Louis Raemaekers, the polemical political artist from Belgium, were also featured in animations although they were redrawn by film artists. Another type of film using crude animation techniques was the series of War Maps made by Kineto. This was a monthly reel showing how battles were fought, by means of a map and coloured flags and arrows, an animated version of the familiar charts published in newspapers during the war. Many American cartoons of a much greater sophistication found their way on to the wartime British screens, from McKay's *Gertie the Dinosaur* to the Essanay cartoons and the *Mutt and Jeff* series. As a consequence many bookers began refusing British product on the grounds that the market was saturated. In yet another area the Americans were to be superior.

One of the peculiarities of the organization of the film industry at this time was that no reliable source existed to indicate the number of cinemas in Britain, but it would seem to have been in the region of 4,000, or about the same figure as at the end of the Second World War. The average size of theatres was, however, a great deal smaller, and the circuits, that is to say chains with more than ten houses, controlled only six per cent. In contrast by 1945 nearly half of all cinemas were circuit-controlled. By the start of the war the trend had veered away from the cosy Bijou towards the large, palatial 'picture palace', a term that was coming into use. Some could seat as many as 2,500 people in plush comfort. In the post-war world it was these vast auditoria with their colonnades and marble pediments which were to fulfil the filmgoing experience.

4 Post-War Crisis

The big new cinemas with their many rows of seats needed films that would draw in the public. Because the trade went for big theatres there were fewer screens available. Had a policy for the construction of a far greater number of small theatres been instituted life might have been easier. As it was there were not enough screens available to provide a constant market for British films. The war ended with America dominating the cinema screen. The advantage of the massive domestic market in America lay in the fact that by the time a film reached Britain it had in all probability recouped its cost and made a profit, so that its British earnings were the cream on top. This factor enabled the United States to offer its product at giveaway prices, seriously undercutting British output which depended desperately on the British market. What also has to be considered is that in almost every case the American film was better scripted, better acted, better photographed and better directed. There was a much more outgoing, adventurous spirit prevailing in the American cinema in the early twenties; the technical quality was there, but so too were the stars and the glamorous publicity that went with them. It is no wonder that the distributors and exhibitors preferred showing American films in preference to the output of the British studios.

It was the beginning of the nadir in British films. With the new peace the industry, already punch-drunk from the battering it had taken in the latter years of the war, could barely rise to its new challenge. There were no new ideas, no advances in cinematic art. Films continued to be produced but they were run-of-the-mill fodder. Will Barker retired from the industry for good in 1919 and of the pre-war producers only Hepworth was a prominent survivor. His first post-war film was *The Forest on the Hill*, from an Eden Philpotts story, with Alma Taylor. This was followed by *Sheba* with Ronald Colman playing a small part. Hepworth's biggest success came in 1921 with *Alf's Button*, from a story by the journalist W. A. Darlington, and starring

the comedian Leslie Henson. It was acclaimed in overseas countries –
a rare honour at that time. Another Hepworth triumph was an adaptation of E. Philips Oppenheim's *The Amazing Quest of Mr Ernest Bliss*.
But, ironically, Hepworth's success was to lead him to downfall, for
he over-reached himself. The Walton studios were modest in size,
consisting of only two stages. Hepworth wanted six and bought the
necessary land. In order to produce his own electricity he bought war-
surplus diesel engines and a generator that had been used in a German
U-boat without realizing that the reassembly costs would be enormous. With the general trade recession money was hard to raise, and
Hepworth was forced to launch a public company with a capital of
150,000 preference shares of £1 and 100,000 ordinary shares. It was
under-subscribed. Hopes that the reputation of the firm would carry
them through this disaster went for nothing. The *coup-de-grâce* came
when he could no longer pay the interest on a debenture issue. As
Hepworth wrote in his autobiography: 'Directly I announced that
fact a receiver was put in charge of the business and I was no longer
of any account in it.'

His last film before bankruptcy engulfed him was *Comin' Thro the
Rye*, a remake of an earlier version of 1916 which had enjoyed a popular success. It was a difficult film. The leading man contracted typhoid
and was out of action for months. Intended for a British Film Week in
1924, it was still incomplete by the time it was due to be shown, and
was exhibited in that unfortunate state. The eventual finished product
was disappointing. But the greatest tragedy was still to come. Hepworth's receiver, doing his duty to the letter, ordered the sale of
everything, including the precious negatives stored in the studio
vaults. The entire output of twenty-four years was boiled down to
recover chemicals from the emulsion to be sold for aircraft dope. A few
odd prints that were elsewhere escaped this fate, but the film historian
has great difficulty in reaching a true assessment of Hepworth's
capabilities beyond contemporary descriptions, for so much no
longer exists. Hepworth himself, his past wiped out, spent most of the
rest of his life making trailers for National Screen Service and died in
1953. The Walton Studios continued in production until the early
fifties. Now a housing and shopping precinct stands on the site, bisected by Hepworth Way.

The fate of Cecil Hepworth is a cautionary tale of the period. It
demonstrated that even the most competent of British film producers
was vulnerable and could scarcely be expected to win through in the

fight to keep the British cinema going. Several of the major American companies had offices in London in 1920. The oldest established were Essanay and Vitagraph, opened in 1912. Fox and Famous Players-Lasky, later to be known as Paramount, came during the war. Jury's distributed Goldwyn pictures in Britain. In 1920 out of a total of 878 films available only 144 were British. Since the running times were on average shorter than those of American films the overall picture was even gloomier than the statistics painted it. By 1923 only ten per cent of films shown were British. By 1926 of 749 films available only thirty-four were British and less than five per cent of screentime was filled by British material. The trade tried hard to protect itself, but it lacked a united voice to speak good sense, and failed to produce good pictures. As early as 1921 attempts were made to combat block booking and it was at a special meeting of the Cinematograph Exhibitors' Association, with Lord Beaverbrook on the platform, that William Friese-Greene, the pioneer inventor of a film camera in 1889, dropped dead after making an incoherent speech from the floor demanding unity within the business. His spectacular funeral was the emotional expression of a shamed industry finding that the old man had died virtually penniless. The eventual outcome was a second Cinematograph Act, but this was not to be passed by Parliament until 1927.

Yet amidst the dreary and unimaginative films being produced in the twenties, a few fresh talents were emerging. George Pearson, who had worked at Gaumont with Thomas Welsh in the early part of the war, had co-founded a partnership, Welsh–Pearson. Their star discovery was Betty Balfour who emerged brilliantly in Pearson's first original screenplay, *Nothing Else Matters*, which appeared in 1920. It was hailed as a great success. The *Daily Express*, recently acquired by Lord Beaverbrook characteristically declared: 'A really great British Film has arrived, as the *Daily Express* always said it would.' Although the eighteen-year-old Betty Balfour was not in the lead, she received the best notices. Pearson also had another young star under contract, Mabel Poulton, and he engaged Thomas Bentley to direct her as Little Nell in *The Old Curiosity Shop*. Her success was an embarrassment to Welsh and Pearson, for the company was too small to promote two stars simultaneously, but fortunately a French producer made a bid for her. It was now a case of finding the right vehicle for Betty Balfour. Eliot Stannard, a screenplay writer, proposed that a music-hall situation act be investigated since it featured a jolly, cheeky girl. Pearson saw the performance, bought the rights of the name and character, and

47

transformed her into a Piccadilly Circus flower-seller. The film was *Squibs*, and was remarkable for the ingenuity used in getting illegal shots of Miss Balfour in Piccadilly with her policeman sweetheart. Sir William Jury (he had acquired the knighthood as a result of his war film career) vetoed an ending in which Squibs, married, was seen settling down with the policeman. But his instinct told him that there was a series potential in the exploits of this new Cockney heroine, and he urged that a sequel be made.

In the meantime Betty Balfour played a charwoman's daughter in *Mord Emily* and a Glasgow girl in *The Wee Macgregor's Sweetheart*. By the time that the latter film was finished the second Squibs subject was ready, and so was the new Welsh–Pearson studio at Winchmore Hill. The new film was *Squibs Wins the Calcutta Sweep* and once again Pearson had to devise intricate plans to film shots of Piccadilly Circus. Authorities at that time were far less tolerant than they are now of the needs of film producers and rarely, if ever, gave permission for main London thoroughfares to be used for location shooting. There were a couple more Squibs films before the series expired – *Squibs M.P.*, in which the heroine was suddenly revealed to be thirty so that she could be elected to Parliament, and *Squibs' Honeymoon* in which Pearson finally married her off to her policeman. With *Reveille* in 1924 Pearson produced an ambitious episodic picture about the aftermath of the Great War partly inspired by Griffith's *Intolerance*. Its climax was the two minutes' silence of Remembrance Day, made effective by the suspension of the orchestral accompaniment at the première, which was notable for the presence of the Prince of Wales.

Reveille was released by Colonel Bromhead of Gaumont. It was he who had collaborated with Cecil Hepworth in organizing British Film Weeks as a publicity ploy to draw attention to the industry. That was in 1924 and had arisen from a proposal of the previous year. The Prince of Wales had attended the inaugural luncheon of the British National Film League, a special body formed to organize Film Weeks throughout the country. Unfortunately the whole venture embarrassingly misfired since there were too few films of any merit to justify such an event. Hepworth himself had failed to get his important film *Comin' Thro the Rye* ready in time for the London Festival. Then, in November 1924, production in all British studios had ceased altogether. It was the blackest period in British film history, even though several new productions were being planned.

An attempt of commendable sincerity to raise the standards of British cinema was made by a small company called Minerva Films. It was started by Leslie Howard, a young actor who had left his native Hungary at the age of thirteen and already epitomized everyone's notion of Englishness, in collaboration with A. A. Milne, the celebrated author; Nigel Playfair, the prominent theatrical figure; Aubrey Smith, the actor; and Adrian Brunel, a young scenarist who had seen war service in Jury's Film Department. The business end of the venture was organized by R. F. Power and Lionel Phillips. The idea was that Milne should write the storylines, Brunel produce the screenplays from these and Smith and Howard perform in the resultant films. Brunel also directed and co-ordinated production to ensure that more than one film could be made simultaneously in the rented studio. It was his first directorial experience. These films were two-reelers, the standard comedy format of the time. Sadly, the work of Minerva was not a success as far as the box-office was concerned because there was as yet in British film comedies no place for West End theatrical humour. The economics of the industry helped to kill this company, the receipts from bookings often taking as long as eighteen months to mature. So Minerva disappeared and its backers withdrew with burnt fingers.

A more spectacular failure occurred when Sir Oswald Stoll, a distinguished theatrical impresario who had turned to films because he felt Britain could do better than contemporary production suggested, premièred *The Prodigal Son* at the Royal Opera House in 1923. This three-hour Norse epic sent the trade to sleep and frightened off the public. It was the nadir of a short film career which had begun promisingly with *Comradeship*, directed by Maurice Elvey in 1919 and starring Gerald Ames and Guy Newall. Elvey probably directed British films longer than any other person – his career began in 1913 and ended forty-four years later. Stoll's film ambitions never exceeded *The Prodigal Son*, and while there were some experiments with the two-colour Prizma process, most of his output was dull, though worthy.

In 1922 Michael Balcon entered film production at Islington. His first film was directed by Graham Cutts and proved to be an outstanding box-office success, almost the only one from a British studio in the early twenties. Balcon came from Birmingham and had formed a company with another young man, Victor Saville, to produce advertising films. At Cutts' insistence they embarked on *Woman to Woman* and hired the American star Betty Compson at the huge salary of £1,000 a week. While the cost of employing her was astronomical, it did enable the film to be distributed throughout the United States and earn a great deal of money as well as prestige. Also in the cast was a then unknown actor, Clive Brook, and Victor McLaglen, who played a bit part. Behind the camera was a young assistant director who had just graduated from title-designing, Alfred Hitchcock. The film was made with money raised by C. M. Woolf, a city financier, who advanced £7,000 capital, and several other backers, including Oscar Deutsch who later founded Odeon Theatres. The film cost in all £40,000 but it recouped this easily. Following his success Balcon embarked on a second feature, *The Prude's Fall*, again with Cutts as director and Betty Compson as the star, but it was a failure. Fortunately for the industry Balcon decided to stay in films and with Graham Cutts formed Gainsborough Pictures, selling its services to Bromhead's Gaumont. The new company took over Islington studios as its headquarters. Victor Saville, meanwhile, left the partnership. The first Gainsborough film was *The Passionate Adventure* with Clive Brook, Lillian Hall-Davies and Victor McLaglen, and directed by Graham Cutts, as would be expected.

An important figure who entered the industry in this period was an Irish ex-RFC pilot and professional billiards player, Herbert Wilcox. He began as a distributor. He formed a partnership with a Newcastle exhibitor, none other than Graham Cutts, and raised £1,400. With this money they filmed *The Wonderful Story*, from a novel by I. A. R. Wyllie, with Herbert Langley, Lillian Hall-Davies and Olaf Hytten. Although praised by the critics it left the public unconvinced. But since in those days there was a gap of several months between trade shows and release dates, Wilcox, on the strength of favourable notices, was able to gain financial backing for further films before the failure was detected. He brought Mae Marsh, the star of D. W. Griffith's *Intolerance*, to England for his second film, a drama, *Flames of Passion*. This scored a considerable success, an exact reverse of Balcon's early production record of a success followed by a flop. Wilcox then entered into a deal with Erich Pommer, the head of UFA from whose Berlin studios some of the great early twenties masterpieces of German cinema had emerged (*The Cabinet of Dr Caligari*, *Metropolis*, *Die Nibelungen*, *Dr Mabuse*), and arranged to produce a film version of *Chu Chin Chow*, which had enjoyed a longer run than any other musical on the West End stage during the previous decade. In spite of the enormous upheavals then affecting the German mark Wilcox managed to complete the film, although it never equalled the success of the stage original. With this film Wilcox experimented with sound synchronization in some theatres, but it was too soon to start making film musicals and again he had pleased the critics more than the public. His next film, *Southern Love*, was set in Spain and shot in Vienna, and given its world première at the Royal Albert Hall, which was turned into a bullring for the occasion. Pommer again offered Wilcox a partnership to produce and direct in Berlin a film version of *Decameron Nights* from Boccaccio, with a cast which included Ivy Duke, a leading British star, Lionel Barrymore, who was brought across from America, and Werner Kraus, a leading German actor. Not only did the film again receive a favourable critical response, it also gained the rare distinction of distribution in the United States.

Michael Balcon then became a co-producer with Erich Pommer. The German cinema's artistic pre-eminence had helped to create a distinctive visual style which exerted considerable influence on some British directors who, although unable to match qualities of story and acting, tried to copy a Germanic style of lighting and editing. In the previous decade the French dominated the cinema artistically, but now in the twenties it was the turn of Germany. During the difficult period of the Weimar Republic, when inflation and unrest haunted the German nation, there was an attempt in Britain to form a rapprochement between the two countries. The first film that Pommer and Balcon collaborated on at the Neubabelsburg studios in Berlin was *The Blackguard*, directed by Graham Cutts in 1924. This was followed by the promotion of Alfred Hitchcock to director status and *The Pleasure Garden*, shot at the Emelka studio in Munich and on location in Italy. An unremarkable and melodramatic story of a good girl married to a bad man, it featured the American stars Virginia Valli and Carmelita Geraghty. Some critics were perceptive enough to appreciate that it signified the debut of a major directorial talent. Hitchcock made another film in Munich, *The Mountain Eagle*, with Nita Naldi, which had an even more melodramatic plot than the first and which, unfortunately like so many films of the period, does not survive. Although Balcon was to continue a business relationship with Pommer throughout the thirties, he only produced these three films in Germany.

During the first half of the decade cinema ownership hardened gradually into circuits. By 1923 there were seventeen circuits with more than ten theatres, the largest being Provincial Cinematograph Theatres. In 1928 they acquired the Tivoli in the Strand, claimed to be the first West End super-cinema when it was opened four years earlier. Because of the failure of the trade to book some of the more interesting films made abroad the London Film Society was founded in 1925, at the instigation of Ivor Montagu, the critic and screenplay writer. Not only was the general trade uninterested in masterpieces emerging from other countries but the British Board of Film Censors adopted an extreme and authoritarian attitude to them. *The Cabinet of Dr Caligari* made in Germany in 1919 by Robert Wiene was banned because of its frightening content, but more sinisterly the masterpieces of Eisenstein and Pudovkin from the new Communist state of Soviet Russia, including *The Battleship Potemkin*, *Mother* and *October*, were rejected as subversive propaganda. Without the Film Society these films would not have been seen at all, but a typically hypocritical instance of official paternalism was shown by the refusal of the LCC to allow a Workers' Film Guild to show *Mother* on the grounds that its subscription was only one shilling and the Film Society's twenty-five shillings. The Film Society attracted a large membership from the intelligentsia of the day; among its founder members were Shaw, Wells, Huxley, Haldane and Augustus John and its board included Iris Barry, Adrian Brunel, Walter Mycroft and Sidney Bernstein. Its first performance was on a Sunday afternoon in October 1925 at the New Gallery cinema in Regent Street, and it continued month after month until the Second World War. By the end of the thirties there were enough cinemas in London specializing in foreign and classic films to make the Film Society's work less essential, but it had met a vital need.

5 The Coming of the Quota

By 1926 the amount of screen time devoted to British films had dwindled to a mere five per cent. Block booking was used as a steamroller to flatten the domestic product. Unfinished American films would be firmly established in the release schedules, given the superior booking power of transatlantic distributors. There was, it now appeared, cause for the government to erect some kind of protective legislation. Political intervention in the affairs of the film industry was by no means new – there had been Entertainments Tax, import duties, and certain Defence of the Realm Act restrictions, but most of all the passing of the Cinematograph Act of 1909 which in providing for the safety and licensing of cinemas had indirectly given birth to the censorship system.

Some believed that the situation in the mid-twenties could be relieved voluntarily from within the business. There was, however, an important reason why this belief was sanguine and naïve. It was not the exhibitors and renters who were suffering, but the British producers. To expect the Americans to relinquish voluntarily their prime position in the English market was to ask more than was reasonable.

In May 1925 the House of Lords debated British films and Lord Newton called for a Committee of Inquiry. It was turned down on the grounds that the Board of Trade was already engaged in its own investigations. In the following years the industry was told that if restrictions such as block booking were not eased government intervention would be inevitable. For a year various ideas were batted around between the Federation of British Industries, who represented the producers on the one hand, and a joint Trade Committee on the other. The FBI demanded a quota system to help British film-makers, and also asked for financial assistance in the form of government-backed loans for new productions, thus anticipating the National Film Finance Corporation which was eventually established in 1948. The joint Trade Committee also asked for a quota which would apply to both exhibitors and renters, and proposed that there should be protection from takeovers by foreign companies.

Unfortunately, a small proportion of the Cinematograph Exhibitors' Association rejected the report, which had been adopted by their Council. For the smaller cinema owner it was a daunting prospect to have to show British films instead of the American ones for which the public clamoured. As so few films were made in Britain anyway, it seemed that quality might well diminish further as the studios rushed out pictures to fill the void created by the quota system. When this brave attempt at voluntary restraint failed the Government was forced to take action, and the Cinematograph Films Act of 1927 came into being. The new act introduced a quota of five per cent for the first six months of its operation, to increase in annual stages to 1935 when the figure would reach twenty per cent, the ceiling until the expiry of the Act. Blind booking was made illegal by requiring that all titles had to be registered with the Board of Trade before any film was placed on hire and after it had been shown to the trade. This terminated the practice whereby forty or more films would be booked in a block containing good, bad and indifferent pictures, some of which may not even have been made. It also became illegal to book more than six months ahead. All these restrictions were imposed with the intention of making room on the exhibitors' books for British films.

The Act was immensely successful. In the year preceding its introduction only twenty-six films had been produced, but a year later there were 128 films made in British studios, seventy-eight more than were required under the terms of the Act. Suddenly there was money available for the cinema and new companies appeared. One of these was British International Pictures, floated by John Maxwell and others in 1926, when it was clear what the outcome of government action would be. It was at this time that the growth of the main circuits really began. What is more, there developed a tendency towards vertical integration, whereby the same company would produce, distribute and exhibit films thereby guaranteeing a showing for its own product. This had already happened and been proved successful in the United States.

For the circuits life was made a great deal easier with central booking and take-it-or-leave-it bargaining with other companies. PCT, the first of the vertical integrations, now had eighty-five theatres, having been established by Dr R. T. Jupp in 1909. The second largest company was Gaumont-British, a company formed from Gaumont,

Ideal Films and W. & F. Film Service in 1927, with twenty-one theatres. Within a year this new company, under the chairmanship of Colonel Bromhead and with the financial backing of the Ostrer brothers, Mark and Isidore, who were merchant bankers of Polish extraction, had merged and built further cinemas to bring its total to 187 houses, adding another 100 in 1929 by taking over PCT. A third Ostrer, Maurice, became a director of Gainsborough with C. M. Woolf as chairman and Michael Balcon as managing director; this production company passed into the mighty Gaumont-British Picture Corporation in April 1928, of which Woolf became chairman on Bromhead's retirement. Three months earlier Associated British Cinemas had been incorporated under the chairmanship of John Maxwell, a Glasgow solicitor who had entered the business as an exhibitor in 1912. Subsequently he became chairman of Wardour Films, a major renting house. Then he turned his interests to production and developed British International Pictures from the chaos he found at the newly opened Elstree Studios, which had been built by J. D. Williams, an American, with Herbert Wilcox as director-in-chief. Maxwell also merged First National and Pathé into a single distribution firm. The ABC circuit and its subsidiaries expanded from twenty-nine cinemas in 1928 to eighty-eight the following year and it was plain that the pattern for the future of the British film business would be the battle between Maxwell's ABC and Woolf's Gaumont-British companies.

The PEP report on the British Film Industry, which came out in 1952, pertinently asked – why did vertical integration not develop on a large scale before 1927 and the Cinematograph Films Act? Their answer was that American dominance and moribund British production had left little to integrate, and that could only have come about if there had been an alliance of British and American interests. Because it was beyond any group to provide sufficient films for each of fifty-two weeks, substantial reliance on American pictures would have been essential. In the United States integration was commonplace, and Paramount, Loew's, Fox and First National had achieved it by 1923. Until the late forties, when anti-trust laws were to divorce studios from the exhibition side of the business, integration was the norm, guaranteeing the power and efficiency of the Hollywood machine.

In Britain, on the other hand, the two main circuits, while representing a small proportion of the total number of cinemas, were able to dominate the market. Invariably they had the best locations for their houses, and where they did not they had the best of the available programmes. Since the end of the twenties the circuit release has provided the normal pattern for filmgoing in almost every urban area in the country with the exception of London's West End, certain large provincial centres, and holiday resorts in season. The circuits' booking power has not only dominated exhibition but been an important factor in production, for without a circuit release a British film cannot expect to recoup its costs. Although numerically the independents are in a large majority most of their programmes are based on the circuit release.

It can be seen that much of the framework of the British film industry today was established well over forty years ago, at the close of the silent era. PEP described this period as the watershed between medieval and modern film history, and it is an apt description.

In America the silent film had reached its zenith; in spectacle with *Ben Hur*, in comedy with Buster Keaton's *The General*, in drama with William Wellman's *Wings*, in epic with De Mille's *King of Kings*. It was the golden age of the silents. Some of the accomplished American technical gloss had rubbed off on the British cinema and there was a marked improvement in the standard of films being produced. One reason was that more money was being spent on directors, writers and stars – the meanness of earlier days, which had helped to relegate British films to the bottom of most cinemagoers' list, had been replaced by a new optimism and a desire to please the public. Although the majority of films remained poor, in the average year's output there were at least a handful of films of which Britain need not have been ashamed.

Two major British directors emerged in the twenties. The first was Alfred Hitchcock, who with his third film, *The Lodger*, an adaptation of Mrs Belloc-Lowndes's Jack-the-Ripper story starring the matinée idol Ivor Novello as the suspect, and June as the near-victim, scored an outstanding success. There was a marked German atmosphere in the lighting and composition and it was clear that the young director's experience of film-making in Munich had been formative. Hitchcock's next film also featured Ivor Novello, *Downhill* (called *When Boys Leave Home* in America), the story of a boy expelled from school after shielding a friend, who drifts downwards through degrees of degradation. The direction overcame the banalities of the story and, when considered in the context of the rest of British output at the time, it is plain that Hitchcock's talent outstripped that of any of his contemporaries. The remainder of his silent output consisted of the disappointing and melodramatic *Easy Virtue*, his last silent film for Gainsborough; the excellent boxing story *The Ring*, made under his new contract at BIP; *The Farmer's Wife* adapted from Eden Philpott's play; then *Champagne*, an indifferent comedy with Betty Balfour; *The Manxman*, from a novel by Hall Caine; and finally *Blackmail*, a thriller of his own choice which was shot as a silent film and then largely remade.

The other director was Anthony Asquith, a son of the former British Prime Minister. He made his film debut with *Shooting Stars*, a murder mystery set in a film studio, which he directed in association with A. V. Bramble. Asquith was only twenty-five at the time and the caution and restraint of many of his later films were not so readily apparent, perhaps still held at bay by youthful bravura. The film was not very popular at the box-office, but it demonstrated many interesting and ingenious technical effects without being over-consciously clever. Asquith had studied technique in Hollywood and consequently had a good grounding in his basic skills. For his next film, a stylish thriller called *Underground*, he was on his own, and his cast included Elissa Landi and Brian Aherne. Asquith's approach to the cinema was always carefully considered, and he displayed a critical awareness towards the medium which contrasted strongly with the cruder attitudes by many of the older types of directors whose views had developed through years of hard grind.

George Pearson had been hard at work through crises and recessions to emerge as one of the industry's leading figures. Throughout the build-up period for the parliamentary bill he had, in his role as President of the Association of British Film Directors, campaigned against the quota law on the grounds that its effect would be to create a glut of inferior pictures—the 'quota quickies' – completely nullifying any attempts to raise the quality of the British cinema. He felt that the legislation was too meagre to be really effective. Time proved him right, although in 1927 he was not able to suggest a more satisfactory alternative course of action. Of his own pictures, one that had intriguing casting was a version of John Buchan's *Huntingtower* with Harry Lauder as the ageing Glasgow grocer who rescues a Russian princess from the Bolsheviks. A release deal was arranged for the film in America where Lauder was a popular figure. Early in 1928 Welsh–Pearson became Welsh–Pearson–Elder and concentrated its production at Cricklewood with a small key staff which included Bernard Knowles, then a cameraman, and Edward Carrick, the art director son of the great theatrical designer Gordon Craig. Pearson made *Love's Option* in Spain and then began a second Lauder film, *Auld Lang Syne*, with the talkie already about to kill the silent film for ever. Lauder was given songs to sing and a crude form of lip synchronization was attempted with wax disc recording. These were transferred to a sound track and the film was shown in 1929 as a silent picture with songs.

Herbert Wilcox, one of the liveliest and most prolific producer-directors, after his adventure at Elstree made *Nell Gwyn* with Dorothy Gish imported from America, and *Mumsie* with Pauline Frederick. This was followed by *Dawn*, with Sybil Thorndike playing Nurse Edith Cavell, whose execution by the Germans in Brussels in 1915 had occasioned a bitter controversy. This latter film became the centre of a fierce censorship row. The Foreign Secretary, Sir Austen Chamberlain, was approached by the German ambassador and told that the release of the film would endanger Anglo-German relations. These views were transmitted to the censor, T. P. O'Connor, and the suggestion made that the film should be banned. O'Connor agreed, although he had not seen the film. Wilcox showed the film to MPs and the press. His supporters ranged from Lord Beaverbrook on the one hand to George Bernard Shaw on the other. Yet even after the BBFC finally saw the picture, the ban 'not fit for showing to British audiences' was confirmed. The film was then shown to the LCC who passed it by one vote, and it was premièred at the London Palladium.

Elstree was now gathering a reputation for Hollywood-style productions. The Hertfordshire studios were modern and well-equipped, on a more generous scale than was customary in Britain. E. A. Dupont, the German director of *Variety*, was lured there to make *Madame Pompadour*, followed by the spectacular *Moulin Rouge* which cost £80,000, and his last silent film, *Piccadilly*. An outstanding figure, who was to direct his best work in the thirties, was Victor Saville, formerly in production partnership with Michael Balcon. Saville made *Tesha* with Maria Corda, the wife of a then little-known Hungarian who spelt his name with a K. This picture had Germanic overtones and was not a success although it was well received by the critics.

The coming of talkies, although a predictable enough development, still managed to catch the film industry unprepared. Elstree were the first studios to become geared for producing sound pictures, although the initial difficulties were formidable. Some pictures that had already been shot had dialogue sequences added to them, for instance Castleton Knight's *Flying Scotsman*, which had a youthful Ray Milland as its leading player, and *Kitty*, directed by Victor Saville with John Stuart and Estelle Brody. Alfred Hitchcock's *Blackmail* was put back on the floor and reshot, although location footage was saved. The heroine, Anny Ondra, was Czech, and incapable of speaking acceptable English, so Joan Barry dubbed her lines live from beyond camera range. The camera itself was fettered inside a stuffy, airless booth, so that its mechanical whirrings would not register on the sound track. The soundproof camera blimps, which liberated the camera once again, had still to appear, and consequently early talkies have a static, dull appearance during the dialogue sequences. Hitchcock, in spite of making what was effectively the first English talking picture, used the sound track in an inventive and creative manner, giving it a relevance to the story. Frequently quoted is his famous isolation of the word 'knife' in an incidental conversation overheard by the guilt-ridden girl who has stabbed a man the night before. *Blackmail* appeared both in sound and silent versions in the midst of a welter of all-talking, all-singing, all-dancing films hastily assembled in the United States and shipped out as fast as theatres were being wired up for the new dimension now added to film entertainment. That many of these pictures were bad and undeserving of screenspace is irrelevant. The new toy swept everything before it with a gathering momentum and by the end of 1929 the silent picture was completely finished; the new, noisy age was in full spate. It meant a completely fresh approach to film-making, a discarding of unsuitable stories and a search for new ideas more suited to the altered medium. It also meant the end of several actors' and actresses' careers, for the early recording machines were insensitive instruments and some voices were not picked up well.

6 The Early Talkies

Sound films were not really new. The idea of moving pictures that talked was as old as the cinema itself. Edison originally developed his Kinetoscope as an adjunct to his other successful invention, the phonograph. There had been many attempts in the first forty years of film history to link gramophone discs with the images on the screen, and it was a device sometimes used for short films featuring music-hall acts. Amplification was a serious problem and until the invention of the thermionic valve had been applied to recording it had been difficult with acoustical horns alone to build up a sufficient volume of sound to fill a theatre. Another and more critical problem was that of synchronization. The perfect interlocking of image with sound was almost impossible in the days of hand-cranked cameras and projectors.

The coming of broadcasting was one of the greatest spurs to the development of talking pictures. In Britain the British Broadcasting Company began regular transmissions in 1922, after a period of experimentation. One of the pioneers of radio was Dr Lee de Forest, an American who for a short time experimented with sound films using discs in London. In the United States D. W. Griffith showed a sound version of *Dream Street* as early as 1921, but the novelty did not catch on. In Germany a sound-on-film system, the Tri-Ergan process, was demonstrated in 1923 and acquired by UFA, who then sat on it. In 1926 a minor Hollywood company, Warner Brothers, bought rights to use the disc system that had been developed in the Bell laboratories under the joint ownership of Western Electric and American Telephone and Telegraph. They christened the system 'Vitaphone' and showed John Barrymore's *Don Juan*, with a recorded orchestral accompaniment, at the Warner Theatre in New York on 6 August 1926. A supporting programme consisted of speech and musical films. *Variety* devoted a special issue to the event, although the industry hoped that it was merely a passing fad which would quickly be forgotten. The following year Warners released *The Jazz Singer*, a schmaltzy Al

Jolson picture in which he sang all his numbers. But as yet there was no spoken dialogue. Then William Fox announced a sound-on-film process, 'Movietone', and the battle for the talkies was on in earnest. The first all-dialogue film, *The Lights of New York*, was released by Warners in 1928, and a ponderous bore it was. Yet it galvanized the whole industry and within a year nearly five thousand American theatres were wired for sound. In Europe a patents row broke out between Fox and the Tobis company which was now exploiting the Tri-Ergan process. Eventually Tobis won but the litigation meant a long delay before sound films could begin to appear regularly in many European countries. In Britain *The Jazz Singer* was premièred at the Piccadilly Theatre in 1928, and it was followed by *The Singing Fool* at the Regal, Marble Arch. Crowds flocked to see these two banal pictures while the entire production side of the industry went into a state of near panic.

With the coming of sound many changes took place in exhibition practice. During the twenties the larger cinemas had graduated from single piano accompanists through musical trios to small orchestras. Suddenly the cinema musicians found themselves out of work, and with the costs of sound equipment adding greatly to the business overheads, unnecessary musicians could be dispensed with as a welcome economy. It was normal for silent films to be issued with complete scores as well as theme tunes; now all this was no more, since the incidental music could be added at source, when the picture was in its final print stage.

A phenomenon of the twenties was the Mighty Wurlitzer, a massive theatre organ with the capacity for imitating orchestras and a host of general sound effects. In some places these monumental machines with their coloured lights and elevating consoles had already taken over from the regular musicians, since all was under the control of one man. The cinema organs remained when talkies came in and many new theatres were equipped with them, the organ interlude forming part of the regular programme until the fifties, when finally this last relic of silent filmgoing disappeared from general use. Even now there are still a few theatres with organs, although their operation is rare and the cinema organist almost an extinct species.

The advent of sound also altered the film itself. Silent films were shot at a basic speed of sixteen frames a second, although in practice this varied up to twenty-two frames. The camera was hand-cranked and operators preferred it that way, for it was actually possible to vary the pace at which a scene was shot and helped to give the silent picture, at its most sophisticated, a flexibility completely lacking in the early talkies. The average projection speed was around twenty frames a second, which is why many silent pictures shown on a modern machine geared at sixteen frames appear to be slow. It was not unknown for projectionists to speed the film up in order to finish the performance by a certain time, and different showings might produce different tempi. All this variation would play havoc with the synchronization of sound, and in any case the basic sixteen frames was too slow for a reasonable recording to be made in the sound-on-film process. A new standard of twenty-four frames per second was determined and henceforth, with the adoption of motor-driven cameras, running times became immutable. Cinemas, however, required projectors capable of showing the rival systems – the Vitaphone wax discs were huge and rotated at the modern LP speed of $33\frac{1}{3}$ revolutions per minute. Sound-on-film won the day because it was a less cumbersome system and did not present the problems of synchronization that plagued the early Vitaphone showings, when so much depended on the projectionist's ability to start the turntable at the right moment. The actual shape of the screen image also changed slightly, as the sound track required a strip at the side of the film. As a result the width of the image on the screen was reduced, producing a squarer shape than previously, an aspect ratio of $1\cdot33:1$. This was to remain standard until the mid-fifties, when widescreen mania swept all cinemas and a new standard was adopted, averaging around $1\cdot75:1$.

The method of film hire also altered. The flat rate which had prevailed until then was replaced by a sliding scale. Hitherto the renter had not shouldered any of the exhibitors' risks, or for that matter gained the increased benefit if the film had enjoyed packed houses throughout its one week run. Now the takings, after the deduction of Entertainments Tax, were distributed between renter and exhibitor according to an agreed percentage, with 'break points' at various stages at which the renter's percentage would be increased. The percentage system proved beneficial to both sides during the talkies boom period and there was no return to the flat-rate system. Another innovation of the period was the double-feature programme which initially was set up as a means whereby the distributor could unload some of the accumulated backlog of silent pictures which no longer could be presented in single screenings. It became customary to slip one of these pictures into a programme alongside the main talkie attraction, and when eventually the supply of silent films had ceased cheap talkies took their place so that audiences, now accustomed to two pictures for their price of admission, would not feel cheated. Inevitably some cinemas, unable to meet the cost of the installation of sound equipment, went out of business, for it was an expensive capital outlay, requiring anything up to £4,000 for the necessary apparatus, and some picture houses were so old and inadequate that the refurbishing was in any case a waste of money.

Another hazard until the industry standardized to a common sound-on-film system was the range of equipment, much of it non-compatible, that was available. In America more than two hundred systems were in competition. The wrong decision could mean that the exhibitor would in a few months be left with an obsolete and expensive array of sound equipment.

At the beginning film production was badly upset by the transition. Films that had been made as silents had ill-considered sound effects and music added to them, while retaining their subtitles. Hitchcock once described the way dialogue sounded in his excellent *Blackmail* as 'subtitles being read aloud'. E. A. Dupont, also at Elstree, the studio first off the mark where British talkies were concerned, embarked on the ambitious *Atlantic*, a story based on the *Titanic* disaster. It was made in three versions, with separate casts, so that it would be acceptable in French and German-speaking countries. Dupont was noted for his Central European temperament and expensive production touches. While his heavy style seemed appropriate in silent pictures it did not help his talkies and the film was not successful, although its two foreign-language versions did much better on the Continent. Dupont next made *Cape Forlorn*, a story set mainly in a Cornish lighthouse, and starring Frank Harvey and Fay Compton. Victor Saville made his all-talking picture debut with a spy thriller, *The W Plan*, starring Madeleine Carroll and Brian Aherne. He also remade the success of the early twenties, *Woman to Woman*. Hitchcock followed *Blackmail* with an adaptation of O'Casey's *Juno and the Paycock* with Sara Allgood and Edward Chapman, and then made an excellent thriller, *Murder*, again with Chapman plus Herbert Marshall as a celebrated actor and Norah Baring as an innocent girl in the condemned cell. It was only his third thriller out of the twelve films he had now made, but it was undoubtedly the genre in which he was most capable of exercising his talent.

During the early talkie days there was a great vogue for filmed variety revues, and they formed the bulk of the first screen musicals. Usually there was no incidental story, merely a string of acts, songs, sketches, chorus numbers, presented as if on a stage. Such films could be made quickly, feature big name stars from Broadway and other showbiz centres, and satisfy the needs of audiences for the all-singing, all-dancing spectacle. Elstree made the first of these films to be shot in England, and invited Adrian Brunel, the director of a successful silent picture, *The Constant Nymph*, to put it all together. The film was completed in twelve days and given the title *Elstree Calling*. Among the many performers were Lily Morriss, Will Fyffe, Jack Hulbert and Cicely Courtneidge, Anna May Wong and Tommy Handley. Hitchcock directed a couple of sketches featuring the cockney comedian Gordon Harker. The film has little to commend it apart from providing an interesting historical record of the state of the West End stage in 1930, and the unfortunate director was not even invited to the première. Nevertheless *Elstree Calling* grossed its costs many times over and was made into eleven foreign-language versions, a rare achievement for a British film.

At other studios the sound film was making headway. Michael Balcon had asked Brunel to make a two-reel musical version of Ketelbey's sentimental *In a Monastery Garden*, in which a male chorus was featured, all in monks' habits. *The Crooked Billet*, Brunel's last film for Gainsborough and shot as a silent, was partially remade with the dialogue springing into life in the fourth reel. Similarly, Anthony Asquith's first talkie, *A Cottage on Dartmoor*, was essentially a silent picture with occasional speech. George Pearson undertook an ambitious American co-production of *Journey's End*, a phenomenally successful stage play by R. C. Sheriff, set in the trenches of the Western Front. Although the film was directed by an Englishman, James Whale, and had a largely English cast, it was made in the Tiffany studios in Hollywood, and became one of the biggest hits of 1930. *Journey's End* foreshadowed the days when Anglo-American co-production would be a regular part of the British scene, although it was unusual in that on this occasion California was the place of production and so, technically, it was an American film.

The tendency to look to the theatre for material to film became as obsessive as it had been ten years previously. The cry now was for words, and the place to go for words was to the playwrights. The static cameras, before blimps and microphone booms had been invented, led to a succession of pictures which were little better than photographed stage productions. In 1930 the more successful ventures included *Young Woodley*, directed by Thomas Bentley in both silent and sound versions, *On Approval* and *Rookery Nook* directed by and starring the Aldwych *farceur* Tom Walls, and *Tell England*, an important film by Anthony Asquith, adapted from Ernest Raymond's novel and including some heroically re-enacted scenes of the abortive Gallipoli landings in 1915.

The latter film was a precursor of a style of stiff-upper-lip filming that was to become a familiar staple of the British cinema in and after the Second World War. This is not to belittle its achievement in 1930 when the realism and neo-documentary presentation of the battle scenes presaged the importance of Asquith's contribution to the cinema. He was one of the first directors in Britain, or for that matter in Hollywood, to break out of the straitjacket sound had imposed on the medium, and the success of *Tell England* gave false hope to the prophets who felt that at last the British industry was beginning to stand on its feet.

But the glut of stage adaptations was beginning to jade the appetites of the filmgoers. It was not so much the style and pace of the direction as the stilted delivery and cinematic inexperience of the actors which was causing irritation, particularly among popular audiences. The British cinema had become a middle-class institution; it was the 'cultured' West End accent that was heard and it was the *mores* of the country drawing-room that were being observed. In Middlesbrough and Smethwick they opted for the classless accents of America, just as they preferred the slicker pace and the glossier technique. It was a time of misery, poverty and unemployment for the working classes on both sides of the Atlantic. Most British films failed absolutely to sense the mood of the audience and equated it with the same people who paid fifteen shillings for a stalls seat in Shaftesbury Avenue. Even George Bernard Shaw, finally consenting to a film version of one of his plays, had a failure. The film was *How He Lied to Her Husband*, and was directed by Cecil Lewis with a cast which included Robert Harris, Edmund Gwenn and Vera Lennox. In spite of Shaw's fastidious interference at every level of production, which he fussed over like a mother hen, the finished article lacked every vestige of Shavian wit and buoyancy. Alfred Hitchcock also got entangled in the french windows and lily ponds of the English gentry with his film version of Galsworthy's *The Skin Game*, but at least

65

there was a strong social conflict, with Edmund Gwenn representing an early exponent of the new technology, anxious to turn the English countryside into a power house of thriving industrial plants.

Victor Saville, whose work at this period was consistently interesting, remade both *Hindle Wakes*, a Lancastrian stage adaptation which at least had more of a grass roots approach to life, and a German musical, *Sunshine Susie*, starring Renate Muller in the same part she played in the earlier version, and Jack Hulbert. In fact it became a vogueish practice to remake films originating in Germany. There was, for instance, *Congress Dances*, remade by Erich Pommer, with Lillian Harvey and Conrad Veidt in their original roles. On the same pattern was *Tell Me Tonight*, directed by Anatole Litvak, with a cast including Edmund Gwenn and Sonnie Hale, as well as Jan Kiepura and Magda Schneider who were in the original version.

Older British film successes were also considered suitable material for remakes; for instance in 1932 Maurice Elvey remade the 1926 Hitchcock film *The Lodger*, again with Ivor Novello in the lead, and Elizabeth Allan taking the part originally played by June. In the same year the new Gaumont-British studios, built on the site of the old Gaumont studios in Lime Grove, Shepherds Bush, were opened. The first film made there was a good one, *Rome Express*, directed by Walter Forde, with a cast that included Conrad Veidt, Esther Ralston and Gordon Harker, and it attracted favourable reviews. The new studios were the result of the Ostrers' control of Gaumont-British and Gainsborough, where Michael Balcon had been left in charge before being invited to take over production control at Lime Grove as well.

During the early thirties Parliament again had to intervene to sort out a difficult situation in the industry. With the closure of many live theatres and their conversion into cinemas – a blight that quickly spread over the West End after the introduction of talkies – there was considerable resentment of the fact that cinemas were open on Sundays, while live stage shows were forbidden under the Sunday Observance Act of 1780. Ways were found of applying clauses in the old Act to cover film performances, with the result that in 1931 the cinemas were forced to stop their Sunday performances. However, vigorous public opposition to this move compelled the Government to recognize a general demand for Sunday films, and so in 1932 a new Sunday Entertainments Act became law. It put the ball firmly in the court of the local authorities, giving them the right to license Sunday cinemas. It also gave the authorities the right to determine what proportion of the takings were to be devoted to charity, as well as stipulating that a further five per cent was to be paid into the Cinematograph Fund, a means for developing the British Film Institute as an educational body, committed to increasing knowledge of the cinema's value as an artistic and educational medium. On average about six per cent of Sunday box-office takings were handed over. Sunday opening itself varied greatly from region to region. In London nearly all cinemas opted for a seven-day week, while at the other extreme, in sabbatarian Scotland and Wales, only about seven per cent opened on Sundays. Because of problems concerned with the transportation of the film itself, Sunday programmes tended to be different from the normal weekday run. Another reason for this was the wish to develop a special Sunday audience. Consequently, for many years Sunday programmes tended to consist of older and cheaper films, which offset the fact that opening hours were shorter and the box-office takings correspondingly less. The passage of the Sunday Entertainments Act did at least legitimate Sunday opening and quelled the factions that had developed in opposition against it. In requiring the local authorities to make the decisions for their own area the Government preserved the principles already established by the Cinematograph Act of 1909. Wherever possible direct state control was avoided in legislation affecting the showing of films. In the thirties there were further pleas from certain factions for a State Censorship Board, particularly as a trend towards violence and sadism was gaining ground in American films, reaching a climax in the gangster cycle which included *Public Enemy* and *Little Caesar*. The BBFC, under its chairman Edward Shortt, who took over from T. P. Connor on his death in 1929, held firm, and eventually the American picture industry voluntarily adopted a 'clean-up' policy with the Motion Picture Producers and Distributors of America, the Hays office, named after its president, Will H. Hays, who had been in charge since its inception in 1922, vetting each film.

7 Boomtime

In November 1931 a young Hungarian who had been a critic and film producer in his native country, and more recently in Paris, arrived in England with a contract to direct two films for Paramount. The first, a comedy called *Service For Ladies*, reintroduced Leslie Howard, and the other was *Women Who Play*. In early 1932 Alexander Korda founded his own company, reviving the disused name of Dr Ralph Tennyson Jupp's Company of 1913, London Films, and was soon joined by his younger brothers, Vincent and Zoltan. The company set to and began producing 'quota quickies', cheap, speedily produced films to meet the demands of the Renters' Quota. The first was *Wedding Rehearsal* which, in spite of its low budget, was well-received. The brothers continued making these films, swapping the direction around between them. Merle Oberon, Robert Donat and Emlyn Williams were among the new performers who found their faces on the screen as a result of Korda's London Films.

In a few short months, with a handful of low-budget pictures, Korda had demonstrated a taste and a capacity for serving entertaining material. It was inevitable that sooner or later he would attempt something more ambitious. He is alleged to have heard a cockney cab-driver singing 'I'm 'Enery the Eighth', although the weight of apocryphal stories about Korda is phenomenal. Nevertheless he was the driving force behind the setting up of *The Private Life of Henry VIII*, a costume biography of the famous monarch which enabled Charles Laughton to deliver one of his earliest virtuoso performances in the cinema, with a supporting cast that included Merle Oberon, Robert Donat, Binnie Barnes and Elsa Lanchester. The cameraman was the lugubrious Georges Perinal, imported from France in his first association with Korda. Money was somehow raised from the City; when it was exhausted Ludovico de Grand Ry, an Italian financier, bailed the company out. Korda held a world première at the Radio City Music Hall in New York, the largest cinema in the world, which had been opened by the legendary showman S. L. ('Roxy') Rothafel in the previous year. With immensely flattering American press notices behind it, the film opened in London two weeks later on 24 October 1933 at the Leicester Square Theatre. The British press went wild in a fury of patriotic excitement. There was an immense attraction in the subject of a lusty, wenching, foul-mouthed, virile English king. Contrary to popular belief, it had not been a wildly expensive picture; its cost was probably less than £60,000, which was small beer by American standards. Its first release grossed a respectable half a million pounds, a valuable figure to be displayed on Korda's balance sheet the next time he approached the City bankers. What is more, the international prestige gained for the British industry for this one film was staggering. Korda was acclaimed as the new genius who could save British films.

And now the vast Prudential Assurance Company was induced to open its coffers. Grandiose plans were set in hand for building an enormous complex of studios at Denham in Buckinghamshire for London Films, which were to cost more than a million pounds. Korda, meanwhile, continued to make films on rented sound stages. His next starred the German actress Elisabeth Bergner, and was directed by her husband, Dr Paul Czinner. It was *Catherine the Great*, and included in the cast Douglas Fairbanks Jr and Flora Robson, as well as Gerald du Maurier and Irene Vanbrugh. In spite of such powerful casting the film failed to achieve anything approaching the same success as *Henry VIII*. In a way it was a direct challenge to Hollywood, for Joseph von Sternberg had just made *Scarlet Empress* with Marlene Dietrich. Although the public failed to take to the Korda film, its taste and worthiness only enhanced his prestige with critics and backers. But this evaporated when his next film, *The Private Life of Don Juan*, appeared. The title part was played by the paunchy, muscle-bound Douglas Fairbanks Sr, his last film, with his best swashbuckling days by now well behind him. The film was a failure, and Korda's persuasive charm was called to good account to keep the Prudential happy. His luck returned with the next film, *The Scarlet Pimpernel*, a romantic costume drama from the Baroness Orczy novel which made nearly half a million pounds on its first run. The director was Harold Young and the cast included Leslie Howard, Merle Oberon and Raymond Massey. Faith was completely restored, and the foundations were laid down on the site at Denham.

Meanwhile, in other studios London Films went on producing pictures. Zoltan Korda directed *Sanders of the River*, a chauvinistic tribute to the paternalism of the British colonizers in Africa. The American director, William Cameron Menzies, was called in to direct a screenplay by H. G. Wells, *Things to Come*, which dealt in a prophetic way with a world that almost destroyed itself in a nuclear holocaust, and sought salvation through the opening up of space travel. With its strident Arthur Bliss score and ambitiously designed sets, its intriguing theme and Wellsian propaganda that humanity's hopes lay with the scientists, it was the sensation of the year. Both this film and *The Ghost Goes West*, a whimsical comedy with Robert Donat, directed by René Clair, had their exteriors shot in the grounds of the unfinished Denham Studios, as did the second H. G. Wells subject, *The Man Who Could Work Miracles*. The day before the studios were to be opened, a fire occurred causing £45,000 worth of damage. The Prudential as well as meeting the building costs in the first place had also insured it with themselves and so had to pay out for the repairs.

The first film to be made completely at Denham was one of the highwater marks of Korda's career, a careful, tender, devoted reconstruction of the life of a great painter, *Rembrandt*, who was played with dignity and compassion by Charles Laughton, with Elsa Lanchester as Hendrijke. Korda did not expect the film to be a commercial success but he wanted the first product of the new headquarters of London Films to be worthy of the industry he had in such a short time managed to transform. Korda was at the summit of his career; he had shown himself to be the foremost producer in Britain, his confidence, ambition, charm and sensitivity attracting attention for British films all over the world. Korda films were made with an intelligent and careful eye on public taste and he was not afraid to run ahead of it. Regrettably *Rembrandt*, an excellent picture, was far ahead of its time and languished in half-empty houses.

But Korda was not the only producer to force the pace between 1933 and 1936. Another remarkable figure was Michael Balcon, who as head of production at Gaumont-British and Gainsborough had already set things rolling with *Rome Express*. In 1933, the year of *The Private Life of Henry VIII*, he was responsible for several interesting films, three of them directed by Victor Saville: *Friday the Thirteenth*, with Sonnie Hale, Jessie Matthews and Gordon Harker; *I Was a Spy*, an accomplished essay into First World War romanticism with Madeleine Caroll, Conrad Veidt and Herbert Marshall; and the best of the trio, *The Good Companions*, with Edmund Gwenn, Jessie Matthews and John Gielgud, an adaptation of J. B. Priestley's novel about a travelling concert party in the north of England. It was the first sound film to receive a Royal Gala Performance. In the following year Balcon capitalized on the enormous and unique talent of Jessie Matthews and put her into musicals where her magnificent legs and high, throbby voice were exploited to great effect. The first was Victor Saville's superb *Evergreen*, an evocation of the Edwardian musical theatre as well as high life in the thirties, with a Rodgers and Hart score. This was followed by *First a Girl*, *It's Love Again*, *Head over Heels* and others, the first two again directed by the prolific Victor Saville. Balcon also lured Alfred Hitchcock away from John Maxwell at BIP and set him to work at directing the kind of films he could do better than anybody else. The first of the Gaumont-British thrillers was *The Man Who Knew Too Much*; it followed an unsuccessful and dismal attempt at a light musical comedy costume picture, *Waltzes from Vienna*, which was one of Hitchcock's worst mistakes, and an area into which he would never venture again. The new thriller, from its shock opening to a thinly disguised version of the Sidney Street siege at its climax, was an exciting work. It starred Leslie Banks, Nova Pilbeam as a kidnapped small girl, and introduced Peter Lorre, the villain of Fritz Lang's *M* and now a refugee from Nazi Germany, to British cinema. Hitchcock followed this film with his even more celebrated version of John Buchan's *The Thirty-Nine Steps*, a far cry from the novel, but a brilliant film with superb counterplaying by Robert Donat and Madeleine Carroll. *The Secret Agent* in 1936 again featured Madeleine Carroll, this time with Peter Lorre and John Gielgud, and was loosely based on Somerset Maugham's *Ashenden*. It was as richly imaginative as the previous two films, but less successful at the box-office. In the same year Hitchcock directed an updated version of Joseph Conrad's novel *The Secret Agent*, and to add to the confusion called it *Sabotage* (*A Woman Alone* in America). The anarchist, now a London cinema manager, was played by Oscar Homolka, and his wife by the American actress, Sylvia Sidney. A notable sequence involved a small boy carrying a parcel bomb in a crowded bus, marred according to Hitchcock by the subsequent detonation, which killed the innocent carrier. It was the last Hitchcock film produced by Michael Balcon.

His tastes, like Korda's, also embraced the elaborate historical type of film. One of the most successful, made in 1936 with Nova Pilbeam playing Lady Jane Grey, was *Tudor Rose*, directed and written by Robert Stevenson, who in another age was to direct *Mary Poppins*.

Rhodes of Africa, in the same year, starring Walter Huston, Oscar Homolka and Peggy Ashcroft, was, in comparison with the quiet stylishness and restrained acting of the first film, a ponderous bore in a style which Hollywood could plainly mount a great deal more successfully. The director was Berthold Viertel, who also made *Little Friend* from a novel by the author of *The Constant Nymph*, Margaret Kennedy, in which Nova Pilbeam, one of the liveliest young actresses of the thirties, was given a big publicity build-up.

Jew Süss, an expensive film for the time, reaching a six-figure budget, was another Balcon period film, directed by Lothar Mendes and starring Conrad Veidt, Benita Hume and Frank Vosper. There was also the continuation of a string of films made on both sides of the Atlantic, featuring the ugly but amazingly popular idiosyncratic actor, George Arliss, in which great men of history were impersonated – for instance Wellington in *The Iron Duke*, which was directed by Victor Saville. If Hitchcock was the king of the thriller in the British cinema of the thirties, Saville was undoubtedly its most important romantic stylist.

Other producers found mileage in costume films. Herbert Wilcox remade his silent Dorothy Gish picture *Nell Gwyn*, with Anna Neagle playing the King's mistress, and achieved the dubious distinction of having it banned in the United States until the distributors had emasculated it to such a degree that a failure was inevitable. Nevertheless, in Britain, although by no means a lavish spectacle, it achieved a good run for its money. It was followed up by Anna Neagle playing Peg Woffington, the eighteenth-century actress, in the equally successful *Peg of Old Drury*.

During this period of the thirties another fruitful and sometimes overlooked genre of British film began to appear in increasing numbers, the broad comedy pictures which featured comedians who had made reputations for hilarious and earthy working-class humour in the music halls. These films were modest in intention – most of them never got near the West End – but they did a great deal to provide a common interest between the producer and the mass audience. Among the comics it is fair to include Gracie Fields, the popular comedienne from Rochdale, who made her film debut in 1931 with *Sally in our Alley*, and through a series of delightful films in the thirties achieved the status of Britain's highest paid star. Typical, for instance, was her 1934 film, *Sing As We Go*, produced and directed by Basil Dean, in which she became a maid in a Blackpool boarding house. Scenes shot in the Lancashire resort, on the 'golden mile' and at the Pleasure Beach, gave a documentary insight into how half the British population lived, while the comedy was rich and human. Also in 1934, another Lancashire comedian, George Formby, made an initial screen appearance – a toothy and gormless young man, son of a famous music-hall star, with a penchant for finding trouble in the most unlikely places. His first film was made in Manchester and was called *Boots, Boots*. He too was to become one of the top box-office draws in Britain. The third great comic to become an established element of the British cinema made his debut in a film about old-time music hall, in 1934, *Those Were the Days*, which was directed by Thomas Bentley. This was Will Hay who a year later appeared in the famous guise of the seedy, uneducated, crooked schoolmaster, Dr Twist, in *Boys Will Be Boys*. The film was directed by Marcel Varnel, a Frenchman who was to become a prime force in the English comedy film of the thirties. His position as the foremost comedy director was rivalled only by Anthony Kimmins, who made most of the Formby pictures.

In 1936 film output in Britain reached the staggering total of 212 features. Yet in spite of both the quantity and quality of the best British films, earnings from overseas markets were minuscule in comparison with the amounts spent on importing films into the country, mostly from America. The British film-producing business was basking in false sunshine and it was not to do so for very much longer.

However poor the studios' prospects were in the mid-thirties, the exhibitors were in an excellent position. New cinemas mushroomed and attracted new audiences. Hollywood's output of excellent pictures was staggering – it was the age of the superstar, of Clark Gable and Gary Cooper, Joan Crawford and Claudette Colbert, Carol Lombard and Jean Arthur, and of course, Fred Astaire and Ginger Rogers. In the ranks of the exhibitors, however, a new and important name had emerged. Oscar Deutsch, an ex-metal merchant who in the early twenties had been chairman of W. & F. Film Service, formed a company in 1931 called Cinema Service. It initially owned six cinemas. In 1933 the company was reformed as Odeon Theatres with a complement of twenty-six cinemas, making it the eighth largest circuit. Deutsch was one of the first British exhibitors to recognize that brand marketing was applicable to the cinema business. He set out to create a readily recognizable corporate image for Odeon, with distinctive lettering, façades and display units. Deutsch embarked on an ambitious policy of building; his intention was to set up a major circuit of up-to-date houses which would outshine their rivals by the luxuriousness of their fittings and the unity of their design. The newly built Odeons were all separate companies in their own right, an arrangement which enabled each theatre to raise its own capital by selling shares to local interests, which would benefit from a good cinema in the locality. After three years the Odeon circuit had become the fourth largest in the country, with 142 theatres, including twenty-nine under construction. But having good theatres was not enough, for Odeon's booking power was inferior to that of the rival circuits, ABC and Gaumont-British. After much negotiation a deal was completed with one of the major American renters, United Artists. This company, unlike its other big American rivals, did not produce its own films, but distributed the work of independent producers. It had been founded in the twenties by Douglas Fairbanks Sr and Charles Chaplin to combat the stranglehold of the big studios. Consequently, although Odeon could now have the bulk of the UA output, there was still an obligation on their part to let other exhibitors have a slice of the cake as well. But at least UA now had a guaranteed base market in Britain, and Odeon a guaranteed film source. Since one of the United Artists's partners from 1935 was Alexander Korda, Deutsch now had the beginnings of vertical integration in the British cinema. The financial arrangements, however, were complicated and created certain problems for the future.

Gaumont-British had greatly increased in size during the mid-thirties, owning 305 cinemas by 1936. ABC had only a few less, 296. John Maxwell, head of ABPC, then announced that he was joining the GB board and that the two circuits would merge. This would have created a giant unit, controlling thirteen per cent of British cinemas and seventeen per cent of seats. But they were the better theatres, mainly first-run houses. Although Maxwell did indeed join the rival board the proposed merger did not occur, possibly because the American interests carried out adroit financial moves to prevent the growth of the monster. Twentieth-Century Fox, the majority shareholders of Metropolis and Bradford Trust, who in turn were controllers of GB, objected to the scheme and formed a new holding company in association with Loew's (MGM). In fact Maxwell remained on the board of both companies until he resigned from GB in 1938 after an unsuccessful legal battle with the Ostrer brothers. In spite of this setback Maxwell's ABC circuit continued to expand, its most important acquisition being the Union circuit, with 136 cinemas in 1937 boosting the total of theatres owned to nearly a hundred more than the 345 of the GB group. Consequently, Maxwell was able to ensure that his exhibiting interests outstripped those of his rivals.

There was another figure, who was to have an almost apocalyptic effect on the British film, now beginning to take an interest in the industry. Joseph Arthur Rank came into films from a wealthy background of Yorkshire flour-milling. An ardent Methodist, the first films he produced were religious shorts. His mission was to make films suitable for church audiences, which would be equal in production standards with the day-to-day output of the normal commercial cinema. There was considerable opposition within the Methodist Church to the use of films for sectarian purposes, and Rank had to fight hard. But in 1934, fired with evangelical zeal, he succeeded in forming a new company, British National Films, in partnership with Lady Yule, the remarkable and immensely wealthy widow of a jute millionaire. Rank initially wanted to make a film of *The Pilgrim's Progress* but this project never materialized. Instead, the first film made by his new company was set in a Yorkshire fishing port and concerned the rivalry between two families. Called *The Turn of the Tide*, it was directed by Norman Walker and starred Wilfrid Lawson, Moore Marriott and Geraldine Fitzgerald, a newcomer who later did well in Hollywood. It pleased both the critics and Rank, who had ensured that although the subject was a secular one its morality would be of a high order. In spite of the prestige of a major placing in the Venice Film Festival the film did not get a wide circuit release and so failed to recoup its costs. It was the beginning of Rank's march towards a situation where he became the most influential force in British films. In order to find a way of getting his films a fair showing he became a backer of C. M. Woolf, who in 1935, after a row with the Ostrer brothers, resigned from Gaumont-British and set up General Film Distributors. This company in a short space of time became very successful, buying, for instance, a quarter share of the American producing company, Universal, which reversed the tendency for American companies to buy their way into British ones. Meanwhile, Rank had become chairman of Pinewood Studios, which had been built at Iver in Buckinghamshire, a few miles from Korda's Denham. In many ways it was superior; the stages were linked by covered arcades and the site included some extensive landscaped grounds, once the estate of Heatherden Hall, which were put to frequent use for exterior shooting.

By 1936 Rank was poised for action. But another crisis was to intervene.

8 Slumptime

Over-confidence had led to over-expansion. British studio space grew at a rapid pace, the number of stages quadrupling in the decade 1928–38, and the amount of floor space multiplying seven-fold. In the year 1937–8 production output achieved a total of 228 films, far more than could reasonably be accommodated on British cinema screens, let alone in overseas markets. One of the bad results of the 1927 Act, as had been forecast, was the predominance of 'quota quickies' in the industry's production record, rather than large, well-made, prestige films. The former were cheap to produce and more likely to yield a profit than quality pictures. In theory they met the obligations of exhibitors and renters to favour the domestic producers, but in practice they contributed to public resentment against British films. It was always hard for a worthy, well-made picture, such as *The Turn of the Tide*, to bulldoze its way on to the screen in the face of Hollywood films and the quickies.

It was not the exhibitors who were to suffer in the crisis. As long as the supply of good American films was maintained, they could not lose. These were the films that the public was eager to see. Consequently, the vertically-integrated companies – the Ostrer's Gaumont-British, Maxwell's ABPC – would survive in spite of the jolt to their production arms.

The extravagant success of Alexander Korda's 1933 picture, *The Private Life of Henry VIII*, had set in train a period of excessive speculation with City firms almost falling over themselves in the rush to get a stake in the new booming business. But there was one factor that had been imperfectly calculated in the eternal optimism of the film-makers. The home market was inadequate and incapable of producing a profit for a reasonably expensive picture – in fact, almost any picture other than a quickie. Access, therefore, to the American market was absolutely essential. And in spite of all efforts this was a target which constantly eluded the British producers. The American companies themselves were not, obviously, interested in the plight of British films, and made little effort to provide any form of reciprocal dealing.

There was another serious aspect to the City's interest in films and that was that the money being poured in was in the form of loans, not capital. In the first ten months of 1936 alone more than £4 million was lent to the British film industry. The only alternative to profitability would be bankruptcy. All the warning signs were present; that they were ignored is a measure of the euphoria of the mid-thirties. Many if not most film companies had made insufficient profit to pay dividends for several years. Waste and inefficiency were legendary and Korda's oft-quoted remark, that when the industry makes money it is in millions, 'and so obviously, when we lose, it must be in millions', was an indication of the unreality and profligacy of this apparently glamorous business.

At the beginning of 1937 a receiver was appointed at Twickenham Studios. Korda ordered salary cuts at London Films. Then came a shock from Gaumont-British – a debit of nearly £100,000 on the previous year's trading. GB would cease to produce its own films, Lime Grove was to shut down, Gaumont-British Distributors was to fold. Henceforth GB News and the Gainsborough films made at Islington would be handled by General Film Distributors. This solemn story continued for many more months, with companies going bankrupt and studios closing. Output for 1938 was considerably less than half that of the previous year and the available studio space was only half-utilized.

The ten-year period of the 1927 Cinematograph Act was nearing its end when the Government in March 1936 appointed a committee under Lord Moyne to investigate and recommend measures to be adopted in a new Parliamentary Bill. After exhaustive evidence-taking and deliberation the Moyne Committee plumped solidly for more protection on a progressively increasing basis. The quota system, the Committee felt, had to a large extent been effective. Mindful of the harm done to the industry by 'quota quickies' it urged the creation of a quality test which a film would have to pass before it could qualify for renters' quota. This test would be administered by a new Government Films Commission. It also wanted to introduce a quota for short films, which had suffered as a result of a loophole in the wording of the 1928 Act. With its recommendations adopted, the

Committee felt that in the next ten year period fifty per cent of screen time would be given to British films.

When put to the trade the Report was received with the same mixed feelings that preceded the introduction of the 1927 Cinematograph Act. As agreement was not possible, Parliament proceeded to enact the legislation as it had done ten years earlier, without the voluntary support of the business itself. The new Act accepted the quota recommendations except for the quality test. The long film quota was dropped to 15 per cent for exhibitors, $12\frac{1}{2}$ per cent for renters in the first year, rising in stages eventually to 30 and 25 per cent respectively. The reason for the initial reduction was that instead of a quality test a cost test had been introduced, and it was felt that production would be bound to drop at first. The minima were £7,500 per film, based on labour costs, and a rate of £1 per foot. With an almost indelicate equation of money with artistic results a system of double and triple quotas was also instituted, so that a film costing £3 a foot counted as twice its length for renters' quota and £5 per foot three times. The Films Commission idea, however, was rejected because it was felt that an enlarged Advisory Committee, now called the Cinematograph Films Council, could do the job in an advisory capacity. Another mild proposal advanced in the Moyne Report, for the Government to set up a film-financing agency, was not covered in the Act. In order that working conditions in the industry should be improved a Fair Wages Clause made it mandatory for employers to offer terms and conditions approximating to trade union agreements. In order that the quota system should not seem too chauvinistic, special provision was made for specialist, 'art-house' type foreign films to be exempted from the requirements, providing that their circulation remained on a small scale.

The new Act could not restore lost fortunes or reopen the closed studios, but one beneficial effect was a new interest from American companies towards production in Britain. The first company to set up a British production wing was MGM, and Michael Balcon, now cut off from GB, was signed up to take control of an ambitious programme of Anglo-American films, each of which would justify its expense by being treated in the United States as a normal MGM product. The first film was suitably transatlantic in tone, *A Yank at Oxford*, directed by the American, Jack Conway, and starring Robert Taylor, Maureen O'Sullivan and Lionel Barrymore with the young British actress, Vivien Leigh. The story, concerning the adventures of a brash Middle West athletics student on a scholarship to the ancient cradle of learning, made a mildly satirical poke at the eccentricities of both Anglo-Saxon nations and was an entertaining box-office success. Balcon, unable to achieve compatibility with Louis B. Mayer, left MGM in disgust and Victor Saville stepped into his shoes. King Vidor, an extremely accomplished Hollywood director, was responsible for the second MGM–British film, an adaptation of an A. J. Cronin novel, *The Citadel*, about a doctor who progresses from the mining slums of Wales to the Adam-decorated consulting rooms of Harley Street, only to lose his ideals along the way. Rosalind Russell came from America to play opposite Robert Donat and Ralph Richardson. The last film, made in 1939, just before the start of the Second World War and the suspension of MGM's film-making activities in Britain, was *Goodbye Mr Chips*, an outstanding world success and an acting tour-de-force for Robert Donat, who was required to span almost a lifetime, from youthful vigour to apparent senility. *Goodbye Mr Chips*, an unashamedly sentimental James Hilton story about a beloved master in an English public school, was directed by Sam Wood, a Hollywood veteran, responsible for among other things two of the best Marx Brothers films, *Night at the Opera* and *Day at the Races*. *Goodbye Mr Chips* also introduced Greer Garson to the screen. Although only seen for a few minutes' running time the impression she made was strong enough to guarantee a lengthy Hollywood career.

What really made the three MGM films stand out from most British films of the time was their technical superiority. They had been made with the gloss and skill of the Hollywood film industry and proved that British technicians under proper guidance could produce work as polished as the Americans. Had the brief MGM period continued, the subsequent story would have been substantially different for all three films had made money, not only in England but in many other countries.

Output in other studios during the two or three years between the beginning of the crisis and the even more drastic upheaval of the war became erratic as the courts filled with bankrupt film men. But by no means were they completely fallow years. Korda, now ensconced in his stately Denham studios, continued to extravagantly hire his directors and stars from abroad (to say nothing of technicians: the standing joke was that the three Union Jacks outside the studios represented the three native Englishmen on the Korda payroll). After René Clair's *The Ghost Goes West*, another celebrated French director, Jacques

Feyder, was brought over to direct Marlene Dietrich in *Knight Without Armour*, from a James Hilton novel about the Russian Revolution. As a film it was not without a touch of vulgarity and was inferior to *Fire Over England*, directed by William K. Howard, with Flora Robson as a tight-lipped, strait-laced Queen Elizabeth, and an excellent cast which included Laurence Olivier, Vivien Leigh, Raymond Massey and Leslie Banks. Korda also brought Joseph von Sternberg from Hollywood to make *I Claudius* from Robert Graves's novel, with Charles Laughton, Merle Oberon and Emlyn Williams. It was an unhappy experience; Laughton suffered desperate agonies in his quest for the interpretation of the part, Sternberg was difficult, temperamental and disliked, and after Merle Oberon was injured in a car accident the film was abandoned, a third of it shot and thousands of pounds spent on massive and spectacular sets. What remains depicts what might have been one of Laughton's greatest performances. Korda also persuaded Robert Flaherty, a giant of documentary films, to make *Elephant Boy* on location with a young Indian, Sabu. Ultimately the film was finished on the backlot at Denham, with elephants pounding through the Buckinghamshire jungle, and the film is far from vintage Flaherty.

Korda's extravagance, flamboyance and penchant for employing so many foreigners, especially Hungarians, aroused xenophobic passions among certain sections of the public, and articles appeared denouncing him as the cause of the British film crisis. Undoubtedly Korda was a brilliant and magnetic force in the cinema. Like many dynamic men he could not do things by halves, and that included his failures which were inevitably more spectacular and more catastrophic than anyone else's. His genius was persuasive and when he turned on the charm even his bitterest enemies melted. Korda rode out the storm with the skill with which he was to survive many others before the end of his career. It was plain that no man had been so successful in raising the British flag in other countries. Like many other exiles who have settled in Britain he was motivated by a patriotism far more passionate than that of many Englishmen.

Herbert Wilcox, born in County Cork, Ireland, has also throughout his long career vigorously waved the British flag. His exultantly triumphant *Victoria the Great* arose from a request by the Duke of Windsor during the brief period in 1936 when he occupied the throne as King Edward VIII. Alexander Korda was for once left at the post. The film was shot in five weeks, a remarkably short time for such a subject, with Anna Neagle playing the Queen and Anton Walbrook Prince Albert. Its treatment was episodic, being based on Laurence Housman's *Victoria Regina*, which was more a series of sketches based on Victoria's life than a play. The film was exhibited to the public at a psychologically appropriate time, and Britain, troubled by a worsening European situation, gladly revelled in a frenzy of nostalgic imperialism. Wilcox followed up the film with *Sixty Glorious Years*, which was the same mixture as before, except that the Royal Family granted permission for certain sequences to be shot at Balmoral, and the whole film was made in Technicolor.

The first British film to be made in the new three-colour Technicolor process, first seen in a full-length feature in Rouben Mamoulian's *Becky Sharp* two years earlier, was the 1937 production from Twentieth-Century Fox, *Wings of the Morning*, directed by Harold Schuster, with a cast including Henry Fonda, Annabella, Leslie Banks and Count John McCormack. 'Wings' was a racehorse and some of the best footage was contained in the documentary scenes of the Derby at Epsom. The new colour process was a welcome addition to the screen and this British film was well-received, it being generally noted that subtler effects were obtained in the soft English light than in American colour films of the period.

Michael Powell, a prolific but unnoticed director of the early thirties, shot an impressive film on location on the Scottish island of Foula, *The Edge of the World*, outstanding for its dramatic photography which captured the quality of the northern climate and the beauty and grandeur of rocks and wild seas. Until then Powell's work had been mainly in quickies, but with this film he revealed himself as a front runner in the new British realist school which was to emerge properly in the wartime forties. An important film of 1937, again set in Scotland, but of a rather more amusing nature, was *Storm in a Teacup* with Rex Harrison and Vivien Leigh, directed by Victor Saville and Ian Dalrymple. In spite of the axiom that 'satire is what closes Saturday night' this film was very successful as well as witty, and demonstrated that British film comedy could sometimes work with subtlety.

In the broader vein George Formby and Gracie Fields continued to be at the top of the box-office popularity ratings. George Formby was a comedian who had adapted particularly well to films, most of which were constructed to a prescribed formula – George trying to hold a job down in spite of appalling disasters beyond his control and trying also to win the girl in the face of opposition from a handsome, accomplished rival. There was always room for a song or two with the banjo (always called a ukelele) and a regular number of hurled pies, whitewash buckets and paint cans. A chase or a sequence in which a machine goes out of control, such as the RAF aerobatic plane in *It's in the Air*, was also mandatory. Most of the George Formby films were directed by Anthony Kimmins, later succeeded by Marcel Varnel, who at this time was concentrating on Will Hay and the Crazy Gang. Varnel's 1937 near-masterpiece of comic film-making was *Oh Mr Porter!* in which Will Hay played an appalling country stationmaster, with Moore Marriott and Graham Moffatt as unco-operative platform staff. Will Hay had a particular skill in evoking sympathy even for the incompetent scoundrels he usually played. In the following year he appeared in *Convict 99* and in a parody, *Old Bones of the River*, as a schoolmaster attempting the Leslie Banks role of the earlier film. Films such as these were not noted for the amounts spent on them but they moved at a crisp pace and demanded little from their audiences beyond the ability to enjoy a good laugh. They were particularly popular in northern England and cinema managers knew that they could pack in bigger audiences than many of the best Hollywood pictures.

Alfred Hitchcock, whose days at Gaumont-British ended with *Sabotage*, made *Young and Innocent* (*The Girl Was Young* in America), an engaging comedy thriller with Derrick de Marney and Nova Pilbeam, for Gainsborough, which continued in business when GB production was suspended. It was that favourite Hitchcock theme, the double chase, with innocent hero, searching for the real value, pursued by the law. At the climax of the film Hitchcock inserted a phenomenal example of his technical bravura, a long shot of a crowded ballroom with a tracking camera ending in a big close-up of a musician's twitching eye, all in one sweep. Hitchcock's last film that properly belongs in the tradition of the Gaumont-British thrillers, although made by Gainsborough at Islington, was *The Lady Vanishes*. A spy thriller set in a mythical mid-European country, it starred Margaret Lockwood, who was becoming the leading young British heroine, and Michael Redgrave. Because of a distribution deal with MGM this film was given a much wider screening abroad and earned a large amount of foreign currency, ensuring Hitchcock's commanding reputation as the best-known British director. Shortly after this film was made he left GB and Gainsborough altogether with the expiry of his contract, and signed a new one with David O. Selznick to go to

Hollywood to make *Rebecca*. Meanwhile he returned to Elstree and Erich Pommer where he shot a highly theatrical version of Daphne du Maurier's historical novel of Cornish smugglers, *Jamaica Inn*. Its cast included Charles Laughton, Emlyn Williams and a new girl, Maureen O'Hara. Laughton had just finished *Vessel of Wrath* for Pommer, the first of several made with capital from ABPC and John Maxwell. Mayflower Pictures had been formed by Laughton and Pommer with the intention of producing pictures on both sides of the Atlantic and *Vessel of Wrath* (*The Beachcomber* in America) had been adapted from a Somerset Maugham story with an eye on the American market, which turned out to be little interested. The following picture, *St Martin's Lane* (*Sidewalks of London* in America), with Laughton, Vivien Leigh and Rex Harrison, was directed by Tim Whelan, an American who made several British films, the best probably being *Farewell Again* the year before. Mayflower Pictures failed to make a big mark in spite of the array of talent signed by Pommer and, when war came, quietly died. Whelan had also been responsible for Korda's first Technicolor film, *The Divorce of Lady X*, which starred Laurence Olivier, Ralph Richardson and Merle Oberon. The subject was surprising at the time, for colour tended to be used more for adventure spectaculars than marital comedies. Korda's other pre-war colour films were *The Drum* and *The Four Feathers*, directed by Zoltan Korda, both of which featured the Empire in its full Victorian splendour; *Over the Moon*, which was a blandly romantic film with lush Venetian locations; and *The Thief of Bagdad*, which actually went into production after the war had started. This film was rich and ingenious in the use of lavish optical effects, and constituted some sort of milestone in the technical development of the British cinema.

Another Hungarian arrived on the scene in the late thirties, with a similar gift for inducing the most difficult people to bow in his direction. Bernard Shaw's encounters with the cinema had been unfruitful and he long held out against requests to film his plays. Somehow Gabriel Pascal got him to agree to the filming of *Pygmalion*, and signed up Anthony Asquith and Leslie Howard to direct the film jointly, with Howard as Professor Higgins, Wendy Hiller as Eliza and Wilfrid Lawson as Doolittle. *Pygmalion* was a much more Shavian picture than *How He Lied to Her Husband*, directed by Cecil Lewis several years earlier. It was well received and regarded as a notable attempt to render Shaw in cinematic terms; valuable concessions had been won from the difficult playwright with regard to 'opening up' the story. Shaw was pleased with the reception and agreed to let Pascal go ahead on *Major Barbara*, which he both produced and directed. Anthony Asquith's last pre-war film was an adaptation of Terence Rattigan's successful stage comedy, *French Without Tears*, which transferred the atmosphere of frivolous matinée romping to the screen with a cast of Ray Milland, Roland Culver and Ellen Drew.

One director whose work was now attracting critical attention was Carol Reed, who had managed to make an episodic collection of experiences of English holiday-makers into a warm, amusing and well observed film. *Bank Holiday* was the prototype for many post-war pictures which showed the fabric of life in holiday camps, stations and airports. There had to be a typical working-class couple (Kathleen Harrison gave the first performance of her well-known 'mum' figure in *Bank Holiday*), a girl out for a good time who nearly comes to a sticky end before she realizes the folly of her ways (Margaret Lockwood) and a plausible young man (Hugh Williams). Carol Reed managed to rise above potentially banal material and confirmed the promise he had shown in *Laburnum Grove* in 1937. Another picture which also fitted into the new pattern of sociological observation was Victor Saville's *South Riding*, from the novel by the tragic young author Winifred Holtby dealing with local politics in a Yorkshire country town; this starred Edmund Gwenn, Ralph Richardson and Edna Best. It was constructed with an eye turned to the realism of the documentary film movement, and its climax was a real event, the Coronation, as seen by the local inhabitants. *This Man Is News*, directed by David MacDonald, with Barry K. Barnes, Alastair Sim and Valerie Hobson, was also an extremely well constructed film with a pace and energy that reflected credit on its writers, Roger Mac-Dougall (who later became a successful playwright) and Alan Mackinnon. A sequel was demanded and the same team went on to make *This Man in Paris*. And as the threat of war became reality Michael Powell recalled the 1914–18 conflict in a well directed picture, *The Spy in Black*, with Conrad Veidt and Valerie Hobson, which dealt with a crisis of conscience in a German U-boat commander.

After Michael Balcon's brief career at MGM had come to an end he became in 1938 a partner with Reginald Baker in a company called Balford, whose purpose was to turn out good programme films at Ealing Studios. On the resignation of Basil Dean, Balcon became head of production at Ealing and started one of the most consistent and worthwhile of all the British film factories. The first picture, *Gaunt Stranger*, had its West End showing as a second feature, but the second, *The Ware Case*, drew more attention. *There Ain't No Justice*, a low-budget boxing exposé, was an incisive examination of the prize-fighting world and marked out the twenty-seven-year-old director, Pen Tennyson, as a most promising socially-minded film-maker. Tennyson's next film for Balcon, *The Proud Valley*, was actually a plea for the nationalization of the coal industry, although it starred the powerful-voiced Negro singer Paul Robeson. It would have been easy for the film to have had a soft centre with such a performer in the lead, yet it retained a trenchant viewpoint. Unfortunately, Tennyson was killed early in the war and made only three films. But on the basis of these, it would be fair to assume that had he lived he would have become one of the most prominent of British directors. *There Ain't No Justice* was greatly under-rated when it was released in 1939 and failed to make money, possibly because it received a very poor distribution.

And so a period not only of British films but a whole way of life came to a close. After September 1939 some changes would be abrupt, some gradual, but hardly anything would remain as it was. It is sad that the film industry fell into the same habits as other media of communication and produced little that could be interpreted as comment on the world situation. No films about the Nazi menace were made before the war; British films kept a silence as close-lipped as any of the appeasers, and spared the German government from the embarrassment of criticism. Even documentaries did not look at the menace threatening the entire world; it was left to the American series *The March of Time* to produce a journalistic account of the events inside Germany, which was frowned upon by the British Board of Film Censors. Similarly the British cinema had nothing to say about the Spanish Civil War, which raged from 1936 onwards. Undoubtedly, commercial pressures prevented a more serious cinema emerging and the feeling that messages were for Western Union was applied as vigorously to British output as to that of Hollywood. The picture palace with its neon façade and gilded auditorium represented for most of the thousands who flocked to it week by week an escape from reality into a fantasy world. The British cinema was a lesser version of Hollywood, with men like Korda, Wilcox, Balcon, Saville, Hitchcock demonstrating that their mastery of it as an entertainment medium was equal to that of the Americans. But with fewer resources, a smaller market and a succession of crises it was impossible for the imitation to come anything more than a very bad second place. If there was an essential British cinema it was an observation of the British people in close-up; the beginnings were there already in *Bank Holiday*, in *South Riding*, in *There Ain't No Justice*, in *Storm in a Teacup*, even in the films of Gracie Fields and George Formby. Here had been found an area in which the British film could develop a uniqueness that borrowed nothing from Hollywood. But bread and butter has always counted in the cinema for more than social consciences, and survival depended on *The Four Feathers* and *Victoria the Great* and *Pygmalion*; it was the box-office subject which could equally well have emerged from the studios of Hollywood that drew audiences and profits.

Possibly the industry was at fault in trying so hard to follow in American footsteps, rather than develop its own indigenous style. But to condemn it on these grounds is to ignore the nature of the problems endured before the war. Had the decision been made when the bubble burst to concentrate on small, low-budget films that had an even chance of making a profit, it is possible that in time feature-film production would have collapsed. On the other hand, that might have happened anyway if the war had not, paradoxically, while closing down studios and recruiting its workers for the armed forces, brought an unexpected salvation from the hard time that had undoubtedly been coming since 1937. The conditions of wartime provided the film industry with a proper role to play in the national life, and the challenge was taken up, producing a miraculous transformation in content, style, subject matter and aesthetics. At last British film had matured and could pass into its golden age of the forties.

9 War and the Golden Age

This golden age did not dawn immediately. At the outbreak of the war the Government in a panic measure closed all cinemas, visualizing the appalling consequences of a bomb falling on a crowded theatre. Only after it became clear that national morale would be better served by allowing people their weekly films, rather than keeping them shut up at home at the mercy of the BBC radio, were the cinemas re-opened. All exterior lights were shut off to comply with the stringent black-out regulations which would apply for almost the duration. It was in fact ten years before the illuminated façades and neon-lights were turned on again, shortage of fuel compelled the electricity supplies to be severely limited until 1949.

During the course of the war the weekly film audience grew until about 30 million people were regular filmgoers in 1945. At the same time cinemas coped with restricted opening hours, depleted staffs, shortage of equipment and the need to maintain fire-watching and ARP. In adversity the British always seem to be at their best and cinema-going was an accepted and welcome ritual for many people who had rarely set foot inside a picture house before the war.

The studios suffered greatly. Two thirds of film technicians were eventually called up and because of requisitioning by the Government the number of studios shrank in the first three years of war from twenty-two to nine. Pinewood, Elstree, Shepperton and Amalgamated were among the large studios to go out of feature-film production. Some studios continued to make films, but for officially sponsored propaganda or training purposes. Most of the requisitioned floor space was turned over to storage or shadow factory accommodation. The number of films that was actually produced dropped considerably, from 108 in 1940 to its lowest figure of 46 in 1942. Although there had been fears from the exhibitors that there would be an insufficient flow of new films to fill the screens, especially since the Government had imposed a limitation of 400 on the importation of new American films as a way of saving dollars, there was no shortfall, partly owing to long runs and reissues. Because of restrictions imposed on competing entertainments, and a shortage of consumer goods, the cinema became an attractive place in which to spend money and get away from the grimness of rationing and warwork. Although box-office takings were to treble in the course of the war, Entertainments Tax was raised three times, so that by 1945 the Exchequer was taking thirty-six per cent of the price of every seat. Consequently, although it was at the zenith of its popularity, the cinema industry was unable to take proper advantage of the situation. In any case, all building of cinemas was suspended. No new ones were permitted and even those in an advanced state of construction remained empty shells until well after the end of the war. Some ten per cent of the total number of cinemas closed, either through bombing or staff shortages, particularly the smaller houses where the loss of two or three personnel to the armed forces could make a major difference.

In wartime production costs for films were greatly increased. By 1944 a film might cost three times as much as it would have done in the immediate pre-war period. The reasons were complex, and Entertainments Tax, and also a wartime Excess Profits Tax, were contributory factors. But there was also a need to raise production values in view of what was happening in Hollywood. There, although production was cut back in quantity, more and more large-scale films were made, often in Technicolor. This meant that British films, still concerned with getting American showings, could not afford to look like 'B' features. Excess Profits Tax was in fact an encouragement towards the production of more expensive films, since the returns could cover costs without getting out of proportion. Wardour Street thinking has often tended to equate excellence with the money spent, and with this in mind certain indifferent 'super-productions' were mounted. Fortunately, with more money to draw upon, it was possible for intelligent directors to initiate the celebrated artistic renaissance. Quite apart from the economic importance to the film industry of a firm foothold in the American market there was in wartime another and perhaps over-riding consideration on a national level for a propaganda voice. The film medium during the Second World War was one of the most effective means of not only informing the public through newsreel and documentary, but altering attitudes with such films as *In Which We Serve* or *The Way Ahead*.

Aesthetically British films improved because there was a situation that could give the cinema a national motive. Too often, before the war, film output in Britain had been in tone that of a small-scale Hollywood; there was little or none of the indigenous style of film-making that distinguishes, say, the French cinema. Now a national style had a chance to emerge, and in spite of all the difficulties of wartime film-making, the shortage of technicians, studio space, and even film stock itself, British films, almost for the first time, came out of the grey twilight and stood for themselves against the best that any other country could produce. Improvisation and ingenuity achieved impressive levels, new techniques were learned and mastered; established methods were often discarded and new ones evolved. Money was spent on better writers, better directors and better actors. As the war continued a heartening public recognition developed of the power of the new British cinema.

All this did not happen at once. The first months of the war saw the tailing off of the last pictures to be shot in the summer of 1939 and the completion of some that were already in execution at the outbreak. Korda's *The Thief of Bagdad*, with its array of technical trickery, ambitious optical effects and monumental animated models, passed through several convulsive stages. Korda replaced directors twice, finally appointing Michael Powell. Korda also scrapped extensive footage already shot at enormous cost, apparently disregarding the fact that there was a war on. Gabriel Pascal, his Hungarian compatriot, was at work on his second Shaw film, *Major Barbara* at Denham. Because he overran the ten-week schedule, almost doubling it, the Government found it impossible to requisition the studios during the panic period of 1940, when every large building was under the threat of being turned into a factory to make parts for Spitfires and Hurricanes. *Major Barbara*, with a cast including Wendy Hiller, Rex Harrison, Stanley Holloway, Deborah Kerr, Robert Morley, Robert Newton and Emlyn Williams, was not the box-office success of its predecessor, *Pygmalion*, and failed to recoup its production costs. Even Shaw himself is said to have lost £20,000 on the venture.

Korda was the first film producer to get a war film on to the screen. A few days before the outbreak he commissioned Adrian Brunel, Brian Desmond Hurst and Michael Powell to direct a propaganda film called *The Lion Has Wings*, with the newly created Ministry of Information footing the bill. Brunel in his autobiography described how politically ill-informed it was, because of the intervention of advisory civil servants anxious not to upset the 'phoney war'. It is said also that the Germans secured a print of it and showed it in their own theatres as an example of the enemy's naïveté. The film was on the screens within a matter of weeks after the start of the war and while its reception in Britain was almost derisory, it did very well in bookings in the United States, although what its effect may have been on American opinion is hard to determine; it certainly made no dent on U.S. neutrality at that stage of the war.

Although *The Lion Has Wings* was a disappointment, several other film-makers turned to war as a film subject. Michael Powell, for instance, who, when directing *The Spy in Black*, had worked with a Hungarian scriptwriter named Emeric Pressburger, collaborated a second time with him on *Contraband*, another spy story with Valerie Hobson and Conrad Veidt. It had an element of Hitchcockian cliff-hanging in a suspenseful sequence in which the heroine had to walk along a narrow, high girder in the blackout in order to escape from the villains. Carol Reed made *Night Train to Munich* and *Gestapo*, Anthony Asquith directed *Freedom Radio* and *Cottage to Let*, about a fifth columnist in a remote country village, before returning to West End comedy with *Quiet Wedding*; and Maurice Elvey brought out *For Freedom*, the story of the *Graf Spee* and its sinking in the mouth of the River Plate. Pen Tennyson's last film was *Convoy*, one of the first war films of real merit, with its realistic view of the life of merchant sea-men. Leslie Howard directed and starred in *Pimpernel Smith*, which was about an apparently absent-minded professor who by brilliant mastery of disguise was able to smuggle eminent refugees out from under the noses of the ridiculous Nazis. Roy Boulting made *Pastor Hall*, based on the experiences of Pastor Niemoller, who was imprisoned and tortured by the Gestapo for opposing the Nazi regime. Brian Desmond Hurst made the immensely popular but sugary story of a Polish pianist who fought as a pilot in the Battle of Britain, *Dangerous Moonlight*. This film featured Richard Addinsell's famous Warsaw Concerto, which became an incessant theme on the radio. But the most important film produced in the period before Pearl Harbor and the American entry into the war was Michael Powell's *49th Parallel*, which was made with Government money. The Ministry of Information had earmarked half a million pounds for the production of helpful feature films. Some £60,000 of the fund was put up for this film, which in the end turned out to be the only one made under this arrangement. In fact *49th Parallel* cost twice as much to make and was bailed out by J. Arthur Rank while the Ministry, its fingers burnt, quietly dropped the scheme. The film was not released until well into 1941, which diminished its effectiveness from a propaganda viewpoint. Nonetheless it made a substantial profit. It was the story of the crew of a U-boat, led by a fanatical Nazi, played by Eric Portman, who are stranded after their submarine is sunk off the coast of eastern Canada. Episodic in treatment, it showed the men's difficulties as they try to escape through a vast, hostile country to neutral America. Laurence Olivier played a Quebecois trapper, Anton Walbrook the leader of a Hutterite settlement of expatriate Germans, Leslie Howard a disillusioned pacifist, Raymond Massey an army deserter who sacrifices his chances of freedom across the border to hand over the last uncaptured Nazi. Much of the film was made in Canada and part of the reason for its delayed completion was due to the fact that Elisabeth Bergner refused to return to Britain for studio shooting. Consequently, her part had to be reshot with Glynis Johns. For all its production difficulties, *49th Parallel* was a thoughtful and intelligent picture and greatly enhanced the prestige of the British film as well as bringing a major Commonwealth country into the foreground.

Some British film people had left England for America at the beginning of the war, giving rise to the phrase 'Gone with the Wind up'. While in many cases it was a calculated absconding from the rigours of wartime Britain to the comforts of southern California, some directors came in for unreasonable criticism. The most notorious, as might be expected, was Alexander Korda, who after *The Lion Has Wings* went to Hollywood and made *Lady Hamilton* (*That Hamilton Woman* in the U.S.A.), with Vivien Leigh, Laurence Olivier playing Nelson. By now Korda had no capacity to raise money for film-making in Britain. The huge Denham studios were no longer under his control. *The Lion Has Wings* was the last film made on his pre-war basis. In Hollywood he could still raise money. Although made in America, *Lady Hamilton* was patriotic propaganda for Britain, which perhaps helps to explain why it was Winston Churchill's favourite film. Many press attacks were made on Korda, yet he is known to have crossed the Atlantic some thirty times during the war and by 1943 he had returned permanently to head MGM's British end. Paul Tabori in his biography of Korda suggests that his frequent comings and goings were connected with political undercover work on behalf of Hungarian anti-Nazis and that this could explain why Churchill in the middle of the war suddenly recommended him for a knighthood, during one of the dangerous trips across the ocean. A cloud of obscurity still hangs over this period of Korda's life and most of the people who could have dispelled it are now dead.

Herbert Wilcox was in Hollywood when the war started, having just filmed his second version of *Nurse Edith Cavell*, this time with Anna Neagle playing the part taken by Sybil Thorndike just over a decade earlier in *Dawn*. An English oak was planted at the old RKO studios in Hollywood to mark the Anglo-American co-production and late in 1939 the new film was premièred successfully at the Radio City Music Hall, in spite of protests in certain quarters that it violated the Neutrality Code. Mindful of the pleas of Lord Lothian, the British Ambassador in Washington, Wilcox switched to the innocuous musical comedies *Irene* and *No No Nanette* for his next Hollywood pictures, returning to England in 1940 to make a biographical film about the life of Amy Johnson, *They Flew Alone*, with Anna Neagle, and Robert Newton as Jim Mollison.

Alfred Hitchcock was also in America at the outbreak of war, making *Rebecca* for David O. Selznick, which won the Academy Award for the Best Picture in 1940. His second Hollywood film was *Foreign Correspondent*, a more topical spy thriller with Joel McCrea as a gauche newspaperman sent to England just before the war to report on the depressing European situation. Blatantly anti-Nazi at a time of American neutrality the film ended with a foretaste of the London blitz. But Hitchcock's British film days were now over and, apart from a couple of short Ministry of Information features made in French later in the war and three unremarkable post-war features, the rest of his output has been American.

Victor Saville was another British director lost to Hollywood, and for that matter to direction, for he had moved into the producer role with *Goodbye Mr Chips*, and in America produced such films as *Bitter Sweet*, *Dr Jekyll and Mr Hyde* and *White Cargo*. When he did eventually return to directing it was plain that his best days had been left behind in the early and mid-thirties.

In spite of the war many films were still unconnected with it, either because they had been started beforehand or because conscious efforts had been made to offer escapism. The hangovers included Carol Reed's excellent, mildly socialistic *The Stars Look Down*, from an A. J. Cronin novel, with Michael Redgrave fighting unjust mine-owners, and Brian Desmond Hurst's thriller, *On the Night of the Fire*, with Ralph Richardson and Diana Wynyard. She was also the star of

Gaslight, a brilliantly executed and macabre film, directed by Thorold Dickinson, from the play by Patrick Hamilton, in which a murderer, played here by Anton Walbrook, tries to drive his wife insane while he searches for the missing loot in a house where he committed the crime. The film was all but destroyed when MGM in Hollywood bought the rights, called in all prints of the first film and scrapped them, then remade it with Ingrid Bergman and Charles Boyer. This version, released in Britain in 1944 as *Murder in Thornton Square*, dissipated much of the atmosphere of terror in the original and seemed born out of an unnecessarily crass act of vandalism.

Plays were, as ever, offering British producers much of their material. Among those filmed during the first part of the war were *Quiet Wedding*, directed by Anthony Asquith from the Esther McCracken comedy; Gordon Harker's repeat of his stage success, *Saloon Bar*, directed by Walter Forde; a remake of Eden Philpott's *The Farmer's Wife*, directed by Leslie Arliss and Norman Lee; and Walter Greenwood's depression story, *Love on the Dole*, directed by John Baxter. The celebrated radio comedians Arthur Askey and Richard Murdoch, whose BBC show *Band Waggon* had been translated into celluloid, were put into a remake of Arnold Ridley's famous comedy thriller of the 1920s, *The Ghost Train*, directed by Walter Forde and slightly up-dated so that the smugglers became Nazi spies.

By 1941 the steady rise of J. Arthur Rank crystallized the industry into the ownership divisions which broadly remained in force until the present time. By a process of taking over other people's white elephants Pinewood Studios had fallen into Rank's hands in 1937. Later he took Denham Studios off Korda's shoulders, three years after they had been built, and a new company, D. & P. Studios, was formed to administrate them both, with Prudential Assurance as one of the backers. Korda went on working at Denham as a tenant, not as owner. Rank's other major studio acquisition was Amalgamated Studios at Elstree, bought to thwart John Maxwell of ABPC who was said to have made overtures to the failing owners, Simon and Paul Soskin, who had made films there since they built them in 1937. With the requisition of Pinewood and Amalgamated during the war Rank was assured of a regular income from these two properties, without the perilous necessity of having to shoot films in them.

On the exhibition side there was an even more spectacular coalescing of the new ingredients of the Rank empire. Since 1938 Rank had

93

been on the Board of Oscar Deutsch's Odeon Theatres. In 1941 Deutsch, dying from cancer, asked him to act as chairman. After his death Rank bought up Deutsch's interests and thus gained control of a circuit of 306 theatres, including the recently acquired Paramount circuit, which although small boasted key locations. A few weeks previously Rank had become chairman of Gaumont-British in succession to Isidore Ostrer who had been obliged to leave Britain for Arizona some time earlier on account of his wife's illness. Rank had succeeded (where John Maxwell five years earlier had failed) in buying out the MGM interest in Metropolis and Bradford Trust, which controlled GB, and also obtained representation for Twentieth-Century Fox on the new GB board, in the shape of its chairman, Spyros P. Skouras. C. M. Woolf, who had left GB six years earlier, returned as joint managing director with Mark Ostrer, an arrangement which proved shortlived, for Woolf, today an almost forgotten figure in spite of the immense influence he had on the industry, died late the following year. Rank now had a circuit of 251 theatres which he continued to administer separately from the slightly larger Odeon circuit. But for intervention on a personal level by the president of the Board of Trade, Hugh Dalton, in 1943 this garnering of exhibition interests might have continued, but even as it stood the aggregate strength of the two Rank circuits was a formidable opposing force to Maxwell's ABC circuit. Maxwell himself died in 1941, and after his death the American company, Warner Brothers, bought forty-nine per cent of his shares, giving them a twenty-five per cent interest in the company. This brought nearly a million pounds worth of dollars into Britain at a time when the Treasury desperately needed them. Thus was established the duopoly which has dominated the British film industry for more than thirty years. It can be said in its defence that it limited the opportunities for American interests to take over in Britain and provided the necessary strength to prevent the wartime collapse of 1914–18. It also imposed its own standards of taste where presentation was concerned and made it virtually impossible for a film to make money if it was unable to obtain a release on one or other of the three circuits. The concentration of power led to the setting up of the wartime Palache Committee to examine the effects.

10 The Documentary Spirit

British documentary films fell outside the scope of ordinary feature production and provided a field in which individual styles could often find an outlet, which in time might spread to other types of film-making. The motives behind the documentary movement were various; it was propaganda for a social purpose rather than profit, and consequently the disciplines of normal commercial pressure were less obvious and less confining. The secret was sponsorship, from Government sources, institutional bodies or large corporations.

The originator of the British documentary movement of the thirties and forties was John Grierson, a Scottish academic who, with Sir Stephen Tallents at the Empire Marketing Board encouraging him, made *Drifters* in 1929, the story of a North Sea herring catch. Grierson had studied film technique with the eye of a scholar, and in his first film he applied his acquired knowledge of editing and construction. A modest two-reeler, the film appeared at a time when the cinema was going through the upheaval brought on it by the introduction of sound. As Forsyth Hardy has noted: 'the feeling of contact with real life, now a commonplace of cinema-going, then had the sharp impact of novelty'. Grierson brought others into his movement, and for the next few years the EMB produced nearly a hundred films. Basil Wright, Arthur Elton, Paul Rotha, Edgar Anstey, Stuart Legg and Harry Watt were some of the film-makers Grierson inspired to work for him in the daunting conditions and low pay of this unglamorous side of the film industry. With the purpose of putting the Empire on the screen many subjects were covered, from Imperial Airways (Rotha's *Contact* in 1932) to the life of Scottish shepherds (Wright's *O'er Hill and Dale*, 1931).

In 1933 the Empire Marketing Board was wound up for political reasons and the film unit was transferred to the Post Office, still under Sir Stephen Tallents. The GPO Film Unit not only set the pace for British documentary in the thirties but also acted as an unofficial training school for documentary producers. The Shell Oil Company set up its own film unit as did a number of other bodies. The outstanding products of this period were Legg's *Cable Ship*, Evelyn Spice's *Weather Forecast*, Anstey's *Six Thirty Collection*, Harry Watt and Basil Wright's *Night Mail*, which featured a verse narrative by W. H. Auden, and Watt's *North Sea* which was about the ship-to-shore radio link. Basil Wright made *Song of Ceylon* for the Ceylon Tea Board and Alberto Cavalcanti came from France, where he had directed *Rien que les Heures*, an outstanding documentary, and made *Big Money*, about the Accountant General's department.

Documentary films became a fashionable method of institutional advertising, with marketing boards, air and steamship lines, gas companies, oil companies and Government ministries sponsoring the work of many directors. Social problems such as poor housing, health, education and industrial spoliation were tackled uncompromisingly and objectively. There was a self-critical approach to national shames, and the films on the whole did not pull their punches, bringing home to the public that in many areas of Britain all was not well. There was, however, a danger that all this cinematic activity could stifle itself, particularly if it became too committed to the sponsors' point of view. In 1937 Grierson resigned from the GPO to found Film Centre, a central advisory body, with Legg, Elton and J. P. R. Golightly. Its intention was to act as a kind of clearing house for ideas, offering investigation and research, advice on documentary generally and supervision of production. Already at this time more documentaries were being made from private revenue sources than Government ones. There were, in fact, by the middle part of the thirties two distinct types of film being made. On the one hand there were the social pictures which commented on contemporary matters; on the other the scientific statements, such as Percy Smith's long-standing stop motion nature series.

Then another kind of film emerged, the first example of which was *The Saving of Bill Blewitt* made for the GPO in 1937. It was about fishing people in a village in Cornwall, but instead of an exposition of pictorial or narrated facts real people were used as actors to get the story across. The intrusion of the message, which was on behalf of the Post Office Savings Bank, was unwelcome, so adroitly had the style been built up by Cavalcanti and Harry Watt. *North Sea* was a direct development from it, moving beyond being merely a publicity film and showing that people re-enacting their own jobs for the camera could lead to a new, vital genre of British cinema. The trawlermen in *North Sea* anticipated many documentaries and semi-documentary features which were to follow during the forties.

The solid achievement of British documentary in the thirties proved to be of immense value when the war started. Something like three hundred films had been made and shown – if not in cinemas, in village halls, schools, lecture rooms and exhibitions throughout the country. Wartime gave greater justification for putting documentaries on the screens that really mattered, those of Britain's 5,000 cinemas. The use of film for exhortatory purposes, to dig for victory, to stop careless talk, to collect salvage and to walk instead of taking a bus, was recognized by the steady flow of Ministry of Information two-minute 'fillers' in every cinema programme, as were the Ministry of Food's amazingly ingenious if unappetizing suggestions in the *Food Flash* series.

The unique talent of Richard Massingham, whose first pictures, *Tell Me If It Hurts* and *And So to Work* had before the war demonstrated his gift for splenetic observation, was used for large numbers of Government-produced shorts. Massingham's plump, bald, flabby-lipped appearance marked him as a representative of middle Britain, a man baffled, bewildered and occasionally deflated by the war effort on the home front. The wit of those now forgotten tiny films was an instance of British genius.

Long documentary subjects, however, were at first slow to appear. Owing to a lack of preparedness, or an unwillingness to co-operate on the part of the government departments involved, the war began with no concrete plans for how to tackle film propaganda. John Grierson had by now left for Canada to perform the valuable task of building up a movement in a country that had hitherto been cinematically backward – Canada's National Film Board was his institution – and so was unable to advise the British government. In Germany the Nazis were very aware of the propaganda value of the film and exploited it with zealous regard. In Britain Cavalcanti was almost alone; he made *The First Days* for the GPO Film Unit, recording the atmosphere of a common peril and a determination to withstand whatever hardships were going to take place, his cameras reporting as matter-of-factly as the photo-journalism invented in the thirties and brilliantly expressed in Britain by Stefan Lorant's new magazine, *Picture Post*. The GPO Film Unit was taken over by the Ministry of Information and became the Crown Film Unit. Its next film was *Squadron 992*, directed by Harry Watt, which appeared in 1940, and was a reconstruction of the raid on the Forth

Bridge and the role of the balloon barrage defences. For security reasons of a somewhat misguided kind its showing was held up, reducing its impact quite considerably. The next film was *Men of the Lightship*, made by a feature director, David MacDonald, who was responsible for *This Man Is News*. It told the story of a German air attack on an unarmed lightship off the Suffolk coast, and its well-observed performances by the real lightship men were somewhat mitigated by the smugly masochistic streak of 'taking it' which had become a feature of national life.

The saviour of the Ministry of Information's film policy was Jack Beddington, an advertising man of great ability, who was appointed head of the Film Division in 1940 in the wake of ineffectual holders of the office. Sidney Bernstein, the owner of Granada theatres, was his honorary adviser. It was Beddington who instituted the policy of shorts to go in every programme, and eventually there was a monthly fifteen-minute film which could be anything from a graphic report from a battle area to a comic lecture by Arthur Askey on how not to catch a cold.

An early and famous Beddington short was *London Can Take It*, made to show the indomitable spirit of London during the blitz. Its commentary was by the American journalist Quentin Reynolds, which helped the ten-minute film secure valuable screenings throughout the United States, a considerable assistance in Britain's campaign for American support. Paul Rotha criticized the film for being too impersonal, too concerned with the background of Britain at war, too little conscious of the ordinary people in the forefront. If this was a fault it was not an enduring one, for successive wartime documentaries were often scrupulous in their grass-roots regard for individuals. There was a demand for longer films which could allow a theme to be developed in more than the most rudimentary black-and-white tones. One of the first was *Merchant Seamen*, directed by J. B. Holmes, which described the progress of a torpedoed ship's crew who survive to sail again.

It was followed by the first wartime documentary to take an offensive rather than a defensive war attitude. Harry Watt's *Target for Tonight* told the story of the crew of F for Freddie, a Wellington bomber, and the routine of a raid on Germany. Psychologically it was well timed, appearing in the latter half of 1941 after the blitz, after the German invasion of Russia and at a time when the war was in a weary stage as far as Britain was concerned. It was shown as a first feature in cinemas not only in Britain but in 12,000 cinemas in the Americas, and was seen there by 50 million people. Its propaganda effect was incalculable, not only for morale-boosting at home but for showing the world that there was no question of Britain being finished. It had been made simply and cheaply, with many sequences mocked up in the fuselage of an obsolete and unairworthy aircraft at the edge of an RAF airfield. An effect of *Target for Tonight* was the sudden interest awakened by feature producers in the power of documentary. J. Arthur Rank, now the tsar of British film production as the Maxwell studios had been requisitioned, approved the recruitment of documentary directors for the production of entertainment features, thus enabling the film industry to benefit from the experience of a body of men who had been able to create films without the customary limitations of the market place to worry about. Ealing Studios, particularly, benefited from the documentary tradition, the first such feature being directed by Charles Frend, a former film editor, with Cavalcanti producing. This was *The Foreman Went to France* with Tommy Trinder successfully playing a straight role, and was about a foreman who persuades his employer to let him cross the Channel to retrieve some important equipment after the fall of France.

Ealing's next film was intended only for servicemen and was made on money put up by the Government. Its purpose was pure propaganda, to bring home the appalling consequences of careless talk. *Next of Kin* showed the progress of an enemy agent through Britain, piecing together the details of a raid on the coast of occupied Europe and passing back the information. When the raid takes place (a Cornish village standing in for France) it is a disaster with terrible casualties. Michael Balcon felt that the picture's message was relevant to civilians as well as soldiers and decided to enlarge the budget himself so that a better film could be made. The abortive Dieppe raid took place before the film could be released and because the similarities were too painful Churchill did not want it to be shown. His decision was reversed, fortunately, by a military committee and the film was very successful. Its considerable profit, however, went to the War Office, after Ealing Studios received back exactly the sum of money that they had invested in it.

The work of Humphrey Jennings, a former painter before he entered film documentary, is probably better known today than that of any of his contemporaries. He had been co-director with Cavalcanti on *The First Drop* and had also co-directed *London Can Take It*. In 1940 and

1941 he had made some impressive and poetic shorts, *Welfare of the Workers*, *Words for Battle* and *Listen to Britain*. In 1942 he took the story of the massacre of the Czechoslovakian village of Lidice and transferred it to Wales as a surrealistic illustration of the Nazi horror in *The Silent Village*. Later he made *Fires Were Started* which was the story of the London Fire Brigade in dockland during the blitz of 1940–41. Jennings's strength lay in his studied assemblage of everyday sights and sounds to build up successive images – his soundtracks were enlivened with snatches of pop songs, radio programmes, overheard conversations, all making a vivid contribution towards an awareness of actuality. His reconstructions in *Fires Were Started* have an authenticity which is heightened by his use of non-professional performers. He was a pioneer of the 'let-it-happen' approach, reducing narration to a minimum or even omitting it altogether, and allowing the action on the screen to tell its own story.

The borderline between true documentary and feature-film semi-documentary sometimes became indistinct. *One of Our Aircraft Is Missing*, which was the story of an RAF crew escaping from Holland after being shot down, was directed by Michael Powell and used a documentary technique, with the flat landscape of Lincolnshire admirably masquerading as the Netherlands. The documentary form was even more vigorously applied in his next film, a shorter work about the Royal Naval Volunteer Reserve, with Ralph Richardson, and called *The Volunteer*.

The outstanding war film of 1942 was Noël Coward's *In Which We Serve*, the story of a destroyer from the day it was commissioned until it was finally sunk and the crew dispersed to other ships. It was based on the real experiences of Coward's friend, Lord Louis Mountbatten, who for the first years of the war had commanded H.M.S. *Kelly*, which went down in the Battle of Crete. Noël Coward produced, wrote, directed and played the lead in the film, a remarkable achievement considering that his British film experience hitherto had been limited to one or two screenplays and a brief appearance in D. W. Griffith's *Hearts of the World* during the First World War. *In Which We Serve* was an archetypal British war film, with the social backgrounds of the officers and men carefully drawn, and showing the burdens duty imposed on everyone from the commander to the lowliest rating. Celia Johnson as the captain's wife made a Christmas day speech to the dinner guests on the life of a naval wife which contrasted with the Christmas leave of the lower orders, exemplified by seaman John Mills. Coward adopted Mountbatten mannerisms for the role, such as the studied care with which all the crew were addressed at crucial moments, and the necessity for the captain to be seen sharing the discomforts of his shipwrecked men. The incident involving Richard Attenborough (in his first film role) as a panic-stricken stoker was taken directly from Mountbatten's own experience. The associate director on the film was David Lean, the cameraman Ronald Neame and the art director David Rawnsley, all of whom later had interesting careers. The impetus Coward got to make the film came from an Italian refugee, Filippo del Giudice, who had earlier set up a company called Two Cities Films, with London and Rome in mind. Del Giudice had no money but he managed to raise a loan from a friend, Major A. M. Sassoon, even though there was no distribution contract. C. M. Woolf nearly financed it but withdrew, although the film was made at Denham. Six weeks after shooting started British Lion agreed to refinance the film and distribute it, and the film was a triumph, setting up del Giudice as an important new entrepreneur in the film business.

Other 1942 films which brought the war into people's consciousness were *Wavell's 30,000*, which was a newsreel compilation showing the war in the western desert; *Ferry Pilot*, a straight documentary by Pat Jackson; *The Big Blockade*, directed at Ealing by Charles Frend, which showed the effects of economic warfare against the Axis; Jack Holmes's *Coastal Command*, which was commended for the excellence of its aerial photography; and *We Sail at Midnight*, directed by Julian Spiro, which was a film tribute to the lease–lend arrangement. At Ealing, Cavalcanti's *Went the Day Well?* was about the occupation of an English village by Nazi paratroopers disguised as English soldiers, in preparation for a major invasion. Parts of the imaginative story were photographed in the style of a military film on tactical exercises. The screenplay was by Graham Greene, and he and Cavalcanti invested the situation with a chilling sense of possibility.

In the following year Harry Watt made the fictional *Nine Men*, also at Ealing. It was about a party of soldiers in the desert who, when cut off from their brigade, defended an old fort against the Germans, and the film owed much to Watt's documentary training. In contrast to it was *Desert Victory*, a narrative account of Montgomery's advance from Alamein. Another combat film was *Malta G.C.*, a graphic depiction of the siege of the Mediterranean island. Leslie Howard, shortly before his mysterious death in a Lisbon–London airliner, directed and narrated a film about life in the women's army, the ATS, called

The Gentle Sex. Episodic in style, it followed the service lives of seven girls of assorted temperaments, all drawn together in one ATS section. Earlier Howard had played the designer of the Spitfire, R. J. Mitchell, in a biographical film called *First of the Few* (*Spitfire* in America) which he had also directed, with David Niven and Rosamund John supporting him in the cast.

The list of films that used the war as a basis for the storyline is a long one. Many were not very good, straining credulity with impossible heroics or pushing suspect values. *Ships With Wings*, which had some of its footage shot on the ill-fated aircraft carrier, *Ark Royal*, fitted this category, as did some of the American attempts at homage to British bravery, such as William Wyler's *Mrs Miniver*, with Greer Garson struggling against the impossible odds of being a British housewife in what looked like a typical Beverly Hills mansion, and *This Above All*, with Joan Fontaine as a WAAF and Tyrone Power as a reluctant hero. Comedy films also took advantage of the war and while the humour tended to be broad rather than satirical, commendable attempts were made to reduce the Nazis to figures of derision. Outstanding in this category was *The Goose Steps Out*, which was directed by Basil Dearden, with Will Hay who played his usual schoolmaster role, this time spying for the British in the disguise of a professor at a German university. Other comedians who were popular in wartime included George Formby, who was still a major box-office attraction; Tommy Handley, a very successful radio comedian who appeared in a film version of his show *It's That Man Again*, directed by Walter Forde, in 1943; Elsie and Doris Waters, who dealt with blitz evacuees in *Gert and Daisy's Weekend*; and Frank Randle who made a series of successful comedies with an army background, usually with Harry Korris, well known as a radio character in *The Happidrome* programme. These films, *Somewhere in England*, *Somewhere in Camp*, *Somewhere on Leave*, and so on, were almost unknown in southern England, although they broke box-office records in the north – a rare example of the successful exploitation of a regional market.

But in spite of the comic spies and the cardboard heroes there was a steady flow of intelligent and unpatronizing films which simply and frankly told the story of people at war. Charles Frend's *San Demetrio London* was the story of a merchant ship on the North Atlantic, limping home after a U-boat attack; *Millions Like Us*, directed by the screenwriting team, Frank Launder and Sidney Gilliatt, was a study of differing civilian types brought together in an aircraft factory under

Direction of Labour orders. *The Way Ahead*, originally intended as an army instructional film called *The New Lot*, to show what happens to raw recruits transferred from civilians to fighting men, was outstandingly directed by Carol Reed. It was one of the best of all wartime films, sparing no sentiment at the end as the entire squad goes into battle and death. *We Dive at Dawn* was a typically sensitive examination by Anthony Asquith of the perils of life in submarines. *The Lamp Still Burns* was Maurice Elvey's tribute to the nursing services, as was Basil Dearden's *The Bells Go Down* to the fire brigades. *The Silver Fleet*, directed by Vernon Sewell and Gordon Wellesley, showed something of life in the occupied countries, with sabotage in the shipyards, as did Harold French's *The Day Will Dawn*, which had a commando raid on a Norwegian port as its climax. Charles Crichton revealed the work of the RAF air–sea rescue teams in *For Those in Peril*. Humphrey Jennings amusingly re-constructed the origins of the Eighth Army's theme song pirated from the Afrika Korps, *The True Story of Lilli Marlene*. John Boulting made *Journey Together*, with Richard Attenborough and Edward G. Robinson, the story of the training of an RAF pilot. William Wyler shot a colour documentary about an American air force Flying Fortress bomber squadron stationed in England, *The Memphis Belle*.

But the most notable Technicolor documentary of the war, filmed in conditions of often extreme discomfort, was *Western Approaches*, made by the Crown Film Unit under the direction of Pat Jackson. It told the story of a score of torpedoed merchantmen, adrift in a cold, grey Atlantic for fourteen days, and used real seamen for its actors. The three-strip Technicolor process required special cameras and at the time there were only four available for use in British studios. Jack Cardiff, who was cameraman on the film, has described how in one of the few scenes where the studio tank was used instead of the real sea the precious apparatus, equivalent to a Rolls Royce in its mechanical precision and complexity, was inadvertently completely immersed. After stripping it was found to be in perfect order, and the soggy exposed film was used to good effect in the final print.

11 The New Era

Even though the war raged, British film output was by no means confined only to war documentaries and war fiction. Audiences were constantly increasing in size, and the cinema had a valuable morale-raising task to perform. Hollywood recognized the need for entertainment and kept up a sustained flow of excellent pictures. The British quota, which at the beginning of the war had actually been in jeopardy, with a few pessimists taking the view that the studios remaining free from closure would be unable to guarantee a supply of product, had been fixed for the duration of the war at fifteen per cent, and exhibitors had experienced no difficulty in maintaining it.

Literary and theatrical sources were still important for producers. Carol Reed made a sprightly version of H. G. Wells's *Kipps*, with Michael Redgrave in the leading role in 1941, and A. J. Cronin's grim novel, *Hatter's Castle*, formed the basis of Lance Comfort's film, which had a spectacular model sequence based on the Tay Bridge disaster. The West End stage success, *Jeannie*, about a young Scottish girl who inherits a fortune, was filmed by Harold French, and the Boultings, Roy and John, made an excellent picture from *Thunder Rock*, a somewhat over-literary play by Robert Ardrey in which an intellectual attempts to escape from the pre-war world chaos by living in a lighthouse on the Great Lakes, peopling it in his imagination with the century-old ghosts of a wrecked immigrant ship.

There was also an interest in historical subjects, possibly activated by a heightened awareness of the national culture in a time of danger. Lance Comfort made *Penn of Pennsylvania*, the biography of the great seventeenth-century Quaker, and Carol Reed directed Robert Donat in *The Young Mr Pitt*, carefully pointing up the analogy between the period of the Napoleonic threat and the isolation of England in the 1940s. It was an episodic film, with a succession of well-known historical figures passing before the camera, but the sincerity of Donat's performance overcame any suggestion that it was merely an historical charade. Thorold Dickinson's *The Prime Minister*, with Disraeli played by John Gielgud, was another patriotic recollection of a greater past era. In 1942 the first major film from J. Arthur Rank appeared, with the avowed intention of raising the cinema's moral tone. It was *The Great Mr Handel*, with the celebrated composer played superbly by Wilfrid Lawson. The film was shot in Technicolor, directed by Norman Walker, and photographed by Jack Cardiff and Claude Friese-Greene, the son of one of the honoured pioneers of the British cinema. In spite of the uplift, the colour, the music and the craftsmanship, the film was a disappointment – so dull that it has never been revived. Nevertheless, its ambitious scope demonstrated the confidence that Rank had in himself and in British films.

Technicolor was used sparingly during the war, largely because of the shortage of equipment and film stock. The next major picture made in colour was Michael Powell and Emeric Pressburger's production of *The Life and Death of Colonel Blimp*, which told the life story of a character inspired by the renowned cartoon creation of David Low in the *Evening Standard*. It was the first picture to emerge from their new company, the Archers. A long, curious film, it presented a very different view of Colonel Blimp, or Colonel Clive Wynne-Candy, v.c., a Boer War veteran, from the one that would be gained from a regular perusal of Low's cartoons. The part was played by Roger Livesey who handled the transitional stages, from a young subaltern to a fat, retired old soldier very well. The story, which showed how Candy developed a lifelong friendship for a former German duelling opponent, played by Anton Walbrook, preached a kind of tolerance not particularly noticeable in films of the period. Deborah Kerr had a triple part, as three young women cropping up in various stages of the hero's long life.

The next time colour was used for a family chronicle picture was in *This Happy Breed*, written by Noël Coward and directed with care by David Lean, his associate from *In Which We Serve*. It told the story of the Gibbons, a lower-middle-class family living in Clapham, from the end of the First World War until the bombing of the Second World War, against a background of national events such as the Wembley Exhibition, the General Strike, the death of George V and so on, woven neatly into the story. Its banalities were submerged by the devoted technique of Ronald Neame's photography which achieved a muted realistic colour unusual for the period, when it was still common for Technicolor films to show off all the polychromatic combinations of the rainbow, and by the warm performances of the excellent cast, which included Robert Newton, Celia Johnson, Stanley Holloway, John Mills and Kay Walsh.

The English scene found its way to the screen also in Anthony Asquith's *The Demi-Paradise*, which used the device of showing the idiosyncrasies of the island race as seen through the eyes of a foreigner. Laurence Olivier played a young Russian ship-designer sent to Britain before the war to arrange the construction of an important vessel for his homeland. Dejected and confused by the apparent inconsequential lunacy of the English character he returns home with relief. When war comes he is sent back and it is on his second visit that he is suddenly and magically converted to appreciate the qualities of Englishness. With its ridiculous village pageant and extraordinary parlour conversation Asquith's film actually contained a hint of satire and self-criticism, unfashionable ingredients for their time.

Another example of national eccentricity was revealed in *Tawny Pipit*, written, produced and directed by Bernard Miles, and for the most part photographed in the open air of the English countryside. It told the story of the discovery of two birds mating in a field and how the whole country followed their every move with bated breath. *A Canterbury Tale*, another Michael Powell film, took a slightly more sinister turn, with Eric Portman playing a character who poured glue over girls' hair in the blackout. It was an episodic film, a modern pilgrimage by several people to the great cathedral, and was evocative in its photography of Canterbury and the Kent countryside.

One of the most pleasant aspects of 1944 film production was the return of Alexander Korda to active direction in Britain. He returned permanently from America to establish MGM–London Films and to reopen the studios at Elstree. He directed a film called *Perfect Strangers*, with Robert Donat and Deborah Kerr, about the problem of a couple resuming their marriage after both had served for three years in the Navy. Although it was a well-made and entertaining film, it was the only example of Korda's work to reach the screen during this period, for after it had been made he split with MGM, leaving the studios he had so assiduously re-established. Korda's flamboyant life was full of such ironies.

An interesting failure of the same year was a film version by Basil Dearden of J. B. Priestley's play, *They Came to a City*. This Ealing film, starring Googie Withers and John Clements, was an experimental attempt at a stylized discussion, but it was lacking in cinematic qualities and was not well received. The same director was on no surer ground with *The Halfway House*, a ghost story about a group of travellers who spend the night at a Welsh inn, which they later discover had been bombed out of existence a year earlier. A far better attempt at the supernatural was Bernard Knowles's *A Place of One's Own*, a period piece from a story by Osbert Sitwell, with ghostly piano-playing in the middle of the night and a well-contrived atmosphere of fear. The sets were the work of Rex Whistler, a promising and stylish artist killed in action after D-Day. *Pink String and Sealing Wax*, a horrific thriller in a Victorian setting, marked the directorial debut of Robert Hamer, although he had contributed an episode to the unusual and frightening portmanteau ghost film, *Dead of Night*, which also featured the work of Charles Crichton, Cavalcanti and Basil Dearden. *Pink String and Sealing Wax*, from a play by Roland Pertwee, showed Hamer's atmospheric skill, and provided Googie Withers with a well-textured ambivalent role as an innkeeper's wife who murders her husband.

Anthony Asquith also made a foray into the realm of Victorian melodrama with his *Fanny by Gaslight* (*Man of Evil* in America), which was taken from a Michael Sadleir novel of wicked lordships and bastard-bearing servant girls. It was one of James Mason's early parts as a suave villain, the recurrence of which was a box-office phenomenon of the mid-forties. This film repeated the casting of the Leslie Arliss romantic Regency melodrama of the previous year, *The Man in Grey*, which also featured Mason, Phyllis Calvert, Stewart Granger and Nora Swinburne, with the addition of Margaret Lockwood. It was the first film in a series of what the critic Francis Wyndham has called Gainsborough Gothic, period films with a strong emotional impact and a vigorous and highly coloured story line. *The Wicked Lady*, directed by Arliss, with Lockwood, Mason, Patricia Roc and Griffith Jones, was probably the *ne plus ultra* of the genre, being concerned with the spicy adventures of Barbara Worth, seventeenth-century noblewoman by day, highwaywoman by night. This was almost a sequel to *Madonna of the Seven Moons*, directed by Arthur Crabtree, in which Phyllis Calvert played a girl suffering from schizophrenia who kept reverting to a gypsy existence. Far less silly, and with a pleasant sense of period, was *Champagne Charlie*, which starred Tommy Trinder and Stanley Holloway as celebrated mid-Victorian music-hall rivals, and was directed by Cavalcanti at Ealing Studios. It fostered some other films which took the turn-of-the-century music halls as a theme, such as *I'll be Your Sweetheart*, directed by Val Guest, with Margaret Lockwood, Vic Oliver and Michael Rennie, and *Gaiety George*, directed by George

King with Ann Todd, Maxwell Reed, Ursula Jeans and Hazel Court, which told the story of the variety impresario, George Edwardes. Lady Yule got back into pictures at the newly reopened British National Studios with a musical called *Waltz Time* which, although not intended for showing to West End audiences, was lavish in its treatment of the syrupy stage musical comedy from which it was taken. Unfortunately, the Twickenham Studios were demolished by a flying bomb just as *Flight from Folly*, a barren musical with Pat Kirkwood, Hugh Sinclair and A. E. Matthews as a comic butler, was finished. The director was Herbert Mason.

A more ambitious picture was produced at Denham under the direction of David Lean from Noël Coward's long-running play, *Blithe Spirit*. It was the third film in which Lean and Coward had joined forces, this time for an amusing comedy with Rex Harrison as a novelist plagued during his second marriage by the intrusive ghost of his first wife, Kay Hammond, and with an invigorating performance by Margaret Rutherford as a medium. Frivolous, diverting and inconsequential, it was filmed in Technicolor which adapted well to a humorous vehicle.

The film that the Lean–Coward team made next was in direct contrast, being a close-up of a frustrated, inhibited, middle-aged affair that took place largely in station buffets, suburban tea rooms and municipal parks. *Brief Encounter* was a totally adult film, expressing an essential Englishness, for it would be hard to imagine French lovers behaving as this pair – the woman returning unfulfilled to a boring, pipe-smoking husband who has not even noticed anything unusual, the man going off to a new job in Africa, never to be seen again. There was a despair and a purity about this pathetic little union and the acting of Trevor Howard and Celia Johnson, with Cyril Raymond as the husband, was of a quality that totally expressed the futility and universal relevance of the situation. *Brief Encounter*, as a study of basic relationships of its time, stands out as a beacon throughout the whole of British cinema. Some of it, however, has badly dated, and the intrusive Rachmaninoff theme on the soundtrack was certainly overdone and represented a piano concerto disease that had affected much of British cinema in the forties, ever since Anton Walbrook had played the Warsaw Concerto in *Dangerous Moonlight*. The specially composed musical insertion (as in Hubert Bath's Cornish Rhapsody in *Love Story*) was a more common way of introducing a piano theme.

An honest attempt at realistic film-making was evident in *Waterloo Road*, which was about seedy life in South London with Stewart Granger playing a new and unpleasant manifestation of the war and post-war scene, the 'spiv'. One sequence, consisting of a savage fight between him and John Mills, marked a distinct rebuttal of any charges that British films were lily-livered. It is still a classic of cutting and camera-work. The director of this film was Sidney Gilliatt. His next film, produced in conjunction with Frank Launder, was *The Rake's Progress* (*Notorious Gentleman* in the U.S.A.) and it gave Rex Harrison an excellent acting opportunity to portray the career of a cad and a cheat who lied and double-crossed his way through pre-war days at his friends' expense, only to meet a hero's death in the war. Told in flashback, the film was notable for its touches of satire and the deceptive charm of its leading character. The supporting cast included Lilli Palmer, Griffith Jones and Jean Kent. It met a certain amount of censorship trouble, particularly in America where at first it was completely rejected. This may explain the weak ending with the unconvincing redemption of the rake, the self-sacrifice which results from the one act in his life that goes against the grain of his character.

Michael Powell wrote, produced and directed *I Know Where I'm Going*, in 1945, with Wendy Hiller and Roger Livesey. It was a love story set on the Isle of Mull in the Hebrides. Herbert Wilcox made a commendable attempt to further Anglo-American relations with *I Live in Grosvenor Square* (*A Yank in London* in the U.S.A.), showing the experiences of an Arizona sergeant (Dean Jagger) stationed in England and coming face-to-face with the upper classes (Anna Neagle and Rex Harrison as her disappointed lover). It was the first of a string of Wilcox films built around London place names. Sydney Box produced and Compton Bennett directed *The Seventh Veil*, a powerful melodrama about a concert pianist, played by Ann Todd, recalling her traumas to a psychiatrist after her hands are burned in a car accident. Her upbringing has been at the hands of a cruel, crippled rich guardian, played by James Mason. Such was the masochistic reaction to Mason that few women found it unconvincing that the heroine should eventually find true love and happiness at his hands. There were several concert sequences, with Eileen Joyce playing the piano for Miss Todd, and the film was one of the box-office successes of the year – convincing proof that success need not be equated with wild and profligate spending.

Such parsimony was very far from the thinking of Gabriel Pascal, who had persuaded Rank to back *Caesar and Cleopatra*, which turned out to be the most extravagant film ever to be made in a British studio. In spite of the fact that filming took place during the war's most crucial stages, starting at Denham a few days after the D-Day landings and continuing through flying-bomb attacks, Pascal went to incredible and absurd lengths to create a super-production from one of Shaw's less promising plays. The cast was huge and costly, led by Vivien Leigh as Cleopatra and the Hollywood actor Claude Rains as Caesar, severely hampered by his difficulties in communicating with the director. Flora Robson, Basil Sydney, Stewart Granger, Cecil Parker, Stanley Holloway and Leo Genn were in the film and several of the bit-part players later became stars in their own right, including Kay Kendall, Michael Rennie, Zena Marshall and Jean Simmons. Curiously, the film also featured two future directors: Michael Cacoyannis (*Zorba the Greek*) was a councillor and Anthony Harvey (*The Lion in Winter*) played the boy king, Ptolemy. Pascal was motivated by an indomitable determination to create the most ambitious British film ever made, and to exploit fully the talent of Vivien Leigh, star of *Gone With the Wind*, which had grossed more than any other film in the entire history of the cinema. It was a proposal that Rank fully supported, and continued to endorse, even when it became all too apparent that Pascal's profligate spending on the film would seriously diminish the financial returns. There is the famous remark Pascal is alleged to have made as the costs soared: 'What does it matter? Mr Rank can sell a few more bags of flour.'

Dogged by poor weather, air raids and a shortage of craftsmen and materials, shooting continued at Denham through the latter half of 1944. Filming had to be suspended for six weeks when Vivien Leigh fell ill, and then Claude Rains was forced to return to the United States before completion, because of income tax problems. In February 1945, by which time both principals had finished their parts, the decision was taken to send a unit on location to Egypt and escape the claustrophobic limitations of Denham. The press had much amusement at Rank's expense when it was learned that the film company had taken its own Sphinx to erect on the edge of the desert – though in view of the fact that the original has become somewhat timeworn since Cleopatra's day it was not such an illogical action. Some 1,200 men and 250 horses from the Egyptian army took part in battle scenes under the blue desert sky. Finally outdoor crowd scenes were shot in the summer of 1945 at Denham, where massive sets had been built to represent Alexandria. The film's final cost is generally agreed to have been £1,278,000, and having been bitten, Mr Rank cancelled plans for backing Pascal's next Shaw film, which was to have been *Saint Joan*. At the end of shooting Mr Pascal was nibbled by a camel and had to be taken to hospital, the final absurdity in the long and intricate production career of his mammoth film. Mr Rank also cut his losses of about £30,000 on *The Snow Goose* by abandoning the film, on which Pascal had already started work.

Although the tendency at the time was to denigrate *Caesar and Cleopatra*, it was by no means the aesthetic disaster that some critics claimed. There were some good performances and the film was excellent visually, with little evidence on the screen to suggest the production traumas. It arrived at the end of 1945, heralded by its notoriety and the critics fell on it, undoubtedly assisting by their lack of enthusiasm the poor performance it achieved at the box-office. It was the end of Pascal's British film career, although he later continued the Shaw series with a modest version of *Androcles and the Lion*, filmed in Hollywood.

If *Caesar and Cleopatra* was an expensive disaster there was an admirable counterweight in the shape of Laurence Olivier's film of Shakespeare's *Henry V*. Another emigré, Filippo del Giudice, was responsible for getting the film made and for obtaining the necessary backing from Rank. This film, too, greatly exceeded its planned budget, and the final cost of just under half a million pounds was an astronomical sum for the period. However, its popularity in many overseas countries brought in an encouraging return on the investment, and its success did much to raise morale within the industry. The plot, with its English soldiers invading France and meeting their enemy on the field of Agincourt, had a calculated topical reference to the events in Europe in 1944-5. In his portrayal of the King, Olivier pulled out all the patriotic stops, ably assisted by the proud surging spirit of William Walton's music. The Agincourt sequence, filmed in Ireland with men of the neutral Irish Army, is one of the most memorable battle scenes achieved in the cinema, inviting comparison with Eisenstein's *Alexander Nevsky*, its charging knights galloping to a score by Prokofiev. But this ambitious film is marred by its shifting settings, from the realistic Elizabethan playhouse at the beginning, with its mixed audience watching a stage performance, to a poetic fantasy treatment of the embarkation at Harfleur, back to a very realistic battle of Agincourt, and then returning to the pretty backcloths and arty designs of the French court scenes. It seemed to be an unnecessarily confusing mixture of styles, irritating in its arbitrariness and diffusing the simplicity of the plot. The acting in the film was creditable, with occasional touches of imaginative casting, such as George Robey in the role of Falstaff, whose death scene was imported from *Henry IV Part 2*, and Robert Newton as an excellent and vigorous Ancient Pistol. *Henry V* was a landmark in British films, a successful attempt at raising a flag on behalf of a national film style, conceived on a level of brilliant, if not audacious, confidence.

Del Giudice, a strangely enigmatic figure for all his flamboyant, lavish manner, formally yielded control of Two Cities Films, his company, to Rank, when the latter stepped in to back *Henry V*. There were still, however, good things to come from his studios. *The Way to the Stars* (*Johnny in the Clouds* in the U.S.A.) could be said to have done for the Royal Air Force what *In Which We Serve* did for the Navy and *The Way Ahead* for the Army. Directed by Anthony Asquith, it showed the life of a wartime airfield that was to know both RAF and USAAF bomber crews. The screenplay was by Terence Rattigan, continuing a collaboration that had begun before the war with *French Without Tears*. The heroics were muted, the focus centring on people to whom the war had brought adventure, love and tragedy. Michael Redgrave and John Mills headed the RAF side of the cast, Douglass Montgomery and Bonar Colleano Jr the American, and Rosamund John and Renée Asherson the civilian. The film incorporated within the plot two short war poems by John Pudney, one of which, 'For Johnny', was presented in a moving scene when John Mills goes through his poetic colleague's effects on behalf of his widow. *The Way to the Stars* was a subtle and authentic view of war at ground level. It made an instantaneous appeal to people who had been through five years of war, crystallizing emotions generally felt, and was one of the best films made by Asquith.

The war drew to a close with governmental eyes once more on the future of the cinema. In 1944 the Palache Committee had made an official study of the effects of the duopoly situation that had developed with the coalescence of the industry into two main groups. Their Report demanded further strengthening of the British film industry, in view of its unique qualities. 'A cinematograph film represents something more than a mere commodity to be bartered against others. Already the screen has great influence, both politically and culturally, over the minds of the people. Its potentialities are vast, as a vehicle for expression of national life, ideals and tradition, as a dramatic and artistic medium, and as an instrument for propaganda.' The Report called for measures to prevent the industry from American domination and, like the Moyne Committee of the mid-thirties, asked for the government to intervene directly with the financing of films, and also to set up a distribution agency with the intention of providing outlets, so that independent productions would not be unfairly squeezed out by the main circuit interests. The government, it urged, should also assist in film export. The Report showed concern over the tendency for 'super-productions' to clog the available studio space for months at a time, and recommended that several medium-budget films for the same cost would in the long run be more beneficial to the industry. It felt that second feature and documentary production could provide a valuable training ground for technicians and actors who might then graduate to first features. The Palache Report also called for the under-taking made by Rank and ABC not to acquire any more cinemas without the consent of the President of the Board of Trade to be given the force of law. The Committee felt that safeguards in the form of controls should be exercised to prevent other circuits from becoming too powerful. While the Palache recommendations were in the main not implemented, they set the tone for the government's attitude towards the cinema in the immediate post-war years.

The war ended in 1945 with the number of paid weekly admissions to British cinemas almost at its highest level of thirty million per week. The following year was a peak in attendance figures, with 1,635 million admissions during the twelve months. In 1945, 67 British films were produced and in the following year this figure leapt to 83 as post-war production got into its stride. The number of American films shown had for most of the war been pegged at around 400, but in the latter years had dropped to around 360.

These were the golden years for the British film industry, although for various reasons, including the wear and tear on theatres during the war, shortages of construction materials and building permits to carry out long overdue renovations, and prohibitive taxation, it was unable to reap the full benefits of the boom at the box-office. Nevertheless, with the greatly improved quality of films being produced in British studios and the showing of international prestige films such as *Henry V* and *Caesar and Cleopatra* (the latter enjoyed a much higher reputation in America than it did in Britain) the industry was hopeful that the new public interest in British films could be sustained to the time when conditions would improve and wartime restrictions be lifted. J. Arthur Rank, in particular, led the wave of new optimism, generously demonstrating his confidence in the future with production going ahead at full steam at Denham, the reopened Pinewood Studios, Lime Grove, Islington, Riverside and Ealing, and with his sponsorship of the broad assortment of producers who had been given encouragement under the commodious Rank umbrella. Ambitious plans for post-war development were announced and attempts were made on the largest scale ever to establish a bridgehead in the American market. The enthusiasm of Rank, while shown by hindsight to have been misdirected at the time, generated a remarkable surge of admiration for the British cinema, which at its best was capable of producing uniquely British films of the calibre of *Brief Encounter* and *Henry V*.

At the same time there was developing a desire to discover and capture the essence of the British people, not only in documentary, but in many characteristic feature films of the period such as *The Way to the Stars* and *Western Approaches*. War had produced a common experience which had tended to dissipate the visibly entrenched class system. There was also fascination in learning what made the other half tick, a curiosity exploited by the film industry. This awareness was by no means limited to films, being more a general mood of the period. It was seen in the radio, which had during the war established its role as the instant communication medium, bringing the voice of the Prime Minister in Downing Street as well as the commentator from the battle zone into every home; and seen too in the press, particularly the successful weekly picture magazines such as *Picture Post* and *Illustrated*. It was a Britain that wanted to know what the neighbours were doing.

12   Peace Has Its Problems

The British film industry was very much at a crossroads. The war had ended with attendances at cinemas at an all-time record level, with goodwill for the domestic product earned at last by a number of distinguished films on view or about to be seen, and with the imminent de-requisition of government-held studio space. There was a need, it was felt, particularly by the Association of Cine-Technicians (ACT, later to become ACTT when television members became included) that the average number of sixty or so films produced in Britain would have to be somehow boosted to 200 in order to maintain an adequate supply for the theatres, and to baulk any further inroads by America on the exhibition side. This object, ACT believed, could be attained by the end of 1947. The Association submitted a memorandum to the Board of Trade in 1946, many of the proposals echoing the Palache Report of two years before, such as the establishment of a film finance corporation, with its own renting organization, a government-owned studio for use by independent producers and a brake on the further acquisition of studios and cinemas by the monopolies. In addition they proposed that the quota system be replaced by a scheme which related film imports to the volume of home production and that consideration should be given either to an *ad valorem* duty or to a limitation of earnings. They also recommended that there should be a veto on the use of studio space by production units which were not all-British in control. This document was noted by the Labour government of the day, and its contents filed for future reference. The new government, elected with a landslide majority in mid-1945, now consisted of men and women to whom the cinema had been a major entertainment, the first government of ordinary picturegoers in British history. Consequently their interest was to be rather more acute than that of previous administrations. Moreover, there were several politicians who fully appreciated the importance of the film medium as a voice for social propaganda. After all, the documentary movement had been largely left-wing in tone and it had played a recognizable part in the awakening of the electorate to oppose the reimposition of Conservative rule.

The most important early post-war change in the composition of the industry, which had remained fairly static during the war years, was the buying out of British Lion, the third largest distributing company, by Alexander Korda who had a year earlier bought London Films from MGM. With Korda's London Films in control, British Lion then acquired the controlling interest in Shepperton Studios, which was the second largest, after Denham. Korda also had a half-interest in the Worton Hall studios at Isleworth. Consequently, he now controlled more studio space than ABPC and was second only to Rank. It was revealed in February 1946 that ABPC had been subjected to another share deal with Warner Brothers, who had bought a further million shares from the estate of the founder, John Maxwell, paying £1,125,000 for them. This gave the American company a $37\frac{1}{2}$ per cent interest in the issued ordinary capital, and there was a general anxiety that the undertaking given to the government that control of ABPC would not pass into American hands was now in danger. The chairman, Sir Philip Warter, gave an assurance that the trustees of Maxwell's estate still retained the voting rights and that the deal meant that Associated British films would have an outlet of about 800 cinemas owned by Warners in the States.

The national press was taking a great interest in the future of British films. The *Daily Mail* launched an annual National Film Award which was to be a British answer to the American Academy Awards, with Silver Star statuettes to match the Oscars. The voting was by public ballot, and the first awards were to *The Way to the Stars* as the outstanding film and to James Mason and Margaret Lockwood as the outstanding actor and actress. The *Daily Express*, recognizing a convenient anniversary, staged a retrospective exhibition, *Fifty Years of Films*, which was put together with reasonable taste at Dorland Hall in Lower Regent Street. Much early film apparatus was displayed, on loan from the Will Day Collection in the Science Museum. Another important promotional venture was a British Film Festival held in Prague in October 1946. Czechoslovakia had not succumbed to the Hollywood salesmen after the war, restricting American imports to a mere eighty films a year, and there was a certain interest in the British cinema there. Unfortunately, it was to last for only two years before the country was completely subjugated by Stalinist policies.

Rank took the initiative to build up the British industry on a large scale. At Shepperton, a mammoth Technicolor musical was made on the reopened sound stages, with the great stage comedian Sid Field as the star. Called *London Town* (*My Heart Goes Crazy* in the U.S.A.) and costing nearly £1 million, it turned out to be a dismal failure, despised by the critics and shunned by the public. Rank bought the Winter Garden Theatre in New York to serve as a showcase for his prestige films. But while they achieved attention in that city from both filmgoers and the press, it was no way to achieve national releases. In Canada things were slightly better, for Rank started his own Odeon circuit which was to consist of over 100 cinemas. He also bought the Kerridge circuit in New Zealand (120 theatres) and the Greater Union Theatres in Australia (82 theatres).

In Britain production, already spread through more than half a dozen studios, was diversified even further. A division was created to produce animated cartoons under the direction of David Hand, an American from the Walt Disney studios. This venture, mismanaged from the start, was to eventually cost Rank half a million. All that emerged from the Cookham studio was a great deal of inferior Disney-style work and a series called *Musical Paintbox*, which mixed rural songs with transatlantic humour.

Rank, still trying to find ways of providing complete programme material besides the main features, started a monthly documentary series which was to be the British rival to the American *March of Time*. It was called *This Modern Age*, each edition being two reels in length and running for about twenty minutes. In fairness, it must be stated that many films in the *This Modern Age* series were highly commendable and no attempt was made to impose an Establishment-minded viewpoint on it. Four times in succession *This Modern Age* won the *Motion Picture Herald* Exhibitors' Poll in Britain for short subjects, in spite of the competition from *The March of Time* and the Disney shorts. But it was never a success commercially, for the budgets were too generous for the potential return and the disinclination of non-Rank exhibitors to show a serious-minded two-reeler too strong.

Pursuing his self-imposed evangelical role as the benevolent tycoon destined to save the industry and lead it to glory, Rank decided that it was necessary to have a children's films division. Its purpose was to supply new, specially-made pictures to the Odeon and Gaumont Saturday morning cinema clubs whose audiences, it was hoped, would be the filmgoers of the future. The general fare at these programmes consisted of indifferent and elderly American comedies or Westerns which had exhausted their normal release lives. Mary Field, who had worked in instructional films and was a director of Gaumont-British Instructional, was given the task of injecting the Saturday programmes with moral content, and to produce special children's films, often in the form of simple adventure stories which had fresh and appealing narratives. The best known of the many films turned out under Rank's children's film programme was made in the Australian outback and was called *Bush Christmas*. It was considered such a skilled piece of work that it won a circuit release in an adult programme, and was shown in forty-one countries. Children's films, however, were yet another field in which Rank was to lose money – a weekly Saturday showing with the audience paying only sixpence per head was a daunting way of achieving returns, even on productions with very low budgets. But Rank persevered in the belief that the social benefits outweighed purely commercial considerations. It was always his hope that the box-office returns to be won by his prestige films in world markets would help to finance these very worthwhile films for the younger age groups.

Rank believed, like the Palache Committee of 1944, that Britain needed a regular flow of cheap supporting films to act as a training ground for the directors and performers in first-feature films, and with this end in view he bought the small two-stage Highbury studios, where John Croydon was installed as producer. Some of the films made under this arrangement were certainly better than the average material then being served up as the bottom half of a programme, but yet again Rank was destined to lose money, largely because the economics of film exhibition only permit a second feature to earn a fraction of what is grossed by the main feature. The so-called 'charm school' associated with Highbury (a pool of young starlets who were to be groomed in the Hollywood manner for future stardom) was also an abortive venture, largely because the girls selected for this treatment tended to be either too genteel or too colourless in personality to achieve any response from the public. Consequently, there was no great eagerness on the part of Rank's producers to put any of these girls into major films, and eventually the Company of Youth (to give its official title) was quietly dropped. It was typical of the Rank approach to lay on elaborate and costly services for the various producers working for him, but to give them sufficient freedom to be able to ignore the services entirely, even though it would mean, ultimately, a failure.

Another Rank innovation, which at the time of its introduction was believed to be the answer to many of the problems facing British film-making, particularly the shortage of studio space, was the Independent Frame system. Devised by David Rawnsley, who had been the art director of *In Which We Serve* and had become the head of the Rank Film Research Department, it was basically a method whereby intensive pre-production greatly shortened the actual shooting time of a film. Sets were to be built away from the stages and wheeled in when required, instead of being built on stage in the traditional way, thus putting it out of commission until the carpenters and plasterers had finished. Elaborate equipment was designed, special ceiling tracks and hydraulic elevators, floor rostrums that were adjustable to any height, and a great number of projection screens, some of which were mobile. Settings were simplified to the point of symbolism. 'An oblong patch of light on the floor, for instance,' wrote Rawnsley, 'immediately indicates the presence of a window in the vicinity, while shadows of various shapes imply the nature and position of the objects by which they are projected.' Actors would stand in a room which wasn't really there at all, perhaps only a table and a chair, with the rest back-projected. A great deal of pre-rehearsal would take place and, in order to save time, every movement of the scenery was carefully plotted in advance with the aid of charts, every line of the script, every bar of the music, was timed exactly in advance. Eventually, it was found to be unnecessary even to use the stars on location; a location unit could use stand-ins for long-shots and shoot material for back-projection in the studio. Independent Frame was disliked by directors because it was an inflexible system, removing a great deal of spontaneity from their work. Some directors, Hitchcock being a notable example, are quite happy to plan everything down to the last detail in advance, but most like to explore a wide range of camera set-ups while actually on the set. There was also a rigidity in the positioning of the actors, a feeling of artificiality, and the system was detested by those who had to perform with it. Great controversy raged for and against the Independent Frame, but eventually it faded away, after losing some £600,000, mainly because the pressure on studio space was replaced by a despairing need to keep them working. For all its faults Independent Frame did manage to anticipate many techniques which were later to become standard practice in television studios, where output has to be maintained at a relentless rate.

British television had initially been in advance of the rest of the world; a high-definition service was started by the BBC as early as 1936, and had continued for three years until the outbreak of war, when it was suspended for the duration. At that time about 30,000 sets were in use and viewers comprised an elite of the population in the London area. In 1946 television started up again, honouring a pledge to the existing licence-holders who had faithfully retained their pre-war receivers, by adhering to the 405-line standard instead of adopting a higher definition. The BBC television service was still very much in its infancy, but it was now possible for it to expand both in numbers of viewers and in areas covered. Rank was interested in the possibilities of television, having the important Bush Radio manufacturing company within his empire, and its more important parent Cinema-Television, set up in 1941 by Isidore Ostrer, who had given the television pioneer, John Logie Baird, vital backing in the early years. Rank wanted to be able to transmit events as they happened to cinema audiences, as well as special programmes, obviating the need for separate film prints to each theatre. However, the BBC had been granted an exclusive monopoly by the Postmaster General for the transmission of television programmes, and it had no inclination to provide a special service for a commercial organization. The government was unwilling to give Rank his own licence on the familiar grounds that if he was made an exception there would be a floodtide of applications. The experimental equipment that Rank had installed at a number of theatres remained unused. This impasse was typical of the early strained relations between the film and television worlds. As soon as the film industry realized that television represented a new and dangerous form of competition attempts were made to prevent the televising of feature films, even old ones which had long ceased to be viable for cinema screening. Television was denied access to the commercial newsreels which had been shown regularly on the small screen before the war, and the BBC was forced to make its own newsreel.

Rank's General Cinema Finance Corporation lost about £1,700,000 on film production alone between 1945 and 1946, a dismal record which paved the way for an even gloomier future. In many respects Rank was extremely unlucky. His public image was very ambivalent. To some he really did stand as a great benefactor, a good and upright man of a kind rarely found in business and most surprisingly in the film industry where sharks and get-rich-quick opportunists allegedly thrived. To them, Rank stood for respectability and rectitude. To others he appeared as a monopolist intent on an eventual sell-out to the Americans. The fact that his films had to adopt a mid-Atlantic attitude in order to become acceptable in America was cited as evidence of the insincerity of his frequently stated intentions to bring stability to the British film industry. In fact he was neither saint nor ogre. One of his answers to the latter group of critics was, disarmingly: 'I don't believe in monopolies. I would like to see more Arthur Ranks in the British film business.' He may well have been right. But because he stood alone he had a rough time at the hands of the Labour government, many members of which openly despised what he stood for. He lacked, too, a really shrewd, experienced film man to warn him off some of the more bizarre and unlikely ventures he insisted on pursuing. Rank's tragedy was perhaps the death of C. M. Woolf in 1941, just as he was beginning to feel his way into the perilous business. Rank's attempt to save the British cinema was, at its apogee, a brave and admirable action, and even those who despised his combination of sanctimoniousness and Yorkshire guile could hardly fail to marvel at the magnitude of his spirit and his unquenchable optimism, which was almost worthy of John Wesley himself. Moreover, Rank gave his film-makers great freedom to develop their own ideas without interference. While some were to let his trust down disgracefully, the most notorious being the appallingly extravagant Gabriel Pascal with *Caesar and Cleopatra*, many excellent directors were given early encouragement under the Rank banner to work out their own styles – David Lean, Ronald Neame and Robert Hamer, for example.

Rank's losses did not pass unnoticed in America. Hollywood has always respected a man who could lose in millions. His unorthodox approach was both intriguing and alarming, and his grip on so many theatres an important bargaining counter. There was, it was felt, far more to Rank than face value would indicate. The success of his films in New York contributed to an awareness of his determination to storm the U.S. citadel even if it was to cost a fortune before it began to pay off. Rank believed that British films would succeed once people had got used to them; this principle held good even on the Odeon circuit in England where takings when he first started had been poor if the programme was an all-British one. Rank also believed that the quality of the films was such that they would attract many people into the cinema who were by no means regular filmgoers.

In 1947 Rank went to America to sell his films and those he was dealing with, realizing that the blunt, honest Yorkshireman was as determined as he was resourceful, began to yield to his requests. While he was there rumours were reported that the Labour government was considering placing a twenty-five per cent *ad valorem* duty on American films reaching England. Rank hurried back to make representations to the government, but was unable to secure an audience with Sir Stafford Cripps, who appeared to be the originator of the tax ideas although Hugh Dalton was Chancellor of the Exchequer. There was at the time a desperate shortage of dollars in Britain and a recognized need to place a curb on dollar expenditure. In the year 1947 something like £18 million was earned by American films in Britain, a large portion of the dollar drain. American producers, aware that some drastic taxation might occur unless action was taken, offered to freeze part of their dollar earnings in Britain, ready for use in production. The next stage was extraordinary and the full story will probably have to wait until 1978 when the relevant Cabinet papers are released. Instead of a twenty-five per cent tax, from 8 August 1947 a massive seventy-five per cent *ad valorem* duty was announced on all films from the dollar area. Moreover, it was to be based on estimated earnings *for payment in advance*. Angrily, the Americans embargoed all new films and stopped their import into Britain. It was a drastic step not anticipated by the government, but there was no climbing down. One theory was that Dalton had expected the Americans to counter-negotiate an increased proportion of frozen earnings and that a satisfactory situation could have been achieved by bargaining, but it was clear that Hollywood had no time for anything resembling an Arab street market. For Rank the blow was a double one – his circuits were now starved of fresh American product, and the arrangements he had made in the States for his films to be shown were rendered void. It is sometimes hard for Americans to appreciate that collusion between the government and business is exceptional in Britain and no one was ready to believe that he was as much in ignorance of the Dalton tax as they were.

The government, having landed Rank in a mess, urged him once again to rescue the British industry, this time by boosting his production to fill the gaps left by the unavailable new American films. It was felt by some that the great opportunity had come. In November 1947 Rank announced a new production programme of forty-seven films, at a cost of £9,250,000. Then came the big snag. The financing of the programme was to be met by Odeon Theatres, who were to buy the share capital and thus become the parent company of General Cinema Finance Corporation. This meant that the investors in Odeon, who were used to regular dividends, because the exhibition side had done well even when production had been in the doldrums, were now expected to participate in the most hazardous side of the film business. Another complication concerned the nature of the two companies. Odeon was public and published its accounts, but GCFC was private, being a branch of Manorfield Investments which was controlled by Rank and his wife. In 1937 a pledge had been given to Odeon shareholders that their company would never take part in film production. However, Rank claimed to have secured the approval of ninety per cent of the ordinary shareholders. A more serious concern was expressed over the price paid for Rank's shares, which was par. Rank, bowing to some criticisms, left £650,000, which had been due to him personally, on loan to Odeon for five years. The moves alienated United Artists, the American company which had in the late thirties given Odeon valuable support, and there was a gradual withdrawal of UA films from the circuit.

Rank's next move was to effect a merger between Odeon and Gaumont under the banner of a new company, Circuits Management Association. The government demanded certain provisos before allowing the deal to go ahead. One was that programmes had to remain separate and not interchangeable between the two sets of cinemas – an unrealistic condition, it was soon realized, since it removed one of the arguments for the merger, which was a more efficient use of booking power. However, it did give a measure of protection to some independent cinema-owners. With a pooled management and a single services division many overheads in the operation of the circuits were reduced.

The effects of the American film embargo were not felt immediately, for Hollywood had stock-piled about 125 new films in Britain in anticipation of trouble. This was enough to maintain a supply until the end of 1947. But in order to fill screen time when this source had dried up, the cinemas were forced to embark on a major programme of reissues. Some reissues do well at the box-office, but when, as in the spring of 1948, several might be playing at the West End first-run cinemas together, the result was very discouraging. It was impossible for the British film industry to fill the gap overnight, since there is usually at least a nine months' gestation period for a film, and apart from Rank, whose production programme had been boosted, it proved very difficult for many producers to raise the finance for new film output. Paradoxically, with the field, in theory, completely empty of competition, it became harder to make films in England.

The reason was simple. Hollywood's retaliatory action had diminished almost to zero the chances of American release and it was felt that the British domestic market was insufficient to earn adequate returns. But the biggest irony was that American distributors were taking as many dollars out of the country as before from the re-issues and from stockpiled films. It was plain that the government had made a gross miscalculation in levelling its tax. The measure had proved to be ineffective in tackling the central problem of the drain on hard currency and it had dealt a savage and unreckoned blow at the British film industry. Yet it was not until March 1948 that the outcome of discussions between Eric Johnston representing the Motion Pictures Association of America, and Harold Wilson, then President of the Board of Trade, were announced. The tax was to be repealed (this eventually happened on 3 May 1948) and for two years a sum of $17 million was permitted to be taken out by the Americans, a figure that could be increased by the equivalent of British film earnings in the United States. The balance of American earnings was to be used for purposes approved by a joint control committee, for production, distribution, and so on, and investment of up to £2½ million outside the film industry. It was estimated that $33 million would be saved as a result of this new scheme.

Bad feeling in the United States resulting from the misconceived tax was scarcely allowed to abate before another bombshell was lobbed into the arena. The exhibitors' quota fixed under the 1938 Act had run out and a new Cinematograph Films Act in 1948 raised it to forty-five per cent for first features and twenty-five per cent for the supporting programme. The renter's quota was abolished in accordance with GATT (General Agreement on Tariffs and Trade), and the percentage was now to be fixed annually to accord with the supply situation. The forty-five per cent quota was received with incredulous horror by the Americans and once more Rank was accused of conspiratorial calumny. That the level was absurdly high was borne out by the fact that a month later Wilson was reporting a 'stoppage' in the film industry because of the difficulties in raising finance.

Now Rank was beginning to slide over the brink into disaster.

13   The Post-War Production Effort

The war had ended with a handful of fine pictures either released or in the course of production. With the gradual reinstatement of studio space and the return of valuable technicians from the armed services there sprang up a strong urge to protect the newfound standing of British films. War stories for a while continued to appear. On the documentary level were *The True Glory*, an Anglo-American newsreel compilation assembled by Carol Reed and Garson Kanin showing the invasion of Europe from D-Day to VE-Day, followed by a reconstruction of the battle of Arnhem, directed by Brian Desmond Hurst, called *Theirs Is the Glory*, and several attempts to show the problems facing a country that had been shattered by war. Probably the best were Jill Craigie's story of Plymouth's blitz redevelopment plan, *The Way We Live*; Paul Rotha's view of the post-war housing situation, *Land of Promise*; and Ralph Keene's exposition of the Abercrombie Plan for London, *The Proud City*. *The Way We Live* achieved a great deal of publicity which resulted in more extensive bookings than was usual for a straight documentary subject.

The war formed the background rather than the main action in the capable Launder and Gilliatt thriller, *Green for Danger*, which had Alastair Sim as a detective investigating a murder in a hospital threatened with imminent destruction from V1 flying bombs. Prior to this Launder and Gilliatt had made *I See a Dark Stranger* (*The Adventuress* in the U.S.A.) which had Deborah Kerr as an Irish girl who gets involved with a German spy ring, then changes her allegiance after meeting Trevor Howard. A pleasantly humorous view of espionage, it was less popular in Britain than in America. *Night Boat to Dublin*, made by Lawrence Huntington for ABPC, with Robert Newton and Muriel Pavlow, also had an Anglo-Irish spy background. Ealing produced *The Captive Heart*, in which Michael Redgrave, a prisoner of war in a German camp, assumed a dead man's identity in order to get repatriated, with ensuing problems when he met the wife. Basil

Dearden directed it, achieving a documentary realism in the sequences showing life in the prisoner-of-war camp. Less successful was Compton Bennett's *The Years Between*, which had Redgrave again returning from a prisoner-of-war camp, this time as an ex-MP who finds that his wife, believing him dead, has taken over his seat in the House. The film suffered mainly from implausibility.

Michael Powell and Emeric Pressburger made a fascinating and highly sophisticated technical exercise, *A Matter of Life and Death* (*Stairway to Heaven* in America), concerning the trial of a young airman for his life in a celestial court, while his body lay on the table in an operating theatre. Earthly scenes were in Technicolor, heavenly ones in monochrome. A huge escalator was erected at Denham, on which the departed soul soared to the clouds. The fanciful storyline, ultimately given some credence as a hallucinatory experience during a desperate illness, was both banal and pretentiously allegorical, with Anglo-American relations obviously on trial. The atmosphere of the operating theatre, the lights and doors swinging along the corridor to it seen through the eyes of David Niven, the airman, was imaginatively achieved. The girl radio operator, who falls in love with him as he brings his stricken plane in to land, was played by an American actress, Kim Hunter, brought over specially for the film. *A Matter of Life and Death* was chosen for the first Royal Film Performance in 1948.

Peter Ustinov, at that time a prodigy of the British cinema, wrote, directed and co-produced at twenty-five a straightforward war film about the radar 'boffins' called *School for Secrets*, with Ralph Richardson. Herbert Wilcox made the first of a series of films featuring his wife, Anna Neagle, and Michael Wilding, this one with a wartime romance as the theme, *Piccadilly Incident*. Basil Dearden made at Ealing a thoughtful attempt to show the effect of prejudice against an ex-RAF man who brings a German wife back to England. This film, *Frieda*, introduced Mai Zetterling to the British cinema.

However, the most outstanding of early post-war films had nothing to do with the war. It was David Lean's *Great Expectations*, by far the richest evocation of a Dickensian novel of the many examples that have been filmed. The film was superbly constructed, from its masterly shock opening, with the escaped convict Magwitch suddenly appearing before Pip like a manifestation of the devil, to the ironic ending when, grown-up, he comes to Miss Havisham's old house, seen for the first time in bright daylight. John Mills played Pip and Bernard Miles the amiable Joe Gargery; Martita Hunt was Miss Havisham, and Alec

Guinness made his first screen appearance as Herbert Pocket. The film was a great success both in Britain and America, and was viewed as proof that British films were going to sustain their promise. It was followed a few weeks later by another major film based on a Dickens novel which had been made at Ealing by Cavalcanti, *Nicholas Nickleby*. The film did not, however, benefit from the comparison, being stagey, fussy and dull in spite of the strong story, with its horrific depiction of life in a nineteenth-century Yorkshire school, Dotheboys Hall. Derek Bond was a likeable but somewhat bland hero, and nearly all the other parts tended to be played as cameos. Cavalcanti abandoned Dickens for his next film, turning to a modern crime story with Griffith Jones as a gang leader, *They Made Me a Fugitive*. In fact, the three main cycles of early post-war films were crime, psychological thrillers (like *The Upturned Glass* with James Mason), and costume melodramas such as *Jassy*, in which Margaret Lockwood appeared in Technicolor in a sequel to *The Wicked Lady*, again produced by Sydney Box, who had taken over production at Gainsborough in 1946, when Maurice Ostrer left, unable to stand the growing interference of Filippo del Giudice, who was trying to unify all of Rank's production companies. Sydney Box had already produced, with great success, a modestly budgeted film, *The Seventh Veil*, which had achieved great public acclaim.

One of del Giudice's better enterprises was a film in Technicolor, directed by Thorold Dickinson, *Men of Two Worlds*, which attempted to show the conflict between an educated African and his people, still clinging to superstition and ignorance. The film had been three years in preparation and had cost £600,000. Much of the footage was shot on location in Tanganyika, with vivid photography of native life and a remarkably accomplished use of colour for the time. Eric Portman gave a sensitive performance as a district commissioner endeavouring to move a reluctant African tribe out from the danger of the tsetse fly, and Robert Adams played the westernized African battling both with the witch doctor and his own roots. A musical score by Sir Arthur Bliss was an additional asset to a well-made film by a director whose career in the cinema only resulted in eight films, most of which, such as *Gaslight*, *Next of Kin* and *Queen of Spades*, were of considerable merit.

Carol Reed's first post-war film, *Odd Man Out*, has become celebrated as a classic of British film-making. It has worn less well than expected, being loaded with effects and performances which now seem high-flown and unnecessarily pretentious, as a mortally wounded Irish gunman endures hallucinations when he staggers from one refuge to another in the last winter hours of his life. James Mason gave one of the best performances of his career, evoking with exquisite care some sense of the conflicts tearing apart the soul of the man. The famous climax, when his girl finds him in the snow by the dock surrounded by police, and draws their gunfire on to both of them, is marred by the indifferent studio quality of the setting, which clamoured for real urban location work, as in the robbery scene near the start of the picture. The film, enhanced by Abbey Theatre acting such as that of W. G. Fay as the priest who gives spiritual succour to the hero, achieved immense critical acclaim, offering a powerful and intense cinematic thesis unusual from a national cinema that generally tended towards bland self-effacement in its output. Reed had attempted and succeeded in an ambitious task, to depict the disintegration of a man's life in the space of a single night, and the inter-relation of other characters, be they mean, treacherous or saintly. The film went over budget by a third as much again, a fact that displeased del Giudice, and before it was released to an enthusiastic reception Reed had moved over to Sir Alexander Korda.

Korda, controller of British Lion and Shepperton studios, was Rank's nearest rival, although the body of production in his care was very much smaller. He viewed Rank's grandiose expansion programme with considerable alarm, having sensed that the whole industry would be in grave danger if Rank over-reached himself. Already a certain amount of the prejudice Rank had aroused in the United States was rubbing off on to Korda, and on British films generally. Yet Korda, having made films in Hollywood, was better known there and had a distribution agreement with Twentieth-Century Fox. His first post-war film, which he directed himself, was a Technicolor adaption of Oscar Wilde's *An Ideal Husband*, with costumes by Cecil Beaton and lush Georges Perinal photography. Its stars were Paulette Goddard, Michael Wilding, C. Aubrey Smith, Hugh Williams, Diana Wynyard and Glynis Johns. Its sets included an expensive replica of Apsley Gate in the 1890s. In spite of the high production values the film was not well received, the transposition of Wilde's theatricality into the medium of film being difficult and unsatisfactory. Korda's other major film at the time was a new version of Tolstoy's *Anna Karenina*, directed by Julian Duvivier, whose most celebrated pre-war film in France was *Un Carnet de Bal*. Vivien Leigh played the part that Garbo had so strikingly performed in 1935, and Ralph Richardson was her husband. The film's dullness was unmitigated by much of the acting,

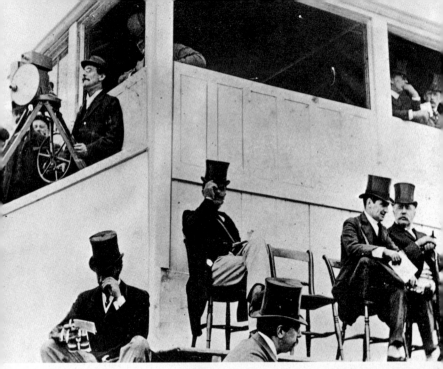

Above Prominent among the earliest pioneers in Britain was Birt Aces who set up his cameras to film the 1895 Derby.

Right Cecil Hepworth's 1905 work *Rescued by Rover*; an early milestone in narrative cinema. It had to be re-shot several times.

Above Robert Paul was one of the most notable pioneers. A shot from a documentary of his, *Army Life*.

Left D. W. Griffith shot *Hearts of the World* (1917) in England. Centre is Dorothy Gish and on the right is the young Noël Coward.

Opposite above American star Betty Compson played in Graham Cutts' *Woman to Woman* (1924), one of the first British box-office successes.

Opposite below Hepworth made *Comin' thro the Rye* in 1916 and 1923. This is the second version, with Alma Taylor.

Above Betty Balfour appeared in Jess Robbin's 1928 film *A Little Bit of Fluff*. It was a remake of a film first made in 1919.

Opposite above Will Rogers and Dorothy Gish came to Britain to appear with Nelson Keyes in Herbert Wilcox's *Tip Toes* (1928).

Opposite below Anthony Asquith's first film, directed with A. V. Bramble, was *Shooting Stars* (1928), a murder mystery set in a film studio.

PLEASE KEEP AWAY
FROM FRONT
OF CAMERA

Above Tom Walls, Robertson Hare, Ralph Lynn and Winifred Shotter in the film of the play *Rookery Nook* (1930).

Right Ondra and John Longden in a scene from the film, *Blackmail*.

Opposite above Anthony Asquith (*kneeling centre, in mourning for the death of his father, a former Prime Minister*) with the production team of *Underground* (1928).

Opposite below The first complete talkie in Britain was Alfred Hitchcock's thriller, *Blackmail* (1929). Hitchcock, with headphones, had voice trouble with his attractive Czech star Anny Ondra.

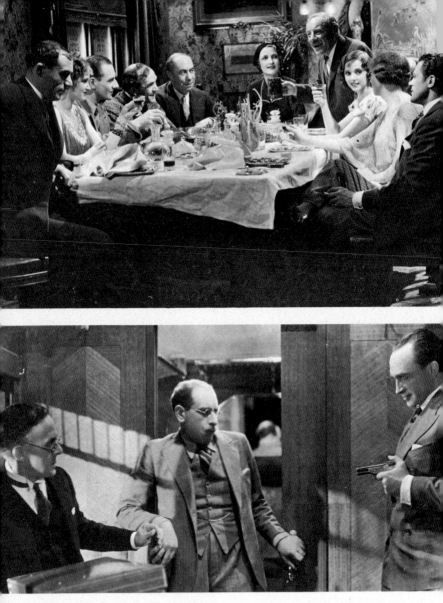

Above Victor Saville made a big impact on the thirties. *The Good Companions* (1933) was a hit, consolidating the success of Jessie Matthews (*third from right*). Edmund Gwenn is proposing a toast, John Gielgud is third from the left.

Below Better things came with Walter Forde's *Rome Express* (1932). Eliot Makeham and Cedric Hardwicke with Conrad Veidt.

Opposite Jessie Matthews.

Left Korda's first great British success came with *The Private Life of Henry VIII*. Merle Oberon as Anne Boleyn is about to be beheaded.

Below Jack Buchanan, a debonair song-and-dance man, was a notable light comedian. He was teamed with Joan Barry in Louis Mercanton's *Man of Mayfair* (1931). Buchanan was one of a handful of British stars to establish an American reputation, but not on account of his films.

Above   *Dark Journey* (1937), directed by Victor Saville, was a spy story set in wartime Stockholm, with Conrad Veidt and Vivien Leigh on opposite sides.

Below   *The Thirty Nine Steps* (1935) was one of Hitchcock's excellent thirties thrillers, in this instance loosely based on Buchan's story. Robert Donat is awoken by the corpse of Lucie Mannheim falling across his bed.

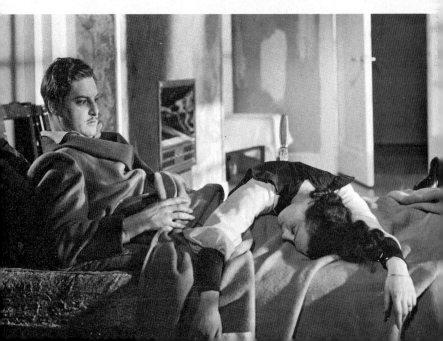

Above Hitchcock at Islington on the set of *The Lady Vanishes* (1938), flanked by Margaret Lockwood and Googie Withers. The film was to introduce Michael Redgrave to the screen.

Below Gracie Fields was one of the top box-office stars of the thirties, playing wry comic roles with unabated vigour. Monty Bank's *Keep Smiling* (1938).

Above Perhaps the most consistently funny comedy team was that of Will Hay, Moore Marriott and Graham Moffat, seen here in Marcel Varnel's impeccable *Oh Mr Porter!* (1937) which was perhaps the apogee of British comic films of the thirties.

Left George Formby in John Paddy Carstairs' *Spare a Copper* (1940). Formby consistently headed the list of most popular male stars in the late thirties, always appearing as an almost moronic but well-intentioned hero.

Above Rembrandt
(1936), directed by
Alexander Korda
himself was a beautiful
succès d'estime with
a powerful
performance by
Charles Laughton.

*Left The Divorce of
Lady X* (1938),
directed by Tim
Whelan, was a comedy
in Technicolor, with
Ralph Richardson and
Laurence Olivier. The
leading female was
taken by Merle
Oberon. It was
another escapist
extravaganza from
Korda's Denham.

Above *St Martin's Lane* (1938) with Rex Harrison and Vivien Leigh, directed by Tim Whelan, was a pleasantly romantic comedy.

Below Sam Woods' sentimental *Goodbye Mr Chips* (1939) with Robert Donat, and Greer Garson making her first screen appearance in the brief role of the school-master's short-lived wife. The story was adapted from a novella by James Hilton.

Above Powell directed Korda's lavish *The Thief of Bagdad* (1940), after several production vicissitudes. The film's chief male star was John Justin.

Below Carol Reed's *Kipps* (1941) with Michael Redgrave and Diana Wynyard was a pleasant adaptation of H. G. Wells' novel about the rise of a country draper.

and contemporary critics felt that Kieron Moore was miscast as Vronsky. Both this film and *An Ideal Husband* were disappointing in commercial and artistic terms and started Korda on a new collision course.

Although it might be thought that the presence of a Labour government would have generated interest in the long film the Boultings made about an ambitious Labour politician, *Fame Is the Spur*, from the novel by Howard Spring, such was not the case, and in spite of an excellent performance by Michael Redgrave it was a failure. There was apparently little public taste for the more serious historical film. *Captain Boycott*, which presented a view of Irish absentee landlordism in County Mayo, a Launder and Gilliatt film directed by Frank Launder, was also a box-office failure, while a melodramatic version of Daphne du Maurier's study of English landlords in Victorian Ireland, *Hungry Hill*, directed by Brian Desmond Hurst, was successful.

After *A Matter of Life and Death*, Michael Powell and Emeric Pressburger turned to India and produced a film about an Anglo-Catholic order of nuns running a school and hospital in the Himalayan foothills, and eventually falling before native superstition and heathen perverseness. The location photography in Technicolor by Jack Cardiff in *Black Narcissus* was a great deal better than the story and lifted the film above the threatening banality. It was a characteristic of the Archers' films that they looked better than they were – technical bravura was applied to thin stories often weak in character detail. They also made, in 1947, a black and white film mainly on location more than a thousand miles up the Amazon, called *The End of the River*. This was a greater disappointment than *Black Narcissus*, being yet another unsatisfactory story, this time directed by Derek Twist.

Far-flung locations were not unusual during this period, and great hopes were pinned on the possibilities of filming in Commonwealth countries. Harry Watt, formerly a veteran documentary director, took a unit to Australia and made a memorable film about a marathon cattle drive that had to be made during the war to safeguard a valuable herd. Called *The Overlanders*, it had an Australian cast, introducing the lean, desiccated figure of Chips Rafferty to the British public. Watt followed this up with a historical film about mid-nineteenth-century Australian gold miners, *Eureka Stockade*. Both these films were produced by Michael Balcon at Ealing, where the output had a character unlike anything else in the Rank Organization.

It was at this time that the famous Ealing comedies were beginning to emerge, characterized by their mild satire at the expense of authority. One of the first to fit the genre was *Hue and Cry*, in which a horde of children unmask a gang of crooks who have been using a comic paper for the passing of coded information. Owing something to *Emil and the Detectives* and to Louis Daquin's *Nous les Gosses*, the film moved brilliantly towards a climax in which it seems as though all the small boys in London converge on a riverside bomb-site to capture and hand over the crooks after Scotland Yard has refused to take the affair seriously. *Hue and Cry* was directed by Charles Crichton and had Alastair Sim in the leading adult part of a recluse creator of boys' adventure stories.

The Ealing approach to film-making placed a considerable emphasis on characterization and the creation of credible characters, a trait that was as marked in the comedies as in the dramatic films. At the end of 1947 an important study of life in London's East End was released, *It Always Rains on Sunday*, which had a story built around the sheltering of an escaped prisoner by his former girl-friend, now a married woman, and his eventual round-up, all in the space of a damp Sunday, while the background of Jewish street markets, coffee stalls, railway yards and the ritual of Sunday dinner pass by in well-observed detail. The director was Robert Hamer, fulfilling the promise he had shown with *Pink String and Sealing Wax*, and his actors included Googie Withers and John McCallum as woman and convict, Edward Chapman as the dull husband, Susan Shaw as the wayward daughter and Patricia Plunkett as the virtuous one, Jack Warner as a police detective, John Slater as a spiv (a designation of the period applied to sharp black-marketeers and petty crooks), and Sydney Tafler as a lady-killing music-shop proprietor. In spite of rather too much studio work for material that would have been better shot on location, the effect was still very convincing, with an excellent use of minute cameo roles shading in the details of Bethnal Green existence.

This was a technique that was used a great deal in British screen-writing where semi-documentary subjects were involved, and a very noticeable characteristic of Ealing films, although perhaps not so apparent in *The Loves of Joanna Godden* which also starred Googie Withers and John McCallum in an adaptation of a novel by Sheila Kaye-Smith about a young woman who inherits a farm on the Romney marshes, in the early years of the century. The director was Charles

Frend, whose next film was to take a rather larger bite at a historical subject.

Scott of the Antarctic was an epic story of a failure, the ill-fated expedition of Captain Robert Falcon Scott to the South Pole, which was beaten to the target by the Norwegian Amundsen and whose members all perished in bitter blizzard conditions. Frend made the film in a straightforward structured narrative, showing the preparations, the gathering together of men and equipment, and the drive and leadership of Scott himself, admirably played by John Mills; then the departure from the lushness of Britain for the barren antipodean ice mass. The build-up was slow and measured, punctuated by Vaughan Williams's atmospheric musical score. It was a splendid and worthy film, but what it gained in terms of prestige it lost at the box-office. The type of Ealing film preferred by the public is exemplified by *Passport to Pimlico*, perhaps the most famous of the great comedy series in which the common man outwitted authority. The plot concerned the effect of the discovery by the inhabitants of a London district that their parish was part of the kingdom of Burgundy, which meant that they were no longer subject to rationing, tax laws or the intrusion of Whitehall bureaucracy. Directed by Henry Cornelius, the film was an amusing attack on a regulation-strangled Britain. But before this new style was firmly established, Balcon produced a routine war film about Belgian spies trained in London, *Against the Wind*, directed by Charles Crichton, with several French stars, including Simone Signoret and Gisèle Préville, augmenting the cast; and a lavish Technicolor film, set in Hanoverian Germany at the start of the eighteenth century, *Saraband for Dead Lovers* (*Saraband* in the U.S.A.), directed by Basil Dearden, with Stewart Granger, Joan Greenwood, Francoise Rosay and Flora Robson.

Sydney Box had claimed, when he took over from Maurice Ostrer at Gainsborough, that production there would soon reach the rate of one film a month. He very nearly achieved this high target in the last flourish of Gainsborough. In 1948, for instance, films with the Box imprint consisted of *Broken Journey*, about an Alpine air crash, directed by Ken Annakin, who had made the portmanteau film, *Holiday Camp*, from a Godfrey Winn script in the previous year; *The Calendar*, directed by Arthur Crabtree, a remake of an Edgar Wallace racing story; *Easy Money*, an anthology of four stories about winners of football pools, directed by Bernard Knowles; *Good Time Girl*, directed by David MacDonald, in which Jean Kent went from bad to worse; *Miranda*, again by Ken Annakin, in which Glynis Johns played a mermaid accidentally caught by a young doctor on a Cornish fishing holiday; *Snowbound*, another David MacDonald film, from a Hammond Innes novel about Nazi treasure in the Alps; Lawrence Huntington's dismal *When the Bough Breaks*, which put Patricia Roc into the hands of a bigamist; and *Daybreak*, directed by Compton Bennett, which Box maintained was so mangled by the British Board of Film Censors as to be hardly worth releasing – an opinion most critics shared. Ken Annakin's *Here Come the Huggetts* reintroduced two characters played by Jack Warner and Kathleen Harrison in *Holiday Camp*, and was the first of a series designed to promote them as the English answer to Dagwood and Blondie Bumstead. Terence Fisher's *Journey into Yesterday* was about the search of an army major for a girl in Germany, and *My Brother's Keeper*, directed by Alfred Roome, had George Cole and Jack Warner as escaping convicts. Then there was *Quartet*, an assembly of four Somerset Maugham short stories, each with a different director – Arthur Crabtree, Ken Annakin, Harold French and Ralph Smart.

It was a varied output, demonstrating extremes in taste and subject matter. In the long Rank twilight Sydney Box, aided by his sister Betty and his wife Muriel, was a dynamic force.

Among the memorable films to emerge in 1948 from the Rank or Filippo del Giudice orbit was Olivier's second Shakespearean foray, *Hamlet*, which unlike *Henry V* was made in black and white. Its style was compelling, with deep focus camerawork by Desmond Dickinson, recalling the work of Gregg Toland in *Citizen Kane*. The costumes were designed by Roger Furse, and William Walton wrote the score. The text was carefully bowdlerized, edited and classified by Alan Dent, for censorship problems had occurred in the United States over the too literal use of the word 'bastard' in *Henry V*. Olivier postured and declaimed; it was a performance of magnificent vocal mastery, but a cold and almost ruthless Hamlet, not entirely pleasing to the critics. Jean Simmons played a delicate and sensitive Ophelia, making much of her short scenes. The film was a display of cinematic virtuosity, far excelling any other attempt at that time to put Shakespearean tragedy on the screen. It may be recalled that as far back as 1913 Sir Johnston Forbes Robertson had acted in a film version of *Hamlet*. Orson Welles's idiosyncratic *Macbeth* was made in the same year, but not shown in Britain until much later.

Rank's Independent Producers' Company, Cineguild, was responsible for *Oliver Twist*, which was directed by David Lean and constructed in the same careful way as *Great Expectations*, evoking the squalor of Dickensian London. As in the earlier film, the opening sequence was striking, as Oliver's mother, heavy with child, struggles across open country in a storm to reach a workhouse, where the hero can be born. The portrayal of Fagin by Alec Guinness was strongly objected to in America on the grounds of anti-Semitism, and the film languished unknown there, losing a considerable revenue. Anthony Newley, who had already had a small part in Peter Ustinov's unsatisfactory adaption of the humorous Anstey novel, *Vice Versa*, was introduced to a wider audience with his playing of the Artful Dodger. Also memorable were Robert Newton as Bill Sykes, Kay Walsh as Nancy, and Francis L. Sullivan as Mr Bumble.

The Archers, another team of Rank's Independent Producers, brought out what is perhaps the only ballet film to have done well on general release. *The Red Shoes* was about a ruthless ballet promoter, played by Anton Walbrook, a young composer, Marius Goring and a beautiful young dancer, Moira Shearer. The theatricality and melodrama of the story were submerged in the masterly sweep of the treatment, its portrayal of the workings of a great ballet company, the relentless drive needed to succeed as a dancer, the sweat and hard work behind the scenes. The film also contained Brian Easdale's complete ballet, choreographed by Robert Helpman, and based on Hans Christian Andersen's fairy story about the shoes that danced their wearer to death, which serves as an allegory for the plot of the film. *The Red Shoes* was written, produced and directed by Michael Powell and Emeric Pressburger; the striking sets were designed by Hein Heckroth, and the Technicolor photography was by Jack Cardiff. Among the great dancers in the film were Helpman, Massine and Madame Rambert, with Ludmilla Tcherina as a ballerina lured away by marriage. With its brilliant colours, exotic locations in Paris and Monte Carlo, and the effectively staged ballet sequences, the film was well-received in an age of austerity, and even more so in America, where it became something of a cult, placing British films high in esteem after the Chancellor of the Exchequer and the President of the Board of Trade had done their worst where Anglo-American relations were concerned. Over the years, *The Red Shoes* became one of the top grossing films in American theatres, a rare honour for an all-British picture.

Launder and Gilliatt, whose Individual Pictures was also under Rank, filmed Norman Collins's long novel about life in the inner suburbs, *London Belongs to Me*, with Richard Attenborough as the ineffective murderer Percy Boon. The compendious cast included such stalwarts as Alastair Sim, Stephen Murray, Fay Compton, Susan Shaw and Wylie Watson. The two producers had a principle of alternating the direction of their films; this time it was Sidney Gilliatt's turn. With a success on their hands, they departed for the South Seas where Frank Launder directed *The Blue Lagoon*, a Technicolor version of H. de Vere Stacpoole's novel of two child castaways who grow up together on a desert island. In spite of the story's possibilities, it was a dull film.

Cineguild's major aberration of 1948 was a stylishly photographed costume melodrama in Technicolor based on a novel by Joseph Shearing, entitled *Blanche Fury*, with Valerie Hobson and Stewart Granger. The director of what was an uninspired series of threatening posturings and flaring nostrils was Marc Allegret.

Beyond the Rank net were the Boultings, responsible for two outstanding films released in 1948. The first was *Brighton Rock*, from Graham Greene's novel about a young murderer and race gang leader. Directed by John Boulting, it moved at a remarkable pace, skilfully creating an atmosphere of terror and corruption, and at its heart was a brilliant performance by Richard Attenborough as Pinky, the desperate boy gangster who marries a sixteen-year-old girl in order to silence her. William Hartnell, Wylie Watson and Nigel Stock portrayed various degrees of sinisterness as his associates, and Alan Wheatley an ex-crook who is pushed off Brighton pier. The Catholic conscience of Pinky is perhaps dealt with superficially by comparison with the book, but in those days censorship problems often emasculated film adaptations. *The Guinea Pig* (*The Outsider* in the U.S.A.) was the other film, directed by Roy Boulting. This dealt with the social problem posed by a clause in the 1944 Education Act which provided for a certain number of grammar-school boys to be awarded scholarships to public schools. Richard Attenborough, then in his mid-twenties, played a thirteen-year-old boy entering a famous public school, and the film follows the adjustment of a working-class youth to a milieu quite different from anything in his previous experience. In the new egalitarianism of the Attlee administration it might have been thought that the burden of the message here was one of outdated snobbery, but the Boultings' mild left-wing sympathies allowed them to keep a firm grip on the situation, so that it would be seen ultimately that the experiment would be of benefit to both sides. Cecil Trouncer played a traditional housemaster and Robert Flemyng a sympathetic young master. The absurdities of school customs and the unnatural inhibitions regarding sex that result from the system were handled in an unexaggerated and convincing way. Adapted from a successful stage play by Warren Chetham Strode, it was a triumph for thoughtful British film-making.

Carol Reed, under his new contract with Korda, directed another outstanding film which helped to restore London Films' declining fortunes, after the débâcle of the costly *Anna Karenina* and *An Ideal Husband*. It was based on a short story by Graham Greene and concerned the belief of a small boy in a Belgrave Square embassy that the butler whom he idolized was in fact a murderer. It was called *Fallen Idol*, and the butler was played by Ralph Richardson, with eight-year-old Bobby Henrey as the small boy. Also in the cast were Michèle Morgan and Sonia Dresdel. The relationship of the boy and the butler was handled with great subtlety and Bobby Henrey's acting was remarkable. As with *Odd Man Out*, Reed chose to consider the psychological implications of the dramatic situation. It is a tidier, more carefully organized film although lacking the bravura of the other work. Another Korda film which was a great success was Anthony Kimmins's *Mine Own Executioner*, adapted from a novel by Nigel Balchin, in which a psychiatrist, played by Burgess Meredith, assumed the guilt of one of his patients, played by Kieron Moore.

The de Grunwald–Asquith–Rattigan team was also successfully active again, this time for Korda, with *The Winslow Boy*, a fairly straightforward transcription of the current theatrical success. The story was based on a real-life incident, the expulsion of a naval cadet from Osborne for stealing a postal order and the subsequent fight by his family to clear his name. In the film Robert Donat took the part of the disagreeable but gifted Q.C. who represents the boy. Asquith's direction was as polished as usual but there was a certain dispersal of the dramatic impact that had made the play such an effective piece of theatre. The last of Korda's 1948 films was an almost unmitigated catastrophe – a long, expensive, Technicolor history, *Bonnie Prince Charlie*, which had an unhappy David Niven playing the lead in what was generally agreed to be a boring waste of money. The subject was not particularly rich in possibilities and the casting of Niven incensed the Scottish audiences who felt he was too shallow a figure to portray a national hero. Anthony Kimmins directed it and no other film by him was quite so mercilessly mangled by the critics and despised by the public.

Associated British were responsible for one of the year's box-office successes. Made under the direction of Harold French, *My Brother Jonathan* was a film version of a novel by Francis Brett Young in which an ambitious young doctor with his eye on Harley Street enters into general practice in a dismal northern industrial town. Michael Denison played the lead, with Dulcie Gray, Beatrice Campbell, Ronald Howard and Stephen Murray in support. It was a sound, unspectacular, faintly heroic film of a kind very characteristic of British cinema in the forties.

Herbert Wilcox continued his Wilding–Neagle partnership. After the less successful 1947 film, *The Courtneys of Curzon Street*, he directed the stars in *Spring in Park Lane*, a light comedy with milord masquerading as the butler for very little reason other than to provide some sort of plot. The pleasantly luxurious settings, with much popping of champagne corks, lifted the film above the austere life most British people were forced to live in the difficult early post-war period. Wilcox was at times a remarkably shrewd showman and his films nearly always divided into patriotic biographies or light comedies about wealthy people.

The nadir of output in 1948 was reached with two films. The first was Maurice Ostrer's amazingly ridiculous *Idol of Paris*, directed by Leslie Arliss, which achieved its greatest notoriety with a sequence showing a duel with whips between two nineteenth-century French demi-mondaines. The other was *No Orchids for Miss Blandish*, adapted from a crime novel by James Hadley Chase and directed by St John Clowes. Worse than any Hollywood 'B' picture, it was a series of indifferently staged killings and beatings in the gangster idiom, set in a pseudo-America. Many local authorities refused to allow the film to be shown in their areas; nevertheless, the press coverage it received enabled it to draw long queues wherever it did play.

The British cinema was meeting the adjustment to the inevitably dull years after the war with a considerable variety of output, but insufficient inspiration.

14 Collapse of an Empire

When Harold Wilson signed the agreement with Eric Johnston of the Motion Picture Producers of America for the terms under which the seventy-five per cent *ad valorem* tax could be lifted, he neglected to ensure that the resumption of Hollywood films entering Britain would be gradual. Consequently, instead of a trickle there was a flood. This meant that after the unhappy spring of 1948, when apart from new British films there had been only revivals available for the public which, coupled with good seasonal weather, had emptied the cinemas, the American competition was by this time very strong. Rank's production programme had been stepped up to no avail, and now the films that had been started at the beginning of the Hollywood boycott were becoming ready for release. In October 1948 Rank reported to his shareholders that the current overdraft position at the National Provincial Bank was in the order of £13½ million. By the following year it had increased to £16¼ million. The situation was so desperate that Rank now contemplated total suspension of film production. In the course of three post-war years Rank had gambled on building up a soundly-based industry and had failed. There was even a certain amount of jubilation over his defeat, the anti-Rank lobby both in and out of Parliament being highly vocal. The President of the Board of Trade himself, who undoubtedly, although unwittingly, was one of the major destroyers of the film industry, said in the House of Commons that it now had 'an excellent excuse for one of its periodic crises'. It was an unnecessary and unworthy sneer. Nearly every move the government had made, even if motivated by the best of intentions, had exacerbated difficult Anglo-American relations and nullified the progress made within the industry to secure transatlantic distribution. Moreover, the government had removed thirty-eight per cent of all domestic box-office takings in the form of Entertainments Tax. That the tax, which in 1938 had taken £39 million from a gross of £109 million, remained at its wartime level for so long was undoubtedly due to the communication failure between Rank, who as the dominating figure of the film business should have been able to state the case, and Labour politicians who were prejudiced against him for doctrinaire reasons. The tax was crippling the industry. To take 1948 again as an example, from a net box-office receipt of £70 million the British producers were left with £7½ million. But since production costs had amounted to nearly twice that, £14 million, the tax was taking from the film industry nearly ten times as much money needed to enable it to break even. It was a policy that could only lead to bankruptcy.

Extravagance was a reasonable charge to be levelled at Rank. He had been taken for a ride by Gabriel Pascal to the tune of £1,278,000 for *Caesar and Cleopatra*; he had spent half a million on setting up an animation unit which proved only that Disney could do it better; Independent Frame, David Rawnsley's novel technique for faster film-making, had cost another £600,000. To be fair, it is arguable that every industry should devote its resources to development and research, but now came the reckoning for that policy. Children's Films and *This Modern Age* were closed down, two of the most worthwhile projects established in the expansive period, but regrettably loss-makers all along. Independent Frame was abandoned. GB Animation was wound up. The loss on general film production was reported to be £3,350,000. John Davis, an astute accountant and tough businessman, now emerged as the man who would save something from the wreckage. Already the recklessly extravagant Filippo del Giudice had been swept away by the Davis broom. The talents of Carol Reed, Powell and Pressburger, Launder and Gilliatt, Ian Dalrymple, Anthony Havelock-Allan, Ronald Neame and David Lean – the creative force of Independent Producers – one by one fell away, most of them joining Korda, who now somehow seemed to represent a beacon of artistic resurrection.

Simultaneously with these troubles, a further cause for alarm was becoming disturbingly apparent. Attendances at cinemas had fallen off by 200 million a year since the peak year of 1946, with a consequent reduction in box-office takings. In 1949 1,430 million people went to the cinema, and the gross taking was £103 million, compared with £118 three years earlier. In 1950 the number of admissions had dropped to 1,396 million, although the raising of seat prices kept the revenue steady at £105 million. By 1952 admissions were down to 1,312 million and there was speculation and alarm as to when the downward trend would level out. At that stage no one was pessimistic enough to imagine that it was only the start of a continuous downward spiral that was to continue for the next twenty years. The reason for the decline initially lay in the fact that since the war most filmgoers had become more discriminating and had begun to go to films they wanted to see, rather then regularly, regardless of what was showing. As post-war conditions slowly improved, other distractions, in the form of alternative entertainments and leisure activities, became a threat to the film business. The summer of 1949 was an exceptionally good one, to the chagrin of cinema managers who prayed for rain and full houses. The television boom had not yet really begun in earnest in Britain, although in America already the number of domestic receivers had reached several millions. The peak years for filmgoing had ended, and the rise of television in the 1950s was almost a *coup de grâce* to the exhibiting business. As attendance fell so did Entertainments Tax, and the Government belatedly recognized that it was necessary to ease the burden faced by the companies. This, coupled with price increases, enabled the film industry to stave off the worst effects of the decline in admissions and to some extent cushioned it from the realities of the situation.

The Palache Report in 1944 had recommended the establishment of a National Film Finance Corporation and a national renting agency to which it would be linked. In July 1948 the President of the Board of Trade announced that the former would be set up, but without the agency. Loans from the NFFC would not be made direct to producers, but through an existing renting organization. There were two possibles, Rank's General Film Distributors and Korda's British Lion. Rank declined the suggestion of a Government loan, preferring at this stage to cut back production, but British Lion, on the other hand, asked for £2 million from the NFFC's working capital of £5 million and, when this proved inadequate for Korda's purposes, had it raised to £3 million. The rest went to smaller companies and the clause restraining direct loans to producers was lifted. In its first year of operation more than fifty applications were approved. The first managing director of the NFFC was James Lawrie who had the difficult task of assessing the consequence of advancing loans, having had virtually no previous experience of the film industry. Although mistakes were made, a number of successful films such as *The Third Man*, *The Wooden Horse* and *The Happiest Days of Your Life* were produced with government money. In spite of this, the government made the bitter discovery already acknowledged by J. Arthur Rank that prestige was not enough, and that it was only too easy to lose a great deal of money backing British films. The NFFC lacked any kind of residual wisdom in film-making, its operation was essentially pragmatic, and Rank actually had an advantage in the capacity to calculate the scale of the risk. The NFFC, while its initial losses amounted to a direct subsidy for the industry (something that Harold Wilson had always denied was the government intention) had, necessarily, to pay lip service to the taxpayer and not hand its funds around with the reckless abandon that characterized certain elements of the film world. This meant that the emphasis for its nominated films was on box-office appeal; they had to play safe in their subject matter and not tackle anything which could be controversial or unpopular. So an element of adventurousness was lacking and many of the films, being of a pot-boiling kind, fell short of reasonable aesthetic standards.

Wilson, aware that there had been no official report on films since 1944 when conditions were vastly different, established not one but two committees in 1948. The first was an inquiry into the commercial distribution and exhibition side of the business under the chairmanship of Professor Sir Arnold Plant, the other was a working party under Sir George Gater to examine the financing of films and 'ways and means of reducing production costs'. Both inquiries began at the end of the year just as the shadows were beginning to lengthen for the industry, and while the committees were sitting the studios were closing down. First Islington, then Shepherds Bush were sold. Production was curtailed at Pinewood and Denham. In February of 1949 only seven of the twenty-six British film studios were in operation and only eleven films were actually being made. Whereas in March 1948 7,253 people were employed in the studios, in March 1949 the number had fallen to 5,139, and in the following year to 4,104. In March 1949 the forty-five per cent quota was reduced to forty per cent, a move to placate the Americans.

Both the Gater and Plant Committees reported that Entertainment Tax was too high. But each committee was handicapped by the terms of its brief, which did not permit any wandering across to the other's territory, and by the poor statistical evidence available to them. Until the Plant Report even the aggregate capacity and numbers of British cinemas were not filed centrally. Since then the Board of Trade has made quarterly reviews which have helped investigations into the business workings. Plant found that there was an absence of competitive trading and rigidity in distribution and exhibition which made for an inability to extract a film's full potential at the box-office. It strongly urged that there should be changes in the machinery of distribution, streamlining procedures and introducing a degree of flexibility. In turn, Gater reported that the film industry practised extravagance on a scale that would not be tolerated in any other industry. The success of British films in the latter war years had attracted a certain type of entrepreneur into the business who lacked basic film experience and who was afflicted with grandiose tastes. The glamour of films was a magnet for the flamboyantly inclined. The absence of forward-production planning was a serious shortcoming, and the lack of detailed study of long-term projects made for a climate of waste. There was in the film business an endemic dichotomy between the artistic and the commercial factions and, while both were essential for its survival, an uneasy partnership existed.

More studios closed. Highbury, Twickenham and British National at Elstree were lost to the industry. The House of Commons debated the situation soon after the publication of the two Reports. Harold Wilson professed an open mind about the conclusions and regarded the occasion as a test of opinion. 'Both Parliament and the country would reject any facile solution of the film industry's problems based simply on handing back in the form of a subsidy money to an industry, admittedly convicted of considerable extravagance, without guarantee that this money would not be swallowed up in further extravagance.' The tone was set. Many felt that even if there was a chance of seeing the money again subsidies were not the answer; the only possible solution was a total restructuring of the entire industry. The exhibitors and distributors were held to be the villains, retaining more of the takings than was justified. There was certainly no cry for a state-owned film industry, in spite of the proposals by ACT for a nationalized circuit that would compete on equal terms with the existing Rank and ABC circuits, and be linked to a state distributor.

The Cinematograph Films Council, the advisory body which had acquired its title in pre-war days after the passing of the 1938 Act, having deliberated for several months, finally accepted the Plant Report's diagnosis of the problems affecting the industry, although it was unable to agree unanimously on all the recommendations. While admitting that present methods were too inflexible the Council felt that the only way to improve total receipts would be to make formula low-budget films although this would damage the creative opportunities of the better producers. It also felt that the Report was unrealistic in believing that free competition was the answer, with government intervention bolstering up any parts of the structure that were liable to collapse. The ACT still called for partial nationalization.

In June 1950 the government set to work to introduce a plan to adjust the rate of Entertainment Tax in such a way that the industry would benefit. The plan was named after the Second Secretary of the Treasury, Sir Wilfrid Eady, who was its principal author. The Eady Plan was calculated to cause a tax reduction of £300,000, but would make available £3 million annually for the industry, half of which would go direct to the producers. The contribution of the other half by the exhibitors, into a production pool, was voluntary. In effect, tax was abolished on seats up to sevenpence and very small cinemas making less than £125 a week were exempted from the levy. Up to 1s. 6d. tax was reduced by a halfpenny. Above that, up to 3s. 9d., the tax was adjusted so that some of a penny price increase would go to the new British Film Production Fund, and the rest to the Inland Revenue. The BFPF was set up to administer the levy and consisted of representatives of various trade factions. Its job was to make payments to producers on 'a purely automatic and objective basis', to quote Mr Wilson, on the basis of the quarterly distributor's gross, i.e. the money earned before fees are deducted. Films less than 3,500 feet were to have the gross multiplied two and a half times to calculate the figure in order to take account of the much lower returns they made, and a small percentage was to be set aside to finance worthy projects, such as the Children's Film Foundation, which was set up under Mary Field, late of Rank's suspended Children's Films. Mr Rank became chairman of the new foundation. The quota also underwent a change during this period, dropping to a more realistic thirty per cent.

Although the Eady Plan ameliorated the producers' problems to a certain extent, it failed to halt losses. So in 1951 it was strengthened and exhibitors were required to pay rather more into the Fund, with corresponding seat-price increases. Entertainments Tax was again slightly reduced. There was also to be some relief for exhibitors who were now hard up against the problems of falling attendances; they were to get some £3½ million annually and the producers nearly £2¼ million more. It was hoped that by means of an augmented Eady Plan the film industry could now become solvent. In this way the principle of government subsidy was established. Hopes that by 1954 profitability could be fully restored were dashed by the continuing admissions slump and the closure of theatres, which created a spiral decline. Consequently the temporary government intervention into the industry's affairs has become a permanent feature and enabled the industry to keep its head above water through very difficult times. The biggest problem concerning the administration of the scheme was its built-in tendency to favour successful producers at the expense of the others. A film that did well at the box-office would get a higher subsidy, although it would be less likely to need it. There was little joy for anyone who wanted to risk his money on something ahead of its times, with the chance of failure at the box-office. Thus cautious film-making was given an official sanction. Certain remedies were attempted, but on a small scale and with scant success. Group Three, for instance, was a company founded to provide worthwhile second-feature material, with John Grierson and John Baxter in control. But that really was not enough to give hope and encouragement to the adventurous, and now there seemed less chance than ever for exciting films to emerge from British studios.

American companies were encouraged by the government to invest in British film-making after 1948 as a means of spending their 'blocked' earnings, after the permissible amount of receipts had been deducted. American-produced films that were made in Britain qualified for the quota and also for benefit from the levy at the box-office. While strident criticisms of the subsequent infiltration from Hollywood were raised, several positive factors had to be borne in mind. Most obviously British studios were in use, and British technicians were given work. Also, of course, the presence of Hollywood stars and directors gained valuable publicity in America for British films. But most important of all, films like *Night and the City*, *The Mudlark*, *The Miniver Story* and *Captain Horatio Hornblower*, *R.N.* were recognized in the course of their wide release in America as British, thus conditioning audiences towards a more general acceptance of British films. Hollywood had at last begun to work outside America. Gradually it became more economical and desirable for the major studios to make films internationally, in Rome, in Paris, in London. And Britain, where a common language and a favourable tax situation prevailed, was recognized as a new base for American operations. Warner (at Elstree), MGM (at Borehamwood), Twentieth-Century Fox and Walt Disney, then in conjunction with RKO, were among the Hollywood companies to work in Britain. Yet another aspect of Anglo-American collaboration was the trend towards a policy of raising finance from an American distribution contract, such as Korda's deal with David O. Selznick which enabled *The Third Man* to be made, and Sidney

Bernstein's partnership with Alfred Hitchcock, under the flag of Transatlantic Pictures.

By the close of this period the purges and economies effected by John Davis at Rank were shown to be effective. By January 1951 the Rank Organization had ceased to lose money and its overdraft had been reduced by £3½ million. Pinewood Studios were now under the wing of Earl St John, an American who had run the Paramount chain of cinemas before the war and before Rank had taken them over. St John organized with the NFFC a production group at Pinewood, securing a rapprochement between the Rank Organization and James Lawrie, who had earlier devoted most of the Fund's capital towards aiding the arch rival Korda. Although Rank's own production at Pinewood was now severely limited, other companies with Rank distribution contracts were using the studios, keeping them open.

15 The Last Brave Fling

The forties ended with industrial decline and a handful of praise-worthy films. From Ealing came Robert Hamer's elegant satire, *Kind Hearts and Coronets*, in which Alec Guinness performed eight roles, assorted in sex and character, all members of the D'Ascoyne family which a young man, Dennis Price, had to eliminate before he could take the ducal title and the family seat. Hamer's direction was sharp, fusing an episodic story into a well-conceived entity. The performances of Dennis Price and Joan Greenwood were cool and under-stated, as well-pitched as Guinness's array of virtuoso turns. Ealing continued their comedy series with *The Man in the White Suit*, directed by Alexander Mackendrick, in which a textile chemist discovers a synthetic fabric which is indestructible and totally dirt-resistant. Instead of being hailed as a benefactor he is denounced by the industry and shunned by his colleagues. The sharper ironies of this film have enabled its moral to survive rather longer than that of many other Ealing comedies. *The Lavender Hill Mob*, also starring Alec Guinness, with Stanley Holloway, was directed by Charles Crichton. It was about a modest, unambitious bank messenger who works out an ingenious plot to make off with a million pounds worth of gold bullion, melted down in the form of Eiffel Tower souvenirs. A trace of self-parody was beginning to become apparent in Ealing films; in this one, a police-car chase sequence in West London was a comic version of a pursuit in *The Blue Lamp*, a serious police film shot in a semi-documentary manner and directed by Basil Dearden, in which Jack Warner as P.C. Dixon is murdered by two thugs in the course of a robbery. The character was revived to become a regular television policeman and Jack Warner still plays the part some twenty-five years later. The script for this film was by Ted Willis, a notable exponent then of the realistic style of screenplay.

Charles Frend directed *A Run for Your Money*, another Ealing comedy with a background of the England v. Wales Rugby International at

Twickenham. But the film fell short of the standard achieved by the studio with *Passport to Pimlico*, directed by Henry Cornelius, and *Whisky Galore*, a comedy based on a Compton Mackenzie story, and directed by Alexander Mackendrick, about an island in the Outer Hebrides during wartime which suddenly finds itself knee-deep in cases of whisky from a wrecked ship. In America, the word whisky was not permitted in the title, which was changed to the very felicitous *Tight Little Island*. In a more serious category, *Pool of London*, directed by Basil Dearden, was a factually photographed crime film set in the London docks, with Bonar Colleano and Earl Cameron, and *Train of Events* a portmanteau collection of stories built around a train crash, directed by Charles Crichton. Ealing Studios under Sir Michael Balcon were in their last remaining years, and at the peak of their reputation. The consistency of their record was a tribute to the taste and enterprise of Balcon who managed, in spite of developing formula films, to maintain a consistent level of freshness and intelligence. He built up a talented and distinguished group of directors in Dearden, Crichton, Frend, Cornelius, Mackendrick and Hamer, all of whom were to develop further on the closure of Ealing.

Rank production at Pinewood began to subside. In 1949 the first stage of the collapse of Independent Producers was in earnest. David Lean made *The Passionate Friends* (*One Woman's Story* in America), one of his most sterile and unadventurous works, with his wife, Ann Todd, playing the lead in the H. G. Wells story of a woman who fails to make an appropriate marriage. Slow-moving and distant in its treatment, it was not a success, and both Ronald Neame who produced it, and David Lean left Rank. It was the break-up of Cineguild, although the company was to make one more film under Lean's direction, again with Ann Todd. It was *Madeleine*, an account of a famous Scottish mid-Victorian murder case in which a 'not proven' verdict was returned against a young woman called Madeleine Smith, who was alleged to have murdered her lover. Both films demonstrated Lean's meticulous assembly of his material, but both died at the box-office and it was with regret on both sides that he left Rank for Korda.

The first four films made with Rank's much-discussed Independent Frame system appeared. The first was *Warning to Wantons*, produced and directed by Donald B. Wilson, who was to initiate all the productions, and starring a French actress, Anne Vernon. A mild and somewhat stagey comedy, the limitations of the method were not too apparent. The second was *Floodtide*, directed by Frederick Wilson, which had a setting on Clydeside, and used a considerable amount of actuality footage which helped to create a realistic atmosphere. *Stop Press Girl*, directed by Michael Barry, was an inept and totally implausible comedy, and *Poet's Pub* was an uninspired film version of Eric Linklater's novel, directed by Frederick Wilson. While an Aldous Huxley story, based on *Young Archimedes* and called *Prelude to Fame*, was being filmed, the axes struck and Independent Frame was abandoned. The director was Fergus McDonnell and it introduced Jeremy Spenser as a young musical prodigy exploited by unscrupulous patrons. The major disadvantage of the Independent Frame system was that it called for an elaborate degree of pre-organizing and once the film was on the floor it was difficult, if not at times impossible, to alter set-ups, thus removing an important part of the director's work-flexibility. Independent Frame was, in its brief period devoted to cinema films, unable to prove itself. Some of its principles were, however, as already stated, to find application in television production.

In 1950 there were the beginnings of a new vogue for Second World War films, a genre that had been out of favour for several years. Two Cities' *They Were Not Divided*, directed by Terence Young, told the story of a group of recruits to the Welsh Guards, from the day they join until the deaths of the two leading players, Edward Underdown and Ralph Clanton, in the final winter of the war as they fight their way through Germany. Against a somewhat sentimental story of English and American comrades-at-arms was a graphic documentary of life in the wartime Guards Armoured Division. Inevitably the war film trend had mainly an American impetus, with such pictures as *Command Decision*, *Battleground*, *Twelve O'Clock High*, *Task Force*, *Go for Broke!* and *Sands of Iwojima*, although the outbreak of the Korean war may have legitimized feelings of nostalgia for the 1941-5 period. For whatever reasons, it was clear that a new cycle had started. An amusing British entry in the field was *Appointment with Venus*, the story of a Channel Island commando raid to liberate a cow. Directed by Ralph Thomas and produced by Betty Box, it was an oblique glimpse of one of the war's more unfamiliar areas of action. Herbert Wilcox, however, having concluded his frothy series of Neagle–Wilding films with the Technicolored *Maytime in Mayfair*, turned to recent history with *Odette*, Anna Neagle adding the heroine who defied the Gestapo to the long list of great ladies she had portrayed. Trevor Howard was cast as Captain Peter Churchill and Marius Goring as a Nazi. The film presented the story as a conventional and straightforward narrative of events, although its sense of purpose was muted by its too obviously respectful attitude. Roy Baker's *Morning Departure* (*Operation Disaster* in the U.S.A.), while not strictly speaking a war film, had a service background, being the story of a submarine disaster and the dilemma facing the remnants of a crew equipped with an insufficient number of escape suits. John Mills and Nigel Patrick kept tight lips as the commander and his lieutenant, and Richard Attenborough portrayed the weakening of moral fibre, a type-casting syndrome dating from his first screen appearance in *In Which We Serve*.

Among outstanding Rank films were Anthony Pellisier's version of a D. H. Lawrence short story of a boy driven by maternal greed to his death, *The Rocking Horse Winner*, with John Howard Davies (who played Oliver Twist in Lean's film), John Mills and Valerie Hobson, and the same director's H. G. Wells adaptation, also with John Mills, *The History of Mr Polly*, which managed to convey the satirical tone of the work quite successfully. As his last film for Rank before moving over to Korda, Ronald Neame made *The Golden Salamander*, with Trevor Howard, Anouk Aimée and Herbert Lom, a well-photographed melodramatic production concerning Tunisian gun-runners.

Rank's loss of Lean and Neame was balanced by the return of Anthony Asquith to Pinewood. After a disappointing film, *The Woman in Question* (*Five Angles on Murder* in America), in which one woman, played by Jean Kent, was seen successively through the eyes of several people, Asquith made, under the Two Cities banner, a film based on Terence Rattigan's one-act play, *The Browning Version*. In this Michael Redgrave played a cuckolded classics master at a public school, with Jean Kent as his unfaithful wife. Redgrave's performance of a failing, pathetic classroom figure was excellent, and the distinctive atmosphere was caught in the carefully observed manner of Asquith's portrayal of familiar English institutions.

Another field in which Rank had been fairly successful was in the compilation of filmed short stories by Somerset Maugham. After the success of the initial selection, *Quartet*, a follow-up was made called *Trio*, directed by Ken Annakin and Harold French. The outstanding story was *Mr Knowall*, in which Nigel Patrick made a notable impression as a shipboard bore on a cruise. As in the first film, each episode was introduced by Maugham himself. The third and last film of this particular cycle was *Encore*, three more stories directed in turn by Pat Jackson, Anthony Pelissier and Harold French. The short episode film was popular in the British cinema at this period, but vanished later, although it remained common in French and Italian production during the fifties and sixties.

But Gainsborough, responsible for the first two Maugham pictures, was running out of time. Sydney Box had gone on what might tactfully be called a year's sabbatical. Among the latter-day Gainsborough productions were the Huggett family series and the deplorably limp David MacDonald film, *The Bad Lord Byron*, which was handicapped by a curious form of presentation in which people associated with the poet, played in the film by Dennis Price, gave evidence in some apocalyptic courtroom. *Christopher Columbus*, an attempt at historical epic, also by David MacDonald, was no more successful. *A Boy, a Girl and a Bike*, directed by Ralph Smart, was set against the background of a Yorkshire cycling club at a time when cycling was a popular pastime, and was enlivened by realistic dialogue written by Ted Willis. The story was, however, trite in the extreme, with Honor Blackman, Patrick Holt and John McCallum involved in a triangle. *Boys in Brown*, directed by Montgomery Tully, was adapted from a play by William Douglas Home on life in Borstal, and *So Long at the Fair*, directed by Anthony Darnborough and Terence Fisher, had an intriguing plot, set in Paris at the time of the 1889 Exposition, and dealing with the total disappearance of not only Jean Simmons's brother but also the hotel room in which he slept.

Only Korda came near Rank in terms of power, although some kind of seesaw principle appeared to operate, so that when one was up the other was down. Recovering from the disastrous *Bonnie Prince Charlie* with Reed's *Fallen Idol* and Asquith's *The Winslow Boy*, he backed Powell and Pressburger's *The Small Back Room* (*Hour of Glory* in the U.S.A.), a Nigel Balchin story about a hard-drinking scientist in wartime who eventually has to defuse an unknown and dangerous German anti-personnel bomb. Emlyn Williams wrote, directed and starred in *The Last Days of Dolwyn* (*Woman of Dolwyn* in the U.S.A.) – the film which introduced Richard Burton to the screen – which was about a Welsh village doomed to extinction under the floodwaters of a new reservoir. The style was too stilted to be entirely successful, and demonstrated the dangers lurking in wait for the actor-director. The second film Carol Reed made for Korda turned out to be an outstanding international success, although three of its four stars, Joseph Cotten, Orson Welles and Valli, had been imported from America, leaving Trevor Howard isolated. Set in post-war Vienna, *The Third Man* conveyed a drab world of control commissions, racketeers and drug traffickers. Welles played the part of a mysterious criminal, Harry Lime, whose mode of hidden transportation was through the extensive Viennese sewer network. By tilting the camera and placing emphasis on huge shadows Reed infused a nightmarish, confused quality into the film which was primarily a study in deception, with Cotten as an American writer who stumbles accidentally into a situation that nearly leads to his death. The story was Graham Greene's, as was *Fallen Idol*. Throughout, from the main title, the sole incidental music was provided by a Viennese zither player, Anton Karas, and his tense strummings were appropriate additions to the feeling of the film as well as becoming extremely popular in their own right. *The Third Man* was very much a film of its time, describing a condition of pain, uncertainty and foreboding. It consolidated Reed's reputation as the leading director consistently working in British studios.

Like Emlyn Williams, Robert Donat also attempted to combine the roles of author, director and actor in *The Cure for Love*, which he adapted from a stage comedy by Walter Greenwood, about a soldier on leave who has to shed a clinging, domineering fiancée, played by Dora Bryan, so that he can marry another girl, a gentle evacuee played by Renée Asherson. The film's background was acutely Lancastrian, with northern dialects looming large, and in spite of occasional good comic moments it failed to advance very far from its theatrical origin. Launder and Gilliatt, whose last Rank film, *The Blue Lagoon*, had in spite of a generally poor reception from the critics been their most successful financially, had now moved their Individual Pictures to be under Korda's wing. Their first picture was a Gilliatt-directed thriller, *State Secret*, set in a mythical middle European country, with Douglas Fairbanks playing a doctor called in to operate on a dying dictator. When the patient dies the hero has to flee for his life, thus turning the film essentially into a chase in the Hitchcockian manner, with Glynis Johns playing the part of a helpful girl cabaret performer who shares the dangers of the situation.

Meanwhile Frank Launder had changed the mood by filming a farcical stage play about a girls' school that had been grafted on to a boys' public school through some civil service mix-up. The resulting collisions, in *The Happiest Days of Your Life*, between Margaret Rutherford and Alastair Sim as the respective heads were played with characteristic vigour and some of the smaller parts established stereotype roles for their performers, such as Joyce Grenfell as Miss Gossage ('Call me Sausage!'), a toothy, hockey-playing mistress, and

Richard Wattis as a bowler-hatted, fumbling man from the Ministry. One of the film's notable achievements was to make a profit for the National Film Finance Corporation; with *Morning Departure*, it managed to recoup its costs entirely in the home market.

Powell and Pressburger turned, after *The Small Back Room*, to historical romance and revived Baroness Orczy's fictional character, the Scarlet Pimpernel, who had been interpreted on the screen by Leslie Howard before the war in a Korda production. For the new film, *The Elusive Pimpernel*, David Niven was chosen to play Sir Percy Blakeney. Although he was then under contract to Sam Goldwyn in Hollywood, the latter was expected to release the film in America. The film was costly, having a final budget of half a million pounds, and was unfavourably compared with the pre-war version. To audiences Technicolor and beautiful photography were no substitute for a fast-moving, tightly directed story. The film was financially disastrous and when Goldwyn refused to handle it a protracted lawsuit was entered into on both sides.

The Archers' other film of that year was no less unhappy. Based on a somewhat bizarre novel (by Mary Webb) about an improbable daughter of nature, *Gone to Earth* was a melodramatic and unconvincing work, unredeemed by evocative Technicolor photography of the Shropshire countryside and a long hunting sequence. The film was to have been distributed in the States by David O. Selznick, and his wife Jennifer Jones, whose beauty covered up her limitations as an actress, was brought over to play the leading part. As had been Goldwyn in similar circumstances, Selznick was disappointed in the film and took Korda to court. But worse was yet to come, for the Archers, Powell and Pressburger, having wasted their talents on unworthy subjects, turned to something much more artistically attractive, a film version of Offenbach's opera *The Tales of Hoffman*. Their hope had been to find a follow-up success to *The Red Shoes*, which had made ballet acceptable on the screen. A score conducted by Sir Thomas Beecham and the Royal Philharmonic Orchestra was in itself not enough, nor were the notable assembly of singers and dancers who appeared in the film, including Moira Shearer, Robert Helpman, Ludmilla Tcherina and Leonide Massine, all of whom had been in *The Red Shoes*, and Robert Rounseville, Pamela Brown, Frederick Ashton, Ann Ayars and Mogens Wieth. The film was indeed long and absorbing, its violent decor and brilliant colour work well ahead of its time, but it none-theless proved to be above the heads of its general release audience.

Possibly it fell a victim to the rigid exhibition system prevailing at the time, which made no concessions to unusual categories of film, even when these would suffer when presented as straightforward weekly programme material. Korda was bitterly disappointed by the financial losses, and as three of the four Archers films made for him had failed at the box-office they and he parted company, thus effectively ending an interesting creative partnership.

Carol Reed also proved to be a disappointment as far as Korda was concerned, when the third film he made for him was released. This was *The Outcast of the Islands*, adapted from Joseph Conrad's novel about a man in the tropics who drifts and ultimately sinks to his destruction. Trevor Howard played the central character with an intensely despairing manner, and in the part of his mistress was a beautiful Algerian actress, Kerima. As far as the box-office was concerned the story lacked the appeal of *The Third Man* and the response was poor, if undeserved. Reed had yet again shown his skill in the handling of a narrative and the creation of mood, in this case that of introspection and waste.

During the same period the Boulting twins produced and directed *Seven Days to Noon* for Korda. In spite of a far-fetched plot about a mad scientist with an atom bomb in his briefcase who holds London to ransom, they succeeded in making the subject credible. The normal tendency would be to treat this familiar boy's paper situation in a tongue-in-cheek manner. Instead, the Boultings gave it the air of documentary realism. *Seven Days to Noon* showed its central character not as a fiendish Carl Petersen-type villain, but as a frightened, desperate and mentally-sick man, living in shabby lodgings. The climax of the film, with many shots of totally deserted London streets and an almost unendurable build-up of suspense, was one of the best examples of this type of filmic nightmare.

Two other Korda films of the period also deserve attention. The first, *The Wooden Horse*, directed by Jack Lee, was based on Eric Williams's account of one of the most ingenious wartime escapes from a German prisoner-of-war camp. Capitalizing on the well-known English fetish for physical exercise, RAF officers made a vaulting horse which was carried out every day into the camp compound. While their colleagues practised physical jerks, a team concealed in the body of the horse dug a tunnel until eventually three men were able to escape through it. The cast included Leo Genn, David Tomlinson, Anthony Steel, Bryan Forbes and Peter Finch. The treatment was in a realistic style, for the story was authentic and Lee was a director who had made several outstanding documentaries. Unfortunately the film's success was to spawn off a number of imitators and within a few years the prison-camp escape story had joined the great gallery of film clichés. *The Wooden Horse* has, as a result, been undervalued and it is hard to appreciate the freshness of its approach when viewing it today.

The remaining Korda film was produced and directed by his brother Zoltan, from Alan Paton's novel of South Africa, *Cry the Beloved Country* (*African Fury* in the U.S.A.). Its theme was race relations, and it contrasted and intermeshed the lives of a rich white man and a black priest living in poverty in a shanty town. Filmed with certain difficulties in Johannesburg, the cast included Canada Lee, Sidney Poitier and Edric Connor among its Negro actors, and Geoffrey Keen, Joyce Carey and Michael Goodliffe as the whites. It was a brave film to make, not merely because of the moral position taken by the original novel but also because it was bound to meet resistance when shown in many parts of the world. Thorold Dickinson's penultimate film, *The Queen of Spades*, with a screenplay by Rodney Ackland (initially the director) and Arthur Boys from a Pushkin story, was Russian in style, with Edith Evans as an old countess who had allegedly sold her soul to the devil. Intense, sombre and occasionally majestic, the film was uncharacteristic and visually over-stimulating. Yet it remains one of the most interesting works of its period.

One of the consequences of the settlement of the Anglo-American film dispute had been the encouragement given to Hollywood companies to make films in Britain. The American industry had shrunk considerably as a result of the extension of television services. In the space of three years from 1946 to 1949 the number of people employed in the studios dropped by almost half and the number of films actually being made dwindled. Britain was not the only other country where assets were frozen, and the Hollywood companies began to consider dispersing production to various other centres throughout the world, mostly in Europe. The number of television sets in use in the U.S.A. rose to about twelve million by 1951, while in Britain only about three-quarters of a million viewers' licences were issued in that year. It was recognized by some that television would use film and that the motion-picture industry would survive if it was able to adapt to changing conditions. In fact, a number of companies had already begun producing filmed series designed for television and not theatrical exhibition. It was the early beginnings of a major new industry.

In Britain, American co-productions started up on a regular basis. In 1949 *Britannia Mews* was made by Fox, directed by Jean Negulesco, with Maureen O'Hara and Dana Andrews. *Edward My Son*, from Robert Morley's stage play, was made by MGM with Spencer Tracy, Deborah Kerr and Leueen McGrath under George Cukor's direction. Robert Taylor and Elizabeth Taylor played together in *Conspirator*, also from MGM, which brought Victor Saville back to direct in England. Edward Dmytryk, a director who was one of the Hollywood Ten, the group which in 1947 refused to tell the notorious Committee for Un-American Activities whether or not they had been communists, was exiled, and made three films in England. The first, *So Well Remembered*, was an adaptation of James Hilton's novel, and was made before the hearings under a Rank–RKO arrangement. In 1949 he directed two films produced by N. A. Bronsten: *Obsession* (*The Hidden Room* in America) from Alec Coppel's play *A Man About a Dog*, in which a murderer keeps his victim prisoner, ready to be dissolved in acid when the fuss about his disappearance has abated, and *Give Us This Day* (*Salt to the Devil* in America), a much more serious work about Italian emigrants in New York during the Depression, with Sam Wanamaker playing the leading role of a man reliving his past as he is buried alive in wet concrete.

Alfred Hitchcock, in partnership with Sidney Bernstein, under the banner of Transatlantic Pictures, returned to Britain to make *Under Capricorn*, with Ingrid Bergman, Joseph Cotten and Michael Wilding. Set in an Australian penal colony and filmed in Technicolor, it showed a number of traces of Hitchcock's long-take method which had been devised for his American film, *Rope*, immediately preceding it. At the time the pace of the film seemed slow, although in retrospect the criticism is not justified, Hitchcock merely anticipating a filmic style some years ahead of its time. He followed it with a more orthodox Hitchcockian thriller, *Stage Fright*, with Jane Wyman, Marlene Dietrich, Alastair Sim, Richard Todd and, again, Michael Wilding, as a detective. The film aroused criticism for its use of a cheating flashback in which an incident was shown happening which later turned out to be a fabrication – a low Hitchcock trick. In spite of such trimmings the whole film was a dull work and marked the end of a particular phase in the director's career. Joan Harrison, who had collaborated with him on many films, produced a Warner film in England, *Your Witness*, directed by and starring Robert Montgomery, who played an American lawyer who gets involved in an English murder mystery.

Jules Dassin, who had directed a realistic thriller about New York police work, *The Naked City*, came to Britain to make *Night and the City* against authentic London backgrounds, with Richard Widmark as a Soho crook, and Gene Tierney. It lacked both the pace and the realism of its American prototype, but was nowhere near so disastrous as another Twentieth-Century Fox venture, *The Black Rose*, a thirteenth-century spectacular of the wanderings of Tyrone Power and his companion Jack Hawkins, through remote areas of Asia. A historical *farrago*, it was a sad work in the honourable career of its director, Henry Hathaway. *The Mudlark*, directed by Jean Negulesco, was also a Fox film, and aroused a certain amount of controversy by featuring the American actress, Irene Dunne, in the role of Queen Victoria. The film concerned the discovery of a chimney boy in the widowed Queen's Windsor apartments, an episode which allegedly led to her re-emergence into the public eye from her royal retreat. In this production Alec Guinness played Disraeli. At Borehamwood MGM made a sequel to William Wyler's celebrated Hollywood film *Mrs Miniver*, *The Miniver Story*. The director, H. C. Potter, failed to repeat the success of the former film, in spite of having Greer Garson and Walter Pidgeon in their original roles. Other films made under Anglo-American agreements during the period include Albert Lewin's decorative and stylish *Pandora and the Flying Dutchman*, with James Mason and Ava Gardner; *No Highway*, directed by Henry Koster from a Nevil Shute novel, with James Stewart as an aircraft research physicist who discovers that a new British airliner is about to drop into the sea with metal fatigue; *Captain Horatio Hornblower, R.N.* made by Warner and directed by Raoul Walsh, with Gregory Peck and Virginia Mayo in a Technicolored version of C. S. Forester's sea adventure stories. Also in the juvenile attraction category was Walt Disney's first completely live-action film, *Treasure Island*, adapted from Robert Louis Stevenson's romance. This latter was one of the most successful fruits of co-operation. Directed by Byron Haskin, it starred Bobby Driscoll as Jim Hawkins and Robert Newton as a memorable Long John Silver, and conveyed the excitement of the classic adventure story more successfully than any of the three previous versions (1918, 1920 and 1934).

The year 1951 was marked by the Festival of Britain, supposedly a commemoration of the centenary of the Great Exhibition of 1851. Its most tangible manifestation was the South Bank Exhibition, in which a great number of pavilions and attractions were shoe-horned into a minute site. The film industry's contribution to the Festival took two forms. In the first instance there was a small film theatre, the Tele-kinema, on the South Bank site, designed by Wells Coates. Throughout the period of the exhibition it showed a programme of British documentaries and stereoscopic and stereophonic films, viewed through Polaroid glasses. Two years later stereoscopy, or 3D, was to become a hysterical gimmick in the commercial cinema, before being abandoned. But at the Festival Exhibition packed audiences saw the system demonstrated in excellent working conditions.

The other contribution of the film industry to the Festival was the production of a film to commemorate the life of William Friese-Greene, the British film pioneer who may have made a crude working camera as early as 1889. The script was written by Eric Ambler, and based on the Ray Allister biography. Robert Donat was selected to play Friese-Greene and an astonishing cast list included many notable actors and actresses in walk-on parts. Laurence Olivier, for instance, was cast as the policeman called in to see the first moving pictures. Ronald Neame produced the film and John Boulting directed it, all for half fees. It was an unhappy venture. The story was an anti-climax, for it was quite unreal to try and make out, as does his headstone, that Friese-Greene was the inventor of cinematography to which, in fact, he contributed little. The story had to be based on his two marriages and his feckless character. During the course of filming Robert Donat, a man of immense courage, fought illness with everything he had. The filming dragged on and eventually the picture was completed and premièred long after the South Bank exhibition had shut its doors for good. The critics were lukewarm and the box-office returns disappointing. The story of Friese-Greene was not worth the telling.

16 Wider Still and Wider

The winter of 1951–2 was a time of major change for Britain. In October the second post-war Labour administration led by Clement Attlee was swept out of office by the Tories. In February King George VI died and Queen Elizabeth II succeeded to the throne. The first event was to mean alterations in official attitudes towards the cinema; the second, which necessitated that a spectacular and magnificent Coronation be staged, was to give the developing television industry the fillip needed to turn it into a popular medium. Admissions to cinemas dropped from 1,396 million in 1950 to 1,365 in 1951, a decrease of 2·2 per cent. Gross box-office takings, however, went up by about three per cent as a result of increased seat prices. Consequently the full implications of the slow decline in audiences were still unfelt. But retrenchment was noticeable within the production side of the industry. The British Lion studios at Isleworth were sold to the National Coal Board, the Warner studios at Teddington went out of use and ABPC's Welwyn studios were taken over by a tobacco company. Denham lay empty awaiting bidders, Highbury and Islington were sold, Lime Grove was acquired by the BBC to become television studios.

One of the new government's more controversial moves as far as the Left was concerned was the closure of the Crown Film Unit, whose work in the documentary field had set a high and often irreproachable standard, on the grounds of economy. It was seen as an assassination on doctrinaire political grounds, a mean revenge for the use made of documentaries to further Left-wing propaganda. The government's case was that the work of Crown was now being adequately carried out elsewhere in specialist units such as British Transport Films, and that the money could be spent in better ways. It was a shortsighted view of the value of documentary cinema, and a decision privately regretted, according to Paul Rotha, by certain senior Tories. Crown was sacrificed in the cause of party politics by a new government attempting to make economic decisions that would offer immediate relief to the taxpayer. Regrettably, no longer-term appreciation of the consequences of such a decision was made, and with the cessation of official film output an important British influence was eliminated in countries overseas.

In 1951 the British Board of Film Censors had adopted a revised system of classification for films, in recognition of changing tastes and needs. Previously, films had been either certified U for universal exhibition, A for adults and accompanied children, and H for horrific pictures, forbidden to children under sixteen. An innocent spectacular adventure such as *King Kong* might have been found in this last category. In this revision A and U were retained, but H was abolished, to be replaced by X, a censorship rating which still eliminated children under sixteen but designed to enable films dealing frankly with adult subjects to be shown where previously they would have been unclassifiable. In the first year of the new certificate's operation more than thirty films were released with X classification, most of them European in origin and preoccupied with sexual themes. In the winter of 1951 ABC and Rank, the dominating circuits, each agreed to release an X certificate film in order to assess its effect on picturegoing. ABC showed *Murder Inc*, a gangster film with Humphrey Bogart as an uncompromising District Attorney, and Rank released William Wyler's *Detective Story*. Neither film did well financially and ABC announced that henceforth only 'outstanding' X films would be shown on the circuit, while Rank banned them completely on the grounds that they broke up family picturegoing.

The effect of these decisions was to seriously influence the type of film that would be made in British studios. It is the practice for production companies to submit scripts to the BBFC in order to anticipate the type of certificate that will be awarded to a finished film. If the censorship rating is considered too severe amendments will sometimes be made so that the film can get a more general certificate. For obviously a distributors' guarantee would be hard to obtain for a film in advance if it was known that it would not get a circuit release. Automatically, then, during this period when X certificates were out of favour with Rank and ABC, films that might have been made, and might have benefited the development of British films, were left alone or emasculated beyond recognition. The most notorious example was a film version of a novel about a London school called *Spare the Rod*. This, if made in its intended form, could only have received an X; as a consequence it remained unmade for years. And, indeed, when a film was eventually produced, it was in a muted, ineffective version.

The pattern of film release was still as rigid as ever, with programme changes occurring weekly, regardless of the quality of the film or the scale of attendances it was attracting. Any departure from this treadmill was alleged to produce such a logjam in the queue of product awaiting screening that it was avoided almost completely. In London the inflexibility was particularly acute. The suburbs, divided into three zones, rotated the programmes rhythmically through a three-week cycle, with south of the river Saturday being the ultimate farewell for most films. Until the 1950s there had been no need in the trade to consider new ways of doing things and only the onset of adversity on the exhibition front prompted any changes at all.

One of the first attempts to modify the pattern was the simultaneous release of Roberto Rossellini's highly publicized *Stromboli* by RKO in a wide number of cinemas throughout the country. The disappointing returns were seen as a vindication for the traditionalists who had deplored the adoption of unorthodox methods. Another blow for those who wanted to see the complacency of the circuit's attitude shaken up occurred when *Chance of a Lifetime* was refused a showing by either circuit. This film, produced and directed by Bernard Miles, was about a group of factory workers who take over the works only to find that running the place is not the same as working in it. An independent tribunal under the Board of Trade ordered that one of the circuits must show it and after negotiation, or coin-tossing, Odeon was chosen. In spite of over-praise from the critics, some of it undoubtedly inspired by anti-Rank motives, the film flopped resoundingly. The release was a fair one and success or failure on the circuit is not a test of aesthetic quality. Nevertheless it was a disquieting experience for opponents of trade inflexibility.

The ACT union itself, in attempting to solve the problem of the loss of livelihood for many of its members, established a film production company of its own and made a feature called *Green Grow the Rushes*, directed by Derek Twist, with Roger Livesey, Honor Blackman and Richard Burton in a story of marshland smuggling and Ministry of Agriculture and Fisheries red tape. The film was released by British Lion. Its box-office failure brought a brave experiment in constructive trade unionism to a close.

In 1953 the 3D mania suddenly arrived. Its origins were in America where, with the showing of *Bwana Devil*, massive publicity was generated to stir up interest. In spite of the indifference of the film it packed in the crowds who watched the action through Polaroid glasses, the same method used in 1951 at the South Bank Telekinema. *Bwana Devil* came to England and was followed by several other films, among them *Fort Ti*, *Sangaree*, *Kiss Me Kate*, and the highly effective *House of Wax* from Warner. Within a matter of months the craze was over as swiftly as it had begun. It was an imperfect system and the Polaroid spectacles proved to be an expensive disadvantage, for patrons assumed that they had been made a present of free sunglasses. The films were on the whole poor, with action suddenly exploding out of the screen for no other reason than to give the audience a vicarious thrill. Most theatres showing the films had to pause for reel changes since two projectors were in use simultaneously. Their speeds had to be carefully monitored, for the slightest discrepancy would spoil the synchronization. Another nightmare was the possibility of a film break, where one reel might have fewer frames than the other. Exhibitors were relieved when the 3D gimmick period was over, but for several months afterwards many Hollywood feature films contained sequences shot from curious angles or featuring objects flying towards the camera – they were 3D films released as flat prints.

What really stopped 3D from making full headway was the innovation of the panoramic screen. Cinerama, a process which involved three projectors showing the combined images of three cameras on a giant curved screen in a specially adapted theatre, had made its initial appearance in New York in 1952, taking the cinema in one giant stride straight back to the fairground. *This is Cinerama* was a mammoth demonstration reel, featuring roller coaster rides and other stomach-turning novelties. The enveloping screen promoted a feeling of actuality, if not of 3D, without the disadvantage of wearing special glasses. The fuzzy lines caused by the picture joins were a minor distraction. While Cinerama in that form could only have a very limited type of display, since the equipment was so costly, Twentieth-Century Fox took up a lapsing patent for another large screen system, CinemaScope, which projected an image that had been squeezed by an anamorphic lens on the camera through a similar projection lens. The ratio of the screen was greatly elongated, from the prevailing 1·33:1 to 2·35:1, so that the shape was that of a letter box aperture.

The first CinemaScope film to be shown in England was *The Robe*, which was premièred at the Odeon, Leicester Square towards the end of 1953. It was quickly followed by *How to Marry a Millionaire* at the

Odeon Marble Arch. But before these widescreen films made their first appearance in Britain there had already been a movement away from the 1·33:1 ratio in many cinemas. So-called panoramic screens were installed, with the effect that the top and bottom were cut from the projected image, giving a pseudo-widescreen appearance to many films, although until production companies began planning their product so that the pictorial composition allowed for expendable portions of the frames, this aroused constant irritation by the loss of vital parts of the action or titles. The new large screens had aspect ratios varying from 1·66:1 to 1·85:1. Most American companies opted for CinemaScope, or their own variations of it, and the whole of Twentieth-Century Fox production, including the films to be made in Britain, was to be shot in this system. Paramount, however, held out and offered its own improved process, a non-anamorphic system under the name VistaVision. During shooting the film ran across the camera aperture horizontally, so that the image on the processed film was turned sideways, resulting in a much larger area. When transferred to a normal 35mm. print there was consequently less grain and higher definition. The finished film could be shown in virtually any commonly used aspect ratio, from the old screen shape to the proportions of CinemaScope, for the action was so planned that nothing essential took place in the top and bottom of the frame. Moreover, VistaVision was a producer's process, not an exhibitor's, and there was no need for the replacement of projection apparatus. The Rank Organization announced that it would use VistaVision for its new productions, rather than CinemaScope. Nevertheless, because VistaVision films were shown on standard-shape screens they did not achieve the same dramatic impact on the public as CinemaScope.

The limitations of the new processes on film-makers was a cause of critical concern. The ultra widescreen of CinemaScope called for an entirely new approach to the composition of the projected image, and it was initially difficult for directors to appreciate how to use the screen horizontally. An additional complication in the early days of Cinema-Scope was the need to shoot simultaneously a standard version of the same film that could be shown in cinemas not yet equipped with the CinemaScope projection apparatus. The confinement of action to the centre width of the screen on other films also presented compositional problems. It was asking a great deal of the lighting cameraman to produce a picture equally acceptable in a ratio of 1·33:1 and 1·85:1.

The effects of this change were a slowing up of film action and a diminution of pictorial style. In fact, it was to be a period of years before the new techniques were properly assimilated and mastered. That there was a change in the method of film projection at this time was explained by the desperation of Hollywood, where the cutbacks resulting from the advance of television had already become crucial. In straitened circumstances many years before Warner Brothers had pinned their faith in the talking picture. Now, exactly twenty-five years later, the widescreen was looked to as the technical achievement which would give the film industry an edge over its new competitor. But after the novelty value had worn off it was plain that filmgoers were not necessarily impressed by mere size; the film still had to have an intrinsic appeal. Moreover, just as talking pictures had their precursors long before *The Jazz Singer*, there had been earlier attempts to broaden the screen dimensions in the early 1930s, notably with Magnascope and Fox Grandeur film, which was 70mm. wide instead of 35mm.

The last films of the immediate pre-widescreen period included a small number of notable achievements. John Huston's first British film, *The African Queen*, with Humphrey Bogart and Katharine Hepburn, was successful on almost every level. The story, from a novel by C. S. Forester about a missionary's daughter and a steamboat engineer fighting a German gunboat singlehanded in Africa during the First World War, was adventurous, suspenseful and ingeniously resolved, and the leading players' performances were rich in compassion and warmth, in spite of the opposing polarity of the characters' social positions. Huston's next film, again made for Romulus–British Lion, was an adaptation of *Moulin Rouge*, a somewhat romanticized novel by Pierre La Mure based on the life of Toulouse-Lautrec. The American actor, José Ferrer, came over to play the leading part, his legs bound up painfully at the knee for the long shots in order to portray the dwarf-like physique of the artist. Huston invested his film with considerable bravura direction, particularly in building up the frenzied atmosphere of the Moulin Rouge music hall during the famous can-can sequence, but he was unable to do much with the trite story. The Technicolor was of a particularly high quality, low-keyed and often monochromatic, A trick of animating some of the best-known Lautrec paintings evoked critical admiration and has been copied to the point of banality since.

Huston's third film during his early 1950s British period was a comedy thriller, *Beat the Devil*, with a plot bearing a resemblance to the first film he had directed, *The Maltese Falcon*, in 1941. The location was shifted to the Mediterranean, but once again it was a story of an assortment of unscrupulous people, swindling each other in a race to acquire African uranium deposits. Bogart and Lorre reappeared, with Jennifer Jones, Gina Lollobrigida and Robert Morley. It was an elaborate joke, not entirely appreciated at the time but now a connoisseurs' item. Some regard it as the first intentionally 'camp' film. Certainly its style is somewhat in advance of its time. Huston's last British film in the fifties was an adaptation of Melville's whaling novel, *Moby Dick*, with Gregory Peck as the one-legged obsessive sailor, Captain Ahab, and Orson Welles in a fleeting but dramatic appearance as the hellfire-preaching Father Mapple. Shot in Ireland and the studio tank, using a muted Technicolor process, the film was over-literary and slightly arid in its treatment, but the ambience of nineteenth-century New Bedford was well-handled.

All four Huston films were Anglo-American in concept with American stars as well as an American director. But the technical contribution was British, and the studio work was shot in England. Consequently it would be unnecessarily chauvinistic to remove these films from any account of the British cinema. By getting a full American release they were achieving results which the average British film only occasionally managed; moreover, they kept studios and workers occupied and helped the balance of payments with the dollar currency area.

American films continued to be made in England, thus ensuring a constant stream of directors and stars from Hollywood. Ted Tetzlaff came over to make *Time Bomb* (*Terror on a Train* in America), with Glenn Ford; Ray Bolger played the lead in David Butler's musical of *Charley's Aunt* for Warner, *Where's Charley?* an adaptation of a Broadway show that did not reach the West End until several years after the film, which did poor business in Britain, was released. Robert Siodmak made the excellent Burt Lancaster swashbuckling satire, *The Crimson Pirate*, a good-humoured thrust at the Douglas Fairbanks school of filming, again for Warner. And Walt Disney followed up the successful *Treasure Island* with more live-action British films, a somewhat romantic historical picture, *The Sword and the Rose*, and a spectacular *Rob Roy*, with Richard Todd as the legendary hero.

At around this period a change took place in the style of the English comedy film. The Ealing comedy with its gentle satirical humour, usually showing the triumph of individuals against the faceless machine of Whitehall, and typified by *Passport to Pimlico*, *Whisky Galore* and *The Man in the White Suit*, went out of vogue. One of the last was

The Titfield Thunderbolt, made in Technicolor by Charles Crichton, which told of the efforts of a group of villagers to keep a country branch railway line open after it had been decided by British Railways to close it down. Full of lovingly photographed rural scenes – it was made near Bath – and quaint eccentric characters, played by Stanley Holloway, Hugh Griffith, Godfrey Tearle as a railway-mad cleric, and Naunton Wayne as a fussy businessman, it was the swansong of a particular kind of T. E. B. Clarke screenplay; and while the English love for railways and old pieces of machinery was acutely observed, the film lacked the punch of its predecessors.

What supplanted the Ealing style was a much broader comic approach. Henry Cornelius's *Genevieve* had as its setting the veteran car run from London to Brighton, with its principal characters a couple whose marriage is on the point of collapse (Dinah Sheridan and John Gregson), and a bragging, oafish friend with a flashy trumpet-playing girl-friend (Kenneth More and Kay Kendall). The old cars in the film are not treated with the reverence of the old locomotive in *The Titfield Thunderbolt*; they are merely hilarious props for the collision of human relationships. It is a type of film nearer the American marital comedy than the whimsicalities of Ealing. Its screenplay was in fact by an American, William Rose, who was later to write *It's a Mad, Mad, Mad, Mad World*. He was also responsible for Alexander Mackendrick's Ealing comedy about the conflict between a Scottish steamboat captain and an America businessman, *The Maggie* (*High and Dry* in America), a neglected yet excellent film and an indication of Mackendrick's promise at that time as a director.

But now it was the end of subtlety. Ralph Thomas's *Doctor in the House*, a broad comedy set in a large London teaching hospital, enjoyed a success far out of proportion to the scope of its wit, with its display of medical student high jinks and total callousness where the patients were concerned. Adapted from a semi-fictional book by Richard Gordon, it was the first of several 'Doctor' films, which were to be the comic series of the fifties, supplanted in the following decade by the 'Carry Ons'. Dirk Bogarde played the leading part, with Kenneth More doing his now familiar lovable oaf characterization, and James Robertson Justice indulging himself as an irascible distinguished surgeon. The first Norman Wisdom film appeared in late 1953, another forerunner of a lengthy series. Wisdom was a comedian who had made his name in television before he turned to the cinema, one of the first stars to achieve that transition. His humour was often maudlin, with liberal doses of Chaplinesque pathos. His characterization was that of the little man in an ill-fitting suit facing a hostile world with infinite good nature and intentions. His first film, directed like many of the succeeding ones by John Paddy Carstairs, was *Trouble in Store*, in which the misunderstood, bullied Wisdom wreaked havoc in a large department store before being hailed as a hero. Jerry Desmonde, an actor who had previously been the stooge to Sid Field, played the harassed and hysterical manager driven to apoplectic fury by Norman Wisdom's incompetence. The new screen comedian achieved a box-office popularity as impressive as that of George Formby two decades earlier, and an annual Norman Wisdom vehicle eventually became almost the sole direct output of the Rank Organization.

Group Three, which had been formed to use money from the British Film Production Fund for training new technicians and feature directors, also turned to comedy for the bulk of its output. Under John Grierson's control it sought its subjects in the traditional English social fabric, as had Balcon at Ealing, but with a more deliberate air of fantasy. Among the early productions were Lewis Gilbert's *Time Gentlemen, Please!*, in which, as in the typical Ealing comedy, Whitehall is the villain, with determined villagers attempting to prove their efficiency and productivity in spite of the problem, an incorrigibly lazy tramp who is spoiling the desired image; *Brandy for the Parson*, directed by John Eldridge, in which a holidaying couple with a yacht are inveigled into handling an illicit cargo; and *You're Only Young Twice*, directed by Terry Bishop, based on a play by James Bridie, *What Say They?* and set in a Scottish university. With the serious and excellent documentary-style reconstruction of the Knockshinnock mining disaster, *The Brave Don't Cry*, acted by members of the Glasgow Citizen's Theatre in support of the principals who included John Gregson and Meg Buchanan, and directed by Philip Leacock, Group Three had made an interesting contribution to British film output, all the more remarkable for the fact that the production budgets were about twenty-five per cent of the normal feature-film cost.

Frank Launder, continuing the farcical approach established successfully in *The Happiest Days of Your Life*, also made a film from a play by James Bridie. Based on *It Depends What You Mean*, it was called *Folly to Be Wise*. This was centred on an army camp brains' trust and the persistence of an ATS girl in seeking an answer to the question of what makes a happy marriage. Alastair Sim played the padre who was also in charge of camp entertainment with a missionary zeal, a fine comic performance, and the cast included Martita Hunt, Miles Malleson, Roland Culver and Elizabeth Allan. After co-producing *Gilbert and Sullivan*, which Sidney Gilliatt directed for Korda, a glossy entertaining musical biography as far from actuality as the average Hollywood film biography, Launder turned to the cartoonist Ronald Searle's demonic schoolgirls and made *The Belles of St Trinian's*, a broadly comic depiction of a feminine Narkover. Again Alastair Sim gave a triumphantly funny performance, this time of the headmistress, long-suffering in the face of such lunacies as the concealment of a racehorse in the dorm. George Cole contributed a memorable Flash Harry role. The St Trinians' formula was another that was to be used for further films. Three more were made between 1956 and 1966.

From the major directors in Britain during the period 1952 to 1954 there were occasionally rewarding films. Anthony Asquith was undoubtedly the most prolific. Abandoning Rattigan for Wilde, he made a Technicolor version of *The Importance of Being Earnest*, with Edith Evans playing her much-loved role of Lady Bracknell, and Michael Redgrave, Dorothy Tutin and Joan Greenwood also in the cast. It was a mannered and intensely theatrical film, performed in the traditional West End style for playing Wilde comedies. The acting was good enough to sustain the cinematic limitations. Asquith's next film had a modern subject, the flight testing of a new aircraft and a plot to steal its secrets by Iron Curtain spies. Compared with David Lean's *The Sound Barrier*, Asquith's *The Net* was inferior, although the flying sequences were handled reasonably successfully. What the film lacked was credibility in its characters and it was a disappointing outcome of a production which promised much better. In his next film Asquith took as his theme a great batsman on the verge of retirement, played by Jack Warner, who makes a last dramatic stand against the Australians. *The Final Test* had a Rattigan screenplay and several famous cricketers in the cast, including Len Hutton, Denis Compton, Alec Bedser, Jim Laker and Cyril Washbrook. The film, occasionally satirical and witty, was in the Asquithian tradition of *The Demi-Paradise* or *While the Sun Shines*, in its gentle mockery of English middle-class attitudes. Asquith's next film in this period was *The Young Lovers*, in which David Knight played a junior American diplomat in London who falls in love with the daughter of an East European ambassador, played by Odile Versois, with ensuing cold war complications. It was unusual to find a love story fashioned from what was usually regarded as thriller territory. The machinery of surveillance, telephone-tapping, tailing and so on is applied to the couple and induces a hysterical atmosphere which eventually causes them to run off to a more neutral country. It is a good Asquithian film, at its best in the first half, the meeting, the onset of suspicion. The last film was *Carrington V.C.*, yet another stage play, this time by Dorothy and Campbell Christie. It concerned the court martial of an officer who embezzled the regimental funds as a protest against his treatment by the War Office over his back pay. The cast included David Niven as Carrington, Margaret Leighton as his wife, and Noelle Middleton as his mistress.

David Lean made *The Sound Barrier* (*Breaking the Sound Barrier* in America) in 1952, with a screenplay by Terence Rattigan. It was the story of an achievement in the air, the conclusion of a problem that had held back aviation technology. The aerial photography was impressive and occasionally poetic, as the credit title sequence demonstrated. The characterization was perhaps conventional, with Ralph Richardson playing a relentless manufacturer, holding science higher than human life, Nigel Patrick as the pilot who crashes to his death, Ann Todd as the wife whose baby is born after the accident and Joseph Tomelty as the designer of the new engine which will take the aircraft through the sound barrier. What made the film work was its impressive construction. Lean's technical skill had reasserted itself after the comparative failure of the slow-moving *Madeleine*. His subsequent film was from a famous play by Harold Brighouse, *Hobson's Choice*, a Lancashire comedy in which a determined woman gets the better of her Victorian father, a Salford bootmaker, by marrying his best workman, a timid, industrious and honest young man played by John Mills. Brenda de Banzie was the daughter and Charles Laughton her drunken, belching father. It was Laughton's first and last British film since *Jamaica Inn* in 1939. He gave a remarkable performance in a barnstorming manner. In one scene Laughton, as an alcoholic disrobing in the bedroom, played it in pantomime, with the actor burlesquing the actions of a fuddled man in a manner worthy of any music-hall stage. There was considerable style in the direction, and a simulation of the period grime of industrial Lancashire.

Hobson's Choice had a point of comparison with Ronald Neame's *The Card* (*The Promoter* in the U.S.A.), which was based on Arnold Bennett's story from the Five Towns saga of novels. Again a sense of period was carefully evoked and a broad comic strain was kept to the surface throughout. Alec Guinness played Denry Machin, an ambitious, charming young man who works his way up to become mayor, with Glynis Johns, Valerie Hobson and Petula Clark as the women who enter his life. Good humour and ebullience were the qualities Guinness projected in his performance and it was a competent example of period regional comedy, never a particularly strong area in British films. Neame made next *The Million Pound Note* (*Man with a Million* in America), a Technicolor comedy set in Victorian London, about a man who is challenged in a wager to live off such a note for a month. The story was Mark Twain's and to play the lead Gregory Peck was brought over from America and placed opposite an actress making her first screen appearance, Jane Griffith. The resulting film was bland and unexciting.

Carol Reed made only one film in this period, *The Man Between*, which in many ways was a reminiscence of *The Third Man*. The setting this time was Berlin, replacing Vienna. The theme, that of abduction and escape from East to West, was presented by James Mason, Claire Bloom and Hildegarde Neff. A simple plot was elaborated with red herrings and contrived locations, such as an open ice rink where the confidential dialogue is bellowed for all to hear. The speed and freshness of the earlier film had given way to a tired reiteration of the same kind of situations. Reed was repeating himself, and *The Man Between* came off the worse for the comparison, in spite of the technical felicity in the depiction of the drab atmosphere of the dismal city.

Lewis Milestone, the Hollywood director whose reputation was established at the beginning of the 1930s with *All Quiet on the Western Front*, made two films in Britain, one a war film called *They Who Dare* starring Dirk Bogarde, about a Commando raid on the island of Rhodes, and *Melba*, a musical biography of the Australian singer, with Patrice Munsel in the leading role and Dame Sybil Thorndike contributing another screen Queen Victoria. Neither film was sufficiently exciting to resuscitate the director's faded glory.

The French director Rene Clément, however, came to Britain to make *Knave of Hearts* (*M. Ripois* in France), and succeeded in combining the Gallic amorous proclivities of a Don Juan (played by Gerard Philipe) with a brilliant and ingenious use of real London locations in a way that no British director had at that time discovered. Clément's use of concealed cameras and sometimes the reaction of passers-by to the activities of the actors was completely genuine. His observation of British behaviour was sharp and pitiless, and for all its humour *Knave of Hearts* was a film with a hard edge. Regrettably, a two-way flow between British and French studios has been slight. Those French directors, such as Clément, René Clair and Jacques Feyder, who had filmed for Korda before the war, and Julian Duvivier who later made *Anna Karenina* for him, represented only the surface of the French industry. If they had been accessible, the creative ideas of French directors could have acted as a valuable stimulus to British production, but invitations and inducements to film in Britain were rare.

17 The Melting Audience

During the fifties the decline of audiences began to accelerate. In 1954 24·5 million people went to the cinema each week; in 1960 only 10 million weekly audiences were averaged through the year. By 1957 increases in admission prices were no longer sufficient to offset the fall in admissions, and gross takings began to diminish as well. In 1954 the gross box-office takings throughout the year amounted to £110 million, leaving a net, after the deduction of Entertainments Tax, of £74 million. By 1960, the net takings had dropped to £64 million, but Entertainments Tax had been lowered sharply in 1957, and in 1960, the last year in which it operated, only £2 million was extracted from the returns.

An even more significant decline in this period was in the number of cinemas open for exhibition. In 1946, the peak year in British cinema history, there were 4,709 theatres showing films. By 1954, 200 of them had closed. But during the rest of the fifties nearly 1,500 cinemas closed, until in 1960 only 3,034 remained open. By 1967, fewer than 2,000 were in business, and by 1971 the figure was 1,552. In certain towns the only cinema was unable to remain open and where the alternative was several miles away many people simply lost the cinema-going habit, thus setting in train the vicious circle that was to wreak havoc in the industry.

The principal cause for the near collapse of film exhibition is commonly assumed to be television. During the fifties television grew at an astonishing rate. In 1952 1,449,000 television receiving licences were issued, but by 1960 there were 10,469,000. The televising of the Coronation in 1953 marked the turning point; it was the big occasion of the fifties which proved the power of television to bring into homes events of magnitude. The public's imagination was fired by the new medium; there was a rush to install sets and many non-set owners watched on communal receivers, demonstrating the drawing power of the electronic picture. Two cinema films, *A Queen is Crowned*, released on the Rank circuit, and *Elizabeth is Queen* on ABC, could only offer Technicolor postscripts to the ceremony. Throughout the fifties new transmitters opened up, increasing the spread of television across the British Isles. In September 1955 the first ITV transmissions began in south-east England, with the Midlands following six months later. Commercial television spurred another receiver installation boom, and for the first time viewers in Britain had a choice of channels. Independent Television stations were more effective than the BBC in securing audiences during the first years and a study of the pattern of cinema closures reveals that the areas that had ITV earliest, with the exception of London, lost their cinemas at a faster rate.

Undoubtedly television did suck away the film audience. But there were secondary factors to account for the increasing unpopularity of the cinema. A shortage of films, partly due to the decline of Hollywood production, where television had already bitten hard, was felt particularly by the smaller exhibitors who lacked the booking power of Rank and ABC. With fewer films to go round the best went to the major theatres, leaving poor pickings for the independents. If the situation was a highly competitive one it meant that the independent was starved of satisfactory product, lost the audience and was forced to put up the shutters. While some independents made attempts to vary the booking pattern so that a successful film could play for longer, there were difficulties in securing prints on a first-release basis. The practice of barring, by which a powerful exhibitor can block any rival within a certain area from showing a film in which he is interested, was one of the most pernicious influences that prevailed. With the emergence of the hard ticket 'road-show' type of presentation incredibly broad barring areas were established; at one time Rank's Gaumont in Glasgow barred the whole of Scotland.

Very large cinemas were as vulnerable as the small ones. Many of the giant 2–3,000-seat picture palaces of the thirties became uneconomic to operate. A large cinema with fewer than a quarter of the available seats occupied presented a depressing sight to the filmgoer. Now that the cry 'Queuing in all parts' faded into obscurity, or redundancy, rows of empty seats became an embarrassment. The Davis Theatre in Croydon, one of the largest in the country, was demolished. The 4,000-seat Gaumont State in Kilburn was bisected, one half becoming a dance hall. The Rank Organization began a policy of ruthlessly weeding out the unprofitable cinemas, which quite often, as for instance at Tolworth on the Kingston Bypass, where a monumental skyscraper now stands, occupied valuable sites in real estate terms. Where silver screens once stood, huge office buildings rose up, or supermarkets, or petrol stations or shopping precincts. The widescreen boom of 1954 temporarily arrested some closures and by the third quarter of 1955 more than half the cinemas in Britain had installed the anamorphic projection equipment necessary for CinemaScope films. In terms of seating this represented a much higher figure proportionately, around seventy-five per cent. In addition some 600 theatres had installed stereophonic sound apparatus. It must be admitted that during the introduction period CinemaScope was a powerful attraction. *The Robe*, the first film generally shown in the process, was the box-office leader of 1953. But eventually the novelty value wore off and, as with the early sound films of *circa* 1929, it became only too plain that the quality of the film itself was the only criterion to attract a reasonable audience. Many of the early panoramic films were badly constructed, limited by the unassimilated new medium and often photographed or projected in such a way that part of the vast screen image was always out of focus.

The introduction of CinemaScope caused a conflict between exhibitors and Twentieth-Century Fox, the American company which held the options on the system. Fox were insistent that CinemaScope and stereophonic sound were to go hand in hand, and that cinemas prepared to change their projection equipment and screens would also have to undertake the cost of rewiring the sound system. This, exhibitors argued, was unnecessary; the full impact of the process was in the projected image and most patrons scarcely cared whether the sound was from an ordinary optical sound track or 4-track stereophonic magnetic recording. The latter was costly and difficult to install and would drain the strained resources of the exhibitors even further. Rank took a firm stand against Fox and announced that no more theatres would be wired for stereophonic sound and that as far as production was concerned VistaVision, the non-anamorphic process used only by Paramount among the American companies, would be the horse that Rank would back. The result was an estrangement between Rank and Fox, who withdrew nearly all their films from Odeon and Gaumont screens. There was even a partial move towards establishing a fourth Fox circuit from out of some of the larger independents such as Granada, but the dwindling number of cinemas made it impossible to consolidate. It did, however, offer a practical demonstration of distribution power that could be used to compel circuits to toe the line.

Eventually, after a period of about two years a rapprochement was reached and Rank once more began to exhibit Fox films.

The major structural change in the organization of the circuits occurred in 1958 when Rank finally completed the merger of Odeon and Gaumont. Henceforth the Odeon release was shown at a number of Gaumont and Odeon cinemas and called the Rank release. The remainder of the two circuits, mostly Gaumont cinemas, took what was called the National release. This rationalization plan involved the draconian purge of many modern cinemas, as well as the more ancient ones. In towns where there were Odeons and Gaumonts one or other, usually the Gaumont, closed. In many instances an Odeon closed and the name was transferred to the remaining Gaumont, e.g. Wimbledon. Or a modern Gaumont was renamed Odeon and played the Rank release, e.g. Chelsea, Hammersmith. What was necessary for the scheme to work to the satisfaction of the auditors was to remove internecine competition. In practice it meant that the National release applied to a mediocre group of theatres, and any film assigned to it was virtually condemned to making a loss. Even the inclusion of a few ABC cinemas in the third circuit was insufficient, largely because Rank's rival circuit realized that the chances for the National release were slight. Rank officially indicated in 1961 that an average expected return for a film on the Rank release would be between £85,000 and £95,000, on ABC release £75,000–£85,000 and on the National release a mere £35,000–£40,000. The result was that distributors were only interested in the Rank and ABC releases, the product that was screened by the National release being mostly that which was left over or unacceptable. In turn there was a decline of audience interest since indifferent films drove the remaining patrons away. Consequently, the third release cinemas closed down even faster than the rest and as the non-Rank exhibitors dropped off as quickly as they could the alternative to Odeon and ABC eventually withered away. Thus the Rank Organization completed the work begun in the late forties when Odeon and Gaumont first combined. The assurance given then to the Board of Trade, that the two circuits would function independently of each other, now no longer held. Lord Erroll, who in 1958 was the Parliamentary Secretary to the Board of Trade, had agreed that a continuation of that ruling was economic suicide for the industry.

Diversification both inside and outside the film business was necessary to keep heads above water. The Rank Organization underwent considerable traumas in the 1950s as it groped for other fields in which to develop interests. Records and leisure shops were abortive, bowling centres in converted cinemas were for a time attractive, but the ultimate key to non-film prosperity turned on Bingo and Xerox copying machines. The attraction of Bingo was the cheap conversion of a cinema to its new purpose; there was no necessity to pull it down and erect a costly new structure. In some places Bingo was introduced gradually, occupying a portion of the week, with films the other. The taste for mild gambling, of which Bingo is a form, prevailed over entertainment and films were ousted. In any case Bingo was far less difficult and more predictable than the showing of films. Local authorities, never particularly attuned to the value of the cinema as a medium of popular culture, willingly sanctioned the use of converted cinemas for Bingo clubs as a prolongation of community life. Bingo was the lazy way out for many cinema-owners, in urban and rural areas alike, and undoubtedly the laxer gaming laws, that enabled the banal game to mushroom, contributed to the premature closure of many cinemas.

It has been argued that too many cinemas have closed since the mid-fifties; conversely, John Spraos in his excellent analysis of the misfortunes of the industry, *The Decline of the Cinema*, suggests that an extreme solution would have been to abandon rural and suburban cinemas altogether, then reduce the numbers of central ones, and spend a great deal of money in refurbishing the remainder to a luxurious standard. The comfort and quality of these theatres, which would then operate exclusively on a long-run basis, would be adequate competition for fireside entertainment. That such a solution would be drastic is not denied, for there is ample proof that audiences contract when availability of cinemas is diminished, and such a policy would render the hazardous film-making business even more risk-ridden in terms of potential profitability. But the pattern of filmgoing in the late sixties, many years after television had done its worst, seemed to demonstrate that a partial move towards such a 'final solution' had already begun. A shortage of cinemas in the West End, many houses being choked up for months at a time with hard-ticket presentations, was matched by a slowly continuing attrition of suburban cinemas.

Returning to the mid-fifties, it is possible to discern another element operating in the scramble to close down unprofitable cinemas. Many stood on prime sites in suburban high streets or at major highway intersections. Office buildings on the same sites could produce a higher site yield. Without doubt some closures were effected which had little to do with declining admissions, but were the result of good offers made for the site by property developers. With insufficient social pressures to keep cinemas open, such closures were carried out almost unnoticed while audiences were allegedly flocking like lemmings to the seductive delights of television. While the Rank Organization always maintained that no cinema of theirs was closed without an alternative one in the same district remaining open (hardly true, for instance, of the south-western London suburbs where seven Rank cinemas in solo positions were shut in the space of five years) some sizeable population centres were left without any cinema at all. In America an audience is more mobile and is prepared to drive several miles for the purpose of watching a film, hence the astonishing post-war boom in drive-in theatres. In Britain, where no drive-in movement was begun on account of poor weather, late summer evenings, lack of available space and reluctance of local authorities to license such constructions, the growth in car-ownership was not matched by larger cinema car parks or more widespread publicity to indicate programmes. Consequently, the trade itself offered little encouragement to would-be filmgoers in towns deprived of cinemas, to make a journey several miles to the next place where there was one. When a cinema was abandoned an audience was also abandoned. The filmgoing habit was one easily lost.

The percentage of closed cinemas was higher for independents than for those belonging to Rank and ABC. While the two groups argued that their presence put a brake on failure, inasmuch that they could keep unprofitable houses going longer, there was a converse factor that although the numbers of cinemas were smaller they were invariably larger and better than the independents. When a major circuit theatre shut down, therefore, the loss was usually greater. The merger of Odeon and Gaumont in 1958 undoubtedly precipitated a closure movement during the consequent period of adjustment. The shrinkage of the circuits was economically justifiable to them, too, in that it enabled some of the more decrepit and unattractive theatres to be shed as an alternative to costly modernization. Far from being saviours of the exhibiting trade, Rank and ABC were able to switch their interests more easily, and to treat their theatres more as pure business assets than community services. With so many cinemas under their control it was possible for them to determine alternative policies on a scale large enough to be viable. The bowling lanes were installed in sufficient numbers to produce an entirely new division, and this too applied to the Bingo clubs and the dance halls which also moved in to many of the former cinemas. Thus there was a diversification incentive. The independent exhibitor, with only three or four theatres, simply lacked the resources to diversify in this way, and was therefore more likely to remain in the cinema business for a longer period before being forced to give up.

The other sanction adopted by the cinema business to stave off the impending disaster was the price increase. As a unilateral expedient higher admission charges are undesirable, because one cinema charging more than the rest tends to lose business. So the upward adjustment has to be made generally, usually on the initiative of the large circuits, who in this way as in so many others set the pace. The theory of the price increase is that while it further diminishes the audience, the percentage lost is less than the volume of higher takings. The large circuits, however, were in a position to fend off higher prices rather longer than the independents. The progressive abolition of Entertainments Duty provided an advantageous cushion to the more prosperous cinemas and price rise decisions were taken only after unofficial talks between Rank and ABC. In this area, typically, a sensible flexibility was absent, and seat prices tended to be the same in all parts of the country, excluding principal city centres, regardless of the audience potential. Smaller independents, exempted from Duty anyway, lacked the advantages of the cushion.

The damage caused by the drastic cutting back of exhibition outlets was felt throughout the entire industry. Fewer opportunities for the employment of cinema workers was followed by less money flowing back for reinvestment in new films, coupled with a heightened risk factor for those willing to invest in production. The 1957 Cinematograph Films Act contained some elements which were to offer hope to the depressed business, notably the consolidation of the voluntary levy and the British Film Production Fund with a statutory Agency, so that the levy now acquired full legal status. The life of the National Film Finance Corporation was also extended by a further ten years, but with the restrictions on its lending powers removed, so that it could now set about paying its way, its role was less a subsidy to the industry, more a specialized bank, to paraphrase the NFFC's 1957 report. The quota was extended not for the customary ten years, but a mere two, in order that the way be left open for a revision of the 1948 Act. But the quota remains, still at the thirty per cent determined by Harold Wilson when he was President of the Board of Trade.

The industry at last won the battle to quash Entertainments Tax, although films were the last public amusements to be subject to it. Its progressive reduction in the late fifties to nil in 1960 considerably eased the deflation of the medium, at least as far as the larger exhibitors were concerned. Although gross takings fell between 1954 and 1960 by forty-one per cent, the net reduction, after elimination of duty, was only fifteen per cent. It is unlikely, in spite of the strength of the exhibitors' case, that had the removal of the Entertainments Duty occurred earlier there would have been much difference in the state of the industry, for other means to absorb the money would have been found. However, the final decision to end the tax was both just and logical, and removed a burden the film business had endured since the dismal year of the Battle of the Somme when the impost had been accepted as an unhappy patriotic necessity. In 1973 the imposition of VAT on seat prices seemed to make a return to the principle of taxing the filmgoer, in spite of industry protests.

Television, with its attraction for the housebound, had yet another apparent menace in store for the cinema. After the growth of the ITV network in the later fifties it was found that the showing of old films in the medium produced remarkable viewing ratings. By 1958 there were around three films a week being shown on British television, a fraction of today's figure, but at that time they were recognized as a further factor in the decline of the cinema audience. In 1957 the backlog of films made by Alexander Korda began appearing on ITV and the BBC announced that it had bought up a huge package of RKO feature films. In spite of their age, there were some excellent pictures now available for the domestic screen and whereas in the earlier days of television the films that had found their way into the transmission schedules had not only been old, but also so bad as to be incapable of any commercial exploitation in the cinema, the situation was now seen to be disturbingly different. It was felt that television corporations should be responsible for their own programming, and not seek an easy way out by showing material designed for another medium, thus causing the unwitting producers and performers to compete against the living cinema. A defence fund was set up on the initiative of Cecil Bernstein of Granada Theatres, who in spite of his television connections reacted strongly to this threat to the cinema. The Film Industry Defence Organization (FIDO) levied a farthing on every cinema seat sold, the resulting funds to be used for the purchase of television rights in British films. Eventually FIDO languished when it became known that the medium of television could in fact extend the commercial life of a film long after its old natural period of release. Today, there is a five-year rule operating, thus preventing the most up-to-date product from reaching the screen, but films are budgeted with their ultimate sale to television in mind. In certain respects television has actually enhanced the cinema by providing air time to specialized works which previously had only been seen by limited audiences, e.g. *Hiroshima Mon Amour*, *Warrendale*, *Kanal*; by keeping alive knowledge and reputations of actors and directors of the thirties and forties whose work would never be seen now except in repertory cinemas or film societies; and by sharpening tastes and attitudes to films. Of course, the contraction of widescreen and colour into the small grey rectangle made at the time a poor substitute for the experience of seeing films in proper projection conditions, and on ITV particularly there are often appallingly bad cuts and insertions of 'natural breaks'. But better surely for old films to be seen on television than to lie undisturbed and unseen in their vaults. The introduction of 625-line UHF transmissions of all programmes and colour using the West German PAL system has greatly improved the technical quality of the television picture, and in areas of good reception a film on the box approaches comparison with the projected image. Television has also been responsible for training or offering initial opportunities to many directors who later acquired distinguished reputations in the cinema.

Various attempts by television to take an intelligent critical interest in the contemporary cinema have been foiled by problems of co-operation with the film business. Film clips of current pictures for use on TV are usually restricted to under three minutes, but they have on occasion been withheld altogether when it was felt that a certain programme was taking too critical a line. Wardour Street can still demonstrate an obstinate refusal to take a modern audience seriously, or to recognize the many possibilities of television to serve as an ally rather than an enemy to the film industry.

18 The Mixed Mid-Fifties

The experimentation with screen shapes and projection systems eventually settled down to a new pattern. The 3D system, using Polaroid glasses, soon fell into disuse, and it was the widescreen which won the day. Most cinemas in the mid-fifties eventually became equipped for the presentation of CinemaScope and other processes that used anamorphic lenses, while ordinary films were shown on widescreens. At the end of 1955 it was announced that of the 4,483 cinemas then open in Britain, 2,896 of them had been equipped for showing CinemaScope films, and secondary versions of films were no longer necessary. Only 546 of these cinemas were also wired for four-track stereophonic magnetic sound, as opposed to the standard optical kind.

During the initial period directors were not happy working with the ultrawide process. One of the first British CinemaScope films, an adaptation by Anatole Litvak of Terence Rattigan's *The Deep Blue Sea*, with Vivien Leigh, Kenneth More, Eric Portman and Emlyn Williams, was an early casualty. The confining melancholic drama, played out in a cheap bed-sitter, seemed to be swamped by the broad embrace of the CinemaScope screen and lost much of its intimacy. The story, about a judge's wife who has gone to live with a shiftless, schoolboyish ex-RAF man, failed to achieve plausibility, in spite of a genuinely moving performance by Vivien Leigh. Michael Powell and Emeric Pressburger were considerably more at ease with the new dimension in their up-dated version of Strauss's *Die Fledermaus*, which retained the original score but featured new lyrics by Dennis Arundell. The setting of *Oh Rosalinda!!* was a four-power Vienna with Anthony Quayle as a Russian general, Mel Ferrer as an American captain, Michael Redgrave as a French colonel and Dennis Price as an English major. The Bat was played by Anton Walbrook and Ludmilla Tcherina was the French colonel's wife, around whom the plot circulated. Excellent choreography and well-designed sets by Hein Heckroth demonstrated that the traumas of *The Tales of Hoffman* had not been in vain.

Experiments were made with a new process, Dynamic Frame, which aimed to become a completely flexible method of presentation. With this system the masking of the screen itself was altered during the course of a film, so that some scenes would appear in a narrow vertical slit and others would encompass the maximum area of a VistaVision frame. Thus the shape of the screen could alter to suit the atmospheric needs of the story. The masking was made at the print stage so that no mechanical effects were needed during projection. D. W. Griffith frequently used vignettes to frame his shots, and Eisenstein in 1930 proposed variable sized images, so the idea was by then not exactly new. The Dynamic Frame was the idea of an American, Glenn Alvey, who persuaded the British Film Institute's Experimental Film Committee and Associated British-Pathé to finance a two-reel film, based on H. G. Wells's short story, *The Door in the Wall*. The film, made in Technicolor and VistaVision, took ten days to shoot and was well received by the critics who saw it. The movements in screen shape were not found distracting and there was a heightened dramatic sense. Derek Prouse wrote: 'it seems very probable that the Dynamic Frame will prove a means of restoring to the screen a spatial eloquence which has in many cases become lost or merely intermittent . . . it preserves flexibility while not denying itself the excitements of grandeur, it can employ dramatic cutting as well as the steady panorama.' Yet this interesting process was never heard of again.

The majority of British films in the mid-fifties were unimpressive. Subject matter tended to be excessively cautious with a leaning towards West End stage successes, popular novels and remakes of earlier, happier films that would have been better left as nostalgic memories. There was also a tendency towards Second World War subjects, a cycle that may well have been set in motion by Charles Frend's 1953 film of the Nicholas Monsarrat best-selling novel, *The Cruel Sea*, with Jack Hawkins as the intrepid Ericson, commander of the corvette *H.M.S. Compass Rose*. Powell and Pressburger forsook the gaieties of Strauss and Offenbach and made *The Battle of the River Plate* in VistaVision with Anthony Quayle, John Gregson and Peter Finch; José Ferrer came to England to direct *Cockleshell Heroes*, with Trevor Howard and he working in Combined Operations; Ronald Neame made an account of one of the more bizarre naval exercises of the war, *The Man Who Never Was*, in which a corpse, complete with bogus invasion secrets contained in a tightly clutched briefcase, was planted on an alien shore.

The RAF received even more distinguished attention. Philip Leacock, one of the directors who served his apprenticeship in Group Three, made a bombing film, *Appointment in London*, with Dirk Bogarde. Lewis Gilbert, who in wartime had worked with the RAF film unit, made a reverential biography of the legless fighter ace, Douglas Bader, with Kenneth More, *Reach for the Sky*, based on the book by Paul Brickhill. The air–sea rescue service received recognition in the same director's *The Sea Shall Not Have Them*. Michael Anderson directed an account of the invention of Barnes Wallis's bouncing bomb which was used to breach the Möhne Dam, with Michael Redgrave as the scientist, and Richard Todd as Guy Gibson, leader of *The Dam Busters*. Anderson's leaden-footed approach to the subject nevertheless won him the coveted task of directing Mike Todd Jr's only enduring contribution to the cinema, the multi-starred epic based on Jules Verne's *Around the World in Eighty Days*. The prison camp story was not forgotten; Lewis Gilbert's *Albert R.N.* (*Break to Freedom* in the U.S.A.); Guy Hamilton's *The Colditz Story* and David Lean's epic *The Bridge on the River Kwai* sustained the genre with Roy Baker's *The One that Got Away* offering a rarity in British films, a German hero escaping from British camps. All these films were based on actual events, as was Lewis Gilbert's account of the capture and torture of Violette Szabo, played by Virginia MacKenna, in *Carve Her Name with Pride*. The same actress also underwent imprisonment by the Japanese in Jack Lee's *A Town Like Alice* (*The Rape of Malaya* in the U.S.A.), based on Nevil Shute's novel. The Army perhaps received less attention than the other services, although the Boultings managed to extract considerable satirical amusement from *Private's Progress*. Herbert Wilcox even managed to make a quite credible war film out of a happening in peacetime, with Richard Todd playing Commander Kerans, captain of the *Amethyst*, a beleagured British ship which made a dash downstream to evade the communists, in *Yangtse Incident*. And Julian Aymes directed *A Hill in Korea*, about the Korean war, in which a group of untried soldiers found themselves pitched into vicious fighting.

An outstanding war film of the mid-fifties was Anthony Asquith's *Orders to Kill*, with a script by Paul Dehn. It concerned the training of a grounded airman (Paul Massie) as a spy and a killer. When he eventually performs the task that he is required to do he bungles it, giving his victim time to make the agonizing appeal, why? The film is concerned with the morality of war and the conscience of the individual when ordered to carry out inhuman orders. By allowing the victim a chance the young spy begins to suspect his innocence and to ask the questions that war has no time for. The film was one of Asquith's best, in spite of occurring comparatively late in his long career. It pointed the difference between the murder of a man in cold blood at close-range and the remote killing of people when flying miles above them in an RAF bomber. Unlike most of the other films in its genre, *Orders to Kill* adopted an attitude to war that was not compounded of heroics and bogus patriotism. By comparison attempts to make the enemy seem reasonable and civilized, as in *The Battle of the River Plate* (*Pursuit of the Graf Spee* in America), seemed false and contrived.

David Lean's interesting and expensive *The Bridge on the River Kwai*, however, was a synthesis of orthodox heroics and unquestioned attitudes. Adapted from a novel by Pierre Boulle, the film is an account of the conflict between a British colonel, played by Alec Guinness, and a Japanese prison-camp commandant, played by Sessue Hayakawa. The prisoners are employed on building a railway to help the Japanese war effort. The colonel must hold together the morale of his men at all costs, and the very act of constructing the huge timber bridge across a jungle river becomes a demonstration of British achievement, an affront to the Japanese. The final absurdity of the situation comes when he dies in an attempt to thwart an Allied commando raid bent on destroying the bridge. It is the most supremely wrongheaded act of courage ever seen in a British war film. In the novel the bridge is not destroyed but remains standing as the final irony, a monument to the fact that no one ever really wins a war. But David Lean, no doubt with the encouragement of his producer, Sam Spiegel, blows up the bridge in a spectacular and breathtaking sequence. The message was lost, but the film was not only the biggest box-office success of the year, but also won the Academy Award. Consequently, *The Bridge on the River Kwai* equivocates between the straightforward epic adventure and the film of ideas. In spite of its ambivalence, the film succeeds in putting across a number of satirical flashes on the nature of war, not least in the relationship between Guinness and Hayakawa who, in spite of their opposed polarity, are very much creatures of a feather, each inflexible in his devotion to an ideal and a rule book.

Also on the epic level was *Dunkirk*, produced by Michael Balcon and directed by Leslie Norman with John Mills, Bernard Lee, Richard

Attenborough and many other veterans of British war pictures. The great retreat, a superbly stage-managed piece of military legerdemain, was reproduced quite realistically in a semi-documentary manner, but carrying with it the inevitable sense of anti-climax as well as the conventional bathetic heroic attitudes underplayed in the traditional manner of this type of film. The technique of weaving individual stories into the totality of a great historical event was a forerunner of the treatment given to D-Day by Darryl F. Zanuck when he produced *The Longest Day* a few years later.

Carol Reed also turned to the war film in *The Key*, after a sentimental foray into the East End with the Wolf Mankowitz fable, *A Kid for Two Farthings*, and the American film of circus rivalries, *Trapeze*. With a script by Carl Foreman, *The Key* is the story of the effect of fear on the men who have to go out in tugs to rescue blazing merchant ships torpedoed in the North Atlantic. A succession of tugboat skippers have held the key to a flat occupied by a refugee, played by Sophia Loren. Each has died in action and it is now the turn of Trevor Howard, who passes the key on to the next in line, William Holden. There is a mystic element about the work, the girl being seen as an evil presage of death, a destroyer of men. The aggrieved official who complains that, according to records, she should have been killed in an air raid, is perhaps more than a humorous inset. At the end of the film, Holden, with all the cards stacked against his return from a particularly difficult mission, finds the girl with the next key-holder. She rejects him and departs for London, leaving him vowing that somehow he will find her. It is a film of disturbing ambiguities and conflicts, undecided as to whether to be a straightforward war story with a reasonably graphic secondary plot concerning the eventual revenge on the U-boat, or a supernatural drama with occult imagery in the ascendant. While better than Reed's intervening films after *Outcast of the Islands*, *The Key* is an uneven though interesting piece of work, enhanced, as was the former film, by the skilful acting of Trevor Howard.

Before making *The Bridge on the River Kwai* David Lean directed Katharine Hepburn in an Anglo-American co-production, *Summer Madness* (*Summertime* in America), which related the romantic encounter of a prim American tourist with a glamorous but heavily married Italian antique dealer. The Jamesian story was filmed against magnificent Venetian locations, and Lean's direction conveyed a sense of place with considerable success. The film's most important attraction, however, was the acting of Katharine Hepburn, who was obliged to make sense of what must surely have been a most unpromising role.

Henry Cornelius, the director of *Passport to Pimlico* and *Genevieve*, made two more films before his death in May 1958, the rather uncharacteristic *I Am a Camera*, an adaptation of a John van Druten play, based on Christopher Isherwood's *Goodbye to Berlin*, and a much more successful film which demonstrated his genial comic sense, *Next to No Time*, which had Kenneth More as a nervous young inventor making the most of the lost hour at midnight on the New York bound *Queen Elizabeth*, when the clock is put back. During this time his self-confidence is at its peak and he is able to enchant the entire ship. It was a pleasant but slightly disappointing valedictory from a director who had shown considerable taste and promise.

Robert Hamer, another director capable of excellent comedy who, like Cornelius, was trained in the Michael Balcon forcing house at Ealing, made two modest films in the period, the masterly *Father Brown* (*The Detective* in the U.S.A.), which had Alec Guinness playing the famous, if unlikely, G. K. Chesterton detective, and *To Paris with Love*, again with Guinness, this time as a widower accompanying his son to the French capital, each plotting to arrange a spouse for the other. Both films, although slight, had flashes of the elegant and witty Hamer style, although they fell far short of *Kind Hearts and Coronets*. Another Ealing director, Alexander Mackendrick, of *Whisky Galore* and *The Maggie*, made what was the last of the Ealing comedies produced in the old studios, an extravagantly dark *comedie noire* called *The Ladykillers*, written by William Rose. Alec Guinness played a sinister and absurd criminal disguised as a professor, who plans a massive robbery, passing off his fellow-villains to his sweet old landlady as amateur musicians. The comic inspiration arose from the juxtaposition of low-class criminality with the genteel respectability of Katie Johnson, whose improbable story at the end of the film is listened to unbelievingly by the patient police. Mackendrick left for America after the film was completed, where he directed for the brief, highly stimulating partnership of Hecht–Hill–Lancaster a trenchant study of Broadway theatrical politics, *The Sweet Smell of Success*.

It was at this time that Ealing Studios closed and were sold to the BBC for use by the television service. The last film to be made there was a routine detective thriller, directed by Charles Frend, and starring Jack Hawkins in one of his overworked Scotland Yard detective roles, *The Long Arm*. With the closing of the studios Sir Michael Balcon ended his eleven-year connection with the Rank Organization, and made a new contract with MGM where he had spent an unhappy period shortly before the war – by now, however, his chief *bête-noir*, Louis B. Mayer, no longer had any connection with the company. For the next three years, Ealing films were made at Borehamwood, and included *The Shiralee*, a Leslie Norman film set in Australia; the same director's *Dunkirk*, which turned out to be the biggest film Balcon had ever been involved in; Charles Crichton's *Man in the Sky*; and Charles Frend's *Barnacle Bill* (*All at Sea* in America), last of the Ealing comedies, with a T. E. B. Clarke story, as usual tilting at local bureaucracy, with Alec Guinness in the lead. At the end of the period the assets of Ealing were bought out by ABPC and the company finally went out of production, its long and fine record among the most honourable in the entire history of British films.

Meanwhile the general output continued in an even more depressing state than before. The success of *Doctor in the House* led to a cycle of 'Doctor' comedies, the second of which, *Doctor at Sea*, had an almost unknown French actress, Brigitte Bardot, starring with Dirk Bogarde. There were remakes of *Vessel of Wrath*, now reverting under Muriel Box's direction to its original and American title, *The Beachcomber*. *The Barratts of Wimpole Street*, with John Gielgud as the unyielding patriarch, was remade by Sidney Franklin. Zoltan Korda's *The Four Feathers* was remade as *Storm over the Nile*, by Terence Young. J. Lee-Thompson remade *The Good Companions* in colour and wide-screen, a youthful Janette Scott failing to achieve the magical impact of Jessie Matthews. The same director was also responsible for the abominable *An Alligator Named Daisy*, a vehicle for the pneumatic Diana Dors. In Lee-Thompson's *Yield to the Night*, Miss Dors was called upon to act the part of a cold-blooded murderess awaiting execution, and gave a credible, sympathetic performance. It was Lee-Thompson's most satisfactory film at that time, with an unusually partisan approach for a British film, firmly siding with the anti-capital punishment lobby. Lee-Thompson's following film, *Woman in a Dressing Gown*, with a Ted Willis script and Yvonne Mitchell as a suburban slut, was a brave attempt at neo-realism, failing through the upper-midde-class inhibitions of its leading actors. *Ice Cold in Alex* was more satisfactory although it was yet another film with the Second World War as a setting, this time the Western Desert in 1942. It told the story of a small party under the command of John Mills, including two nurses, who, cut off in the retreat, have to make their lonely way back to Alexandria. Both this film and *Woman in a Dressing Gown* gained awards at the Berlin Film Festival, a demonstration at least of a growing international respect.

One of the most poignant failures of the period was that of Charles Chaplin, who came to Britain in 1957 to make his first film in the country of his birth. *A King in New York* was a flat, off-centre attack on America which was naïve and over-simplified in its approach to the problems of witch-hunting and the cold war. In the sixties Chaplin was to make a further and even more disastrous attempt to film in Britain with *A Countess from Hong Kong*. While each film had occasional moments of Chaplin genius it was perhaps a pity that the excellent *Limelight* of 1953 could not have been Chaplin's last statement on film.

Another unique figure in the cinema as a director is Sir Laurence Olivier, whose attempts at putting Shakespeare on the screen brought considerable prestige to British films in the forties. In 1955, backed now by Korda, he made a third Shakespearean film, *Richard III*. In terms of his own performance it was undoubtedly the best, his Richard a deformed, spidery villain in total command of the mechanistic court intrigues until his final downfall at Bosworth. With Olivier were Gielgud, Richardson, Claire Bloom and Pamela Brown. An intense, almost intimate film, it held together more consistently than *Henry V* and was less swamped by heavy effects and settings than *Hamlet*. It also provided a magnificent record of some great Shakespearean acting. For his next film, *The Prince and the Showgirl*, Olivier rather surprisingly turned away from Shakespeare to Terence Rattigan, adapting his stage play *The Sleeping Prince*. The showgirl of the title, who at the 1911 Coronation of George V gets involved with the Regent of a Ruritarian country, was played by Marilyn Monroe, who was brought to London from Hollywood with considerable publicity. Her performance was a delightful portrayal of knowing innocence, and admirably counterpointed Olivier's wooden, arrogant Prince. It was however an unsuitable choice for him to direct, and the film lacked the necessary lightness to keep it afloat.

During the fifties the American director Joseph Losey (*The Boy With Green Hair*, *The Lawless* [*The Dividing Line*, G.B.], *The Prowler*) began making films in Britain. Exiled from Hollywood by the McCarthy witch-hunt, his first British film, *The Sleeping Tiger*, was directed under a pseudonym, a special arrangement made for the benefit of the distributors. It was a Freudian melodrama about a psychiatrist with a bad marriage, and Losey made what he could of an unpromising script. His next British film, *The Intimate Stranger*, was credited to yet another fictitious director, and was an ingenious study of warped pathology, concerning an American film-editor working in England who has a bogus past romance planted on him by a rival anxious to discredit him. Both these films were low budget and shot on an impossibly tight schedule. As programme fillers they were hardly noticed, except by the most discerning critics who saw a spark of the unique inspiration characterizing Losey's work, a concern for the most pessimistic motivations of humankind, an obsessive fatalism which drives his characters on, almost forcing them to self-destruction. The first British film to which his own name was attached was *Time Without Pity*, a loose adaptation of the play *Someone Waiting*, by Emlyn Williams. In this film Michael Redgrave plays an alcoholic whose son is being executed for a murder he did not commit. Seeking the real murderer he allows himself to be shot so that there is sufficient incriminating evidence to stop the execution. The film is a race against time; with twenty-four hours to go the father desperately pursues every avenue in an attempt to stop the hanging, approaching a newspaper and an MP opposed to capital punishment, but all to no avail. Only when he confronts the real murderer, a self-made bully (Leo McKern), does his chance of success appear. The conflict is essentially a battle for mastery: the murderer aware that although his guilt is known there is nothing the other can do to save his son. The opportunity was not lost on Losey to establish a powerful subjective statement. In spite of the limitations of budget, *Time Without Pity* was crammed to an almost baroque extent with imagery and incident, a lively approach to a complicated, almost metaphysical subject, the power of time.

His next film was *The Gypsy and the Gentleman*, made for Rank. It was a curious choice of material for Losey, a heavily melodramatic Regency story full of gambling hells and madhouses. Deverill, played by Keith Michell, marries Belle, a gypsy (Melina Mercouri), without telling her that he has squandered his fortune. He is inveigled into committing his younger sister into Bedlam to cheat her out of a will, but when eventually he learns that his wife never loved him he drowns both her and himself. Losey was able to make a stylish and interesting film from such an uncharacteristic subject, but that he did it with a certain amount of distaste is evident from the fact that he left the dubbing to someone else.

In the neglected area of animated cartoons two films in the mid-fifties offered a certain encouragement to followers. The first was the John Halas and Joy Batchelor full-length version of George Orwell's horrific fantasy, *Animal Farm*, in which a hideous parody of totalitarian attitudes gradually emerges and erupts into a violent and cataclysmic climax. Appearing in the year preceding the Russian oppression in Hungary, it was the first time, at least in Britain, that the cartoon medium had been used to tell a serious story. Regrettably, the visual style was not equal to the brave conception and many of the images emerged as sub-Disney anthropomorphism. The ability to break away from the Disney style has always been a difficulty for animated-film-makers, daunted no doubt by the fact that the field was for many years so dominated by one studio that many techniques were learned there and disseminated.

However, Richard Williams, a young Canadian artist, produced in 1958 a half-hour cartoon, *The Little Island*, which visually owed nothing to Disney. Moving entirely away from the notion that the animated cartoon was an extension of the comic strip, a view that must have persisted from the time that Winsor McCay in the States first animated *Gertie the Dinosaur* in 1909, Williams treated his work in the manner of an abstract impressionist. Three little men inhabit an island; each has a vision reflecting his own particular belief, respectively Truth, Goodness and Beauty, each represented in an individual and expressive style. Eventually Goodness and Beauty antagonize one another and grow into warring monsters. Then the bomb on which Truth has marked the score explodes. *The Little Island* was an astonishing personal achievement, almost a single-handed creation, and its stylistic range so extensive that it represented a very formidable landmark in the development of film cartoons. The message of Williams's work was that communication between people with fixed ideas was negligible, and it was expressed with wit, imaginative invention and technical accomplishment. Sadly, his talent was channelled into the more profitable paths of television commercials, feature film credit title sequences and short subject humorous cartoons. The film was given a sparse and timid release by Rank, and even withdrawn from cinemas when it was found that audiences were not responding as quickly to it as they would to *Tom and Jerry*.

19 The Critical Imperative

The fifties ended with the British cinema in a critical state on both the artistic and the economic level. Some of its great figures had gone for ever, Korda himself dying in 1956. A giant in every sense, his failures had been realized on as monumental a scale as his successes. Many of the best directors, such as Thorold Dickinson, who had become a don at London University, were either no longer making films or had succumbed to the temptations and opportunities of Hollywood. Ronald Neame, David Lean, Carol Reed, Alexander Mackendrick all moved off to California, in most cases their contribution to a developing British film complete. The guaranteed successes at the box-office were the comedies of Norman Wisdom, the 'Doctor' films and a new series, which began in 1958 with *Carry on Sergeant*, and was quickly followed by *Nurse, Teacher, Constable*, and endless profitable variations on a basic risible theme. To this had to be added the large number of films aimed at a teenage and pre-teen public, many cashing in on the fifties rock 'n roll craze, with *Six-Five Special, The Tommy Steele Story* and others. There was also a tendency towards horror films; particularly noted for their achievements in this area were Hammer Films, with *The Curse of Frankenstein, Dracula* and many others.

The X Certificate, introduced at the beginning of the decade as a device to permit more adult treatments of subjects previously either completely taboo or only seen in a highly bowdlerized form, was now in danger of being swamped with inane rubbish, and had in any case long fallen into disrepute, a badge of guaranteed salacity. Tragically, some of the more promising work from America during this period, particularly those films which had moved forward in their perception of public awareness, were given X certificates, and quite often cut by the BBFC. The blue film session in *The Bachelor Party* was eliminated in the British exhibition print, so that all that was seen were the faces of the men enjoying a pornographic movie. Similarly many of the films produced in Europe, where a genuine revolution in taste was occurring, reached Britain with damaging excisions. The X certificate, tarnished by its associations, failed as a protection for works of merit.

This lack of seriousness and any sense of experimentation was typical of the industry at this time, even when experience in both France and America was moving totally in the opposite direction. While Hollywood was producing *Marty* and *A Hatful of Rain*, while in France Bresson was making *Un Condamné a Mort C'est Echappé*, Britain was producing the entertaining but irrelevant Quatermass science fiction films of Val Guest, taken from Nigel Kneale's television series, and the Boultings' diversionary *Brothers-in-Law*. While a large production such as *The Bridge on the River Kwai* could achieve outstanding box-office success, it was not as a result of its being British. To an American audience it would have appeared to be an American film and films of this expense and scope were only permissible on such terms.

Yet the glimmerings of an artistic revolution were at hand. In France a group of critics under the tutelage of André Bazin, and associated with the review *Cahiers du Cinema* began making modest films to fit their theories. As financial backing grew, their films became more ambitious. Among these film-makers were Jean-Luc Godard, Claude Chabrol, François Truffaut and Jacques Rivette. Attaching a label to their output, the French press called it '*la nouvelle vague*' – the new wave. Accepted ideas were turned aside, spontaneity counted more than technical gloss. It was the time of hand-held cameras, jump cutting, blurred soundtracks, impromptu acting. Their work represented the emergence of a completely fresh approach to film-making, a palliative to the exhausted, worked-out conventions to be found in the great majority of international productions. The new wave was one signal, but there were others nearer home.

In 1956 the Royal Court Theatre staged *Look Back in Anger*, an untidy, rhetorical attack on established values by a new playwright, John Osborne. It was the most significant moment on the post-war stage. In dealing its hammer-blows at the complacency and caution of West End theatre, *Look Back in Anger* and the English Stage Company opened an encouraging window for a new generation of playwrights, actors and directors. Another portent occurred shortly after the *Observer* newspaper staged an exhibition in London commemorating the sixtieth anniversary of the movies. The amateur, almost philistine, critical approach demonstrated in the exhibition so incensed Lindsay Anderson, a left-wing critic and editor of the review *Sequence*, that he delivered a polemical attack in the British Film Institute's quarterly magazine, *Sight and Sound*. The article, a combination of theoretical assumptions, personal pique and deeply-felt concern, failed to bring the film critics of the national press to heel, largely because the *credo* quoted derogatorily by Anderson, of Alistair Cooke in 1935, expressed an attitude held generally by critics under the full encouragement of their editors: '. . . I am without politics and without class. For a film hero I am prepared to take John Barrymore, George Robey, a Battle-ship, Mickey Mouse, or an Italian Straw Hat. I hope that everyone who wants to make a lot of money in films will make it, that every girl who aches to become a star overnight will become one . . . My malice extends only to those who have a dull talent . . .' What Anderson should have been complaining about was the lack of awareness among the general public of the value of the cinema. It is a chicken–egg argument, most newspapers subscribing to the attitudes which promote circula-tion and keep readers happy. Hardly surprisingly, film criticism has never received its due in Britain, unlike the way things are ordered in France, many writers being only temporarily interested before moving on to more profitable fields. In all its history in Britain the cinema has fought against its second-class status. Yet at the same time it must be confessed that some sections of the business have acted almost as though they have a vested interest in its continuing mediocrity.

Lindsay Anderson's essay was timely, arriving at a moment of intellectual reawakening. His theme of artistic commitment, the adherence to a defined value and purpose in a work, became almost a cult-belief. Yet in spite of the trappings of fashionable trendiness surrounding the philosophy, which was popularly, and in ignorance, associated with an ill-assorted group of writers such as Kingsley Amis, John Wain, John Braine and Colin Wilson – the 'angry young men' of the daily papers – the value of Anderson's words went deeper. A critical position was established, the values of the film as art were restated with considerable power, and a challenge was made for a partisan cinema which would not equivocate but would fully recognize itself as a force for the elucidation of human creativity and imagination. It was a provocative thesis, an approach calculated to antagonize and numb the adversary.

And there were repercussions. Free Cinema, a term invented to describe certain films made under the financial aegis of the British Film Institute, showed at the National Film Theatre a number of interest-ing documentaries which demonstrated new talents. One of them,

O Dreamland, about a coastal resort in south-east England, had been made by Anderson himself as early as 1953. In the first Free Cinema programme in February 1956 this film and *Together*, by Lorenza Mazzetti, a story about two young deaf mutes living in the East End, were coupled with *Momma Don't Allow*, the work of Karel Reisz and Tony Richardson, with photography by Walter Lassally, a short documentary about a suburban jazz club in North London. These films almost certainly would not have been made but for the BFI fund, except for the Anderson film, which cost less than £100. Two of them were shot on 16mm. and all were put together by individuals rather than the large teams which would have been required if the ACT had been involved. The success of the initial showings led to more ambitious films being shot under the Free Cinema label. The Ford Motor Company sponsored another Anderson film, *Every Day Except Christmas*, which was about Covent Garden Market, and this was followed by *We Are the Lambeth Boys*, directed by Karel Reisz, who had moved away from the British Film Institute to become Films Officer for Ford. *We Are the Lambeth Boys* was shot in a Kennington Youth Club and showed something of the life of young people in a dense, working-class area of London, the action observed by the camera in a ciné-verité style – the Saturday dance, the school hymn singing, the working environment, the contact between boys and girls, even a spontaneous and spirited debate on capital punishment. These films, made without considerations of the commercial cinema to inhibit them, provided Anderson, Richardson and Reisz with an arena in which their voices could be heard. All were to move into making feature films, and Richardson and Anderson were also to devote a lot of their talent to the theatre.

At the Venice Film Festival in 1955 the prize for the best short-story film went to a half-hour version of a Wolf Mankowitz play, based in turn on a Gogol story, *The Bespoke Overcoat*, with Alfie Bass and David Kossoff. It was the first film to be directed by Jack Clayton, who had begun a long apprenticeship in the mid-thirties and had worked his way up to the position of producer. Clayton's first long film is usually regarded as a turning point and harbinger for a new, honest approach in the British cinema.

Room at the Top was adapted from John Braine's first novel, about an ambitious young man in a local government office in a large and bleak northern town who makes a set for a wealthy industrialist's daughter, and when thwarted turns to an older married woman. Eventually he is forced into marriage with the girl, the older woman meeting her death after a drinking orgy. The character of Joe Lampton is ambivalent, bitter, his social animus perhaps deriving from a slum childhood and a war spent mostly in a prison camp, but driven forward by a kind of confident, day-dreaming quality, a refusal to admit the impossible. His eventual translation from the cobblestones of the lower end of the town to the tudorized gables at the top is meant to show his sublimation of life's values to ambition. He has destroyed one life and knowingly goes into a loveless marriage accompanied by the material comforts for which he has always hankered. It is, in his terms, not a bad jail sentence. In retrospect, Braine's book is hardly as startling as it may have seemed at the time. The stance is a traditional, stolid one of disapproval. In the film the tight-lipped and rather frigid performance of Laurence Harvey does not explain the character's motivation. Donald Wolfit, as the industrialist, delivers an impressively theatrical portrait of a nineteenth-century mill-owner, although the performance hardly fits this particular film. Simone Signoret, as the older woman, is not too happily cast, either, volatile Gallic temperament not mixing well with Yorkshire reticence. But the critics' admiration was mainly on account of the love scenes between Harvey and Heather Sears; at last someone in a British film actually admitted that the sex act was enjoyable and for the first time such dialogue was passed by the British Board of Film Censors. What seemed startling in 1959 had by ten years later become banal, but *Room at the Top* was at least a turning point in this sense. A far more satisfactory film had been made from Braine's novel than was produced out of the more important staging post of the fifties protest, *Lucky Jim*. The Amis novel was turned into a farcical comedy by the Boultings, in the style of their *Private's Progress* and *Brothers-in-Law*, doing for Redbrick universities what the other films had done respectively for the army and the law. They even used Ian Carmichael again in the leading role. A harmless and entertaining film in its own right, it was a regrettable dilution of the power of its original.

The Horse's Mouth, a novel by Joyce Cary about an artist whose only values were in his art, while antedating Braine and Amis was very relevant in its theme of protest and dissatisfaction with the established order. Alec Guinness played Cary's single-minded creation, Gully Jimson, in a film directed by Ronald Neame, with the paintings of John Bratby standing in as the work of the artist. A thoughtful, well-meaning film, dominated by a technically magnificent performance by Alec Guinness, it did not fully succeed, largely on account of the slightness of its attack.

Tony Richardson's first full-length film was *Look Back in Anger*, made for Woodfall, a company established by himself and John Osborne for film production. It appeared three years after Osborne's play had startled audiences at the Royal Court Theatre, and in the intervening period much had happened to alter the original impact. Jimmy Porter's frequent histrionic outbursts were considerably trimmed for the film version, which was written by Nigel Kneale, author of the gripping Quatermass science fiction serials on BBC television. The only survivor from the English Stage Company production in the film was Mary Ure, as Porter's wife, Alison. The leading part was taken by Richard Burton, somehow older, almost more thoughtful than the stage version of Jimmy Porter. But most significantly, the introduction of Ma Tanner, a character only referred to in the play, not only provided Edith Evans with an opportunity to display her most moving performance, but gave the film a firmness and definition missing in the original, brilliant though it was. The agony of Jimmy Porter, his refusal to adopt the self-deceit of social values, became credible and immediate in his exchanges with her. As a first film, *Look Back in Anger* was a triumph, even if some visual devices, such as the overlapping dissolves, tended to show a close study of what was the trend-setting gimmickry currently used in France. Such crudities, however, were easily cancelled out by the quality of the acting, including Claire Bloom as Helena, Alison's actress friend, and Gary Raymond as Cliff, Jimmy's friend. The photography by Oswald Morris tended to hold the action in close-up, emphasizing the claustrophobic nature of the relationships. *Look Back in Anger* expressed a new vitality and sense of attack in the cinema, and the film was to exercise almost as much influence on its medium as the play on the theatre.

Richardson next collaborated with Osborne and Nigel Kneale to film *The Entertainer*, Osborne's second play. Laurence Olivier repeated his stage role of Archie Rice, the fading, anachronistic comedian reduced to treading the boards of a dingy seaside resort before half-empty houses. His son is involved in the ill-conceived Suez affair, where he is eventually killed. Rice lusts after a teenage beauty contestant on the pretext of extracting money from her parents for a new show, to the disgust of his daughter. Signing cheques he cannot honour, he is ruined by the end of the film. Osborne's play was a statement on the decay of the country as a whole, the Suez incident and the broken-down performer serving as a microcosm of social degeneration. The allegorical spirit of the play was muted in the film version and

Suez, after the pre-title opening, was referred to only briefly. The acting was theatrical in style, with Olivier's performance calculated with a monumental precision – puffed face, drooping eyebrows, leering mouth, on stage the most convincing of bad comics, desperately milking an unresponsive audience for laughs. Joan Plowright as the returned daughter, Alan Bates, Albert Finney and Shirley Ann Field as the beauty contest girl, performed with a clear sense of purpose. It was again an extraordinarily rich film, full of unfulfilled promise, still marred by similar faults found in Richardson's first film; but it was alive, it was possessed of a vital force and at moments it was filled with deep compassion.

In the same year as *The Entertainer* came Karel Reisz's first full-length film, *Saturday Night and Sunday Morning*. It was adapted from Alan Sillitoe's novel set in his native Nottingham. The central character, Arthur Seaton, played in the film by Albert Finney, is a hard-drinking, red-blooded, rebellious young factory worker, sowing his seeds in every direction until finally trapped into conformity and marriage on a new housing estate, a fate he resents, hurling a defiant stone at the trim new houses. The theatricality of Richardson's two Osborne pictures was replaced by a totally believable, almost spontaneously observed realism, a view of a regional setting in a style never previously revealed. The factories and backstreets, canal banks and pubs, in which the action took place, were not studio reproductions, but genuine Nottingham locations, stocked with real live inhabitants who could never be mistaken for fugitives from Central Casting. Albert Finney in the main part played with a gusto and an instinct which instantly gave the situations a veracity unusual in feature films. Insolent and self-confident, but without the consuming ambition of a Joe Lampton, Arthur Seaton signified the emergence of a new folk-hero, the new breed of British working man, combining high wages with a disdain for being told what to do, irresponsible as long as he can get away with it, a creature who has to enjoy his freedom before he loses it to nappies and rent books. Rachel Roberts played the wife of a workmate, made pregnant by the rammish Arthur, and Shirley Ann Field the dull, pretty girl he is eventually ensnared by. Karel Reisz directed the film with a sureness and modesty which resulted in an accomplished work. In only one sequence, at a fun fair, when two soldiers seek Arthur on the roundabouts and dodgem cars in order to beat him up, does Reisz depart from a four-square camera approach; as a consequence he remained in total control of his material, and this first feature film remains to this date his most satisfying.

Woodfall, formed by John Osborne and Tony Richardson and Bryanston Films, joined a company of independent producers that made this trio of films and linked up with British Lion, the third British-controlled distribution group which unlike Rank and ABC lacked a circuit of its own. After his brief period with MGM Michael Balcon was persuaded to take the chairmanship of Bryanston, and in the course of four years some £3 million worth of business from the company flowed through British Lion's accounts. This company had endured a difficult time during the fifties, its misfortunes stemming from the time that Korda, when he was in control, received a £3 million government loan. In 1954 an official receiver was appointed and British Lion faced extinction. A new company was formed early in 1955 and the National Film Finance Corporation took the 600,000 shares valued at £1 each, which had been left as assets of the old company, thus wiping out the £3 million debt. But it meant that the new company was owned by the government. At the beginning of 1958, shortly after the resignation of Sir Arthur Jarrett as managing director of the NFFC and the appointment of David Kingsley, who was already managing director of the NFFC, to succeed him, a new injection of creative strength was given to the management. New board members appointed were John and Roy Boulting, Sidney Gilliatt and Frank Launder, and John Woolf. Thus for a time it looked as though the much-sought 'third force' had a strong chance, and that the independent producers had a new outlet for their product. It was, in time, to prove illusory, owing to the absence of a releasing circuit. British Lion had to join the queue with other distributors for a place on the two circuits, and after the demise of the short-lived and useless National circuit there was considerable pressure.

Another independent production team releasing through British Lion was the combination of Richard Attenborough and Bryan Forbes. Forbes, an actor turned screenwriter, and Attenborough, an actor respected within the industry for his professionalism, made as their first film *The Angry Silence*, directed by Guy Green. It was a story of industrial relations, the effect of a political agitator fermenting a dispute which resulted in a man being sent to Coventry and made a victim of the violence of the mob. Set in a realistic Midlands environment, the screenplay was by Bryan Forbes and Richard Attenborough played the scapegoat, with Pier Angeli as his anguished wife. The dialogue, use of locations and acting all showed the new mood of contemporary awareness, engendered by the pioneering *Room at the Top*. There was more than a passing resemblance to Kazan's *On the Waterfront*, with the ultimate demonstration of the collective guilt of the workmen, when the young thug who causes the hero to lose an eye is hauled before a workers' meeting after himself being beaten up. Where *The Angry Silence* fails is in naming its true enemies, in showing exactly what the strike is all about. The agitator is too shadowy, too implausible a figure to be taken seriously; he is merely a melodramatic plot appendage, diminishing the quality of the film from genuine involvement in a major contemporary situation to sensational titillation. The compromise weakened the film's impact, but *The Angry Silence* was still a welcome addition to the new cinema of realism, and was actually made on a budget well below the average for a first feature.

After writing and appearing, again with Attenborough, in Basil Dearden's amusing and ironical thriller, *The League of Gentlemen*, about a robbery organized and carried out by ex-army officers led by Jack Hawkins, Bryan Forbes directed *Whistle down the Wind*, an adaptation of a novel by Mary Hayley Bell, written by Keith Waterhouse and Willis Hall. Hayley Mills plays a young girl on a farm in Lancashire who believes that an escaped prisoner found hiding in the barn is Christ, largely as a result of the expletives he utters on discovery. The film combined its allegorical depiction of the betrayal of Christ with an insight into the secret child-world of fantasy and make-believe. Some of the symbolism (the prisoner at the end of the film standing silhouetted with outstretched arms on a hill while he is frisked by the police capturers, for instance) was pretentious and overstated, but the dialogue of Hall and Waterhouse had an edge to it which combined well with the hard, beautiful photography of Arthur Ibbetson.

Another playwright of the post-*Look Back in Anger* theatre was Arnold Wesker, whose play, *The Kitchen*, was filmed by ACT Films and directed by James Hill with a little-known cast on a low budget offered by the NFFC. The kitchen was that of a London restaurant and the film observed the cosmopolitan miniature world that existed among the tureens and baking tins. That so much emotional carnage could occur behind the scenes in an unsmart restaurant in one day required considerable imaginative effort, and the director kept the film moving through sharp close-ups and over-emphasized images. The result was a film which went slightly too far, although in the idiom of its period it was an acceptable enough attempt.

In the more traditional area there were some good things in the years from 1958 to 1961. Don Chaffey's 1958 film *The Man Upstairs*, another product of ACT Films, featured a recurring plot theme, the lonely man in a back room who goes berserk. Like *Le Jour se Lève*, the man harangues the world from an upstairs window after having committed violence (in this case he has pushed a policeman down the stairs). The man was played by Richard Attenborough, who effectively conveyed the desperation and defeat of the spirit endured by someone feeling responsibility for the death of a working colleague.

Joseph Losey's three films of the period were each of interest and power. *Blind Date* in 1959 was at first glance an ordinary suspense thriller concerning a corpse mis-identified by a young Dutchman who finds himself involved in a murder case. In Losey's hands it became a study of transient feelings and police corruptibility. Adopting his familiar disdain for stereotypes, he made everyone in the film suspicious and vaguely unpleasant. His next, *The Criminal*, in the following year, was by far his best British film at that time. Again his material was conventional, a familiar story of crooks, prison life and hidden loot. The central part of a tough underworld leader was played by Stanley Baker, with an excellent conflict situation built up between him and the chief warden of the prison, Patrick Magee, whose attitudes to his job seem little different from those in his care. Losey's mastery of banal material was never more effective than in this film, which had a pace and attack of unique quality. Some scenes, particularly the prison riot, had an intensive emotionalism obscuring the bereft storyline. Alun Owen's dialogue was another of the film's many assets. Losey's last film of the period was delayed for nearly two years after completion before being released in 1963. This was *The Damned*, a strong, fable-like work in which a group of radioactive-contaminated children are raised in a grotesque experiment. The cast included Macdonald Carey, Alexander Knox, Viveca Lindfors, Shirley Ann Field and Oliver Reed.

Sapphire was an unusual detective story, directed by Basil Dearden, which went some way towards examining the colour problem in Britain. The murdered girl is half-Negro and Scotland Yard has to work through her coloured boy friends in the ambience of clubs and lodging houses until the murderer is found and confesses. The direction of the film was crisp and routine, but the story was sufficiently different from the typical product in its genre to invoke interest. Two years later Dearden directed *Victim*, produced in association with Michael Relph, and, like *Sapphire*, written by Janet Green. Dirk Bogarde played a barrister blackmailed by a young homosexual who commits suicide when arrested. He then faces the dilemma of choosing between exposure of a homosexual ring in which he is involved, that will inevitably ruin his career and marriage, and keeping quiet. He chooses the former course, pursuing the blackmail spiral to its conclusion, well aware of the scandal that will result. A combination of conventional thriller, and for the time a daring revelation of homosexuality on the screen, hitherto one of the British Board of Film Censors' most celebrated taboos, the film succeeded in spite of occasional lapses into melodrama. Dirk Bogarde's sympathetic performance to some extent mitigated some of the propagandizing qualities that the film exhibited, with its careful marshalling of arguments to show that many homosexuals could not help it and were often innocent victims of blackmailers.

Jack Cardiff, a cameraman turned director, made a stolid attempt at filming D. H. Lawrence's *Sons and Lovers*, with Dean Stockwell in the part of Paul Morel, the miner's son who breaks out from his parental domination. Trevor Howard played the father and Heather Sears was Miriam, the girl he loves and eventually spurns. Carol Reed's *Our Man in Havana* was a much more felicitous literary adaptation, adapted from Graham Greene's novel by the author himself, with Alec Guinness as a bumbling, amateur spy peddling plans of vacuum cleaners, believing them to be acceptable as mysterious mountain installations, and getting himself into ever deeper water. Noël Coward contributed a richly humorous performance as an unflappable and incompetent member of the Foreign Office's local staff. It was Reed's best film since *The Third Man*, ten years earlier, which had been another Graham Greene partnership.

Sir Carol Reed's return to form was unfortunately not followed through. After working for a brief time on an MGM remake of their mid-thirties classic, *Mutiny on the Bounty*, he was replaced by Lewis Milestone. Ronald Neame, after his success with Alec Guinness in *The Horse's Mouth*, used him as a hard-drinking Scottish colonel in *Tunes of Glory*, whose command is being taken over by an unimaginative and regimentally-minded successor, played by John Mills. Guinness eventually drives the newcomer to suicide and then goes out of his mind. The story, set in a grim castle-like barracks in a Scottish town, was by James Kennaway, and in the small part of Guinness's daughter was Susannah York, making her first film appearance. The chief value of the film lay in the head-on collision of two opposing temperaments, and the performance of John Mills was a convincing proof of his stature as a British film actor, achieved by devoted and reliable work over the years.

Among films made in Britain by American companies during the period, one of the most notable was Mark Robson's *The Inn of the Sixth Happiness*, the story of Gladys Aylward, an English missionary in China during the Japanese invasion, which starred Ingrid Bergman and Robert Donat, playing his last part before death after years of torment. *Suddenly Last Summer* was directed by Joseph L. Mankiewicz, and starred Elizabeth Taylor, Montgomery Clift and Katharine Hepburn. It also featured one of the most remarkable sets ever built in a British studio, a 1920s New Orleans house designed by Oliver Messel. The screenplay, based on a Tennessee Williams one-act play, with its themes of mental breakdown, homosexuality and even cannibalism, was by Gore Vidal. *The Guns of Navarone*, directed by J. Lee Thompson from a war book by Alistair Maclean, was a hard-ticket epic with Gregory Peck leading a handful of guerrillas against an apparently impregnable Nazi fortress, and eventually destroying it. Hardly the most novel of themes, the film attempted to analyse the nature of courage and survival, but the higher issues were swamped by the *Boys' Own Paper* style with its emphasis on adventure and spectacle. Lewis Gilbert's *Sink the Bismarck!* was a more successful war film, the centre of action being the Admiralty War Room, where Kenneth More as Director of Naval Operations plots the destruction of the German battleship and the deployment of British warships with the intensity of a fanatical chess-player. His coldness and unwavering sense of discipline we later learn are the result of the loss of his wife in an air raid. In spite of the repetition of the familiar war film stereotypes, the tension and excitement of the final chase were well-stated and the model work in the Pinewood studio tank was technically of a very high order.

In the area of humour the British cinema continued to extract box-office returns from agreed formulae, not without success in many instances, to the pleasure of producers. The Norman Wisdom films, the 'Carry On' films, the 'Doctor' films and to a less regular extent the 'St Trinian's' films formed the main comic series. Some comedians, such as Jimmy Edwards (*Bottoms Up*), Charlie Drake (*Petticoat Pirates*) and Spike Milligan (*Postman's Knock*) were lured from radio and television, but none of the films managed to make the best of their comic gifts. The Boultings, however, succeeded best with comedy. Continuing their attack on the various echelons of the establishment they went for the Foreign Office in *Carlton-Browne of the F.O.*, which featured one of Terry-Thomas's most entertaining film performances as a dim-witted diplomat sent to butter up a forgotten colony where valuable mineral deposits had been discovered. In the role of a plotting Prime Minister was Peter Sellers, who reappeared in the Boultings' next film, *I'm All Right Jack*, in a caricature role that became a classic stereotype, that of Fred Kite, a bone-headed, idealistic shop-steward. The film poked fun at one of the most sacred of all British Institutions, the Trade Union movement, with Ian Carmichael, again in his *Private's Progress* character, playing an aspirant to a managerial career in industry confronted by the implacability and agitating genius of the shop stewards. Latching on to the fashionable targets of the day, strikes, TV panels, management remoteness and stupidity, advertising, the class war and even nudism, the Boultings' production was highly contemporary. Unfortunately, their shafts often went wide, satire being supplanted by facetiousness, and in this film particularly it is hard to find a properly defined point of view – the workers are shown to be slothful, stupid and occasionally malevolent, but then the bosses are two-faced and unscrupulous. The acting of Sellers, Dennis Price as the most double-dyed of the businessmen, and Irene Handl as Kite's wife was of an exceptionally high order.

The Boultings had filmed the first Kingsley Amis novel, *Lucky Jim*, but it was Sidney Gilliatt who made the second, from a script by Bryan Forbes. *Only Two Can Play* was the screen version of *That Uncertain Feeling*, and Peter Sellers played the part of John Lewis, the Welsh librarian who becomes involved with the wife of a rich town dignitary, played by Mai Zetterling; the similarities with *Lucky Jim* were considerable, Richard Attenborough's performance as the pseudo-intellectual bore being a repeat of the Terry-Thomas role in the former film. Adult dialogue, sex jokes, horrible lodgings and grimy Swansea streets helped to locate the film, even if Sellers did play yet another mimicking part with a funny voice.

Peter Sellers had by now become almost a cult, and the film was a huge box-office success. However, his presence was not sufficient to redeem Anthony Asquith's polished and dull adaptation of Shaw's *The Millionairess*, written for the screen by Wolf Mankowitz. Sophia Loren was miscast as the Shavian heroine and Sellers now performed his Indian doctor act. Ponderously acted, sumptuous in style, the film was a disturbing illustration of the decline in Asquith's talent. Mankowitz's previous work in films had included the adaptations of his stories *A Kid for Two Farthings* for Carol Reed, and *Expresso Bongo*, directed by Val Guest, in which Cliff Richard starred as the youth exploited as a pop-singing discovery by an unscrupulous agent, played by

Laurence Harvey. The failure of *The Millionairess* was a reminder that another screen version of a Shaw play, *The Devil's Disciple*, made in Britain by no less considerable a group than Hecht–Hill–Lancaster, and directed by Guy Hamilton, was also a disappointment, in spite of the acting presence of Sir Laurence Olivier in the role of General Burgoyne. Burt Lancaster was clearly ill at ease in the part of Pastor Anthony Anderson, an early American freedom fighter. Guy Hamilton's touch was far more assured in his comedy *A Touch of Larceny*, in which James Mason played a man who pretends to defect to the Russians with vital secrets in the hope that when branded as a traitor by the press he can reappear and collect heavy libel damages. George Sanders played a diplomat and rival for the girl (Vera Miles), who suspects that a fraud is being carried out.

20 Scares of the Sixties

With cinemas closing by the hundred it was pleasant to find at the end of the fifties that a handful of new cinemas had been opened or were being planned. In London's West End, Columbia opened a new theatre in Shaftesbury Avenue in the basement of an office block, which was designed to be the London showcase for their product. The Empire, Leicester Square, shortly afterwards closed down and reopened as a smaller, more modern cinema, sharing premises with a Mecca dance hall. Later, the Gaumont, Haymarket was to close, its building converted into an office block with a basement cinema. The large structures of the twenties and thirties were no longer economical units unless they could maintain near-capacity audiences. Smaller cinemas had lower overheads and could sustain long runs. It was the beginning of a trend which was to continue through the decade, with the turning of the Plaza into Paramount and Universal, with the new Odeon in St Martin's Lane and the rebuilt Odeon at Marble Arch, and the twinning of the Warner Theatre. The pattern was repeated in the provinces, too, and several rebuilt twins were put into operation following the successful opening of two new Odeons, working in tandem, at Nottingham on the site of an old Rank theatre.

A greater flexibility was also introduced into the release pattern, a demand made by many interested filmgoers for several years. Films that were successful on the circuits were actually retained for second and even third weeks, or re-released shortly afterwards. A number of Greater London theatres occasionally played pre-release films simultaneously with their West End showing, using a system that had originated in New York, with the Premier Showcase presentations. Unfortunately, the multiplicity of administration difficulties prevented this method from going as far as it might, and it was used only for exceptional films. Another pre-release system concerned the long-running road-show films such as *The Sound of Music*, *Dr Zhivago* and so on, which were given seasons in certain suburban theatres, running for several weeks before later being generally released. In some theatres 70mm. equipment was installed, but few independents could afford to leap on to this particular bandwagon, largely because the presence of another theatre in the locality could 'bar' product. Some bars were ridiculous and outrageous. For example, the Astoria in Purley was barred by cinemas in the West End, fourteen miles away, from showing 70mm. films simultaneously, and the Gaumont, Manchester, extended its 70mm. bar to cover the whole of Lancashire, thus preventing an independent in Morecambe from showing a film at the same time, even though it was able to offer a twenty-week run throughout the holiday season. Even more ridiculously, as has already been stated, the Gaumont, Glasgow's normal 35mm. bar of fifty miles was extended to cover the whole of Scotland, a blanket coverage which was eventually reduced to twenty-five miles.

In London, the normal three-week releasing period for all films, by which each programme played the first week in the north-west suburbs, the second week in the north-east (and certain south-western localities), and the third week in south London (a measure introduced during the war years in order to lessen the number of release prints needed) was ended and a return made to the pre-war two-week release, the first week north and the second week south of the Thames. This move was not the result of increased generosity on the part of the exhibitors, but an indication of how total numbers of cinemas had dwindled. As far as the filmgoer was concerned it was a backward step, since a film he might be prepared to travel to see was now available for only two-thirds the time it would have been before the change. This, coupled with the general disappearance of second-run theatres, which were either closed or absorbed into the main release group, lessened the opportunities for seeing a desired film and, although the remarkable growth of the Classic circuit in the sixties was a positive effect, it was usually months or years before a film would be reshown in their theatres.

In the mid-sixties an attempt was made to alter the traditional close of programmes on Saturday night, by making Friday a programme change day as in the West End, where it was normal to open a new film on a Thursday or Friday. It was thought that cinemagoers would prefer to see a new film on Friday nights, pay-day for the majority of the working population. The experiment was, however, short-lived, since it was found that weekend audiences dropped. In any case, the Saturday–Sunday programme break meant that two separate shows were available at the same theatre during a weekend, and this was preferable to the exhibitors.

Another experiment which was retained was the split release, whereby a film considered less popular than average was shown in only half the available cinemas on a circuit, the other half playing a similarly blighted film, or revivals. This limited form of release made it much harder, if not impossible, for a British film to make any money, but the circuits' answer would be that the alternative was that the film would not be shown at all. It was argued that such a method of presentation helped to compensate for the demise of the National circuit. It did call in to account a certain skill in picking films and in assuming the degree of their popular appeal. Consequently, first ABC and then Rank built up a small group of provincial theatres into a pre-release circuit which would offer some guidance to the London programmes. It was after disappointing provincial returns that the Beatles' cartoon film, *The Yellow Submarine*, was withdrawn from a blanket London general release in spite of favourable critical reviews, and, later, an enthusiastic reception in the United States. It was still the big circuits who had the power to call the tune.

However, it would be unfair not to point out that the reluctance with which unusual films were shown in the fifties was relaxed to a certain extent. Once Rank had a total ban on X certificate films, but this was gradually relaxed as more and more worthwhile films appeared in the X category. It was still rare for a foreign-language film to get a circuit booking, but occasionally they showed up in split releases. Certain excellent films were denied even that privilege; Truffaut's *Fahrenheit 451*, made at Pinewood, had a handful of bookings; Albert Finney's *Charlie Bubbles* was barely seen outside the West End, in spite of good reviews, and Jack Gold's *The Bofors Gun* was similarly buried. A British Lion film of some merit, Desmond Davis's *The Uncle*, was refused a showing in or out of the West End, and remains unseen to date, nine years after production, except on television.

Ambitious refurbishing programmes for the circuit cinemas were put into operation. Some were made smaller, or re-seated, so that there was more leg room and fewer seats. Both Rank and ABC recognized at last the need to make their remaining houses attractive and modern. The old gilt and plush mammoth Trocadero at the Elephant and Castle was pulled down and replaced by a starkly elegant new Odeon in a startling concrete design by Erno Goldfinger. Rank not only opened new West End Odeons at Marble Arch and St Martins Lane but re-modelled the Odeon, Leicester Square, and the Leicester Square Theatre, in the former case destroying one of the best examples of thirties cinema interior decoration at a time when its art-deco charm was just becoming recognized, and replacing it with the self-conscious design gimmicks of the sixties.

Two reasons led to the establishment of cinema clubs in the West End, such as the Compton, where continental films were shown to 'members-only' audiences. Firstly, there was the lack of small public cinemas with highly specialized programmes, and, secondly, the situation regarding film censorship. While the British Board of Film Censors had, with the passing of time, slowly become more liberal, an astonishingly high number of films were altered at the Board's insistence, and in some cases totally rejected. The club performances did not require a certificate from either the BBFC or the local licensing authority. Much of the material shown in this way was hardly worth seeing, but no doubt it gave pleasure to a few. Yet the position of the film censor became more and more invidious as the sixties progressed, and when finally, in 1968, the Lord Chamberlain's grip on the theatre was abolished, Lord Harlech, the President, and John Trevelyan, the then Secretary and active functionary of the Board, were left on a precarious limb. It was argued that censorship protected not only the industry from unreasonable prosecutions, but young people from exposure to corrupting influences, and society generally. There is no written code of practice, it having been decided years earlier that an enlightened form of censorship could not exist if it was bound by case law and precedents. In that respect, at any rate, wisdom was shown.

Yet one of the most disturbing aspects of the British system is the fact that judgements are often made on aesthetic grounds and that certain words, actions or implications are given greater freedom in films of 'merit' than in less worthwhile productions. Which means that the censor is also expected to be a critic and to interpret the degree of artistic integrity expressed in a given work. Film-makers usually submit scripts in advance of shooting to the BBFC for general guidance. These are often returned with suggestions for modifying certain scenes to ensure an X, A, or U certificate as desired. While Mr Trevelyan's taste and acumen were admired throughout the industry, it was disturbing that he, and not the film-makers themselves, was in a position to determine the pace at which the British cinema could move. For many years, in fact since its introduction in the early fifties, it has been felt that the X certificate had shortcomings in that it provided too wide an umbrella for films to be classified under and that a more discriminating certificate was needed, possibly with an age limit of eighteen rather than sixteen years. In this way fewer films would need to be cut or rejected, if the notion of having a film censor at all has to be endured.

During the latter part of the sixties there was a considerable body of opinion in favour of abolishing the office completely, and making films liable, as with books, under the Obscene Publications Act. While in the new permissive climate of the times such a move would appear to have logic, the industry itself might be unwilling to take the risk, regarding its voluntary policing system as the only alternative to an authoritarian degree of interference. Nevertheless, the public rows between producers and the censor grew in number, filling yards of newspaper columns with cantankerous and unnecessary dispute. In mid-1969, Mr Trevelyan announced that it was proposed to eliminate the censorship letters A, U and X, and to replace them with numerals from 1 to 4 to indicate the category of the film. Such a change was overdue, even if only partly meeting the objections to film censorship. It was not put into effect because it was felt to be too confusing for the public. Instead, a new category, AA, was introduced and modifications were made to the entire classification system. It meant that the age for admission to X films was raised to eighteen, although conversely children could attend A showings alone, with parental permission. Silvio Narrizano halted a showing to the press of his film *Blue*, having not seen what had been perpetrated on it by the censors' shears until that moment. Mr Trevelyan himself appeared before the press and explained his reasons for removing a fleeting and harmless glimpse of pubic hair in the Swedish film, *Hugs and Kisses*. A few seconds cut from *Rosemary's Baby* were left in for the press show, but Fleet Street remained uncorrupted. Four minutes were required by the BBFC to be removed from *The Killing of Sister George* in a lesbian love scene. However, the Greater London Council, in granting a local X certificate, only demanded a forty second cut, while to compound the lunacy of the workings of censorship the nearby county of Berkshire allowed the film to be shown within its boundaries with no cuts at all. Such inconsistencies, far from indicating the degrees to which people in neighbouring geographical areas were susceptible to the corrosive influence of the cinema on their psyches, merely threw the censorship system into ridicule and disrepute.

In spite of the continuing decline in audiences and cinemas, there was an encouraging trend towards the specialist 'art house' type of theatre. In London's West End the number of cinemas regularly showing continental films multiplied. By 1972 there were fifteen of them and this total did not include the cinemas specializing in nudist and pseudo-pornographic films of poor quality. The Academy, a pioneer in the showing of non-English-language films, split into three parts during the sixties, with three auditoria of varying sizes on the same premises. The luxurious and well-designed Curzon, in Mayfair, built in 1934 in a modernistic Netherlandish style, was pulled down and replaced by an equally luxurious theatre in the lower depths of an office building. Many news theatres, which once mushroomed across Central London in the days when newsreels were plentiful, were converted for showing either programmes of continental films or old features that had exhausted their general release possibilities. More and more provincial cinemas regularly screened foreign films. Several towns outside London were sites for regional film theatres, which were started up by the British Film Institute as local branches of the National Film Theatre. Since 1957 the National Film Theatre has been located in a purpose-built theatre under the southern end of Waterloo Bridge, after five years in the old Telekinema, a leftover from the South Bank exhibition of the Festival of Britain. The regional film theatres began modestly, some operating in borrowed university halls and other places, on occasional evenings, but by 1968 there were twenty-three in operation throughout the country, although the building programme for purpose-built theatres suffered an economic setback when the Government trimmed the expenditure.

The opportunities for seeing classic films from the whole spectrum of world cinema were further enhanced by showings on television, particularly on BBC-2, of so-called minority interest works. Many films have been shown in this way and not in the cinemas at all; others have commanded far higher audiences in one television exposure than during the course of a long West End art house run. Another indication of awakening interest in the serious cinema was the proliferation of books published towards the end of the sixties, in contrast with the handful produced in earlier years. Several publishers produced series, Studio Vista with Moviebacks and Picturebacks; Secker and Warburg with Cinema One; Zwemmers with an extensive range of paperback volumes devoted to film subjects; Lorrimer, which specialized in publishing filmscripts and many others. There was an awakened sociological interest in the output of the fan magazines of the forties, most of which failed to continue publishing once the decline set in. The film star stills, posters, even campaign books issued to the trade with a new movie, became coveted cult objects and many serious artists (in Britain David Hockney and Peter Blake; in America James Rosenquist and Andy Warhol), turned to the idioms of golden age film publicity as a thematic inspiration for their art. Many film figures of the thirties and forties whose work had been accepted as routinely competent in its time were astonished and gratified to find themselves taken up by film societies and invited to lecture on the significance of their work, which may have consisted of B picture westerns.

Another interesting manifestation of the period was the emergence into the open at last of the private collector. The preservation of films is fraught with difficulties. There is the instability and vulnerability of film stock, which has to be kept at an even temperature to avoid the consequences of the emulsion becoming sticky and detaching itself from its base. Many important films have rotted away, forgotten in rusty cans, only to be discovered too late, after serious deterioration has rendered the print unfit for projection. Another problem concerns that of the laws of copyright, which when applied to films are complicated and difficult to work. Experience has shown that it is better to err on the side of caution.

Many films are denied showings because it is not possible to unravel the current copyright-holders from a maze of transactions over the years. Companies which go out of existence can hand their rights over to another company which might also disappear, thus producing a whole chain of inherited responsibilities until the eventual position is so obscure that no one can make an accurate assessment of it. A large number of films, often in massive lots rather than individually, have been sold to television, creating new copyright problems. The National Film Archive makes an attempt to preserve the best of contemporary films and a committee of critics and members of the British Film Institute convenes regularly to decide on the preservation list. Owing to the high cost of prints and the smallness of the fund available for film purchase only a fraction of the material does in fact find its way to the vaults of the National Film Archive, and that which does is often the result of donations from the film industry, who might supply a used print free of charge. An attempt was made in 1969 in a Private Member's Bill to achieve a statutory deposit system similar to that applied to books entered in the British Museum, but with the cost to be met from a special levy, so that the film-makers could be paid for their prints. But a book is a relatively inexpensive item compared with a film print. An ordinary 35mm. black and white print costs around £250. A 70mm. print in colour is nearer £2,500. When a print is deposited in the National Film Archive, in its vaults at Aston Clinton and Berkhamsted, it is normally not shown – a dupe projection print has first to be made, entailing further expense. It is, in view of all the hazards, not surprising that many films do not survive in any form and others survive merely as fragments.

But the work of the National Film Archive has independently been supplanted by many individuals who have collected films or film stills as a hobby, and continued it as an obsessive urge to save what was in danger of being lost. The most prominent are Philip Jenkinson, whose regular television appearances have done a great deal to generate an interest in old films; Kevin Brownlow, who has virtually single-handedly reconstructed the work of the great French film-maker, Abel Gance; and John Kobal, whose outstanding private collection of film stills contains much material no longer held by the originating studios, which regularly purge their files of accumulated and outdated photographs for the sake of the space they take up.

The Rank–ABC domination of the exhibition side continued and during the sixties was subjected to an intensive scrutiny by the Monopolies Commission. Their report was published in October 1966. It found that there were certain aspects that were felt to be disturbing.

... the dominance of ABPC and Rank, and the rigidity of the industry which results from this and from the practice of barring, are detrimental to the service which the industry gives the public. In the first place film production is not governed directly by consumer choice and film-makers are not free to make the films that they believe in, subject only to the willingness of the public to see them. Instead, production is effectively determined by the policies of only two companies without the check of competition. Admittedly, we have no reason to think that they do not act conscientiously and seek to meet what they believe to be the public demand. But the public's task cannot be anticipated, and we believe that the public would be better served by a freer market.

However, the Commission was caught in a difficult dilemma when it came to suggesting remedies, admitting that any drastic measure would hasten a total collapse. Inevitably the measures they eventually suggested were not particularly draconian. They found that conditional hire, lack of competition and barring were against the public interest and recommended that the two organizations should extend the practice of flexible booking, in giving trial runs to films whose appeal to the public was in doubt and in giving partial bookings to films of clearly limited appeal. They called for a reduction in any bar outside the West End to no more than four weeks, and for any exhibitor to have a right to bid after that time. They called for an end to conditional hire. They also asked for Rank to discontinue the practice of giving regular weekly bookings to its own documentary films and that they should book documentary and other short films on their merits. There was one dissentient to this particular clause among the Commissioners; he took the view that Rank were entitled to choose the way they filed their own programmes.

This last clause was aimed at the *Look at Life* series, which began in 1959 as a replacement for the two newsreels, Universal and Gaumont-British, closed by Rank as an economy measure. *Look at Life* was a weekly colour featurette on a topical subject, lacking the incisive depth approach of the old *This Modern Age* series, more like a superficial popular magazine article. The blandness of its treatment of subject matter was usually inoffensive, undramatic and unintentionally amusing. Apart from colour it offered nothing more than a concentrated item from a typical television magazine programme. Through the years the *Look at Life* team went on churning out their weekly subjects, later reduced to thirty-nine a year, but in 1969 *Look at Life* itself was closed down after 507 editions, not as a result of the Monopolies Commission verdict but because it was no longer economical to keep it going, even with a guaranteed number of bookings. Its closure came quite soon after that of *Pathé Pictorial*, a similar short-subject series made in colour, which was generally shown on the other circuit. Of the five newsreels which had once regularly appeared on British screens, only one remained, Movietone, and the great majority of cinemas no longer bothered to show newsfilms. In America the newsreel had become completely extinct by the sixties and in Britain much of the material shown was of a less topical magazine feature type rather than spot news, except when some planned spectacle (a state visit, a royal wedding or a major sporting event) took place which provided an opportunity to get colour film into the cinemas a day or two later. Although colour transmissions began on the second BBC television channel in 1967 it was not until late 1969 that the two main British networks were able to switch from monochrome, and sets capable of picking up the new signals were at first few and expensive. So there was still a slight point in favour of cinema newsreels in colour. It is worth noting that their existence ensured that certain historical events were still recorded on 35mm. film, for television newsfilm was normally shot on 16mm., with much lower standards of definition. But the preservation of actuality for posterity could be an expensive exercise.

The Monopolies Commission's suggestions were for the most part tame, only because the Report recognized the disastrous consequences that might result from any drastic remedy. The recommendations were sufficiently mild to be practicable, but they made no real difference to the situation.

The ACTT, on the one hand, called for the withdrawal of Britain's application for entry into the European Common Market, and on the other urged the establishment of a third circuit, under national owner-ship, to provide an outlet for the independent film-makers who were being crowded out. In 1962–3 the number of British films playing in ABC and Rank theatres was just over fifty per cent of the total, twenty per cent more than quota. Yet there were still many films unable to get bookings or delayed for an unreasonable length of time before being shown, thus incurring heavy interest charges. One such film, which took more than a year to find its way to the cinema, was Sidney Furie's *The Leather Boys*. Apart from the investment problems of such a delay it was argued that a film could date or fail to catch the mood of the audience, which is always a constantly shifting factor. The actors and the director concerned could also find their careers temporarily stalemated. The main problem with the Third Release idea was the lack of theatres available to form such a circuit; it was partly for this reason that the National release collapsed, and since its disappearance the attrition of exhibition outlets had continued at a steady rate. Yet in 1969 there was still strong feeling on the left that a government-owned circuit would have to be established, but by that time the solution was seen in terms of requisition or nationalization of part or all of the Rank and ABC theatres.

To the continuing story of crisis in the sixties, successor to crisis in the fifties, which in turn supplanted crisis in the forties, there was the débâcle of British Lion, the third British distributing force and the only one to lack a circuit on which to show its product. The National Film Finance Corporation had an extensive stake in the company for historical reasons. In late 1963 it became apparent that the chairman of the NFFC, Sir Nutcombe Hume, who was a known advocate of non-participation in the film industry by the government, was planning to sell the company to a selected bidder. The first step was for the NFFC to exercise its option to buy, for £795,000, the shares held by the Board members appointed in 1958, David Kingsley, the managing director, the Boultings, Frank Launder and Sidney Gilliatt. The option to acquire these shares after five years had been one of the requisites for the re-established company. At the same time the NFFC were required to offer the Board the option to buy the company, but established a tight time limit of little more than a month. On 20 December the British Lion case was discussed in the House of Commons and a government statement was made that it was believed the company would be better off in private rather than public hands. The opposition case was endorsed by the five directors, that only through the guarantees of public investment could British Lion maintain its independence. A small group of Tory MPs, led by Iain Macleod and Angus Maude, were ranged with the film-makers, the film unions and the Opposition, in deploring the proposed sale. Then on 29 December a bombshell was dropped, when it was revealed that the only bidder to come forward was Sydney Box, who led a group which included Lord Willis, with the backing of Standard Industrial Trust. Great optimism prevailed; it was expected that the mechanics of the sale would be completed inside three weeks.

It was at this point that second thoughts seemed to occur. Sir Michael Balcon wrote to the NFFC offering to put up a competitive bid amidst considerable publicity. The government gave an assurance that the final decision would be made without indecent haste. The *fait accompli* with Sydney Box was unscrambled, and it was laid down that the bidder for British Lion would have to find £1,600,000 and give the NFFC assurances that the Shepperton studios would be kept open for independent production. The bids now came in thick and fast. Balcon brought in Tony Richardson and John Osborne, with whom he had been associated through Bryanston and Woodfall, and also Brian Epstein, Joseph Janni, John Schlesinger and the American distributor and exhibitor, Walter Reade. Leslie Grade was joined in a competitive bid by John Woolf and Sam Spiegel. John Bloom, an ill-fated washing-machine millionaire, headed a group containing the talents of impresario Jack Hylton, Anthony Mann and Terence Young. The Federation of Film Unions entered a bid. The most bizarre was that of Edward Martell's Freedom Group, a right-wing political body.

In February 1964 Edward Heath announced in the Commons for the government that the NFFC would hold a special share in the company which would prevent its voluntary liquidation or sale, and could veto the disposal of the studios. Acrimony was rampant, writs for slander passed between aggrieved parties, the Boultings throughout kept up a brilliant propaganda campaign with unabated zeal. There were many references to Crichel Down, an earlier and notorious example of a government's high-handed disposal of a public asset without reference to democratic principles.

Eventually it was announced that the consortium headed by Sir Michael Balcon was the successful contender for British Lion. With the existing Board and the new names associated with the project Balcon took the studios over, announcing the intention of instituting an annual production programme of between ten and fifteen films a year. The rift between British Lion and the two circuits was to be healed, although the company would not betray its principles of independence. The Shepperton studios would, in spite of their development potential, be retained for film-making. The company would trade competitively with both Rank and ABC. The presence of Walter Reade in the new set-up was part of a campaign to secure showings in the United States. With a heavy sigh of relief most of the parties concerned in the British Lion affair concluded that the outcome was reasonably hopeful and that the company had fallen into the best possible hands.

To Balcon's disappointment he found that his talents had only been needed by the new company during the setting-up period and once in business his intentions of initiating a heavy production programme were not observed. Many of his colleagues felt that the risks in getting films booked on to either of the two circuits were too high. Balcon, feeling that the company had been acquired on a mandate to make films and to support independent producers, considered that in the circumstances he could no longer continue as chairman and resigned. Lord Goodman was appointed in his place. In his autobiography, *Michael Balcon Presents . . . A Lifetime of Films*, Sir Michael wrote:

If I had known how the whole adventure into British Lion was going to turn out there would have been no justification, except on principle, for any interfering over the original Sydney Box deal for control of the company. I could have saved myself a great deal of work and worry, and in the end severe disappointment. I have no reason to believe that Mr Box would not have done just as much by way of actual film-making as was now the official policy of British Lion.

Later Walter Reade withdrew from British Lion, his shareholding being taken over by Max Rayne, who then became deputy chairman.

David Kingsley and Joseph Janni got rid of their shares and later still, in 1968, it was announced that the company's structure would be amended to permit the financial participation of the general public. Its valuation when this was completed was £3 million, a significant increase from the £1,600,000 purchase price of the company four years earlier. As a production company its output has been severely limited, its record of 1958–64, when it set the pace for the industry's revival, being replaced by caution and playing safe, either by producing films such as *Till Death Us Do Part*, or by not making films at all.

Two economic factors that could not be escaped determined the industry's production policy: the first that no film could succeed without a circuit booking and even then would be unlikely to make a profit in the domestic market; the other that anything up to ninety per cent of the films made in Britain derived their financing at least in some part from American sources. On the whole this system was more objectionable in principle than in practice. It enabled studios and technicians to stay in work and it also meant that many films were treated equally on American screens, even though their British character may not have been intrinsically apparent – although there were many exceptions.

The attraction of Eady money, the intention of which had never been to help finance the runaway American production but which nevertheless had no means of excluding them, even if it was proved desirable, gave considerable financial advantages. One of the hazards was the uncertainty of the continuation of American interest in Britain as a production centre. An improvement in the conditions attached to filming in Hollywood could result in a mass withdrawal similar to that which occurred at the outbreak of the Second World War. An almost total collapse of the British industry would then be inevitable as time was to show. In Hollywood itself the runaway productions were viewed with considerable alarm, particularly as there was a similar fear of unemployment in their studios. Should an American fund be set up in the future on the same lines as that in Britain the inducements to producers might be sufficient to set them scurrying back to take advantage of it. Suddenly the British film industry would be depleted. Eady money at least ensured that the American-financed films made in Britain relied on the employment of many British craftsmen and technicians, and for this reason Britain was a more attractive film centre than other European countries. But that attraction could only last as long as the Americans used Eady money. Demands to make it harder for American films to qualify were self-defeating. The dilemma was cruel. The only real solution was to raise the level of British-financed production gradually, a difficult enough task at any time, and during a period of protracted economic restraint almost impossible. The American system of film financing is a great deal less complicated than the British. Instead of 'front money' and 'end money', with all its caveats and paperwork, it is normal for an American company to make a full 100 per cent advance for a project which it finds attractive. Even the National Film Finance Corporation found such competition was rendering its role superfluous. To combat the trend it negotiated an agreement with the Rank Organization for each party to put up £500,000, with the National Provincial Bank coming in for a third £500,000, thus creating a fund permitting loans up to a million and a half pounds, the films concerned to be decided by the NFFC and released in Rank cinemas. But however welcome, such a new source of finance meant that even more production was to be tied to one circuit.

In 1966 a further depressing fiscal burden was added to the film industry in the shape of the government's Selective Employment Tax, applied to the service industries. SET was another factor rendering exhibition difficult, for the tax had to be paid on a *per capita* basis for every employee. Obviously, film exhibition was not being singled out for victimization; this particular tax fell widely across the national business life and was one of the most unpopular measures of the Labour Government. The Conservative party gave an assurance that on their return to office it would be abolished, although it was not until late 1971 that the phasing out of the tax was begun.

Some elements of the film industry looked with interest at the rival medium, television. Many film companies had extensive interests in it – Rank through Southern, ABC in ABC TV, later to become Thames, Granada Theatres in Granada Television, Balcon in Border TV and so on. FIDO, the scheme to keep cinema films off the box, had failed, but there was still a five-year bar which, while preventing recent films from being seen, also stopped the production by television organizations of cinema films. The delay was harder on the independent producer who could not afford to wait five years before getting the additional return on capital for a television sale.

In 1965, after protracted discussions, a limited experiment in pay television was begun. The system consisted of a slot meter coupled with a domestic cable-TV receiver. When a coin was inserted the picture unscrambled. Pay-TV, the only company which eventually survived to conduct the experiment, relied on cinema films for the bulk of its output, with a six-month bar. Part of the profits were to be distributed to cinemas in the pay TV area if diminished audiences resulted. Bravely, Pay-TV, a consortium financed by British Relay who supplied the land lines and sets, ABC and British Home Entertainments conducted the experiment, in Westminster, Southwark and Sheffield. It was impossible to make a profit in three such small areas and when after two years the company asked the Postmaster General for a licence to extend it and was refused, pay television came to an end. Similar experiments in North America had also foundered. Pay-TV was not to be an answer to the film industry's troubles.

21 *Nouvelle Vague* or *Déjà Vu?*

The brief period of 1959–63, with its new hopes in film output – Tony Richardson's *Look Back in Anger* and *The Entertainer*, Karel Reisz's *Saturday Night and Sunday Morning*, the Attenborough–Forbes combination which produced *The Angry Silence* and *Whistle Down the Wind* – continued to display work of interest and excellence. Richardson followed his previous success with an adaptation of Shelagh Delaney's play, *A Taste of Honey*, which was a depressing account of a Salford girl who is made pregnant by a coloured sailor, lives with a young and kindly homosexual and is eventually driven out by her mother, who has in turn been abandoned after a brief marriage. That such unpromising material should produce a film of warmth, humour and occasional beauty was a tribute to the acting, particularly that of Rita Tushingham, in her first film part, and Murray Melvin. Occasionally, the visual impact was swamped by an over-conscious stylization, so that long sequences seemed to consist of Jo wandering along lyrically photographed canal banks, or walking wistfully among groups of playing children.

Richardson had meanwhile made and failed in an attempt at filming in Hollywood, his subject being an adaptation of Faulkner's *Sanctuary*, which seemed nerveless and disappointing. His next British film was *The Loneliness of the Long-Distance Runner*, from a short story by Alan Sillitoe, about a Borstal boy who quite deliberately fails to win a cross-country race in order to spite authority, in this case a platitudinous, wrong-headed governor, played by Michael Redgrave. The picture also introduced a new face to British films which, like Rita Tushingham's, lacked the conventional film-star gloss, but instead had a fascinating ugliness. It was that of Tom Courtenay. Again Richardson allowed style to swamp content. The story was told in a confusing series of flashbacks, suggesting reasons for the central character being in Borstal. The photography by Walter Lassally was lyrical and mysterious, with its treatment of early morning solitary runs through misty woods and dew-laden grass. Fashionable borrowings from French prototypes, mostly Truffaut's *Les Quatre Cent Coups*, were incorporated almost like nervous tics; for instance, the reiterated device of the dialogue of the next scene overlapping on to the one preceding it, or jump cuts, or speeded-up action used not because they were relevant to the point of the film, but because they provided a veneer of trendiness. Such irritations detracted from the worth of the film and have consistently marred Richardson's skill as a director.

His next film was a costumed historical work, far removed from the contemporary provincial scene of his earlier pictures. It was *Tom Jones*, from Henry Fielding's magnificent eighteenth-century novel of the adventures of a lively young man born on the wrong side of the blanket. His hero was played by Albert Finney with verve and energy. It was a bawdy, romping film with great gusts of lascivious humour, its stately homes run amok by pigs, its comic squire falling under his horse as he tries to spur it into action, its lovers munching apples in a sexually inflammatory manner. The cast, particularly High Griffith's Squire Western and Edith Evans's Miss Western, performed in the spirit of the work, that of a promiscuous charade, always entertaining and visually interesting thanks to Lassally's camera work, but marred as before by the intrusion of jump cuts, freeze frames, speeded-up movement, titles over dialogue scenes and actors addressing the audience directly – in short the whole bag of fashionable self-indulgent tricks. In particular, a lengthy stag hunt sequence loses itself because it turns into a crude piece of anti-blood sport propaganda. As a film *Tom Jones* had an interesting history, failing to get an initial circuit booking. Finally, United Artists came to the rescue and played it at the London Pavilion, where it proceeded to break records. When it was eventually given a proper release it proved to be one of 1963's biggest box-office successes.

Among new directors to emerge in this period was John Schlesinger, who had since going down from Oxford been employed as an actor, and as a BBC film producer for the *Monitor* arts programme. He made a short documentary film for the British Transport Commission, called *Terminus*, depicting a day at Waterloo Station, which attracted sufficient critical attention to get a subsidiary booking on the Rank circuit. His first feature film was *A Kind of Loving*, from a provincial novel by Stan Barstow, with Alan Bates as a bored young man who drifts into marriage with a dull girl he has made pregnant, and his eventual realization that the trap has closed. The theme, close to much that had already been seen, may have seemed unpromising, but Schlesinger managed to keep the interest alive without recourse to sentimentality or obviousness, or for that matter a Richardsonian retreat into trendy cliché. Certain aspects of the English scene were faithfully observed – the office dance, the ITV quiz, the off-season seaside resort. The script was by Willis Hall and Keith Waterhouse, who were also responsible for the next Schlesinger film, *Billy Liar*, which had its antecedents as both a novel and play. The mood of the new piece was much more one of satire, a feeling established immediately with the credit title sequence in which the camera flashes past serried rows of suburban houses, while Godfrey Winn intones record requests on the *Housewife's Choice* programme. Billy Fisher (Tom Courtenay) is an inveterate daydreamer, retreating into a fantasy world when the problems of his day-to-day existence in a Northern undertaker's office become too much, which is frequently. A free-wheeling and interesting girl (Julie Christie making an early film appearance) persuades him to go south to London, but his nerve fails him at the last minute. As a study of a compulsive liar, with dreams of uniformed despotism mixed up with the complications of his real life, Tom Courtenay manages to contain what could be a wild caricature. But *Billy Liar*, although more entertaining than *A Kind of Loving*, lacked the roundness of tone of the earlier film, and veered wildly in its moods between high satire and straightforward observation. The intrusion of Julie Christie into the ambience of Wilfred Pickles and Mona Washbourne seemed mistaken, her particular form of swinging Chelsea dolliness being anachronistic and her attraction to the hero unlikely. Nevertheless, the film was a convincing consolidation of Schlesinger's power as a director.

The first feature film to be directed by Lindsay Anderson also appeared in 1963. It was *This Sporting Life*, adapted by David Storey from his novel about a league rugby-playing miner. Richard Harris was the leading actor and Rachel Roberts played the widow with whom he lived. As a study of a hopeless, incompatible relationship, leading as it does to an inevitable tragedy, the film must count as one of the finest ever to emerge from a British studio. The hero, a man of force and violence, seeking his outlets on the rugby field and in the monumental orgies of beer-swilling that follow, is shown to be a guilt-ridden weakling, incapable of comprehending his communication failure with the woman he loves. The human theme is carefully and thoroughly explored, the characters emerge as real and believable, the detail is as studied and vivid as the broad concept. In the sequences on the rugby field the visual images achieve beauty and poetic heroism, with the slowed-down movement of hulking players colliding and crunching off one another like muddy giants in some medieval war. The film failed at the box-office; all kinds of reasons could be produced – unsuitable publicity, a theme too scaring for audiences to accept, or just general insensitivity to material of real worth. The pre-conditioning of the northern scene in the Woodfall films had made the genre into something of a cliché; there had been too many with the authentically photographed backgrounds and accents, producing an anti-reaction among filmgoers. It was more than five years before Anderson made another full-length feature. Perhaps an improvement in taste had occurred in the interim, for *If.* . . . was a magnificent and resounding box-office success.

Richardson, Schlesinger and Anderson succeeded in getting films away from the studios and into real streets, real buildings: *A Kind of Loving* was shot in Stockport, *This Sporting Life* in Wakefield. Undoubtedly part of the retreat to the north was a desire to throw off the southern studios and southern values. The provincial scene, so long ignored in the cinema, had now become an integral part. Not all regionally-based films were made in the north, however, which was something to be grateful for. Clive Donner, whose early films showed warmth and skill in the handling of children, emerged as a director of promise with *Some People*, a story of teenagers in Bristol, which had been conceived as a propaganda piece for the Duke of Edinburgh Award Scheme. A conventional treatment of the potential delinquents who turn to the Youth Club and the Award Scheme as an alternative to terrorizing motorists on ton-up motor-bikes and smashing up property, it managed to treat its banal theme with considerable warmth and humour. Kenneth More was saddled with the somewhat unbelievable role of an aerospace scientist who is organist and choirmaster when off duty, and represents the other side of the generation gap. One of the tearaways was a youthful David Hemmings.

Donner's next film was made on the minute budget of £30,000 in a derelict house in Hackney, and was produced by Michael Birkett. It was Harold Pinter's screenplay of his own play, *The Caretaker*, with Alan Bates and Donald Pleasence, who had played the same parts in the theatre, and with Robert Shaw augmenting the small cast. It was one of the most successful translations of a play into film, largely because no attempt was made to open it out, the action mostly taking place in the confined space of a real, cluttered attic. Donald Pleasence's performance as the unpleasant tramp, lured into the house by the Robert Shaw character to be the caretaker, and thus arousing the jealousy of Alan Bates as his brother, was magnificent. The editing, constantly coming into close-up and cutting rapidly from one shot to another, was perhaps too fussy for the nature of the film. The smallness of the cast was a reminder that Pinter had established his playwrighting skill in the confined medium of television. *The Caretaker*, with its low budget, was deliberately designed for a limited release and was an attempt to prove that a circuit booking was not absolutely necessary for a film. But in spite of a long run at the Academy in the West End it failed to get its money back.

Donner's next film was frankly commercial, again with Alan Bates as an ambitious gatecrasher into the wealthy upper classes. *Nothing But the Best* was an attempt to expose the empty and brittle affluence of the early sixties, with its tastes pre-packaged by television programmes and colour supplements ('Is Rembrandt hip or square this year?'). The screenplay, by Frederic Raphael, contained many funny lines and was particularly successful in outlining the character played by Denholm Elliott, a seedy ex-public-school conman who teaches our hero the manners and methods needed to marry the boss's daughter, played by Millicent Martin, with Harry Andrews as her father and head of the smart West End estate agency which employs him. One or two neat camera tricks fitted the acidly satirical style of the film – a long close-up of hero and heroine for instance, clinched in dance on what appears to be some dark night club floor revealed in a long track back to be the deck of an empty barge with a portable record player.

Donner's *Here We Go Round the Mulberry Bush* of three years later was also about a young man trying to get somewhere, but in this instance the object of his goal was the end of his virginity, the film being the story of an adolescent boy, modishly set in a Home Counties new town, trying to make out with the local birds, in between studying and coping with the indifference and indolence of his working-class parents. Denholm Elliott was excellently cast in a small but immensely funny part, of the permanently sozzled father of a posh girl-friend. The story was from a novel by Hunter Davies, in part undoubtedly autobiographical, although Donner wisely moved the location away from the north west to the south east.

That working-class comedy could move to London from its provincial exile was demonstrated in 1963 with *Sparrows Can't Sing*, which was directed by Joan Littlewood, from the play she had earlier presented at Stratford East by Stephen Lewis – who also incidentally played a part in the film. Affectionate and exuberant in its portrayal of the modern working-class cockney, it contained some pleasant performances by James Booth as a seaman back from two years at sea, looking for his attractive and sprightly blonde wife, Barbara Windsor, and Roy Kinnear as the fat, put-upon brother of the man she has gone off to live with. *Live Now, Pay Later*, directed by Jay Lewis, was a satirical study of the suburban hire-purchase mentality, with Ian Hendry as a smart salesman who eventually meets his nemesis. *The Leather Boys*, directed by Sidney Furie, a young Canadian film-maker who had migrated to Britain, had Rita Tushingham in the role of a wife deserted by her husband for a homosexual relationship. Set in a London of motor-bike caffs and cheap lodging houses, the film was sharp and bitter in tone. It was delayed for a year before it finally got a booking on the ABC circuit.

Sidney Furie also directed *The Young Ones*, which was favourably received as an attempt at a British musical. The putting-on-a-show theme, with its group of youngsters determined to make good in face of opposition from their elders, was hardly startlingly original, but the young cast was a good one, led by Cliff Richard and the Shadows, and the numbers were put across with spirit. A more ambitious Cliff Richard musical, *Summer Holiday*, was made as a follow-up, and directed by Peter Yates. In this the same (or a similar) group of youngsters took an old London bus off on a trip across Europe to Greece. Furie returned to the genre of the Cliff Richard musical in the following year, with *Wonderful Life*, this time with the exotic locations of the Azores providing the colourful background. Meanwhile, he had made *The Boys*, a courtroom film about four youths on trial for murdering a garage hand. The action rarely moved outside the Old Bailey and the effect of the film was sombre and dramatic, marred slightly by the casting of Richard Todd as prosecuting counsel and Robert Morley as the defence.

On an altogether gentler level, the work of Desmond Davis, who had been the camera operator for some of Tony Richardson's earlier films, attracted attention. The first full-length feature he directed was *The Girl with Green Eyes*, from a novel by Edna O'Brien, with sensitive performances by Rita Tushingham and Lynn Redgrave, and Peter Finch playing a middle-aged writer having an affair with the first of the two girls in Dublin. The photography by Manny Wynn was excellent, evocative, atmospheric, while the direction, though borrowing many of the fashionable tricks of the Richardson days, used them with a degree of restraint. Davis made another film shortly afterwards called *The Uncle*, a study of the relationship between childhood and the adult world. This film was not given any bookings outside Plymouth, where it was largely shot, and that such a well-made, intelligently acted and directed piece of work remained unseen was a telling criticism of the monopolistic power of the circuits and the impotence of British Lion when it came to dealing with it. Davis returned to the more conventional love story genre in his next film, *I Was Happy Here*, which had Sarah Miles as a girl returning to the Irish coastal village where she was born. The mood was absurdly and disastrously shattered by *Smashing Time*, which reunited Lynn Redgrave and Rita Tushingham, this time playing a pair of provincial dolly-birds attempting to take London by storm. Made sharp by prods at the world of pop singers and promoters, public relations men and gossip reporters, the film was curiously old-fashioned in spite of its relentless pursuit of mid-sixties contemporaneity. It was Davis's most ambitious work and undoubtedly his most disappointing – a glaring example of the fizzling out of the Woodfall movement that had begun with the sixties, pretension submerging invention.

Karel Reisz, whose *Saturday Night and Sunday Morning* seemed to be one of the most sincere and effective attempts at the provincial protest genre, turned to a well-known theatrical warhorse for his next film, the grisly thriller by Emlyn Williams, *Night Must Fall*, which did not appear until 1964. The delay was in part owing to his abortive attempts to make with Albert Finney a film about the nineteenth-century Australian criminal, Ned Kelly. Using Finney in the role of the psychopathic Danny, who hacks a woman to pieces in between working hours at a country hotel, Reisz dressed the story with strong psychological images and tried to build up an atmosphere of horror just beneath the surface, rather in the manner of Hitchcock's *Psycho*. The main trouble was that Finney's performance suggested abnormality immediately and his attractiveness to women was slightly implausible. In any case the plot, depending on horrific coincidences, was too stagey to bear anything more than a straightforward treatment. A promising opening, with the camera wandering through a thick wood, discovering the murderer hacking away at his victim, proved to be deceptive. *Night Must Fall* was a great disappointment after the director's previous work. His next film, *Morgan, A Suitable Case for*

Treatment, also delved into mental breakdown, this time exploring schizophrenia, with David Warner playing a young artist who identifies with a gorilla and builds up a series of disturbed fantasies. It was another film of the social misfit, but Morgan Delt is a far more advanced case than Arthur Seaton or Jimmy Porter or Jim Dixon. As a study of mental disintegration, the film was far more successful (and certainly funnier) than *Night Must Fall*, and additionally was graced with the presence of Vanessa Redgrave in the part of the wealthy and incompatible wife.

The primary study of psychological disintegration in the early sixties was Peter Brook's interpretation of William Golding's pessimistic novel, *Lord of the Flies*, which traces the change of a group of schoolboys, shipwrecked on a tropical island after some future nuclear Armageddon, from normal human beings into primitive savages. A microcosm of the outer world, the island society rejects the wise Ralph and the weak Piggy, following instead the bullying leadership of Jack, who believes in the rule of fear. Brook achieved immense realism by shipping a group of boys, most of whom had never acted before, to a remote island, and allowing something of the society depicted in the book to develop. Instinctively the boys did find their leader and did gradually alter their standards. Brook shot the film in sequence, often using improvised dialogue and action. The horrific power of the book, one of the most compelling of its decade, was perhaps muted when translated into filmed images, but *Lord of the Flies* was a potent and shocking adaptation, a parable of extraordinary ferocity and acuteness. Brook had difficulty in getting his film shown – another black mark for the two main circuits.

Certain other films crept into the new wave category simply because they dealt with social themes – Peter Glenville's *Term of Trial*, for instance, which introduced Terence Stamp as a recalcitrant youth giving a middle-aged schoolmaster, played by Laurence Olivier, a difficult time. Olivier's performance of a man trapped into a compromising situation with a young girl, Sarah Miles, rose above the script, which required him to make an astonishing plea from the dock, when on trial for raping her. The film contrasted with Leslie Norman's *Spare the Rod*, from Michael Croft's novel, also set in a dismal slum school with the familiar youthful delinquents pitted against sadistic or despairing teachers. The filming of this novel had been delayed for years until a version acceptable to the British Board of Film Censors could be created. Inevitably, the result lacked the fire of the original work, being a fairly straightforward rampage through the box-office version of the blackboard jungle. Donald Pleasence, as an embittered headmaster, conveyed a sense of the despair of the situation and Max Bygraves's performance as the young and idealistic new master provided a reasonable amount of sincerity; but the direction was bland and unexceptional.

Ken Hughes's *The Small World of Sammy Lee* attempted to get under the skin of the Soho of small-time crooks and strip shows, with Anthony Newley playing a man desperately trying to raise sufficient money to avert a bookie's collection agents from slashing him to shreds with their razors. Adapted by Hughes from his own television play, the film moved at a frantic pace, the camera following the fast-talking central character relentlessly until the climax, when having failed to meet the debt he is beaten up and discovers that his money has been left by one of the thugs as a gesture of compassion. A tortured, interesting film, underrated both at the time of its release and since, it is undoubtedly the best film by Ken Hughes, a director with a lengthy record of unpretentious programme-fillers, and more recently the juvenile epic *Chitty Chitty Bang Bang* and the historical exercise *Cromwell*. He was also responsible for the better of the two Oscar Wilde films that appeared within a few weeks of each other in 1960, his starring Peter Finch and called *The Trials of Oscar Wilde* (*The Green Carnation* in the U.S.A.). The other, *Oscar Wilde*, was directed by Gregory Ratoff, with Robert Morley playing the unfortunate playwright.

A director trained by television who made a feature debut in the early sixties was Ken Russell, best known for his *Monitor* work. His first cinema film, *French Dressing*, was a comedy which failed to be particularly funny, about an English seaside resort which tries to emulate Cannes by holding its own continental film festival. It was ground covered many times in Ealing comedies with more directness and less disguised humour. A mixture of satire and slapstick put together in a pretentious and undisciplined manner, it demonstrated that effective screen comedy is a difficult and elusive quality to capture. Jeremy Summers's *The Punch and Judy Man*, a comedy built around Tony Hancock, one of the greatest of all British comedians who had made television his most successful medium, also missed its target, largely because Hancock's personality was too strained and introspective to externalize his performance effectively, and yet so strong that it swamped the direction and the literate script (another seaside town story, by Philip Oakes). Hancock's earlier film, *The Rebel*, directed by

Robert Day, had been made on relatively orthodox lines as a broad comic romp, but he had found this kind of film-making unsatisfying. *The Punch and Judy Man* was a brave attempt to provide a great comedian with a deserving vehicle. Its failure ended Hancock's career in the cinema, returning him to television, which he ultimately and tragically found too limiting.

Cliff Owen's *The Wrong Arm of the Law*, another comedy, succeeded where the others had failed. It had as its basis a superb situation, an underworld run on brisk, welfare state lines with paid holidays for crooks and luncheon vouchers, suddenly threatened by a gang of unscrupulous Australian villains who disguise themselves as the police when they carry out a job. Crooks and police collaborate to drive the new gang out of business and a twenty-four-hour crime truce is staged. One of the most pleasant inventions in the film is an underworld conference run like a trade-union meeting. The central part, gang-leader Pearly Gates, who doubles up as a West End couturier, was played with great verve and confidence by Peter Sellers, while the part of an impossibly stupid Scotland Yard inspector was taken by Lionel Jeffries with a rich comic talent. *The Wrong Arm of the Law*, in spite of occasional unevenness in the writing, was genuinely funny and original.

Sellers had established himself as the leading comic actor of the British cinema during the late fifties and early sixties, occasionally venturing into serious roles, such as that of the racketeer in John Guillermin's *Never Let Go*, or the Indian doctor in *The Millionairess*. In the Boultings' *Heavens Above!*, which after their satirical prods at the army, the law, trade unions and the foreign office was directed at the church, Sellers played a northern liberal clergyman who by clerical error is assigned to a stuffy middle-class country parish, which he proceeds to shock by upsetting its traditions, appointing a Negro churchwarden, for example. But the approach was too heavy-handed and crude to elevate the film artistically higher than the robust and ever-successful *Carry On* series, which under the direction of Gerald Thomas appeared with great frequency, usually with the same cast of perennials, Charles Hawtrey, Hattie Jacques, Kenneth Williams and Kenneth Connor.

22 The Old Faithfuls

In the new climate older directors were tested hard. Some, such as David Lean, became associated only with the large-scale international epic, the type of film that would be shot in 70mm. and shown in a handful of theatres around the world for the first year or so of its life, and which, of course, was only made possible by American finance. Such a film was his monumental *Lawrence of Arabia*, co-produced with Sam Spiegel and written by Robert Bolt. Financed by the profits of *The Bridge on the River Kwai*, *Lawrence* took four years to make and had a budget in the £4 million class. Mostly shot on location, it was successful in creating a feeling of the Middle East, the hazy heat of the desert, the hot sand sending up rippling waves of light and mirages. Lawrence was played by Peter O'Toole, physically too tall, but nevertheless as convincing as is possible in such an enigmatic role, and the film left the interpretation of its subject's character tantalizingly ambiguous – dreamer, mystic, idealist, charlatan, he seemed all of these. Lean's direction was careful, episodic and organized to provide climaxes rather too regularly. It was an unashamed commercial film, over three hours long with a driving energy to sustain its audience through the adventures of its hero. Omar Sharif made his western debut in his most satisfactory part as Sherif Ali, Lawrence's Arab colleague, and a number of distinguished actors popped up either in Arab disguise (Alec Guinness, José Ferrer, Anthony Quinn) or as British military figures (Jack Hawkins as Allenby).

Following the success of *Lawrence of Arabia*, Lean and his screenwriter Robert Bolt set to work on a 70mm. version of Boris Pasternak's *Dr Zhivago*, filmed in Spain with a cast which included Alec Guinness, Ralph Richardson, Julie Christie, Tom Courtenay, Rita Tushingham and Omar Sharif. In spite of the English weight of its cast and production, it was outside the technical quota necessary to enable it to be classified as a British film, and accordingly took the U.S. nationality of its distribution company, MGM. It was a notable film, like *Lawrence* photographed by Freddie Young, who simulated the broad and expansive steppes on the plains of Spain. Unashamedly romantic in tone, rather than a re-creation of the despair voiced in Pasternak's powerful novel, it had a lyrical score by Maurice Jarre to reinforce the wet-eyed mood.

Carol Reed, after his successful *Our Man in Havana* and his unfortunate experience with MGM over *Mutiny on the Bounty*, turned to a somewhat lightweight thriller for his next film, in which Laurence Harvey played an aviator who faked his own death in order that his wife (Lee Remick) could collect the insurance money for them to live out a comfortable exile. The coincidental appearance of a young insurance agent (Alan Bates) in their Spanish retreat creates unforeseen complications and eventual panic. The central part of the film was concerned with the change in character that overtakes the fugitive as he assumes his new identity and adopts that of an outgoing, free-wheeling wealthy Australian. *The Running Man* opened well, with a memorial service for a still living man, but it disintegrated into a rather flaccid widescreen travelogue, below Reed's usual calibre. The director's film-making activities were unseen for a further five years, but with *Oliver!*, his first musical, of Lionel Bart's version of Dickens's novel, he created a lively image of early Victorian London and achieved the distinction of an Academy Award for the best direction of the year. The film was greeted more enthusiastically in the United States than in Britain, but Ron Moody's gaunt Fagin was favourably compared with Alec Guinness's in the David Lean version of twenty years earlier.

Anthony Asquith, who died in 1968, was responsible in 1962 for *Guns of Darkness*, a melodrama with a background of Latin American politics. In spite of a script by John Mortimer and a cast which included Leslie Caron and David Niven the film was a feeble tail-off to a distinguished career. It was followed by *The V.I.P.s*, a *Grand Hotel*-type drama set against the background of London Airport, which was also disappointing, although a glossier and more expensive production. Not only was the format an old-fashioned one, but the screenplay, by Asquith's seasoned collaborator, Terence Rattigan, explored a number of immensely trite situations arising when a group of transatlantic travellers, each facing certain problems, are forced to stay at the airport hotel overnight when fog makes their flight out impossible. The cast included Richard Burton and Elizabeth Taylor, Maggie Smith, Orson Welles, Margaret Rutherford and a number of other well-known screen faces engaged in relatively minor parts. As box-office entertainment the film was successful, but in style it was a throwback to another age. Asquith also made a straightforward record of four items in the repertoire of the Royal Ballet, with the dancing of Margot Fonteyn and Rudolf Nureyev carefully laid down in amber for a future generation. *An Evening at the Royal Ballet*, made for British Home Entertainments, did not seek to be more than an observation of a performance on the stage of the Royal Opera House, Covent Garden, and as a film made no fresh contribution to the medium.

Asquith's last completed work was another Rattigan collaboration, *The Yellow Rolls-Royce*, an elaborate and expensive confection, built up of several episodes in the life of an elegant motor-car which passes from a marquess to a gangster and then to wartime Yugoslavia where it is used to transport freedom fighters. The style of the film was flat, lifeless and stifling, the dramatic coherence shaky. The all-star cast, which included Rex Harrison, Jeanne Moreau, Shirley MacLaine, George C. Scott, Alain Delon, Ingrid Bergman and Omar Sharif coped as well as it could with the unpromising material, but it was a disappointing finale to a fine and lengthy career.

Of other directors who had been at work in Britain in the 1930s, Michael Powell probably remained the most prominent. His *Peeping Tom* of 1959, a study of a psychotic murderer who photographed his female victims in their death-throes, enraged the critics of the day, although in retrospect it was an early statement of themes which were to emerge more strongly in the sixties, when the Moors murders and the Boston Strangler became obsessive topics. Regrettably, Powell's next film went back to some vanished concept of belief in the power of the Empire and the rightness of established order. *The Queen's Guards* was a pompous and tiresome exercise in misplaced chauvinism and bore little relation to what else was going on at the time in films. Powell's next film was made in Australia. *They're a Weird Mob* was a women's magazine story lurking behind a tough hide, attempting to show the problems of an immigrant trying to settle in his new country. It was, one hoped, only a temporary twilight for a man who had been a powerful force in British cinema.

Although Jack Clayton did not direct his first full-length feature, *Room at the Top*, until 1958, he had been employed in films since the mid-thirties. In 1961 he was responsible for *The Innocents*, which had been adapted from the celebrated Victorian ghost story, *The Turn of the Screw*, by Henry James. Deborah Kerr was cast in the central role of the governess responsible for two young children apparently possessed by the spirits of her deceased predecessor and lover, the valet. Clayton, opting for a Gothic treatment, with dark corridors, ghostly voices, curtains flapping in the wind, candles blowing out, still managed to construct a film of elegant and chilling dread, closer in feeling to the horror films of the Hammer studios than Jamesian enigma. Accepted as a ghost story with Freudian overtones, *The Innocents* was successful. Deborah Kerr's performance as the ageing, determined governess running full-tilt into an atmosphere of unremitting evil was suitably disturbing. The photography, by Freddie Francis, was a remarkable evocation of the foreboding and heaviness of a mid-Victorian summer.

Clayton's next work was scripted by Harold Pinter, from the novel by Penelope Mortimer. *The Pumpkin Eater* was about a much-married woman with several children in a despairing search for domestic protection. Her marriage to Jake, a successful and unfaithful screenwriter, is floundering, and she undergoes psychiatric treatment. An unpleasant friend of Jake's pours out the full details of her husband's affair with his wife and after a bitter fight the marriage explodes. The film was pitched on an emotional summit for its entire length and while the acting, of Anne Bancroft as Jo, Peter Finch as Jake, Maggie Smith as his uncaring mistress and James Mason as the vile and insulting friend, was of a sustained high level, the effect was a kind of Swiss Cottage grand guignol, a nightmare atmosphere of madness and absurdity, too strained to be entirely credible. The intrusion of a demented woman under the next drier at a hairdressing salon, and a breakdown in Harrod's food hall, were the kind of effects sufficient to send the whole structure toppling. *The Pumpkin Eater*, an actor's picture, while treading the paths of Antonioni failed to keep its cool.

Our Mother's House, which followed, again wandered into a psychological jungle, this time with a basic horrific situation, that of a group of children who bury their mother, dead after an illness, in the garden to avoid being sent to an orphanage, and somehow convince the daily help that she has gone away. In spite of looking after themselves adequately, suspicions are aroused and the father turns up, grasps the situation and capitalizes on it, spending the dead woman's savings. When the children learn that none of them are his, each being illegitimate by different men, one of the girls kills him with a poker. All this takes place in a large house at Croydon. Inevitably, the story's implausibilities, a kind of combination of the two previous Clayton films, mars its total effect, but again the director's hold on his actors and the beautifully composed photography of Larry Pizer, with its carefully observed images of the changing seasons, demonstrated the romantic quality of Clayton's work. A director of exceptional talent and promise, he has yet to make a completely satisfying film.

There is an analogous quality in much of the work of Bryan Forbes. He shows a similar interest in psychological motivation, or the distorting lens of childhood, as in *Whistle Down the Wind*, the first film he directed after a long career as an actor and screenwriter. His *L-Shaped Room*, from the novel by Lynne Reid Banks, as a kind of horror fable set in the contemporary and squalid world of Notting Hill bedsitterland, in which the main character, a girl played by Leslie Caron, achieves the birth of her child after several attempts at abortion. The film was not particularly successful, its storyline being diffused and deliberately designed to shock genteel susceptibilities. *Seance on a Wet Afternoon*, however, was a mature and accomplished work, containing two outstanding acting performances – those of Kim Stanley and Richard Attenborough as an overbearing medium and her meek husband. A plot involving the kidnapping of a child, so that the medium can 'divine' its whereabouts, goes awry. The film treads the borderline between sanity and madness, demonstrating the narrowness of the separation between them. Regrettably, this excellent film failed to make a satisfactory impression at the box-office. After Forbes directed *King Rat* in Hollywood he made *The Whisperers*, which again contained a virtuoso acting performance, that of Dame Edith Evans as an old-age pensioner suffering from illusions of being spied upon and delusions of grandeur; her crooked son conceals in the house some stolen money and the old lady, finding it, assumes it to be her long-awaited legacy. The film is a study of the loneliness of old age and the unintentional heartlessness of national welfare.

In 1969 Bryan Forbes was appointed managing director of the Associated British Picture Corporation and became the studio head at Elstree, under the new parent company, Electrical and Musical Industries, who had acquired ABC after a protracted takeover bid. The appointment was a refreshing one in that a studio head with experience of acting, writing and directing now existed; his task in revitalizing the studios and getting new films off the ground without dependence on American money was indeed formidable. Not only was Forbes well-equipped creatively, and it was his stated intention to continue to direct films himself, but he showed an interest in getting to grips with labour relations in the studios, making himself much more approachable and willing to discuss grievances with the working force than any of his predecessors. It was hoped that his appointment would open a new range of possibilities for the industry, and certainly morale at ABPC was greatly raised in the opening months of the new regime, marked by a deluge of scripts from aspirant screenwriters, agents and stars anxious to form part of the new production programme. Regrettably, optimism was short-lived and Forbes withdrew in 1971.

One of the longest-serving directors in the sixties was Val Guest, who had been involved in films since the earliest days of talkies, first as an actor, then as a scriptwriter, then as a writing director and finally as a producer. His list of film credits consisted almost entirely of light-weight comedies, with a few near-horrific war films such as *The Camp on Blood Island* and *Yesterday's Enemy*, interspersed with *Carry on Admiral* and *Up the Creek*. After a hard-edged police thriller with a fashionably grimy Mancunian setting, *Hell Is a City*, in which Stanley Baker played a detective, tough in a pseudo-American idiom, Guest's most interesting film was a science-fiction attempt, *The Day the Earth Caught Fire*, set in the immediate future and based on the premise that a hydrogen bomb had knocked the world off its axis and sent it into a fresh orbit towards the sun. Shot against an authentic Fleet Street background, using the *Daily Express* offices (and the ex-*Express* editor, Arthur Christiansen, playing himself) the film built up an atmosphere of mounting terror as a balmy summer gives way to tropical heat, and good process work gave an impression of what London would look like if it had the climate of the Persian Gulf. Edward Judd as a hard-drink-ing reporter and Janet Munro as a girl in the Civil Service, whom he pumps for information on the true state of affairs, gave credible performances and the film had both pace and originality in treatment, as well as an intriguing theme.

Jigsaw, a mystery involving a dismembered body found in a seaside house, bearing resemblances to the Mahon case of the twenties, was a study of patient police detection, with Jack Warner playing an old superintendent and Ronald Lewis his young and energetic assistant. Mostly photographed against a background of Brighton, the film did not move beyond mechanical entertainment, the locations remaining as passive backdrops. The following film, *80,000 Suspects*, was set in Bath, using real locations as much as possible, where a smallpox epidemic breaks out against a background of the marital troubles of a doctor played by Richard Johnson and his wife, Claire Bloom. A strong injection of melodrama, with the original carrier of the disease setting fire to the house and incinerating herself inside it, contrasts with the documentary-like sequences of the official moves to stop the spread of the epidemic. *Beauty Jungle* (*Contest Girl* in America) attempted to expose corruption within the beauty queen business, with Janette Scott as a typist lured into the circus and Ian Hendry as a reporter who becomes her manager when she turns into a full-time professional. This film lacked the punch of the previous ones and was mostly unrelieved tedium. *Where the Spies Are* was a routine thriller which attempted to capitalize on the James Bond craze and starred David Niven as James Leasor's espionage character, Dr Jason Love, complete with his rare Cord car.

In 1962 the first of the James Bond films had appeared. Directed by Terence Young, it was *Dr No* and was shot in Britain and on location in Jamaica, on a relatively low budget. Bond, one of the archetypal fictional heroes of the fifties, had been created by Ian Fleming, whose habit it was to produce a new Bond book every spring. They were notable for their overt sadism and the sexual licence of the protagonist, who in some respects was closer to a clubland hero of Buchan or Sapper. The villains were always immensely exaggerated: Dr No was a kidnapper of space rockets, which he diverted from Cape Canaveral by means of a complex clandestine tracking station hidden in a redoubt on one of the Jamaican keys. The film Bond was Sean Connery, who brought a touch of roughness to the character that was absent in the Fleming stories. The film was decorated with many bizarre devices, such as an attaché case which was really a murderous weapon, elaborate and imaginative sets by Ken Adam, a series of expendable blondes and exotic locations. It was an immense success and obviously the first of a series.

The production values escalated further with the next film, *From Russia with Love*, which followed the format of the first. Guy Hamilton relieved Terence Young of the chore of directing the next one, *Goldfinger*, which had its villain organizing a raid on the gold reserves of Fort Knox, but Young returned for *Thunderball*, most of which appeared to be shot underwater in the Caribbean, where a stolen bomber lay, bearing nuclear warheads. Lewis Gilbert directed the next Bond film, *You Only Live Twice*, although Fleming's first Bond novel, *Casino Royale*, the rights of which were not owned by Harry Saltzman and Albert Broccoli, the producers of the Connery Bond, was given a curious and unsuccessful comedy treatment by a motley collection of directors consisting of John Huston, Ken Hughes, Val Guest, Robert Parrish and Joe McGrath, all of whom strived too hard to burlesque the Bond genre. After *You Only Live Twice*, the most successful of the Bond films financially, Sean Connery decided to retire from the role, feeling that it was handicapping his development as an actor, and for the next Bond film, *On Her Majesty's Secret Service*, the part was taken by George Lazenby, who failed to make any impact. Connery returned for *Diamonds Are Forever*, as positively his last appearance in the role, and after much public searching the producers appointed the tried-and-true hero-figure Roger Moore to play Bond in *Live and Let Die*.

The success of the Bond films spawned innumerable imitations, most of which were puerile, but *The Ipcress File*, adapted from Len Deighton's excellent thriller, with Michael Caine as his contrasting, shabby, down-at-heel agent, the antithesis of James Bond, was given a very satisfactory treatment by Sidney Furie. Less successful was a sequel, *Billion Dollar Brain*, which was directed by Ken Russell, with occasional extravagant touches, such as the disappearance of an entire army under the Baltic ice, an effect surely borrowed from Eisenstein.

Basil Dearden also made intriguing use of the espionage genre in *The Mind Benders*, in which an isolation technique, whereby a man is induced to abandon many of his senses by prolonged immersion in a tank of water, is used to produce a Jekyll and Hyde effect on its subject. Dirk Bogarde and John Clements made a suitably sinister pair as victim and security officer. *A Place to Go* was set in Bethnal Green, and produced as usual by Michael Relph. It was a cautious attempt by this team at the new realism, with Rita Tushingham and Mike Sarne making the best of an unpromising working-class setting. Dearden and Relph also produced in the same year (1964) *Woman of Straw*, in which Sean Connery, Gina Lollobrigida and Ralph Richardson took part in an unusual thriller whereby a rich man's wealth becomes a magnet for his unscrupulous nephew, who uses the older man's Italian nurse as an unwilling accomplice to get at the money. The same team's *Masquerade*, a thriller about the kidnapping of the young heir to an oil-sheikdom, with Jack Hawkins as a cynical and ageing Foreign Office strong-arm man who makes an attempt to cheat the government at its own skulduggery, was also fashionably appropriate in its mood, containing such well-worn sequences as the narrow suspension footbridge in imminent danger of collapse.

Khartoum, the most interesting of Dearden's films in the 1960s, was an American co-production from United Artists and told the tragic and futile story of General Gordon, played in a firm and thoughtful manner by Charlton Heston. His was one of the best performances in a British film during the decade, contrasting oddly with that of Sir Laurence Olivier in the same film, who played the Mahdi with rolling eyes and a curious accent, thus calling too much attention to technique and not enough to the feeling of the character. A prologue set the scene excellently and was directed by the famous still photographer, Eliot Elisofon, who briefly conveyed the enormity and mystery of the desert. Dearden's later films of the sixties, *Only When I Larf*, from a Len Deighton story, in which Richard Attenborough plays a skilful confidence trickster and master of disguise, and *The Assassination Bureau*, with Diana Rigg as an Edwardian lady reporter and Oliver Reed as the head of an international consortium that monopolized political murder, were both comedy thrillers of a lightweight and unexceptional kind.

23   Visiting Firemen

During the sixties the British cinema was richly endowed with the work of numerous major directors from other countries, mostly from America. Some, like Joseph Losey, had become completely British in feeling, severing connections with their homeland; others, such as Dick Lester, found the British climate a more satisfactory one in which to pursue their film career. In addition to the foreign directors who made their homes in Great Britain, many, such as Preminger, Truffaut, Antonioni, Zinneman, Wilder and Godard, came to make a film in British studios.

Of the expatriate Americans, Joseph Losey was by far the most established and important. His films, rich in an almost baroque manner, concerned themselves with the observation of human weakness and decay, using symbolism and analogy when heavy stylization ran dry. *The Servant* (1962) describes the encroachment of a rich young man's valet to become an indispensable and ultimately destructive element of his life. A screenplay by Harold Pinter, based on a novel by Robin Maugham, gave Dirk Bogarde a magnificent acting opportunity as the sinister and ambiguous manservant Barrett, while James Fox provided a finely detailed exercise in upper-class ineffectiveness as the young man whose moral strength is insufficient to resist the corrupting force of the other man. The first two-thirds of the film are beautifully assembled, a mounting atmosphere of menace, moving with a rhythmic progression. Then Losey allows the atmosphere to disintegrate, exploding it into a series of contrived and unconvincing effects as the plot apparently fights desperately towards a resolution. *The Servant* is a fine Losey film, marred as so many are by his love of ornamentation, which can overload his situations to the point of absurdity.

King and Country (1964) was a simpler, more direct film, made on a tight shooting schedule and scarcely moving outside its one main setting, that of a Passchendaele dugout in 1917, where Private Hamp is tried by court-martial for walking from the guns in battle, and is sentenced to be shot. Death is an inevitable and ever-present force hovering over the entire film, and while the luckless Hamp awaits his fate the soldiers try and execute a rat in a ghastly symbolic parallel of the primary event. No attempt is made by the court to take account of mitigating circumstances; the morale of the battalion is of greater importance than one man's life. The defending officer, another skilful performance by Dirk Bogarde, can make no impression, in spite of the weight of his sympathy swinging round to the accused during the course of the trial. He, too, is as much a prisoner of the situation as Hamp and it is he who, burdened it would seem with the guilt of the situation after the firing squad has fumbled the execution out of misplaced compassion, has to put a last bullet through his head. Tom Courtenay as Hamp gave the characterization needed, a semi-articulate terror-stricken scapegoat, caught up in an act of obscenity as appalling as the war itself. This was Losey's great attack on the meaning of war when it becomes a universal experience and young men like Hamp through no wish of their own find themselves in circumstances which are completely beyond anything they have contemplated, and are unable to opt out. *King and Country* is a plea for the individual will, a cry for freedom against a man-made death.

Losey's next film, *Modesty Blaise* (1966), represented a complete change of mood, into the area that had already been exploited by the Bond films. Modesty was a successful strip cartoon character, played in the film by Monica Vitti, with Terence Stamp as her platonic assistant, Willie Garvin, and Dirk Bogarde as Gabriel, the deadly master criminal. The film was a burlesque of the genre, played out against a fashionable op-art background, with extravagant visual gimmicks and internal jokes – an oil sheikh whose suite at the Ritz is crammed with pin-tables and boxes of biscuits, Gabriel's exotic drink with a live fish floating in it – and mocked the ephemera of the mid-sixties. Regrettably, the spy-film send-up was an already established type of film and Losey's excursion into this area exposed him to the very vulnerability of the medium he was trying to satirize. Amusing, inconsequential, visually elaborate and richly laced with sex and violence, the film missed its target because the Bond films had more than an adequate touch of self-parody themselves.

With *Accident* (1967) Losey returned to his introspective approach and produced his most satisfactory film, a triangle with two Oxford dons lusting after an Austrian girl student who becomes engaged to another undergraduate, later killed in a car crash. The screenplay was by Harold Pinter (who plays a small part as a TV producer) from a novel by Nicholas Mosley, and the film was photographed by Gerry Fisher in a very naturalistic colour, conveying with great beauty the atmosphere of the English summer. It is the simplest and most direct of Losey's works, relieved from the usual baroque imagery. Only one sequence, an improbable and obscure team game, fought in the hall of a stately home, betrays his failing for indulgent effects. Dirk Bogarde as tutor to the two students, anxiously awaiting his moment to seduce the girl, seeking solace with a former girl friend in London (a small part by Delphine Seyrig), produces an accomplished performance, as does Stanley Baker as his bouncing, extrovert and basically pitiful rival. *Accident* examines the conflicts and guilt of the middle-aged man, the fading of a life of promise, the ambiguities of relationships.

Boom! (1968), with Richard Burton and Elizabeth Taylor in an adaptation by Tennessee Williams of his play, *The Milk Train Doesn't Stop Here Any More*, moved back into an earlier Losey mood with a confrontation between a wandering poet and the richest woman in the world, dying on her Mediterranean island, in which the one seeks power over the other. *Secret Ceremony* (1969), also with Elizabeth Taylor, moved in a similar area. In this film a young, wealthy and mentally retarded girl, Mia Farrow, attempts to establish an ageing Catholic prostitute as a replica of her dead mother, and the woman plays along with the charade until, ultimately, tragedy ends the deception. Both these films, falling once again into Losey's style of baroque symbolism, fail to produce situations that convince or concern their audience.

Stanley Kubrick's first three films completed in England, *Lolita* (1961), *Dr Strangelove* (1969) and *2001 : A Space Odyssey* (1968), were all interesting and important. The first, an adaptation by Nabokov of his celebrated novel, was unusual in that apart from a few establish-shots, it was made entirely in Britain, although set in the United States. With a despairing seediness, James Mason played Humbert Humbert, the New England professor who forms a wild, lusting affection for the early teenage daughter of his landlady, taking her on a marathon journey across the country after her mother's death. Peter Sellers as Quilty, Humbert's rival for Lolita, a playwright who makes a fetish of impersonation, produces a comic performance, even hilarious in death-throes when shot by the enraged professor. Kubrick made *Lolita* less of the expected exercise in salacity than a cool and intellectual analysis of obsessive behaviour.

Dr Strangelove, or, How I Learned to Stop Worrying and Love the Bomb, besides having the longest title ever used for a British film at that date, was in Kubrick's words a 'nightmare comedy', in which an insane U.S. general launches an all-out nuclear attack on Russia and seals off his base from the outside, causing consternation in the Pentagon. Eventually, one of the bombers gets through to its target after it has been disclosed that the Russians have a 'doomsday machine' which will render the whole world uninhabitable the moment a nuclear weapon hits Soviet territory. The Texan bomber pilot rides his bomb down to the ground, waving his hat as though on a bucking bronco, and then on the soundtrack Vera Lynn's voice sings 'We'll meet again . . .' Peter Sellers plays three parts – an ineffectual RAF Group Captain, the apologetic American President, and the manic Dr Strangelove, an ex-German scientist still unable to prevent his false arm from occasionally jerking in a Nazi salute. A brilliant anti-war film, bitter in its examination of the ultimate possibility of a nuclear confrontation, *Dr Strangelove* held its savage course all through without any flagging from its terrifying proposition.

Kubrick's *2001 : A Space Odyssey* tackled a theme as awe-inspiring as the destruction of the world, the exploration of the universe beyond it. Its prologue, set in prehistoric times before the evolution of man, showed the arrival of a mysterious black slab among a colony of apes; it seemed to possess some kind of power to transmit intelligence, for later the apes devise a means of defending their waterhole against the encroachments of a neighbouring tribe. A bone is tossed in the air and in a sudden cut is transformed into an orbiting space station at the turn of the twenty-first century. A similar slab has been found on the moon and has been discovered to be sending signals to Jupiter. A monumental space expedition is mounted, with two astronauts operating a huge spaceship, their three colleagues in a state of hibernation and kept alive by the latest and most complex computer, Hal. In flight Hal asserts its authority by causing a minor fault and the deaths of all crew members except Bowman (Keir Dullea) who disconnects the computer's memory. During the approach to the destination the spaceman falls into a timewarp and the dimensional meaning of everything he has known until then ceases to apply. He finds himself in

Above Michael Powell and Emeric Pressburger made an ambitious hands-across-the-sea type film with *49th Parallel* (1941). Glynis Johns (*left*) played a Hutterite girl in a Canadian prairie settlement, menaced by itinerant U-Boat men.

Below Leslie Howard played Mitchell, the Spitfire designer, in his own film, *The First of the Few* (1942), with David Niven. It had a notable musical score by William Walton.

Left Captain D (Noël Coward) with his wife, Celia Johnson.

Below John Mills, as Able Seaman Shorty Blake, with Kay Walsh. *In Which We Serve*, written, produced and directed by Noël Coward, also used the talents of David Lean and Ronald Neame. As a study of a ship's career in war it was impressive and stiffly stoical. It was the biggest box-office success of 1943.

Above   Anthony Asquith's *Fanny by Gaslight* (1944) with James Mason showed a nostalgic interest in the customs and costumes of Victorian England, a relief from the drab war-weary time in which it was made.

Below   Laurence Olivier's *Henry V* (1945) was a magnificent, costly, spectacular homage to Shakespeare.

Above David Lean's *Blithe Spirit* (1945) with Kay Hammond, Rex Harrison and Constance Cummings, was a finely wrought rendering of Noël Coward's long-running play, an occult comedy of two wives.

Below The Gainsborough Gothic period was at its height with *The Wicked Lady* (1945), here with Margaret Lockwood and Patricia Roc.

Above Anthony Asquith's *The Way to the Stars* (1945) was almost the *In Which We Serve* of the Royal Air Force, and one of the most sensitive of war films. Its cast included Michael Redgrave and Rosamund John.

Below Rex Harrison was an unprincipled bounder in *The Rake's Progress* (1945) directed by Sidney Gilliat. Here with Lilli Palmer. The ending with the rake's redemption was a false note.

Left The renaissance period of British cinema was in full cry with David Lean's *Brief Encounter* (1945) with Celia Johnson and Trevor Howard.

Below The last film Alex Korda directed was *An Ideal Husband* (1947) from Oscar Wilde's play. Here is Korda on the Shepperton set with Glynis Johns and Hugh Williams.

Above Richard Attenborough was the young psychopath in the Boultings' version of Greene's *Brighton Rock* (1947), with Carol Marsh.

Below Herbert Wilcox provided escapism with an Anna Neagle–Michael Wilding series. *This is Spring in Park Lane* (1948) with milord Wilding pretending to be a butler.

Above Laurence Olivier both appeared in and directed *The Prince and the Showgirl* (1957) with Marilyn Monroe, the only film in which she was to appear outside America.

Opposite above *Passport to Pimlico* (1949), directed by Henry Cornelius, was in the typical idiom of the *genus* Ealing comedy. Prominent here are Raymond Huntley, Stanley Holloway, Basil Radford and Naunton Wayne.

Opposite below Brenda de Banzie, Charles Laughton and John Mills in David Lean's *Hobson's Choice* (1954), a comedy set in Victorian Lancashire.

Left Jack Clayton's *Room at the Top* (1958) allegedly presaged a new style in British films. Here are Laurence Harvey and Heather Sears in a famous scene.
Below Richard Burton and Claire Bloom in Tony Richardson's *Look Back in Anger* (1959) from John Osborne's apocalyptic stage play at the Royal Court three years before.
Opposite above Shirley Ann Field and Laurence Olivier in Tony Richardson's *The Entertainer* (1960), the second Osborne play to be filmed under the Woodfall banner.
Opposite below Leslie Caron in Bryan Forbes' *The L-Shaped Room* (1962).

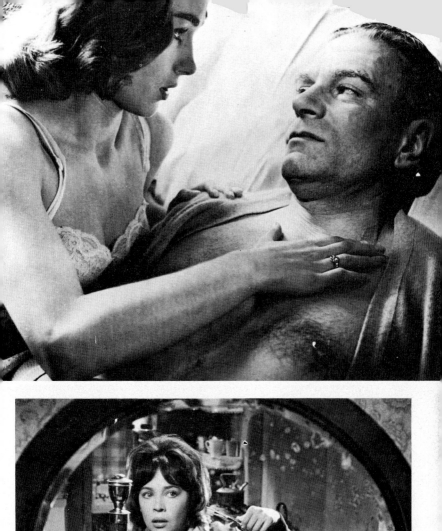

Above Albert Finney as a psychopath and Susan Hampshire in *Night Must Fall* (1964), directed by Karel Reisz, from a play by Emlyn Williams filmed in Hollywood 1937.

Opposite above The Beatles in their second film *Help!* (1965), directed by Dick Lester.

Opposite below *The Knack* (1965) was a Dick Lester whimsicality. Here with Michael Crawford, Rita Tushingham and Donal Donnelly.

Above　The most consistent box-office returns of the sixties came via the James Bond thrillers starring Sean Connery. This is *Goldfinger* (1964), directed by Guy Hamilton, the third to be filmed.

Below　Anita Pallenberg, James Fox and Mick Jagger in *Performance* (1970) directed by Donald Cammell and Nicolas Roeg.

Opposite above　Roeg was also responsible for *Walkabout* (1971) with Jenny Agutter and Lucien John as two children stranded in the Australian outback and then saved by an aborigine youth, David Gumphill.

Opposite below　Ken Russell, here with Twiggy on the set of *The Boy Friend* (1972), encouraged more controversy than any other contemporary British director with his outrageous and excessive 1971 film *The Devils*.

Above Vanessa Redgrave as Mother Superior of the convent at Loudon. The film stirred up a hornet's nest.

Below Stanley Kubrick films Malcolm McDowell attacking Adrienne Corri in *A Clockwork Orange* (1972), a horrific, savage glimpse of the near-future.

a strange apartment where he rapidly passes through life into old age. As he dies a slab appears before him and his regenerated foetus takes its place in the universe.

The production values of this ambitious film were on an unprecedented scale. Many large American corporations projected their planning more than thirty years in order to predict what everyday objects would look like at the end of the century, and glimpses of the uniform of a Pan Am stewardess on a moonliner, or Howard Johnson's Earthlight Room in the space Hilton, as well as several hundred words of complicated instructions on how to use a space toilet, provided considerable humour. The interior of the space ship was made weightless because Kubrick had it shot within a centrifuge, built specially for the film at vast expense by Vickers-Armstrong. Every detail was carefully researched and depicted, and some of the process work, such as the docking of the Pan Am clipper into the satellite hangar, was breathtaking and faultless in its execution. Yet in spite of the technical gloss, *2001* goes far deeper than a mere exercise in lavish film-making. It attempts to describe the final loneliness of man and the result of exploration to the edge of his soul. An astonishing accomplishment, *2001* was one of the seminal films of the sixties.

The American-born director Dick Lester effectively began his film career in Britain, having emigrated from American television. Among his earliest work was a comic short, *The Running, Jumping and Standing Still Film*, made in one day with few props but the help of some of his friends, including Peter Sellers and Spike Milligan. The film had arisen out of Lester's work directing Goon-show type programmes on Independent Television. His first feature was a routine assemblage of musical turns, entitled *It's Trad, Dad*, and connecting with a current fad in the world of pop. Its treatment was noted as being unusually lively for that type of picture. Lester's next film was *Mouse on the Moon*, again a routine work, and sequel to Jack Arnold's Ruritanian comic fantasy with Peter Sellers, *The Mouse that Roared*. The film which established Lester's reputation as a disciple of the new sixties trendiness, was *A Hard Day's Night*, which featured the Beatles, still at their apotheosis, the Beatlemania period having been one of the social phenomena of the preceding year. The plot was nebulous (an excursion to London from Liverpool for the sake of a television programme) and was merely an excuse to string together a number of Beatles songs. Lester's treatment was, however, visually exciting, eschewing conventional devices for the presentation of the musical numbers, and the film was enlivened by a witty script by Alun Owen, loaded with satirical references to contemporary trends.

The following year Lester made *The Knack*, an adaptation by Charles Wood of Ann Jellicoe's play, about a sex-starved young man sharing a house with a relentless womanizer who apparently never fails. Lester's film extended the play into a film with an almost Godardian attempt at ciné-verité, using live street interviews deploring the licence enjoyed by the younger generation, and a lengthy sequence in which Rita Tushingham wanders the streets of London crying 'Rape' to all and sundry. Visual gags of an expert kind abounded, for instance, a motorist getting out to help an apparently pregnant girl across the road, then finding that his vehicle has been pushed out of sight by the cars behind. Michael Crawford played the diffident man and Ray Brooks the voracious one; with Rita Tushingham they made a well-balanced trio, and in some of the enclosed scenes Lester demonstrated a sensitivity in handling his cast. The photography by David Watkins was also fresh and adventurous, and in spite of certain blemishes, *The Knack* was an exciting cinematic event.

The second Beatles film, *Help!*, benefited from being shot in Eastman Colour and had a complicated plot involving the pursuit of Ringo by Eastern religious fanatics determined to recover a sacrificial ring which has somehow become stuck on his finger. The locations were far flung, ranging from Salisbury Plain to the Alps and eventually the Bahamas. As before, the film was rich in visual gags: a dark hand attempts to seize the ring when Ringo puts his hand into a letterbox, the four Beatles enter four suburban front doors in a long terrace and appear inside in a vast room created by knocking down the inner walls of the four houses. The photographic treatment was inspired by both television commercials and colour supplement advertisements, with soft filters, out-of-focus backgrounds and even the screen image tilted completely sideways so that the musical numbers were miniature visual pyrotechnic exercises.

But it was apparent that a measure of slickness in Lester's work was overtaking the power of the content. *A Funny Thing Happened on the Way to the Forum* was a frenetic attempt at filming a straight musical from the theatre, a Plautus plot made into a modern New York Jewish comedy, while retaining its ancient setting, with Zero Mostel in the lead, as a slave attempting to gain his freedom. The film, shot in Spain, was classified as an American production in spite of a considerable amount of British talent involved in its execution. It was also the last film in which Buster Keaton appeared. *How I Won the War* was Lester's anti-war film, a combination of broad comedy and violence, shot with a grim satiric energy, a failure of a film because the message became muddled beneath a series of contrived effects, many of which failed to work, like a series of weak revue sketches. His next and best film, *Petulia*, was made in the U.S.A. with the English star Julie Christie, and after that Lester returned to Britain to make *The Bed-Sitting Room*, an unsatisfactory return to the Goonish humour of earlier works.

Sidney Lumet, a distinguished American director, made two interesting films in Britain during the 1960s. *The Hill*, with Sean Connery, Ian Bannen and Harry Andrews was a bitter war film, set in a desert detention camp, and was a meticulous study of a deliberately created sadistic system, shot with a claustrophobic eye for detail. The central point of the camp is an artificial mound up which the prisoners are forced to scramble in the sweltering sun by the ruthless R.S.M. The screenplay was by Ray Rigby, co-author with R. S. Allen of the original play. Lumet's other film was in the genre of the spy thriller. *The Deadly Affair*, with James Mason and Simone Signoret, is a workmanlike, unglamorous and totally consistent work, shot in drab and realistic colour by Freddie Young and written by Paul Dehn from a novel by John le Carré. Martin Ritt had also worked in the John le Carré world with his version of the best-known work, *The Spy Who Came in from the Cold*, which had Richard Burton as the shabby agent in East Germany, recalled to go through a series of squalid experiences before a confrontation with his arch enemy, the East German counter-espionage chief, played by Peter van Eyck.

John Huston, who in the early fifties had made several British films, including *The African Queen*, *Moulin Rouge* and *Moby Dick* was responsible for two films in Britain in the sixties. The first was the thriller, *The List of Adrian Messenger*, a very personal and stylized murder mystery played out against a deliberately old-fashioned background of East End dockside pubs and massive country houses, enlivened by the fleeting appearance of several major American stars such as Frank Sinatra, Burt Lancaster and Tony Curtis in unrecognizable disguises. The film followed the classic pattern of detective thrillers, the central character, played by George C. Scott, patiently unravelling his clues until eventually the killer, a master of disguise, is literally unmasked. A combination of private joke and methodical exercise,

Adrian Messenger was a curious work, more in the spirit of *The Maltese Falcon* or *Beat the Devil* than most of Huston's films, but missing some of the spirit of both by dint of the ponderousness of its treatment.

Having adopted Ireland as his habitat, it is not surprising that Huston should choose to film there, and *Sinful Davey* used its Irish locations as substitutes for early nineteenth-century Scotland. Ostensibly the biography of Davey Taggart, a young pickpocket bent on capping the deeds of his celebrated father, who had perished on the gallows in the year of his birth, the film was an almost Disneyesque romp through a series of action adventures bult around the likeable hero, played with gusto by John Hurt. Like *Adrian Messenger* the film used the grand disguise as a plot device. Taggart, insinuating himself into the Duke of Argyll's ball and skilfully removing every vestige of jewellery from all the ladies he dances with, or dodging with great facility the heavy-footed officer of the law, played by Nigel Davenport, who is constantly pursuing him, and finally cheating the hangman through the devoted contrivance of his friend McNab (Ronald Fraser) and his girl Annie (Pamela Franklin), was a popular, delightful miscreant, a fact recognized by the genial Duke (Robert Morley), who sees to it that the condemned cell is furnished like a stately home. This is Huston at his most whimsical, a baffling film for critics expecting something more significant in his work.

A far more serious historical film was Fred Zinneman's magnificent interpretation of Robert Bolt's play (the screenplay was also his) of the downfall of Sir Thomas More, *A Man for All Seasons*, designed by John Box and photographed by Ted Moore, with a style finely evoking Tudor England. A long and distinguished cast included Paul Scofield as Sir Thomas More, Robert Shaw as Henry VIII, Leo McKern as Thomas Cromwell and Orson Welles as a powerful Cardinal Wolsey. Visually entrancing and sensitively directed, the film's major limitation seemed to be in the style of its dialogue, which was bland and unexciting for such a tragic theme.

Stanley Donen, originator with Gene Kelly of some of the best MGM. musicals of the late forties and early fifties, such as *On the Town* and *Singin' in the Rain*, has made several British films, starting with the insipid comedy of stately home infidelities, *The Grass Is Greener* (1961), unredeemed by a cast which included Cary Grant, Deborah Kerr, Robert Mitchum and Jean Simmons. *Arabesque* (1966), a spy thriller with Gregory Peck and Sophia Loren, although shot and set mostly in England, counted against quota as an American film and was loaded with all manner of chic pictorial effects, Donen demonstrating a weakness apparent from an earlier thriller with Cary Grant and Audrey Hepburn (*Charade*, 1964) for shooting his images indirectly as reflections in mirrors or other shiny surfaces, thus dissipating the narrative energy. *Bedazzled* (1967) found him on different ground in a comedy built around Peter Cook and Dudley Moore, whose act had become well known on television. An updated version of the Faust legend, with Peter Cook as the Devil in the disguise of a seedy opera-cloaked George Spigott, and Dudley Moore as a girl-hungry short-order cook, it was aided by Eleanor Bron as the same girl appearing in a number of disguises. Based on a screenplay by the two comedians, the film was an extended series of television sketches, amusing enough for Moore–Cook addicts, but painfully inadequate for anyone not drawn to their particular school of humour. *Two for the Road* (1967), in spite of a novelettish script by Frederic Raphael, was Donen's most successful British work – an itinerant film in which an architect (Albert Finney) and his wife (Audrey Hepburn), on their travels, recall previous journeys before they became bored with their marriage. An entertaining and glossy picture, it had the benefit of excellent location photography by Christopher Challis and a romantic score by Henry Mancini, to say nothing of Audrey Hepburn's extravagant wardrobe which included items by Foale and Tuffin, Ken Scott, Paco Rabanne, Mary Quant and other illustrious names of the so-called swinging sixties.

It was this world that the leading Italian director, Michelangelo Antonioni, attempted to capture in his first British film, *Blow-Up*. The central character, a young, rich, petulant photographer played by David Hemmings, was himself very much a symbol of the period, and is established at the start, having slept in a dosshouse so that he can gain photo-reportage material for a book, driving away in a Rolls-Royce. While photographing in a London park he sees a man and a woman embracing. The woman runs over to stop him taking pictures but he returns to his studio. The woman appears, demanding the negatives, and he gives her a substitute roll. On developing his picture he is startled to find what appears to be a man with a gun in the bushes–and, in a later shot, a body. Rushing back to the park in the middle of the night he finds the body, but on his return to the studio all his pictures have disappeared. When he returns to the park in the morning the body, too, has gone. It all might never have happened. And to emphasize the thinness of the gulf between illusion and reality the photographer, leaving the park, takes part with some students in an imaginary tennis match, without a ball or racquet, yet with the sounds of a game being heard on the soundtrack. It is a study of the fallibility of modern communication, the obscuring of truth by modern iconography. The world beyond the trendy fashion photographer's ambience ceases to have permanence or meaning. As an attempt at a thriller style, the film was less successful than it might have been, lacking the precise cutting of a Hitchcock or the unambiguous symbolism of a Lang. But Antonioni attempted merely to work within the genre, finding it a convenient means of establishing his point. David Hemmings succeeded in a long and difficult role, as the photographer, but for Vanessa Redgrave the task of providing a semblance of plausibility for the actions of the woman proved beyond her capabilities. *Blow-Up*, while an interesting work and a fine debut in an alien tongue, was by no means the most successful of Antonioni's works.

The same, regrettably, must be said for the film François Truffaut made at Pinewood in 1966 under a short-lived policy by Universal to bring European directors to British studios. *Fahrenheit 451* was from Ray Bradbury's science-fiction novel about a world in the future which no longer permits books, and the struggle of an independent thinker to defeat the regime. Oskar Werner played a fireman (in this future period the firemen were employed in starting, not extinguishing, fires – of books), who begins to read the works he is ordered to destroy. Betrayed by his wife, one of two roles played by Julie Christie, he is lured by another girl in her image to a different community, a primitive tribe of forest-dwellers, all of whom have chosen to commit a classic literary work to memory, so that it can be transmitted to future generations. The film followed the usual Truffaut introversion, the close-up of a loner against an implacable society, the individual who seeks an alternative to the society in which he finds himself – a theme distinct in his work from his first feature, *Les Quatre Cents Coups*. Eschewing the methods usually employed in science-fiction films, with complex and far-fetched gadgetry and costumes, the world in this film looked disturbingly normal, although it was meant to be a long way into another age. The neat housing estates and modish clothes worn by Julie Christie are of our own time – it is the behaviour and the sterile attitudes of people that are alien, although they are really extensions or projections of contemporary attitudes. Science fiction is essentially fable-like and this Bradbury story is an excellent example, though curiously, less spectacularly conceived in film terms than in the original book.

Roman Polanski, the young Polish director of *Knife in the Water*, has made the bulk of his work in Britain, beginning with the gruesome and nightmarish horror of *Repulsion*, in which a psychotic young girl left alone in a flat has hallucinations, murders her boy-friend, barricades herself in, then cuts the landlord's jugular vein with a razor. Polanski's greatest skill in this film lay in his treatment of incipient madness – distorting furniture and wallpaper, dwelling closely on curious domestic shapes, a crinkled potato, a skinned rabbit. Catherine Deneuve as the girl was able by a vacant and wide-eyed performance to mirror her disturbed condition with a realism so intense that it seems surprising that none of the other members of the cast notice that anything is wrong. Polanski's second British film, *Cul de Sac*, also built up an atmosphere of nightmare lunacy, but with a plot that strained credulity to its ultimate limit its impact was greatly blunted. A pair of gangsters on the run barricade themselves on a remote island and terrorize the occupants of the only house. The master of the house is a pathetic and effeminate weakling with a beautiful and selfish wife who is plainly bored by him. One of the gangsters forms a third part of the triangle, as in *Knife in the Water*. Donald Pleasence, Lionel Stander and Françoise Dorleac (Catherine Deneuve's sister) made what they could of the unlikely material and Gilbert Taylor's location photography of Holy Island, off the Northumberland coast, was impressive, but the film was disappointing. Polanski's next, *Dance of the Vampires*, followed a more conventional and overt approach to the horror genre, and was not without considerable black humour.

Jean Luc-Godard's film made in Britain, *One Plus One*, which featured the Rolling Stones, was fragmentary and eccentric and the subject of considerable controversy during the 1968 London Film Festival; it remains a curiosity, a poor example of his work.

Joseph Strick's *Ulysses*, made in Ireland, qualified under quota as a British film, and turned out to be inevitably a reduction of a masterpiece, James Joyce's novel being spread over so broad a canvas that it defied any attempt to constrict it to the screen. A cherished long-term project, *Ulysses* was more celebrated as a watershed for a new censorship attitude than as a film. The BBFC refused to give it a classification, and it played to local authority certificates. Certain municipal and county councils banned it outright, but the GLC allowed it to play in its full version. Molly's soliloquy, beautifully delivered by

Barbara Jefford, explored language hitherto unheard in the British cinema, but, in spite of the fierce controversy brewed by the press, the film was boring, worthy, undramatic and only very mildly outrageous, in pitiful contrast with the grandeur of its original.

Among the veteran directors of Hollywood who filmed in Britain in the later sixties were Otto Preminger, George Sidney and Billy Wilder. Preminger made a brisk, conventional thriller about a kidnapped child, *Bunny Lake Is Missing*, filmed with sufficient brio to cause one to overlook the implausibilities of the plot. Genuine locations in and around Hampstead and Trafalgar Square contrast with absolutely fanciful interiors, such as a toyshop packed with broken dolls, and the mews flat of a curiously indulgent character acted by Noël Coward, who keeps a rack full of whips, one of which he alleges belonged to the Marquis de Sade. Keir Dullea is called upon to play a psychotic and Laurence Olivier a police detective, with Clive Revill as an able assistant, and an excellent performance by Anna Massey as a young schoolteacher. By no means Preminger's best, the film nevertheless bore the marks of a shrewd and professional entertainer.

George Sidney's large-scale musical, *Half a Sixpence*, was an adaptation of a successful stage show based on the H. G. Wells novel *Kipps*, with Tommy Steele retained in the leading role of the orphan draper who rises to a higher station and over-reaches himself. A director as experienced in putting across lavish musical spectacle as Sidney could be relied upon to offer an exhilarating film, and *Half a Sixpence* combined considerable brashness in the staging of its production numbers, particularly 'Flash, Bang, Wallop!' and 'Money to Burn', aided by Gillian Lynne's energetic choreography, with an intelligent and sensitive use of a number of English locations, such as the Pantiles at Tunbridge Wells standing in for Folkestone. Tommy Steele's performing presence, brimming with effervescence and gusto, demonstrated a maturity as a musical actor, unjustified by the bulk of his screen work.

It must be recorded that at least three major productions by American companies in Britain had to be switched to other countries. Joseph L. Mankiewicz, after a protracted and costly wait for the wet Buckinghamshire skies to clear and give a semblance of the Nile, scrapped the footage of *Cleopatra* shot in England, and made the film in Italy. William Wyler began *The Collector* in England, but finished the film in Hollywood, and Richard Fleischer's *Doctor Doolittle*, which used the Wiltshire village of Castle Combe as the port of Puddleby, finally gave up on account of the weather, rather than the opposition of some of the locals, and the film was finished in California. The English climate has rarely been on the side of film-makers and the costs of keeping units waiting for the rain to stop have often nullified the savings in production costs.

24 Hope Springs Eternal

The latter half of the sixties was remarkable for the number of emer-
gent British directors, materializing in an even more prolific array
than the resurgence of 1959–63. Television turned out to be the most
fruitful training ground and many of the new names appearing in the
British film industry had crossed the divide from home entertainment.
Among this breed were Ken Loach, Jack Gold, Peter Collinson, Kevin
Billington, Silvio Narrizano, Peter Watkins, Philip Saville, Ted
Kotcheff, Ken Russell, Joseph McGrath and Christopher Morahan,
but the list could go on. In addition, there were brave individual
attempts to establish reputations. Anthony Harvey, an editor of some
experience, made a short feature, *Dutchman*, set on a New York sub-
way train, in which a white girl accosts, insults and finally kills a
young Negro. The shooting schedule was a week, and apart from some
establishing shots of stations was filmed entirely on one set, with
Shirley Knight and Al Freeman Jr as his cast. A remarkable and savage
film, establishing within its one hour running time an atmosphere of
hate and evil from a centuries-old conflict, the film was an auspicious
start to a directorial career; and it led to Harvey being contracted to
direct *The Lion in Winter* from James Goldman's play about the visit
of Eleanor of Aquitaine to her husband, Henry II, at the Christmas of
1183. This featured a virtuoso performance by Katharine Hepburn,
supported by Peter O'Toole in a role somewhat more middle-aged than
he was.

Another director who fought against the odds to get a film made was
Donn Levy, who began *Herostratus* in 1962, and finally had it shown
in 1968. A sustained *tour de force*, the film's theme was that of a young
poet who gets an advertising agency to promote his impending suicide
as a protest against the values of the consumer society. Using various
experimental techniques (blank screen between shots instead of
'transitional opticals', subliminal cutting, highly stylized colour and

an exploration of psychological disturbance), the film had extraordinary power and feeling.

Perhaps even more remarkable, in terms of an exhaustive and single-minded pursuit of an ambitious objective, is the story of how *It Happened Here* came to be filmed. Kevin Brownlow and Andrew Mollo, a trainee film cutter and a military enthusiast respectively, began the film on an amateur basis in 1956, when they were both in their teens, shooting it on 16mm. It was the account of what might have happened in Britain had the Nazi invasion taken place in 1940. Gripped by the intriguing possibilities of this theme the two young film-makers expanded their conception and spent several years raising money to shoot further sequences, eventually, with the assistance of Woodfall, moving into 35mm. By 1964 the film was complete, and had cost £7,000, a remarkably modest sum for such an ambitious work. It managed to create a fictional historical event with such graphic realism that much of it looked like a newsreel, unearthed from some archive. Both of its directors were sticklers for realism, insisting on the most minor details being correct with greater exactitude than many feature films with a budget a hundred times the size. Many of the crowd scenes were shot with unpaid performers, and their enthusiasm garnered much voluntary talent. The film first appeared at the Cork Film Festival in 1964 and in 1966 was shown commercially at the London Pavilion, but with a ciné-verité sequence, in which genuine British fascists playing Nazis aired their views spontaneously in the course of an interview, removed by order of the distributors, United Artists, for fear of repercussions on the grounds of anti-Semitism.

The theatre was also a fruitful source for future film directors. The young former director of the Royal Shakespeare Theatre, Peter Hall, made his film debut with an adaptation of Henry Living's *Eh* (its title expanded to *Work Is a Four-Letter Word*), in which David Warner played a misfit in a near-future technological society, with Cilla Black making an inconspicuous debut as his gormless but devoted fiancée. The treatment seemed to owe more to Marcel Varnel's George Formby comedies than to René Clair's work on the same theme, and while making a brave attempt at a satirical exposure of the nightmares of the modern world, the target was fumbled. Hall's next film was an adaptation of a Royal Shakespeare performance of *A Midsummer Night's Dream*, performed in a soggy, autumnal location with grotesquely post-synchronized dialogue taking the edge off the performers' delivery. In spite of a cast which included David Warner as

Lysander, Diana Rigg as Helena, Judi Dench as Titania, Ian Holm as Puck, Paul Rogers as Bottom and Barbara Jefford as Hippolyta, the result was a heavy-handed *farrago* which made Shakespeare's lightest and most fanciful of plays look dull and unattractive, inviting unfavourable comparisons with Max Reinhardt's pre-war Hollywood version, which had Mickey Rooney as Puck and James Cagney as Bottom.

But before dismissing Peter Hall's contribution to the cinema, consideration must be given to his third film, *Two into Three Won't Go*, a study of a collapsing marriage and the infiltration of a rootless girl into the relationship, who acts as a catalyst for the eventual disaster. Rod Steiger as a travelling businessman constantly attuned to the possibility of an itinerant sexual encounter, Claire Bloom as the childless, intelligent wife coping on her own in settling into a new house on a soul-less suburban executive estate, and Judy Geeson as the girl hitch-hiker, a contemporary child, awarding marks to her lovers for their sexual prowess, lying compulsively and without purpose, gave excellent moving performances, aided by Peggy Ashcroft as the wife's fading, dotty mother and Paul Rogers as a lecherous hotel-keeping old army friend of the husband. The film had something of the quality of *Brief Encounter*, a futile, destructive affair played out in a quintessentially contemporary English setting. It represents Hall's maturest and most capable screen work.

Peter Brook, a giant of the theatre, whose film ventures had been singular in their determination (*Moderato Cantabile* was filmed in France, *Lord of the Flies* was made only after immense difficulties in raising the money, and even after completion was only released following painful and protracted negotiation), turned his stage production *The Persecution and Assassination of Jean-Paul Marat as Performed by the Inmates of the Asylum of Charenton under the Direction of the Marquis de Sade* from the play by Peter Weiss into a film, retaining the theatricality of the original. This could be justified on the grounds that the *Marat/Sade* was already a multi-level *divertissement*, a confusion of reality between the events of the play within a play and the lunatics acting it out. The film is more than a mere record of a theatrical performance, being a fusion of the two mediums into an integrated artistic work. Brook later made *Tell Me Lies*, an assembly inspired by his Aldwych production *Us*, an indictment of the Vietnam war. A strange and contorted attack on British complacency, ignorance and impotence, the film lacked the Brechtian passion that had made the stage performance a memorable theatrical experience; it was merely a collage of documentary discussion, newsreel and enacted incident. Brook's next film essay was a version of *King Lear*, photographed in Denmark in a freezing landscape with Paul Scofield movingly portraying Shakespeare's ageing monarch.

Sir Laurence Olivier's astonishing performance of *Othello* for the National Theatre in John Dexter's production was recorded on film in an absolutely straightforward studio production by Stuart Burge in 1966. Cinematically unremarkable, the film is valuable as a lasting reminder of a controversial and fascinating interpretation of Shakespeare's tragic hero. Franco Zeffirelli, after making *The Taming of the Shrew* with the Burtons in Italy, made *Romeo and Juliet* with genuine teenagers in the roles – sixteen-year-old Leonard Whiting and fifteen-year-old Olivia Hussey, with considerably fresher results than the Renato Castellani film of 1954, which used Laurence Harvey and Susan Shentall in the same parts. Zeffirelli's film was hardly faithful to the text, but had considerable zest and attack and achieved its ends by breathtaking camera work and flowing narrative.

Also to be considered in the context of theatrical directors working in the cinema is Peter Glenville, a former actor, whose first film was *The Prisoner* (1954), with Alec Guinness and Jack Hawkins, and who later made *Term of Trial*. His *Becket*, with Richard Burton performing with Peter O'Toole as Henry II, was an adaptation of Jean Anouilh's play. It was a very literary film, preserving lengthy chunks of the original dialogue, and moved at a pedestrian pace relieved only occasionally by a startling visual effect. *Hotel Paradiso*, Glenville's next film, remained unshown until 1971. It was followed by his version of Graham Greene's novel set in President Duvalier's Haiti, *The Comedians*, a co-production of U.S.A., Bermuda and France.

The Royal Court, scene of the renaissance of English theatre in the mid-fifties, contributed several talents to the British cinema, particularly John Osborne, Tony Richardson and Lindsay Anderson. Richardson's work after *Tom Jones* was largely disappointing: there was a misplaced attempt in Hollywood to film Evelyn Waugh's *The Loved One*; the disastrous *Mademoiselle* and the feeble *Sailor from Gibraltar*, both with Jeanne Moreau; and *Red and Blue*, with Vanessa Redgrave. Only in his long-term project, *The Charge of the Light Brigade*, did his full power reassert itself. It was a diatribe against the values of Victorian England and the wilful cruelty of the military authorities in the Crimea. The *mise-en-scène* was constructed with care and a good eye, the dialogue by Charles Wood was splattered with a mixture of modern and period expletives, and Trevor Howard as the bristling, faintly eccentric Lord Cardigan and Sir John Gielgud as Lord Raglan contributed interesting and vastly enjoyable performances. As a view of history it was an odd and occasionally quite inaccurate film. Cartoon interpolations by Dick Williams, while brilliantly executed in the manner of nineteenth-century political cartoons, appeared to be devices to bridge lacunae in the narrative, and the exposition of the final disaster quite failed to produce a plausible explanation for the astonishing mistake. The battle scenes found Richardson at his worst, unable to produce a coherent sequence, resorting instead to violent camera movement and distorted sound to cover up the inadequacies. A well-tried theme, this was the fifth film to deal with the ride of the six hundred into the 'Valley of Death' at Balaclava, and while a not unworthy attempt, it had glaring faults, and was another infuriating example of Richardson's shortcomings as a serious director.

Lindsay Anderson, unlike Richardson, has shown no inclination towards a prolific cinematic output. Between *This Sporting Life* and *If. . . .* he made only one other film, a forty-one-minute segment of what was to be one part of a three-decker, the other episodes to be directed by Tony Richardson and Peter Brook. *The White Bus* was an interesting and ambiguous experiment, not succeeding because its images were too gnomic for immediate comprehension. It is a study of alienation, almost an autobiographical reminiscence of its writer, Shelagh Delaney, returning from London to the Northern town in which she was brought up. Seen in isolation, the film disappoints; how it may have fared had the others been completed one cannot know. The Richardson story later became the unfortunate *Red and Blue*.

But with *If. . . .* Anderson reached out to the peak of achievement in the British cinema and made a film which must count as one of the most powerful ever made by an English director. A study of a rebel in an English public school, it showed an individual making a protest against authority, a cry which turns eventually into anarchy and armed insurrection, with parents, masters and prefects subjected to guerrilla gunfire from the rooftops on Founders' Day, an ending recalling Jean Vigo's classic *Zero de Conduite*, which had more than one resemblance to Anderson's film. The school, with its archaic, meaningless customs, its pseudo-progressive headmaster mouthing platitudes about the need for accepting the challenge of social change, the authoritarian rule of the prefects, represented a microcosm for the whole of English society. The school was Britain, its staff and prefects symbols of the establishment, the hero and his two young colleagues voices of dissent. Appearing in the year when world-wide student protest movements sparked off considerable revaluations of the accepted order, *If....* achieved weight by its excellent timing. But regardless of journalistic topicality, the film had the power of passion in its statement, a strong, political, committed force not merely unusual, but virtually unknown within the British cinema. That the film emerged, not without production difficulties owing to financial shortfalls, was to the credit of Paramount, who distributed and secured an excellent run at one of their new Piccadilly Circus theatres, and also persuaded ABC to give it a general release, with success, thus proving that an intelligent film can be marketed to the British public, whatever the traditional beliefs in Wardour Street.

Of other directors who blazed into life at the beginning of the decade, John Schlesinger probably retained most of his initial reputation. His *Darling* (1965) forsook the industrial North for the world of tele-pundits, public relations men and *dolce vita* of the affluent metropolis, using Julie Christie as a girl on the make, easing her way through the chic social areas into an ultimate stage of pampered boredom as the wife of an unfaithful Italian aristocrat. The script by Frederic Raphael was astringent and cultivated, peppered with references to the fickle values of the mid-sixties.

Julie Christie was cast in Schlesinger's next film, a long-standing project, as the heroine of Thomas Hardy's poetic paean for a rural England already rapidly vanishing in his day, *Far From the Madding Crowd*. Organized in the epic manner, the film attempted an evocation of the country scene in mid-Victorian England, using delicate colour photography by Nicolas Roeg, and an engaging assembly of rustics, led by Alan Bates as the staunch shepherd, Gabriel Oak, who wins Bathsheba after many vicissitudes. Peter Finch was well cast as Boldwood, the withdrawn, brooding neighbour who, driven crazy by love for Bathsheba, eventually resorts to violence. Less successful was Terence Stamp's Sergeant Troy, the dashing cavalry man who secures the heroine, her farm and her inheritance and then squanders them. Hardy always depicted his characters as puppets in the hands of some higher determinism, with violence and passion lurking just beneath the smooth surface. Schlesinger, while constructing a visually attractive film, failed to get under this surface; his performers mostly move as puppets, without revealing the mainspring of their motivation. Consequently Bathsheba, one of the most powerful of Hardy's heroines, appears to be merely fickle and vacillating. Schlesinger's next film was an American one, made in New York, the excellent *Midnight Cowboy*.

Karel Reisz also entered the area of the large-scale high-budget international picture with *Isadora*, a biography of Isadora Duncan, the American dancer whose art and life was always good for columns of newspaper copy in the earlier part of the century. Advocate of free love, worshipper of the Russian revolution and fanatic of an ideal embodied in Greek classical dancing, Isadora was a woman of undoubted genius and charismatic power, barely suggested by Vanessa Redgrave in Reisz's film, which makes her into a boring, tedious and insufferable person few would have wanted to be in the same room with. The eccentric casting of James Fox as Gordon Craig and such touches as the Angel of Death, a mysterious stranger at the wheel of a red Bugatti who flits in and out of the scenes in her later years, and eventually drives her off to the sudden and horrific death as her trailing scarf gets caught in the rear wheel and breaks her neck, gave a grotesque air to the film which at times seemed about to topple into total absurdity. Ambitious and costly, with a script by Melvyn Bragg and Clive Exton, neither exactly lacking in talent as writers, *Isadora* nevertheless missed the essential quality of its subject and lost, too, the simplicity of approach which had made Reisz's *Saturday Night and Sunday Morning* one of the most encouraging signs of reawakening in the British cinema. It suffered also by comparison with the capable low-budget television film made for the BBC by Ken Russell two or three years before.

Bryan Forbes, another director to emerge earlier in the decade, continued his career with *The Wrong Box*, an amusing if somewhat heavy-handed treatment of a novel by Robert Louis Stevenson and Lloyd Osbourne about a tontine of £100,000 and the struggles of various avaricious characters to acquire it. In spite of a cast which included Peter Sellers as an absent-minded doctor given to picking up a kitten and using it to blot his wet ink, Ralph Richardson as a garrulous and appalling bore, Wilfrid Lawson (his last screen role) as a magnificently decrepit butler, Peter Cook and Dudley Moore as two nephews intent on laying hands on the fortune, and an amazing cast filling minor parts, with even Tony Hancock in a completely wasted role, the film gives the impression of assembly in haste. After *The Whisperers*,

Forbes made *Deadfall*, a thriller in a tradition begun by *Rififi* some years earlier, with Michael Caine as an energetic cat burglar and Eric Portman as a homosexual mastermind. In spite of the customary tension scene in which a daring jewel robbery is carried out with the precision of a moon landing, the film was too enmeshed in its pretentious atmosphere to offer much satisfaction. Before taking over as the production head at Associated British, Forbes completed *The Mad Woman of Chaillot*, a star-studded adaptation of Giraudoux's play, ornate and allegorical, a self-consciously old-fashioned film.

The Boultings, after so many send-ups of cherished British institutions, turned in 1966 to straightforward northern working-class comedy, with Bill Naughton's own adaptation of a play, *The Family Way*. It told of the early marital problems of a young couple, played sympathetically by Hayley Mills and Hywel Bennett, whose failure to consummate their union becomes common knowledge throughout their town. John Mills gave a comic performance as the boy's father, and the supporting cast included Marjorie Rhodes, Wilfred Pickles, Avril Angers and Liz Frazer. The film managed to avoid the pitfalls one would associate with this type of subject, and to convey a reasonably convincing view of life in a northern town.

Twisted Nerve retained the Hayley Mills and Hywel Bennett partnership, but in a vastly different film. A study of a psychotic youth given to retreating into a sub-normal alter ego, it shows him fastening on to a young girl and later murdering her mother with an axe. The film aroused controversy by its glib association of mongolism with psychopathic violence, an unthinking, false conclusion which was bound to cause distress to families affected in this way. But apart from the poor taste that led to this sensationalist attitude, prominent not only in the film but in the advertising campaign which accompanied its West End screening, it was a poorly constructed and predictable thriller, the camera used to make its points with the delicacy of a sledgehammer.

A director emerging in the sixties without an apprenticeship in television, something of a rarity in the new age, was Michael Winner, whose path after graduating from Cambridge had been via teaboy, through fifth-rate featurettes to second-rate nudist films, and eventually, after some disastrous first features (*The Cool Mikado*, *West 11*), to a well-made and stylish film, *The System*, filmed entirely on location in a west of England resort, with Oliver Reed as the leader of a group of young men who use his job as an outdoor photographer as the basis for a girl-hunting scheme. A script by Peter Draper helped the astringency of its outlook on English girls on holiday. Winner's next film was *You Must Be Joking*, an account of an army initiative test with Terry-Thomas and Lionel Jeffries providing their customary comic performances. An amazing, if somewhat obvious, succession of old jokes, the film was enlivened by the director's constant application of fashionable cinematic tricks, a Winner characteristic, which usually comes off, thanks to the totally unselfconscious manner in which they are employed. *The Jokers* developed Winner's comic style with a robbery of the Crown Jewels making the authorities look foolish. The intention of the miscreants, Oliver Reed and Michael Crawford, is not to steal the regalia but merely to borrow it, an act which is not felony in spite of the confusion into which it throws the police and the military. Written by Dick Clement and Ian Le Frenais, whose work on television (*The Likely Lads*) had achieved considerable success, the film moved at a fast, good-humoured pace and demonstrated a lineage from the *Passport to Pimlico* style of Ealing comedy.

I'll Never Forget What's 'is Name was a much harder and sharper comment on the world of advertising, an attempt at depicting the cynical values prevailing in the communications business, with Oliver Reed as an adman retreating from his expensive job to work on a struggling literary magazine, only to find it bought up by his erstwhile and odious client, played by Orson Welles. Back in the advertising world again, the hero makes a television commercial so honest in its statement that he feels sure it will destroy the product – instead it wins an award coveted by the client. The script was again by Peter Draper and was full of acid comments on its characters – the hero is vastly unlikeable and appallingly callous towards his wife. A reunion at his minor public school ends in the same bullies and the same victim re-enacting their roles of twenty years earlier. The message of the film appears to be that beneath the superficial values of the adman's culture there is nothing much – life is disillusion. The negative approach of the film is unsatisfying and ambiguous.

Winner's next film, *Hannibal Brooks*, again starring Oliver Reed, moved towards a more whimsical approach to a curious subject, a wartime escape from a German prison camp across the Alps into Switzerland, with an elephant. A quirk of casting put Reed in the part of the elephant-obsessed escaper and Michael Pollard, the pudgy-faced third member of the *Bonnie and Clyde* gang, in the role of an escaped American, now leading a private guerrilla army. The reverse casting, plus the mixture of bloodshed and high farce, made the film an uneven and difficult mixture to classify and the unsureness of the director's intentions was very apparent. The film which followed was *The Games*, a drama played out around the Olympics with Stanley Baker as an unyielding coach, Michael Crawford as an ultimately rebellious athlete and Ryan O'Neal as his ambitious American rival. Winner's rapid and effervescent career at least demonstrated an ability to garner the talents of exceptional performers such as Orson Welles.

A similar skill was apparent in the first film directed by Richard Attenborough, at the comparatively mature age of forty-five. After a long and distinguished film career as an actor (his first appearance, it should be recalled, was a panic-stricken stoker in *In Which We Serve*) and as a producer of such films as *The Angry Silence*, *The L-Shaped Room* and *Whistle Down the Wind*, in partnership with Bryan Forbes, it was not until 1968 that he was able to direct a film himself. His choice was *Oh! What a Lovely War*, a Brechtian entertainment of a few years earlier that had been staged by Joan Littlewood, and was intended as a diatribe on the folly of the First World War, using songs, diaries and commentaries of the period in a kind of dramatic anthology. The theatre performance re-enacted the whole ghastly tragedy on the stage of a seaside pier, the actors wearing the traditional white clowns' costume under their khaki service dress caps. Attenborough took the film completely into the cinematic dimension, shooting all the action in and around Brighton, retaining the seaside atmosphere of the summer of 1914. The Western Front was spread out across the South Downs, the sea often faintly visible at the rear of some shot showing the mud and misery of the front line in the foreground. Like a mammoth pageant, a vast cast including many of the best known names in the British cinema appeared, said their line or two and vanished. Yet so well did John Mills as Haig, Laurence Olivier as French, Michael Redgrave as Wilson, John Clements as Von Moltke and Vanessa Redgrave as Mrs Pankhurst, and many others, integrate with the film, that it was more than a star-spotting charade: it was an ordered and coherent totality.

The songs of the war were used with brilliant orchestrations by Alfred Ralston to extract the maximum poignancy and futility of the sacrifice. Particularly outstanding was Maggie Smith's rendering of the recruiting song, 'I'll Make a Man of You', which revealed her glamorous soubrette at the conclusion, when the able young men of the audience are safely in the hands of the colour sergeant, as an over-painted, frowsty whore. The songs were often simple parodies by the soldiers of contemporary melodies – in the words by anonymous hands the most pathetic cries of all, the anger directed not at politicians or even generals, but at sergeants, or merely the acceptance of some situation ordained by fate – 'We're here because we're here.' At the film's conclusion the crosses march across the downs until they stand thousand upon thousand, as far as the eye can see, and the sound-track resounds to a pastiche of Jerome Kern: 'And when they ask us / how dangerous it was / oh, we'll never tell them / no, we'll never tell them. / We spent our pay in some café / and fought wild women night and day / Was the cushiest job we ever had. / And when they ask us / and they're certainly going to ask us / the reason why we didn't win the Croix de Guerre / oh, we'll never tell them / no, we'll never tell them / there was a front – but damned if we knew where.' It was a film that moved in a new direction and enlarged the horizon, and, while marred by occasional lapses of taste, it had an overall power and effectiveness that made it a rich and exciting cinematic experience and marked a notable, if belated, debut as a film director by Richard Attenborough, together with the work of Len Deighton on the screen-play. He removed his credit after differences with Attenborough, but nevertheless the film bore his mark.

Lewis Gilbert's *Alfie*, with Michael Caine as a Bill Naughton hero of the times, amoral, working-class, hard-edged, sexually athletic, was the foster parent of a number of films in this genre. Ken Loach's *Poor Cow*, from a Nell Dunn novel, a dismal description of the mis-fortunes of a working-class girl involved with a young criminal, was the best, using television techniques to push the narrative forward – titles within the film, straight interviews to the camera – an indication of the training Loach had received in the TV medium, culminating in his outstanding drama documentary, *Cathy Come Home*, which featured Carol White, the star of *Poor Cow*, in a poignant image of homeless-ness. Loach's next cinema film, *Kes*, with its Yorkshire setting, an uncompromising story of a boy's love for a kestrel, developed the unambiguous style of attack that characterized the earlier film.

Released at around the same time as *Poor Cow* was Peter Collin-son's *Up the Junction*, another film with television origins, being based on a television play by Nell Dunn, a collection of short observa-tions of life in Battersea. The film had an element of unreality in that it never adequately explained why a rich girl from across the river should choose to go and work on a factory level among working-class girls; the explanation that she gives to the boy she encounters – that it is here where the real people live – sounds patronizing and implausible. In spite of Suzy Kendall's performance as the 'posh' girl, and Denis Waterman as her boy-friend, who ends up in jail after trying to impress her with a stolen sports car, the film had an air of spuriousness. Christopher Morahan's *All Neat in Black Stockings*, from a novel by Jane Gaskell, who like Nell Dunn was a middle-class writer with a passion for the working-class, was in the same territory – in this case having Victor Henry as a window-cleaner who makes a mess of an affair with a girl cursed with a toffee-nosed mother.

Another forerunner in the genre was *Georgy Girl* (1966), directed by Silvio Narrizano from the novel by Margaret Forster, which was notable for the excellent performance of Lynn Redgrave as a tall, ungainly,warm-hearted and put-upon girl, suffering mainly from the selfishness of her attractive flatmate, played by Charlotte Rampling. Most of these films belonged to a style that can, for want of anything better, be called 'Swinging London', being based on the climate of permissiveness that began to prevail during the period of Roy Jenkins's Home Secretaryship. Abortions, unmarried mothers, promiscuity, four-letter words and other elements of the brand image of the permissive society became almost mandatory ingredients in films, the BBFC relaxing its standards bit by bit, but holding firmly to a policy of restricting the showing of films dealing with drug addiction. Even pubic hair became a forgotten taboo after the already mentioned deletion from the Swedish film *Hugs and Kisses* had demonstrated the ludicrousness of this type of censorship.

Peter Collinson of *Up the Junction* made *The Penthouse* in the previous year, a brutal and horrific study of two intruders in a flat occupied by a girl, played by Suzy Kendall, and her lover, who spend the subsequent time torturing the man and raping the girl. A tasteless and voyeuristic film, it showed the rough edge of Collinson's approach. His *The Long Day's Dying* was an anti-war film, centred on four commando soldiers in the Second World War, and showing their reaction to death in close-up – marred by facile violence and effects, and far less effective in its thesis than Losey's *King and Country*. Later Collinson made *The Italian Job*, an amusing exercise in organized crime, involving a massive robbery in Turin, masterminded by Noël Coward as a privileged British convict and noted mostly for the flamboyant stunt driving of a team of Mini-Coopers, designed to transport the stolen bullion from the scene of the crime. Michael Caine provided yet another performance of the cockney character operating on the fringes of the law, as in *Alfie*, the Harry Palmer films from Len Deighton's spy novels, and *Deadfall*.

Peter Yates, whose first directorial credit was for the amiable Cliff Richard musical, *Summer Holiday*, and who was also responsible for the film version of N. F. Simpson's *One Way Pendulum*, made a spectacular incursion into the world of the criminal with *Robbery*, supposedly based on the Great Train Robbery of 1963 in which a mail train carrying vast quantities of used banknotes was stopped and raided in perhaps the most notorious British crime that did not involve a murder. A brilliantly executed car chase through London streets at the opening of the film, which starred Stanley Baker as the leader of the gang, was a forerunner of the same director's celebrated chase sequence in his subsequent film, *Bullitt*, made in California, with Steve McQueen pursuing criminals at ninety m.p.h. up and down the steep streets of San Francisco. Like Collinson and Loach, Yates is a former television director.

Kevin Billington began his career making film items for the BBC, particularly the *Tonight* Programme, and moved on to direct major television documentaries on subjects such as Madison Avenue and the Guards Brigade. His first feature film was in contrast to much of the work of the television-trained new directors. *Interlude* was unashamedly romantic; the love affair of an internationally acclaimed conductor, played by Oskar Werner, and a young girl reporter on the *Evening Standard* initially sent to interview him, played by Barbara Ferris. The genealogy of this type of film went back into the mid-forties, a comparison made more apt by the frequent infusions of abbreviated classical music references (cf. *The Seventh Veil*, *Love Story*, etc.). On face value it would seem to be a curious choice of subject, an unfashionable women's magazine type of story. Billington handled it in a semi-documentary manner, using not only real locations such as the Royal Festival Hall and the Café Royal, but making all the references genuine ones, so that the girl is not for instance only working for the *Evening Standard*, a real newspaper, but also for a well-known specific section of it, the Londoner's Diary, rather than following the usual film habit of introducing fictitious journals such as the *London Globe*. Verisimilitude assisted the novelettishness of the plot and the film was an interesting debut.

Jack Gold also trained with the *Tonight* team; his first feature film, *The Bofors Gun*, was a work of remarkable integrity, and contained a virtuoso performance by Nicol Williamson as an intractable and violent Irish soldier determined to make life impossible for an ineffectual national serviceman, Lance Bombardier Evans, in charge of the guard duty, played by David Warner. Adapted by John McGrath from his own play, the action takes place on a gun site in Germany during the mid-fifties. Gunner O'Rourke, driven by a manic destructive force, is resolved to kill himself and thus ruin the guard commander's chance of a commission and a ticket out of the dismal camp. The action is confined to this one dreadful night, with Evans covering up O'Rourke's drunken escapades, losing the respect of the others, equivocating on the central issue of his motive for not reporting the insubordination. Gold's handling of actors was shown to be sure and a good cast, which included a superb portrayal of a kindly old sergeant by Peter Vaughan, gave the film an overall assurance and distinction. In spite of excellent reviews, it received few bookings on the Rank circuit, who were also the distributors.

The same was true of the first film directed by Albert Finney, *Charlie Bubbles*, which did not appear in Britain until after receiving critical acclaim and a good run in New York and other American cities. Finney played the central character, a successful and wealthy writer who feels isolated from his origins and on impulse takes off in his Rolls-Royce, accompanied by his American secretary, for Manchester, where he was brought up. He sees his estranged wife and takes his son to a football match which they watch from within a hermetically-sealed directors' box. There is a total failure to reach the same wavelength as the boy, and the film is a study of alienation, dexterously and confidently presented. At the conclusion of the film a surrealistic note appears; the writer having failed to communicate beyond himself sees a balloon in a meadow near his wife's house, and heaves himself into the basket to float away from his problems. *Charlie Bubbles* is strongest in its observation of the relationship with his wife, played by Billie Whitelaw. As a visual description of an arid marriage it is remarkable.

Of the remaining television directors, Philip Saville (*Oedipus*, *The Best House in London*), Joseph McGrath (*The Bliss of Mrs Blossom*) and Peter Watkins (*Privilege*) are worth some attention. Watkins's case is a peculiar one. Having achieved a considerable reputation with an uncompromising re-enactment of an ancient Highland battle in the BBC's *Culloden*, which used vivid locations and local men as the warriors, he made a documentary of the future, attempting to show what would happen if Britain were involved in an all-out nuclear war. The resulting film, *The War Game*, was considered too strong, too horrific, to be shown on television, and the BBC shelved it amidst a storm of disapproval. Eventually they agreed to allow the unprecedented to happen, for the film to be shown in selected commercial cinemas, and to be distributed by the British Film Institute. The notoriety and controversy excited by the film probably obscured its true quality. It is a cleverly produced piece of tendentious propaganda, achieving its effects by forcing an observation of a catastrophe too horrific to be considered; in other words, exploiting the deliberate back-turning of most people when they consider the effects of a nuclear holocaust. The weaknesses of Watkins's style, for all its skilful use of documentary techniques learned in television, were only too apparent in his first cinema film, *Privilege*, which dealt with the elevation of a pop singer by a cynical totalitarian government, into a pseudo-Christ figure who could serve as a distraction from too close a public attention of official policy.

The sixties ended with a new generation of film directors firmly in position, and the British film industry, in spite of continuing vicissitudes, likely to survive somehow as long as the process of making films on celluloid or its equivalent remained in use. Anthony Crosland, President of the Board of Trade, announced that the NFFC would be given a new lease of life, its depleted funds made up with public money to something like the original sum.

Of the directors who stood behind the great, brave days of the forties, when the British cinema enjoyed a unique national character, few remained. Asquith, Cornelius, Jennings and Hamer were dead, Dickinson lost from films to academe, David Lean and Carol Reed directors only of mammoth international roadshow pictures. Only the Boultings and Ronald Neame, whose excellent *The Prime of Miss Jean Brodie*, with Maggie Smith and Robert Stephens, emerged from Muriel Spark's novel, were still making films implicitly English in character. Even Michael Powell, who followed the success of his Australian film, *They're a Weird Mob*, with the delightfully observed and wittily written comedy about an artist who seeks seclusion on the Great Barrier Reef, *The Age of Consent*, would appear to have moved on from the essentially English character of his *Colonel Blimp*, *A Matter of Life and Death*, and even *Peeping Tom*. But this impression may be altered if ever his film version of Graham Greene's *The Living Room* reaches the screen.

25 The Last Challenge

It has been calculated that the number of cinemas open in the whole of Britain by the beginning of the seventies is equal to those in the London area only a quarter of a century earlier. A mere 1,552 remain of a total that once approached 5,000. Admissions have sunk from an annual rate of 1,514 million in 1948 to a mere 193 million. However, the industry, ever optimistic, began to feel relief in 1971 that the average age of audiences, for so long depressingly near the teenage level, was advancing. It was a crumb of comfort and a just reward for the concerted attempts that were at last being made to modernize patterns of distribution and exhibition.

Suburban cinemas of the inter-war years continue to close at a high rate, but while many sites are still being turned into supermarkets, office blocks, service stations and shopping centres, there is now a halt in the declining total number of cinemas, for many of the shut-down theatres are subsequently subjected to rebuilding programmes, opening later as small 'twinned' or even 'tripled' complexes. The advantages of the arrangement are manifold. An architectural re-design enables the auditorium shape to correspond with the widescreen format that has prevailed since the mid-fifties. The smaller size of the theatre makes cinema-going less of a lonely pastime, for the audience of a few hundred that looks so small in a cinema with 2,500–3,000 seats now fills its space to capacity. The cinema complexes need only one projection room with considerable manpower savings and periscopes are often installed to enable each auditorium to receive its picture from the same source. Automated equipment is often installed, relieving the functions of a projectionist still further. A single foyer and combined box-offices also make cinema operation more economic. But there is an overwhelming advantage to the patron – the extended choice of films available and the consequent greater flexibility of programming. Where three cinemas are brought together under one roof it is possible to have extended runs, probably with

70mm. projection apparatus, in one auditorium, a standard release in another and to keep the third for more specialized audiences.

Another exhibition tendency is the appearance of theatres operating entirely on 16mm. Not only are the running costs greatly reduced, but the range of available films multiplied. And with developments such as Super-16 beginning to come into use there is obviously a new type of exhibition method awaiting exploitation. New small theatre groups, led by the Classic circuit, are beginning to establish 16mm. houses, sometimes as one cinema in a triple complex, at other times in separate locations, usually where no cinema has previously existed, such as a new shopping precinct.

Changes are also taking place in circuit control. ABC became part of the massive EMI group, along with Elstree studios and the British end of the MGM distributing arm. The new management put into hand a large number of conversions to twins and triples throughout the country, and in a short period was able to boast a considerable lead over their sluggish competitor, Rank, who nevertheless effected major improvements in many of the key release cities. Rank has disposed of a number of cinemas they could no longer make pay to other cinema interests, reversing their original fifties policy when the first great wave of cinema decimation occurred. The Classic group is one of the beneficiaries of the new attitude and has acquired several former Odeons, boosting it into the third largest exhibition group in Britain. Classic was eventually taken over by Tigon, which had made its fortunes in the highly profitable area of Soho skin films, and under the astute leadership of its chairman, a property tycoon, Laurie Marsh, was poised to give Rank and ABC a genuine run for their money. By 1971 Tigon had achieved the enviable objective of vertical integration, having set up a production organization. They also had a multiplicity of other interests, including the burgeoning business of television cassettes. However, in 1973 Laurie Marsh withdrew from the film scene and it was clear that Classic was of more value to the group as High Street real estate than as cinemas.

Shortly before the Labour government, which had been in office since 1964, went to the country in June 1970 a new Films Act was put through Parliament. This maintained the quota at thirty per cent and provided for the infusion of a further £5 million into the National Film Finance Corporation, over the period up to 1980. The NFFC had, since it was established in 1948, lost over £5 million of its original £6 million investment, and so the new money was designed to restore the status quo and provide the basis of a revolving fund to help film production through the 1970s. The new Tory government, elected in June 1970, decided not to honour this part of the Act and instead offered to pay a sum of £1 million, provided that the Corporation itself could match it with a further £3 million raised in the City. So the Conservative 'lame duck' philosophy, which had already acquired considerable notoriety in its application to other sectors of British industry, was now applied to films. It became stated policy for the government to get out of the business side altogether, and it was with this intent that encouragement was offered to the NFFC to seek private enterprise finance. Inevitably, there have been angry cries against the so-called philistinism of the Tories which recalls an occasion nearly twenty years earlier when another Tory government, newly elected after a long Labour innings, closed down the Crown Film Unit. John Terry, the NFFC's managing director, set to with a will in his endeavours to form a consortium to keep the NFFC afloat, but it was with the very real threat that failure would end the Corporation for ever. One of the most useful services performed by the NFFC in the period leading up to the government decision was to devise a way of changing the traditional methods of film finance, so that the 'end money' concept, which was the Corporation's risk finance, be replaced by a more equitable system. At the beginning of 1971 a new arrangement was established with British Lion and Anglo-EMI. It made over to the investors seventy-five per cent of the distributor's total receipts until they had recovered 1·35 times their principal investment. After that they were entitled to fifty per cent of the total receipts, with twenty-five per cent going to the producer in lieu of the previous 'producer's share of profits', and twenty-five per cent of such total receipts would belong to the distributor to be applied in meeting its commissions, overheads and expenses.

During its lifetime the NFFC was denied total effectiveness as a financing force through the limitations placed on its available capital. The film industry has tended towards heavy investment in multi-million dollar spectacles, having found that when these held public attention the profits could be very large indeed. The top-grossing films of all time, as listed annually by *Variety*, are nearly all examples of epic-spending, led by the greatest filmic bonanza of all, *The Sound of Music*. John Woolf of Romulus was a producer who had several films financed by the NFFC and who has been able to make favourable returns from them. In the mid-sixties he approached the Corporation for a large loan to make *Oliver!* from a successful stage musical. The money required was far beyond the NFFC's resources and so Woolf went to Columbia instead, who gave him 100 per cent backing. In view of the subsequent success of the film it is clear that the NFFC would have become completely solvent if they could have made the investment.

Similarly, it has been the case that producers, after receiving early support from the NFFC, have later gone elsewhere when they have achieved success. The highly-profitable *Carry On* series was initially backed by the NFFC but after its remarkable money-making capacities had been demonstrated on several occasions the producers sought their support from other sources. The NFFC has had to place commercial considerations high on the list of priorities, although in the first twenty-one years of its existence it was able to show a profit only six times. The type of film in which the NFFC has shown interest has varied from the untried and experimental to the most basic of commercial fodder. Heading the 1970 list of films financed by the Corporation was *I, Monster* and *Up Pompeii*, although also on it were Maurice Hatton's *Praise Marx and Pass the Ammunition* and Kenneth Anger's *Lucifer Rising*. The number of British films financed by the NFFC had dropped from twenty-eight per cent in 1963 to a mere two per cent in 1969 and seven per cent in 1970. In 1968 some eighty-eight per cent of the films made in Britain had been backed by American money, but in 1970 this total had dropped to sixty-six per cent with 1971 falling lower still with the withdrawal of American support from the British industry.

The hope was that the overall costs of film-making could be brought down. As the 1971 Report of the NFFC stated:

It is the Corporation's conviction that film production in Britain will expand and opportunities for employment increase in direct proportion to the lowering of costs. Here the major contribution must be made by top talent, which has for too long been forced to seek the maximum cash fees obtainable owing to the remoteness of 'profits'. But this tendency can be reversed if top talent is remunerated through a share of the distributor's gross receipts, or by an investment of fees in accordance with the Corporation's new lending policy. When the astronomical fees disappear there will be every reason for other fees to descend to a saner level and for out-dated crewing and other practices to be modified.

And to exemplify the kind of gesture that would be needed to achieve this happy state of affairs the Report cited the case of *Under Milk*

Wood, directed by Andrew Sinclair from Dylan Thomas's radio play, which was two-thirds financed by the Corporation and one-third by a firm of merchant bankers. Its stars, none less than Richard Burton, Elizabeth Taylor and Peter O'Toole, were used to receiving fees of a considerable magnitude, but on this occasion were prepared to work only for a share of the profits – an example of the high-mindedness needed to pull the industry through. The fact that the film's box-office potential, even with its formidable casting, was questionable, means that such noble experiments are unlikely to be repeated on anything like the scale which would give substance to the NFFC's optimism.

The withdrawal of American finance and the shrinking of the Hollywood distribution field in London (Warner and Columbia, Paramount and Universal merged their interests, for instance) meant that if production was to be sustained at around fifty features a year a considerable change of heart was needed. The appointment of Bryan Forbes, a film-maker, as head of production at Elstree, was seen as a step in the right direction, even though it was clear from the start that his area of operation was going to be heavily circumscribed by the EMI establishment, led by Bernard Delfont. Forbes lasted in his post a mere eighteen months but during his brief period of office he was able to set up a programme which contained a mixture of films best forgotten, and others that were not only artistically satisfactory but actually generated some interest at the box-office. The first batch of three to emerge under the programme were all poor, which was unfortunate for it made the task of selling the notion of a truly independent British film industry even more difficult. There was *Hoffman*, in which the director, Alvin Rakoff, ruthlessly demonstrated Peter Sellers' limitations as an actor when divorced from a film-maker with the skill of a Stanley Kubrick. Then *The Man Who Haunted Himself*, a curiously old-fashioned film based on an Anthony Armstrong ghost story written in the 1920s and which turned out to be the last film to be directed by Basil Dearden, who in 1971 was killed in a motorway car crash. Finally, *And Soon the Darkness*, an attempt at Hitchcockery by Robert Fuest, telling of the disappearance and murder of one of a pair of English girls on holiday in France, in a sunny but unappealing part of that country, spoilt because the director made the mistake rare in Hitchcock of constantly altering the point of view of the story.

Fortunately for the reputation of both Forbes and the studio the next batch showed considerable improvement. It included Lionel Jeffries's pleasant evocation of an Edwardian children's classic, *The*

Railway Children, with Jenny Agutter playing the leading role of a young middle-class girl coping with a sudden domestic upheaval to the remote fastnesses of Yorkshire when her father is unjustly sent to prison, against a background of beautifully photographed steam-hauled trains passing by green fields; *Tales of Beatrix Potter*, another children's classic and a cinematic novelty, with members of the Royal Ballet performing in animal disguises mimed versions of some of the stories to a musical pastiche of Victorian tunes arranged by John Lanchbury; *The Raging Moon*, Bryan Forbes's own film in which two paraplegics, Nanette Newman and Malcolm McDowell, have a desperate love affair in wheelchairs, ending inevitably in tragedy, but made with a sensitivity that generally avoided sentimentality. Some films in the first year's programme took so long to reach the screens that they were in danger of becoming stillborn, such as *Mr Forbush and the Penguins*, beset by production programmes and not shown to the public until the end of 1971, and *The Breaking of Bumbo*, directed at short notice by the author of the original novel, Andrew Sinclair, when the original directing team, Kevin Brownlow and Andrew Mollo, withdrew after a dispute with the producer. Sinclair's film was muddled and excessively studio-bound, and the original story of a National Service Guards officer who rebels during the Suez crisis was unsatisfactorily updated and made him affected by agitprop and student unrest. It has still, at the time of writing, not been released.

With Mike Hodges's crisp thriller, *Get Carter*, Elstree was on firmer ground. Its use of Newcastle locations and Michael Caine's powerful playing of a crook involved in a gang feud were a palliative to the soft reputation of much of the MGM–EMI product. Later, the same director's *Pulp* effectively used Caine as a Mickey Spillanish writer caught up in a real-life plot as far fetched as anything he had written. The mood of *Get Carter* was echoed in Michael Tuchner's *Villain*, in which Richard Burton played a ruthless criminal and planner of a wage grab. His performance was seen as drawing inspiration from the real-life Kray brothers, East End gangleaders who had recently been given lengthy jail sentences after a reign of terror. Peter Hall also made an attempt with a thriller in soft rather than hard terms, *Perfect Friday*, but the result was a disappointingly conventional bank robbery with David Warner as a feckless aristocrat called upon to impersonate a bank inspector.

Robert Fuest, a director who had graduated to films via television, having been responsible for some creditable work on *The Avengers* series, made an enjoyable spectacle out of a macabre horror story, *The Abominable Dr Phibes*. The film was aided by excellent art deco sets by Brian Eatwell and the incomparable Vincent Price in the title role of the mad, disfigured doctor intent on eliminating all those present at an inept and fatal operation on his wife. To achieve his ends each victim is sent to eternity with a different part of the curse of the Pharaohs. Its sequel was *Dr Phibes Rises Again*, in similar mood. Before making *Phibes I* Fuest had been engaged on a dismal version of *Wuthering Heights*, which while presenting no more of the story than the much-admired William Wyler version of 1939, did so with considerably less style and passion. Literary classics, as a result of TV serializations, had suddenly become vogueish, and Delbert Mann made another Brontë story, Charlotte's *Jane Eyre*, with Susannah York, and George C. Scott as Mr Rochester. Both this and *David Copperfield* were made directly for American television, and even shot to allow for the insertion of commercials, but for theatrical distribution outside the United States. Neither captured the flavour of their predecessors made in Hollywood, and *David Copperfield* was only noteworthy for its bizarre casting, which included Sir Michael Redgrave as Peggoty and Sir Ralph Richardson as Micawber, a performance that was bound to invoke unfavourable comparisons with the definitive treatment of the character by W. C. Fields in the Cukor version. Christopher Miles made a foray into D. H. Lawrence territory with *The Virgin and the Gypsy* and managed to assemble his material with considerably more sensitivity.

The theatre is still a spring from which the British film drinks thirstily, although changes in the style of the West End stage are reflected in such films as *Entertaining Mr Sloane*, directed by Douglas Hickox, and *Loot* by Silvio Narrizano, both plays originally by Joe Orton, an iconoclastic and savagely funny dramatist. The first film was excellently served by Beryl Reid, Peter McEnery and Harry Andrews, while the second, with a script by Ray Galton and Alan Simpson and acting of an exaggerated kind by Richard Attenborough, Lee Remick and Hywel Bennett, paid a reasonable tribute to the Orton vision of a mad world. Anthony Page's *Inadmissible Evidence* presented Nicol Williamson in a film version of the part he played in John Osborne's stage play, and while the film dissipated much of the intensity of the original through the requisite 'opening-out', the decay of the early middle-aged solicitor, Maitland, still offered the nightmare image of a man trapped by circumstances into rejecting everything that he cared about. Bill Naughton's *Spring and Port Wine* was also filmed, with James Mason in the leading part of a rigid Northern father forced into learning home truths about the young generation. A slight film, directed by Peter Hammond, it was relieved from tedium by Mason's performance. Peter Medak made *Joe Egg* from Peter Nichol's play about a couple with a chronically handicapped child, and the effect was more successful than his following work, an ambitious version of Peter Barnes's play *The Ruling Class* with Peter O'Toole as an aristocratic scion moving from an insane identification with Christ to an allegedly sane one with Jack the Ripper.

Some of the large-scale productions that fell into the epic spectacle category, usually denoted by 70mm. projection and an intermission in the middle of the film, included David Lean's first film since *Dr Zhivago*, *Ryan's Daughter*, with an original screenplay by his earlier collaborator, Robert Bolt, and starring Bolt's wife, Sarah Miles. Set in Ireland during the First World War, it was about a local girl who deserts the village schoolteacher to whom she is married for a British officer, and the opprobrium that arises from her act. In spite of a spectacular storm sequence, with giant waves battering a rugged coast, the film suffered from being an intimate story inflated by Panavision 70 to grotesque proportions. Herbert Ross directed a musical version of *Goodbye Mr Chips*, with Peter O'Toole, and Petula Clark in the Greer Garson role, enlarged and transformed into a musical comedy soubrette. The sentimentality of James Hilton's original story seemed anachronistic and the film was at times acutely embarrassing, even though an attempt was made to produce a natural musical, with no production numbers as such, and most of the songs murmured on the soundtrack during Peter O'Toole's numerous introspective reflections. Harry Saltzman, with Benjamin Fisz, created an epic from *The Battle of Britain*, directed by Guy Hamilton, and using just about every Hurricane and Spitfire in the world that could still be flown. The large cast included Michael Caine, Christopher Plummer, Kenneth More, Michael Redgrave, Susannah York, Robert Shaw, Trevor Howard, Patrick Wymark and Laurence Olivier in the key role of Air Chief Marshal Dowding. To a certain extent the film was reverential of the achievement of the summer of 1940, but lacked soul. In spite of an alleged enormous effort to get its period details right there were many irritating solecisms which helped to damage the verisimilitude. William Walton was commissioned to write the music, but in the event only part of his score was used, in a battle sequence, which was effectively turned into a bloody aerial ballet, the only sound accompanying the explosions and wheeling aircraft on film being Walton's music. The aerial photography was generally excellent and one of the best efforts of a cameraman who specialized in air-to-air shooting, Skeets Kelly. He was to lose his life on his next film when his helicopter plunged into the Irish Sea during the shooting of *Zeppelin*, the indifferent and melodramatic adventure yarn of the First World War, directed by Etienne Perier.

Historical subjects of a more remote order still attract attention, most notably with Hal Wallis's production of *Anne of the Thousand Days*, directed by Charles Jarrott, with Genevieve Bujold playing Anne Boleyn to Richard Burton's Henry VIII – an attempt to repeat the formula of *Becket*; and Ken Hughes's *Cromwell*, with Richard Harris playing the title role like a seventeenth-century Castro, and Alec Guinness a long-suffering, weak-willed Charles I. Another film set in the seventeenth century was James Clavell's *The Last Valley*, which was about the Thirty Years War. Omar Sharif, a scholar, and Michael Caine, a professional army officer, pitted their philosophies against each other in a quiet Alpine valley where they took refuge from the destruction that had laid waste the rest of Europe. The collision between the scholar's idealism and the captain's pragmatism produced an exchange of ideas rarely found in a film of this type. Clive Donner's *Alfred the Great*, with David Hemmings racing through Saxon Britain like a rampaging rugger player, was marred by its racy modern dialogue and the literal blood-and-thunder style of its direction. Ronald Neame provided another version of the perennial Dickens story, *Scrooge*, this time as a musical in the *Oliver!*, tradition, with snow-strewn London streets filled with leaping ragamuffins. The central performance by Albert Finney mustered considerably more sympathy for the crabby character than had previously been seen, and a number of flashback scenes to Scrooge's younger days offered a motivational insight that is usually avoided. It was a tolerable film, avoiding the deluge of sentiment associated with the novel. Billy Wilder's long-awaited attempt at interpreting another archetypal figure from the pages of English literature, *The Private Life of Sherlock Holmes*, was a curiosity, a fresh vision of the master detective, played by Robert Stephens, with Colin Blakely as Dr Watson, revealing the ambivalence and weaknesses as never before. Much of the film was a Wilder joke, the lengthy sequence discussing the possibility of Holmes being homosexual, and based on the celebrated

273

Shavian riposte to the suggestion that he and Isadora Duncan should pool beauty and brains to produce a perfect child, 'Her brains, my beauty!' Although the first impression was disappointing, in spite of I. A. F. Diamond's witty screenplay and an expensive outdoor set at Pinewood of Baker Street, which succeeded in looking like an expensive outdoor set, it was a film that one could grow to like.

Crime attracted another American director, but in his case real-life rather than fictional. Richard Fleischer, whose previous examinations of celebrated murder cases included *Compulsion*, based on Leopold and Loeb, and *The Boston Strangler*, came to Britain to make *Ten Rillington Place*, an account of the crimes of John Christie, a compulsive killer of women in postwar Notting Hill and the cause of the wrongful execution of Timothy Evans. The psychopath was played convincingly by Richard Attenborough, with John Hurt as Evans, and while the film went no further than official records in attempting to define the nature of Christie's sickness, it was a grim work, overtly loaded with anti-capital punishment propaganda, and a reasonably accurate attempt to capture the atmosphere of its period. The film was inspired by Ludovic Kennedy's book. Sam Peckinpah also chose a gruesome theme for a film he made in Britain. *The Straw Dogs* was an exercise in bucolic Grand Guignol, with Dustin Hoffman as a mild American professor in a rented house in Cornwall. After his attractive young wife, played by Susan George, undergoes violence and rape at the hands of malevolent villagers, he turns to violence himself and dispatches the intruders in an orgy of bloodletting. The stomach-turning horror of the final scenes of the film provoked outrage from several film critics who normally set their caps firmly against censorship, with Alexander Walker of the *Evening Standard* in the vanguard, but received approbation from the public, who queued delightedly to see it.

Stanley Kubrick's *A Clockwork Orange*, passed by the BBFC without cuts, also had an outraged reception. Kubrick's film, based on an Anthony Burgess novel, was set in the near future and described a world only slightly extended from the one familiar now. The story of a young murderous thug with an engaging disposition, superbly played by Malcolm McDowell, who is treated in prison to modify his ultra-violent nature, and then made use of by the government and its opposition in a manner as callous as his earlier criminal life, had a horrifying logic. The film was divided into sections identified by snatches of music which ranged from Beethoven's Ninth Symphony to Gene Kelly's 'Singin' in the Rain', both of which had relevance to the plot. The film, for Kubrick almost a pot-boiler between *2001* and his long-planned Napoleon project, with *Barry Lyndon* intervening, nevertheless assumed the status of a seminal comment on the nature of social madness.

Lindsay Anderson echoed the Kubrick film with *O Lucky Man* in which McDowell, playing a character with the same name as the hero of *If.* . . . made a progress through an England corrupt at every level. An astonishing, powerful, angry film, the looseness and indulgence of its construction hampered its impact, but it was a further endorsement of Anderson's stature as a film-maker.

Joseph Losey chose a violent situation for his film of Barry England's novel, *Figures in a Landscape*, in which two fugitive soldiers flee together through an unnamed country, pursued by an enemy who constantly buzzes them from a helicopter. It was in the allegorical nature of the film to be non-specific about its setting and the intentions of its characters – it is a dreamlike drama of pursuit and the relationship of the two men, the tough bravado of the older one, played by Robert Shaw (who wrote the screenplay), and the middle-class superiority of the other, another fine performance by Malcolm McDowell, who survived. It was a film of menace and ambiguity, and a typical Losey exposé of life's foundations. It was less important than Losey's later film, *The Go-Between*, from the novel by L. P. Hartley, a harking back from old age to an Edwardian past, ' . . . a foreign country, they do things differently there'. Michael Redgrave played the old man recalling a summer as a youth out of his depth as a guest in a school friend's stately mansion, becoming involved with an unlikely love affair between one of its occupants and the village smith, when he is cajoled into acting as messenger for them. The experience scarred him so deeply that he was never able to marry. The couple were played by Julie Christie and Alan Bates, and the boy by Dominic Guard. The summer landscape of Norfolk has never been photographed so evocatively and Losey's obsessive interest in British class behaviour and interaction, as seen in *The Servant* and *Secret Ceremony* for instance, was again a dominant part of the structure.

Ken Russell, whose film of D. H. Lawrence's *Women in Love*, with Alan Bates, Oliver Reed, Glenda Jackson and Jennie Linden, aroused much public interest, not least for its celebrated nude wrestling scene, was for part of its length a reasonable interpretation of the novel and always excellent to look at. He followed it with a wild life of Tchaikovsky, *The Music Lovers*, a bravura piece of considerable eccentricity, paralleling some of his more excessive biographies of composers that he made for BBC television. His next film was *The Devils*, out of Aldous Huxley and John Whiting, and purporting to be an account of events at Loudon during the reign of Louis XIII. Possibly the most outrageous British film ever made, it did not let up for a moment, not from its opening shot of the king, clad in a Soho stripper's non-costume, performing a dance as Venus before a transvestite court, to the final incineration of Oliver Reed as Grandier, the proud, sensual, defiant priest, his flesh blackening and popping at the stake. The result was an orgiastic super-abundance of revulsion, an assault on the audience so violent that the original point of Whiting's play, a study of the means by which a man awkward for the state's intentions could be removed, was shrouded, obscured by the spectacle of nude nuns and plague pits, torture and madness. Having done his worst Russell next turned to the inoffensive pastiche of a twenties musical, *The Boy Friend*, casting the matchstick-thin model, Twiggy, as his female lead, and offering his second-hand impressions of Busby Berkeley. This in turn was followed by *Savage Messiah*, purporting to be a study of the vorticist artist Gaudier-Brzeska, and marking a return to a more intimate style, with Scott Anthony and Dorothy Tutin.

Another film remarkable for its violent effect was Donald Cammell and Nicolas Roeg's *Performance*, with Mick Jagger playing a pop singer living in secluded luxury and James Fox as a young hood seeking refuge from gangland intimidators in his ménage. Held up by its distributors for a lengthy period, it was finally shown in a re-edited form with some of its violence modified. It was a bewildering film, partly because of the deliberate attempt to confuse identities. The pop singer and the gangster see in each other an alternative version of themselves, an effect accentuated when even their appearances are swapped. Roeg later went to Australia and made the savage and beautiful *Walkabout*, the first film to display successfully the weird otherworldliness of the Australian outback landscape. The plot described how a teenage girl and young brother were abandoned by their father who then committed suicide in the wilderness, after city life had become too much for him. At the determined insistence of the girl the two set out to walk across the desert as though on a Sunday stroll, both neat in their school uniforms. *En route* the girl, played by Jenny Agutter, meets a young aborigine on his walkabout, and an unlikely *ménage à trois* is established, isolated from civilization. He followed this film with the sumptuously visual, occult romantic work *Don't Look Now*, with Julie Christie and Donald Sutherland in a Venetian setting.

John Boorman's *Leo the Last* examined identity, having Marcello Mastroianni as a faded scion of European princeliness, convalescing in a large mansion located somewhat strangely in a seedy London cul-de-sac. He observes the plight of the people around him through a telescope and resolves to give his house to the poor by blowing it up in a spectacular fireworks display, and thus at last make contact with the real world. Stylistically and visually rewarding, the film was shot in muted, desaturated colour, the nearest thing to a black and white film after the point when Wardour Street had decreed that all films should be made in colour, regardless of subject, in order to satisfy sales to colour television (which relentlessly persists in showing black and white films from the thirties and forties, and, it is to be hoped, will continue to do so). Boorman's *Zardoz*, a projection into the future and a parable of man's ultimate downfall, was in many respects as ambitious and thought-provoking as Kubrick's *2001* in the previous decade.

Stylistically interesting was Tony Richardson's *Ned Kelly*, made in Australia after his not altogether satisfactory Nicol Williamson film, *Laughter in the Dark*, based on Nabokov's novel. Mick Jagger played the nineteenth-century outlaw and folk hero, not without protest from local chauvinists, in a not unlikeable manner, but the social protest framework of the story was continually strained by the director's fondness for lyrical irrelevance, slow-motion sequences, out-of-focus flora in the foreground and the usual panoply of visual tricks which mar Richardson's work. The final battle, with the outlaw grotesquely garbed in crude armour advancing against a fusillade of bullets, his own weaponry confusingly switching from shotgun to pistols, produced a memorable image, but the film failed to jell, and its allegory of modern society was stated too ponderously to have much effect.

Dick Clement, after the strange and not unimpressive comedy thriller, *Otley*, entered Iris Murdoch country with *A Severed Head*, adapted by Frederic Raphael, and with Richard Attenborough as a cliché-spouting psychiatrist blandly usurping Ian Holm's wife, played by Lee Remick, and driving him into the grip of a fearsome female don played by Claire Bloom. The credit titles emphasized the puppet-like qualities of the leading characters and the pace was taken at the cracking rate of farcical comedy. John Schlesinger essayed into this middle-class world in a rather more weighty fashion with *Sunday, Bloody Sunday*, a triangular plot involving Peter Finch and Glenda

Jackson as rivals for the affections of an ambisextrous youth, played by Murray Head. The screenplay by Penelope Gilliatt carefully sketched its world, seemingly dividing its characters into the sort of people who read *The Times* and those who read the *Guardian*. Peter Finch, a Jewish homosexual doctor with a fondness for Mozart and traumatic recall of his *barmitzvah*, and Glenda Jackson as an unsettled divorcee, gave utterly convincing performances. The ambivalent character of the young man, an abstract sculptor enjoying a trendy success, was drawn so that he could casually enjoy the dual relationship and then eventually opt out by removing himself to New York, leaving both his lovers to their grief. An intelligent, unsuperficial approach made this Schlesinger's most mature feature film and confirmed him as one of the most powerful forces in modern British cinema.

Peter Yates, having, like Schlesinger, achieved success with a film made in America, in his case *Bullitt*, made a film called *Murphy's War*, with Peter O'Toole, which had more than a passing resemblance to *The African Queen* of twenty years earlier. O'Toole played a mechanic from an aircraft carrier, shipwrecked towards the end of the Second World War, who uses ingenuity, initiative and courage to attack the U-boat which sank his ship. The trouble is that he goes on fighting after the German surrender and the impulse to destroy the U-boat has eclipsed all the other issues. John Dexter in *The Virgin Soldiers*, from a novel by Leslie Thomas, also examined the theme of conflict. His film was set in Malaya during the emergency period and dealt with a group of National Servicemen caught up in a situation not of their choosing. An individual, a loner out of step with the world, was presented in Richard Sarafian's *Vanishing Point*, with an ex-policeman driving a souped-up car at speed from Colorado to California, pursued after a couple of traffic infringements by the full vengeance of the forces of law and order, and ultimately meeting a meaningless death in a road block. The film was something rare, being wholly American in subject and location, yet made by a British company and crew. As the fugitive speeds across the desert he becomes a symbolic folk hero and is guided by an extrasensory soul disc-jockey in a small-town radio station. The virtuosity of the driving recalled Peter Collinson's *The Italian Job*. The spectacular chase formula was given a variation in Geoffrey Reeve's *Puppet on a Chain*, the vehicles on this occasion being power boats, and the location the narrow crowded canals of Amsterdam.

The inspiration of the tycoons of Wardour Street has become so threadbare that a large percentage of production has turned over to cinema versions of established television successes. In this category are such situation comedies as *Up Pompeii*, with Frankie Howerd cavorting in an Ancient Roman setting (its medieval sequel was *Up the Chastity Belt*), *Dad's Army*, a gentler nudge at the risible ribs of the wartime Home Guard, *Please, Sir!*, a glimpse of a secondary modern Narkover, and the most successful British film of 1971 at the box-office, *On The Buses*, followed by *Mutiny on the Buses* in the following year and *Holiday on the Buses* after that. Even the satirical BBC programme, *Monty Python's Flying Circus*, was turned into a cinema film, *And Now for Something Completely Different*, regrettably not the case, since every item in it had already been seen on the small screen. The fact that all these films, without exception, have been financially successful is not only a dismal index of public taste, but a direct encouragement to Wardour Street not to exercise too much imagination.

Other films, particularly the *Carry On* series, which by mid-1975 had reached a total of twenty-seven films, pursue an English fondness for *double entendre* and innuendo, the nadir of which was reached in *Percy*, which was about a penis transplant, although Roy Boulting's *There's a Girl in My Soup*, adapted from a long-running sex comedy, was not far behind. Warren Mitchell, renowned for his Alf Garnett role in *Till Death Us Do Part* on television and in Norman Cohen's film, switched his characterization to that of an odious suburban insurance man on the make in *All the Way Up*, directed by James MacTaggart, and Jim Clark had fun at the expense of au pairs in *Every Home Should Have One*, which starred the goggle-eyed comedian, Marty Feldman. Kevin Billington attempted a humorous film with *The Rise and Rise of Michael Rimmer*, with another television comedian, Peter Cook, but it was not altogether satisfactory. Dick Lester also failed, though more nobly, to realize the promise of his earlier work, and his film *The Bed-Sitting Room*, based on an iconoclastic play and starring Spike Milligan, with its blunt humour and sledgehammer direction was little short of a disaster. Gerry O'Hara's *All the Right Noises*, dealing with a lower-middle-class love affair between a stage electrician and a teenage actress, an understanding wife forming the apex of the triangle, was one of the more felicitous attempts of the time at light domestic comedy, albeit in familiar territory.

Ken Loach's *Family Life* seemed to close the book on British urban social values. Simply the story of a girl driven mad by her nagging, puritanical mother and weak, short-tempered father, it boldly stated the unmentionable truth, that family life was a destructive force, a self-perpetuating insidious myth. Everyone involved with the girl, from boy friend to psychotherapist, was axe-grinding in his own interest, even with the best motives. The ultimate shot shows the girl reduced to a totally catatonic state on display to a classroom of students, while the lecturer blandly asks: 'Any questions?' The screen-play by David Mercer was consciously propagandizing the methods of R. D. Laing, and the film was shot in a flat, documentary-like style, the camera as eavesdropper, a technique Loach learned with tele-vision and work such as *Cathy Come Home*. Another film from the same company, Kestrel, which owed much to television method was *The Body*, directed by Roy Battersby and produced by Tony Garnett, a study in close-up of most human functions, with some quite extra-ordinary photography of internal organs actually at work, but marred by a somewhat purposeless approach.

Memorial, producers of *If. . . .* and *Charlie Bubbles*, were respon-sible for *Gumshoe*, with Albert Finney playing a Liverpudlian bingo caller, entranced by the ambience of forties thrillers, which leads him into an impersonation of a Bogart-style private eye and immersion in a genuine thriller situation. Directed by Stephen Frears from a screen-play by Neville Smith, the film was refreshingly lively and effective, even if nearly everyone who came into contact with Finney effort-lessly assumed the idiom of the dialogue. The supporting cast of Frank Finlay, Billie Whitelaw and Janice Rule ably held the film on its narrow tightrope.

In 1971, the year following the introduction of revised censorship ratings, together with the new AA certificate, John Trevelyan resigned the secretaryship. His successor, Stephen Murphy, came from the Independent Television Authority, where he had been a Senior Programme Officer. His settling-in period was watched with great interest to see if any major policy changes were to be implemented, and quite quickly controversy arose over the passing of Peckinpah's *The Straw Dogs*, admittedly with cuts, and the refusal of a certificate of any kind for Andy Warhol's *Trash*, on the doubtful grounds that it glorified drug-taking, while a far more meretricious British film, *Extremes*, which featured drug addiction, was passed. On the other hand a controversial East European film, *W.R. – The Mysteries of the Organism*, was passed without a single cut. There was also a con-siderable backlash of anxiety over Ken Russell's *The Devils*, which was banned outright by a number of local authorities, but this film had been the responsibility of Murphy's predecessor. It was difficult to muster general public opinion in favour of abolishing the censor altogether, in spite of the removal of stage censorship, owing to sustained pressure in the opposite direction generated by such groups as the Festival of Light, Lord Longford's anti-pornography committee, responsible for a fatuous report in the autumn of 1972, and Mrs Mary Whitehouse, whose activities were directed mostly at suppressing anything that did not meet with her approval. In 1973 Murphy's position was rendered even more uncomfortable by the controversy surrounding Bertolucci's *Last Tango In Paris* which was passed with one small cut. The Greater London Council attempted to classify rather than censor films, and the censorship issue promises to be lively for some time to come.

The British Film Institute also underwent a difficult period. Increasing discontent with policies led to the formation of a members' action committee. Their objections were to the failure of the governing body to encourage new film-makers and criticism, and to the traditional and establishment-based approach of the BFI Membership of the governing board was narrow, the governors appointed directly by the Minister for the Arts. There was no representation by the body of membership on the Board of Governors at all. There were few governors who had any direct concern with film-making, and two of them, Lindsay Anderson and Karel Reisz, resigned in despair during 1970. At the Annual General Meeting that year, presided over by the then Chairman, Sir William Coldstream, the action committee presented motions for the resignation of all the governors. These were defeated and a subsequent postal ballot of all the members provided overwhelming support for the regime. But during 1971 more trouble occurred and there were mass resignations in the Education Department, following decisions to curb its activities and publications. Sir William Coldstream was succeeded by Denis Forman, a former director of the BFI, and at the 1971 AGM a confrontation was made with the action committee. On this occasion eleven governors were voted out of office, although the Minister, Lord Eccles, had on the same day appointed four more to fill vacancies created by other retirements and resignations. The Minister could, in any case, reinstate all the deposed governors if he chose. The membership was again consulted in a postal ballot, thus restoring the status quo. But in 1972 it was agreed to allow members to elect two of the governors.

The National Film Theatre, under heavy fire for the commercial nature of some of its programmes, opened NFT2, a smaller adjoining theatre, in 1970, thus enlarging its opportunities for showing lesser-known works. The objectors to the programming were sometimes reluctant to face the fact that the NFT was supposed to be self-supporting, and therefore needed audiences. Later, an even smaller theatre was added to the South Bank complex, for private screenings. The main event at the National Film Theatre each year continued to be the London Film Festival, when an international assembly of work seen at other festivals was compiled and shown to NFT audiences. A newer NFT attraction was the series of John Player lectures, arranged under the sponsorship of the tobacco company, at which various eminent figures in films addressed audiences, answered questions and showed examples of their work. They ended in 1973.

In 1970 the National Film Archive joined forces with *The Sunday Times* to present an exhibition at the Round House at Chalk Farm to celebrate seventy-five years of cinema. The exhibition was divided into twelve genres and was staged in the building's circular gallery. The auditorium was reserved for day-long screenings of a remarkably broad collection of films, many receiving their first public showing. Each evening there was a celebrity event, and those appearing at Cinema City, as the festival was called, included Harold Lloyd, who opened it in the presence of Princess Alexandra, Richard Burton and Elizabeth Taylor, Louis Malle, Gene Kelly, Shirley MacLaine, King Vidor, Colleen Moore, George Stevens, William Wyler, John Frankenheimer, Norman Mailer, Luchino Visconti, Franco Zeffirelli, Peter Sellers, Spike Milligan, Roman Polanski, Peter Hall, John Schlesinger, Herbert Wilcox and Anna Neagle, Ralph Nelson, Omar Sharif, Robert Bolt, Richard Fleischer, Richard Attenborough, Mervyn LeRoy, Michael Powell, Joseph Losey, John Addison, Dmitri Tiomkin, Marty Feldman and George Axelrod. The opening film was the first public screening in Britain for some thirty years of Harold Lloyd's *The Kid Brother*, and Cinema City closed with Charlie Chaplin's *The Circus*. A strike of newspaper wholesale delivery drivers, resulting in the disappearance of newspapers from London during the first fortnight of the three-and-a-half-week run of Cinema City, depleted audiences; and significantly, after the restoration of the press to normal, there were capacity houses nearly every night. The choice of the Round House produced considerable criticism in view of its seedy, brutally basic atmosphere, which was like that of a large, dusty warehouse (it was built in the early days of railways as an engine shed) and the very serious acoustical problems it presented. Regrettably London in 1970 was still without the ideal exhibition centre for a venture of this kind, and in some ways even the event itself was premature, for although the creative strength of the industry responded superbly to the occasion, much of it was dissipated in preaching to people already converted to films. The National Film Archive faced the terrifyingly massive task of copying most of the collection on to stable acetate film and little money with which to carry out the job. Shortly after Cinema City Lord Eccles announced a massive increase in the grant for this purpose and the work was put in hand. The possibility of setting up a proper study centre for the film came a little closer, although it was difficult to see how the NFA, unsatisfactorily wedded to the cumbersome BFI could achieve this end in the immediate future.

The establishment of the long-awaited National Film School took place in 1971 and the first principal was Colin Young, a Scotsman who had been the director of the celebrated film school at the University of California, Los Angeles. It would not be until the mid-seventies that the success of this venture could be judged. The BFI Experimental Film Fund, one of the most controversial areas of Institute activity, was used to help young film-makers within the limited amounts of money available. One of the most promising, Barney Platts-Mills, was made a governor of the BFI at the age of twenty-seven, having directed *Bronco Bullfrog* and *Private Road*.

In 1972 production continued to slump with little money available for new productions, and the industry faced the loss of British Lion's Shepperton Studios, now owned by a property company, Barclay Securities. In real estate terms Shepperton was a valuable investment, but its closure, following the shutdown of MGM at Borehamwood in 1970, would have left Britain with only Pinewood and Elstree, the latter idle after *Murder on the Orient Express*. A retreat from the studios had been in progress for years, both in Britain and America. But, as production centres, the studios are essential, not merely as sound stages, but as laboratories, recording studios, editing suites, property and wardrobe departments, and administrative offices. Without identifiable headquarters the film industry could easily become an itinerant, maverick, homeless creature, its position made even more insecure.

By the end of 1973 the crisis of production, hampered now not only by financial shortfalls, but by a generally bad industrial situation, had reached the stage where only half as many films were being made compared with the same time in the previous year. The ACTT strengthened their demands for the full nationalization of the industry, with workers' control and no compensation for the former owners. They conveniently ignored the fact that even a government would find it hard to compel the public to go to see films they did not wish to see. The producer Leon Clore proposed a plan whereby Eady money, instead of being returned to the successful producers (who were the people in least need of it) would be channelled into a fund for general investment in the industry, after a sum of not more than 15 per cent had been paid out to the original producers, who would now be obliged to use the money for further film financing. In this way there would be investment available for the kind of film that has no commercial chance under the present system. The proposal produced a lively trade controversy.

The British film industry stands poised on the edge of the television cassette revolution and the changes that may come about as a result of the introduction of a fourth television channel. But such challenges have, ironically, been its mainstay from the beginning. The industry has stumbled from crisis to crisis, throughout its seventy-five years or so of history, has endured the depredations of the financially unscrupulous and the artistically incompetent, and suffered the onslaughts of entertainments tax, television, bingo, and a dozen other natural enemies of the cinema. Yet each setback, each disaster, has somehow compounded the resilience of the medium. The cinema, written off many times, has always come bouncing back ready for the next round. No matter how many barriers are erected to prevent new talent from seizing its chance, be they restrictive practices imposed by the unions or narrow appreciations of what will interest an audience on the part of the front men in Wardour Street, somehow a spirit has managed to exert itself – a spirit that could have something in common with the national character. The British film has often been preoccupied with the guarded tolerance and scorn of official bullying that every Englishman feels is his ingrained natural quality. That such an easy-going nation as this can produce a *Brief Encounter* on the one hand, a cry against the machinery of the conformity and the quiet life, and *If. . . .* on the other, a voice bitter and angry questioning the validity of all our values, is proof that there is a national cinema – a living being, however sickly, that needs to be cherished.

A Biographical Guide to the British Cinema

LINDSAY ANDERSON (1923–   ). Director, born Bangalore, India.
The leading maverick of the British cinema, Anderson has always been a passionate advocate for commitment, deploring not only the uncaring approach of other film-makers, but the ignorance and insensitivity of most critics. At Oxford he was a founder editor of *Sequence*, which began as the magazine of the Oxford University Film Society, and later continued in London until 1952 as Britain's leading critical periodical devoted to films. His films have been relatively few, only three main features throughout his career, but all are major works, *This Sporting Life* and *If. . . .*, which like his 1973 work, *O Lucky Man* was the British Cannes entry. Most of his creative career has been spent in the theatre, notably at the Royal Court, London.

Films. Short subjects: *Meet the Pioneers* (1948), *Idlers That Work* (1949), *Three Installations* (1952), *Wakefield Express* (1952), *Thursday's Children* (1953), *O Dreamland* (1953), *Trunk Conveyor* (1954), *Foot and Mouth* (1955), *Every Day Except Christmas* (1957), *The White Bus* (1966), *The Singing Lesson* (Poland, 1967). Features: *This Sporting Life* (1963), *If. . . .* (1968), *O Lucky Man* (1973), *In Celebration* (1975).

KEN ANNAKIN (1914–   ). Director, born Beverley, Yorks.
A varied career in the Civil Service, as a salesman and as a journalist, gave Annakin a broader experience of life than most British directors, and his first feature, *Holiday Camp* (1947), was made on the 'slice of life' principle. His subsequent output has been generally reliable, but rarely remarkable. He is one of a select band of British directors trusted by Hollywood, and much of his recent work has been for American companies.

Films. Short subjects: *London 1942*, *A Ride with Uncle Joe* (1943), *Combined Cadets*, *The New Crop* (1944), *Three Cadets*, *Pacific Thrust*, *Fenlands*, *Make Fruitful the Land* (1945), *It Began on the Clyde*, *We of the West Riding*, *English Criminal Justice* (1946). Features:

Holiday Camp (1947), *Miranda, Broken Journey, Here Come the Huggetts, Quartet* (one episode) (1948), *Vote for Huggett, The Huggetts Abroad, Landfall* (1949), *Double Confession, Trio* (1950), *Hotel Sahara* (1951), *The Planter's Wife, The Story of Robin Hood* (1952), *The Sword and the Rose* (1953), *You Know What Sailors Are, The Seekers* (1954), *Value for Money* (1955), *Three Men in a Boat, Loser takes All* (1956), *Across the Bridge* (1957), *Nor the Moon by Night* (1958), *Third Man on the Mountain* (1959), *The Swiss Family Robinson* (1960), *Very Important Person, The Hellions* (1961), *Crooks Anonymous, The Fast Lady* (1962), *The Informers* (1963), *Those Magnificent Men in their Flying Machines* (1965), *The Battle of the Bulge* (U.S.A., 1965), *The Biggest Bundle of Them All* (U.S.A., 1966), *The Long Duel* (1967), *Monte Carlo or Bust* (1969), *Paper Tiger* (1975)

ANTHONY ASQUITH (1902–68). Director, born London.
Son of the first Earl of Oxford and Asquith and nicknamed 'Puffin', he went into films as soon as he went down from Oxford University, going to Hollywood to learn technique. His first film, co-directed with A. V. Bramble, *Shooting Stars* (1927), was a silent, but attracted attention for its innovations and effects. Shortly afterwards he was directing films in his own right, one of the first and most effective being *A Cottage on Dartmoor* (1929), his first talkie. The bulk of Asquith's work was tasteful, good-mannered, literary and discreet. He made several films in collaboration with the playwright, Terence Rattigan, both of original screenplays such as *The Way to the Stars* (1945) and adaptations such as *The Winslow Boy* (1948). He also filmed three of Shaw's plays and Wilde's *The Importance of Being Earnest* (1952). He was one of the most English of directors, portraying the middle and upper classes with affection and gentle satire, perhaps seen at its best in *The Demi-Paradise* (1943). He was a staunch upholder of workers' rights in the industry, and a major figure in the history of the film trade union, the ACTT.

Films. *Shooting Stars* (co-dir.) (1927), *Underground, The Runaway Princess* (1928), *A Cottage on Dartmoor* (1929), *Tell England* (co-dir.) (1930), *Dance Pretty Lady* (1931), *Marry Me* (screenplay only) (1932), *Letting in the Sunshine* (screenplay only), *Lucky Number* (1933), *The Unfinished Symphony* (1934), *Moscow Nights* (1935), *Pygmalion* (co-dir.) (1938), *French Without Tears* (1939), *Freedom Radio, Quiet Wedding* (1940), *Cottage to Let* (1941), *Uncensored* (1942), *The Demi-Paradise, We Dive at Dawn* (1943), *Fanny by Gaslight* (1944), *The*

Way to the Stars (1945), *While the Sun Shines* (1947), *The Winslow Boy* (1948), *The Woman in Question* (1950), *The Browning Version* (1951), *The Importance of Being Earnest* (1952), *The Net*, *The Final Test* (1953), *The Young Lovers*, *Carrington V.C.* (1954), *Orders to Kill* (1958), *The Doctor's Dilemma*, *Libel* (1959), *The Millionairess* (1960), *Guns of Darkness*, *Two Living, One Dead* (1962), *The V.I.P.s*, *An Evening with the Royal Ballet* (1963), *The Yellow Rolls-Royce* (1964). Shorts and documentaries: *Guide Dogs for the Blind* (1938), *Channel Incident*, *Rush Hour* (1940), *Welcome to Britain* (1943), *Two Fathers* (1944), *On Such a Night* (1956).

RICHARD ATTENBOROUGH (1923–   ). Actor, also producer/director, born Cambridge.

After training at RADA Attenborough entered films in 1942, playing a panic-stricken stoker in Noël Coward's (q.v.) *In Which We Serve*. This experience led to a certain amount of typecasting, broken by occasional forays into the underworld as a vicious psychopath. (*Brighton Rock* [1948] was the definitive role in this genre.) During a long career he has been a mainstay of the industry and an actor who can always be relied on to bring to a part a polished characterization. In 1959 he also began to produce and a number of distinguished films (*The Angry Silence*, *Whistle Down the Wind*, *The League of Gentlemen*, *The L-Shaped Room*, etc.) were made under his aegis. The first film he directed, *Oh! What a Lovely War*, was a brilliant exercise in *déjà-vu* perception.

Films. *In Which We Serve* (1942), *Schweik's New Adventures* (1943), *The Hundred Pound Window* (1944), *Journey Together* (1945), *A Matter of Life and Death*, *School for Secrets* (1946), *The Man Within*, *Dancing With Crime* (1947), *Brighton Rock*, *London Belongs to Me* (1948), *The Guinea Pig*, *The Lost People* (1949), *Boys in Brown*, *Morning Departure* (1950), *Hell is Sold Out*, *The Magic Box* (1951), *The Gift Horse*, *Father's Doing Fine* (1952), *Eight O'Clock Walk* (1954), *The Ship that Died of Shame* (1955), *Private's Progress*, *The Baby and the Battleship* (1956), *Brothers in Law*, *The Scamp* (1957), *Dunkirk*, *The Man Upstairs*, *Sea of Sand* (1958), *Danger Within*, *Jet Storm*, *I'm All Right Jack*, *SOS Pacific* (1959), *The Angry Silence* (also produced), *The League of Gentlemen* (also produced) (1960), *Whistle Down the Wind* (only produced) (1961), *Only Two Can Play*, *All Night Long*, *The Dock Brief*, *The L-Shaped Room* (only produced) (1962), *The Great Escape* (U.S.A.) (1963), *Seance on a Wet Afternoon* (also produced), *Guns at Batasi*, *The Third Secret* (1964), *The Flight of the Phoenix* (U.S.A.) (1965), *The Sand Pebbles* (U.S.A.) (1966), *Dr Doolittle* (U.S.A.) (1967), *The Bliss of Mrs Blossom*, *Only When I Larf* (1968), *Oh! What a Lovely War* (co-produced and directed only), *David Copperfield* (1969), *The Magic Christian*, *The Last Grenade*, *A Severed Head* (1970), *Loot*, *Ten Rillington Place* (1971), *Young Winston* (directed) (1972), *Brannigan*, *Conduct Unbecoming* (1975).

ROY BAKER (1916–). Director, born London.
Baker learned his craft at Gainsborough before the Second World War. On returning from the armed forces he directed his first film, a thriller called *The October Man*, with John Mills. A workmanlike and reliable film-maker, he was responsible for some films made in Hollywood at the beginning of the fifties.

Films. *The October Man* (1947), *The Weaker Sex* (1948), *Paper Orchid*, *Morning Departure* (1950), *Highly Dangerous*, *The House in the Square* (U.S.A.) (1951), *Inferno* (U.S.A.), *Don't Bother to Knock* (U.S.A.) (1952), *Passage Home* (1955), *Jacqueline*, *Tiger in the Smoke* (1956), *The One that Got Away* (1957), *A Night to Remember* (1958), *The Singer Not the Song* (also produced) (1960), *Flame in the Streets* (also produced) (1961), *The Valiant* (1962), *Two Left Feet* (also produced) (1963), *Quatermass and the Pit* (1967), *The Anniversary* (1968), *Moon Zero Two* (1969), *The Vampire Lovers*, *The Scars of Dracula* (1970), *Dr Jekyll and Sister Hyde* (1971), *Vault of Horror* (1973).

SIR MICHAEL BALCON (1896–). Producer, born Birmingham.
An elder statesman of the British film industry, Balcon was responsible during his long career for the production of some 350 films, the first of which was the 1922 production, *Woman to Woman*, directed by Graham Cutts. Balcon was founder of Gainsborough and produced the first films of Alfred Hitchcock (q.v.). Later he became head of Gaumont-British, and after the cessation of production by that company joined Metro-Goldwyn–Mayer to launch a programme of British-made films. After producing *A Yank at Oxford* Balcon left and became responsible for production at Ealing Studios. The years that followed were his most fruitful and during his time the Ealing product became synonymous with a certain type of film – at first war films with a realistic root, later the distinctive Ealing comedies. Balcon gathered many talents under the Ealing umbrella, the most notable of whom were Alexander Mackendrick, Robert Hamer, Charles Crichton, Henry Cornelius and

Charles Frend (qq.v.) and established a remarkable *esprit de corps* within what became a very individual portion of the Rank Organization. Among the films that were made at Ealing were *Kind Hearts and Coronets*, *The Lavender Hill Mob*, *Passport to Pimlico*, *The Man in the White Suit*, *The Cruel Sea* and *The Ladykillers*. In the mid-fifties the studios were sold to the BBC and production moved to the MGM studios at Borehamwood, collapsing after six more films had been made. Balcon helped to set up the independent co-operative company, Bryanston, and was chairman of British Lion during the critical period 1963–6. Until 1971 Balcon was Deputy Governor of the British Film Institute. Throughout his career he was always concerned with fostering new talents.

DIRK BOGARDE (Derek Van Den Bogaerd) (1920–). Actor, born London.

Bogarde's initial acting experience was in the theatre. He became a Rank contract actor in 1947 and was given a starring role in *Esther Waters*. Over the years his performances have matured and varied to the extent that he is regarded as one of the most versatile of British actors. In recent years he has worked with directors of perception such as Losey (q.v.) and Visconti, culminating with the latter's poetic *Death in Venice*.

Films. *Esther Waters* (1947), *Quartet* (1948), *Once a Jolly Swagman*, *Dear Mr Prohack*, *Boys in Brown*, *The Blue Lamp* (1949), *So Long at the Fair*, *The Woman in Question* (1950), *Blackmailed* (1951), *Hunted*, *Penny Princess*, *The Gentle Gunman* (1952), *Appointment in London*, *Desperate Moment* (1953), *They Who Dare*, *Doctor in the House*, *The Sleeping Tiger*, *For Better or Worse*, *The Sea Shall Not Have Them* (1954), *Simba*, *Doctor at Sea*, *Cast a Dark Shadow* (1955), *The Spanish Gardener* (1956), *Ill Met by Moonlight*, *Doctor at Large*, *Campbell's Kingdom* (1957), *A Tale of Two Cities*, *The Wind Cannot Read* (1958), *The Doctor's Dilemma*, *Libel* (1959), *Song Without End* (U.S.A.), *The Angel Wore Red* (U.S.A.), *The Singer Not the Song* (1960), *Victim* (1961), *H.M.S. Defiant*, *The Password Is Courage* (1962), *The Mind Benders*, *We Joined the Navy*, *I Could Go On Singing*, *Doctor in Distress*, *The Servant* (1963), *Hot Enough for June*, *King and Country*, *The High Bright Sun* (1964), *Darling* (1965), *Modesty Blaise* (1966), *Accident*, *Our Mother's House* (1967), *Sebastian*, *The Fixer* (U.S.A.) (1968), *Oh! What a Lovely War*, *Justine* (U.S.A.), *The Damned* (Italy) (1969), *Death in Venice* (1970), *The Serpent* (France) (1972), *The Night Porter* (Italy) (1974).

JOHN AND ROY BOULTING (1913–   ). Directors/producers, born Bray, Bucks.

The careers of the Boulting twins have been inextricably linked since their entry into films during the thirties. For a considerable part of the time they alternately produced and directed each other's films. In 1937 they founded Charter Films and made a number of thoughtful works, reaching their peak with *Brighton Rock*, *The Guinea Pig* and *Seven Days to Noon* in the immediate postwar years. After *Private's Progress* (1955) they concentrated on comic attacks on British institutions, characterized by a mildly satirical treatment. Both brothers have been active campaigners on behalf of the industry and are directors of British Lion.

Films directed: JOHN: *Journey Together* (1945), *Brighton Rock* (1947), *Seven Days to Noon* (1950), *The Magic Box* (1951), *Private's Progress* (1956), *Lucky Jim* (1957), *I'm All Right Jack* (1959), *Heavens Above* (1963), *Rotten to the Core* (1965). ROY: *Consider Your Verdict* (1938), *Trunk Crime* (1939), *Inquest*, *Pastor Hall* (1940), *Thunder Rock* (1942), *Fame Is the Spur* (1947), *The Guinea Pig* (1948), *Singlehanded*, *High Treason* (1951), *Seagulls over Sorrento* (1954), *Josephine and Men* (1955), *Run for the Sun* (U.S.A.) (1956), *Happy is the Bride*, *Brothers in Law* (1957), *Carlton-Browne of the F.O.* (1959), *Suspect*, *A French Mistress* (1960), *The Family Way* (1966), *Twisted Nerve* (1968), *There's a Girl in My Soup* (1970), *Soft Beds, Hard Battles* (1973). Shorts and documentaries: *The Landlady* (1938), *Dawn Guard* (1941), *They Serve Abroad* (1942), *Desert Victory* (1943), *Tunisian Victory* (co-directed) (1944), *Burma Victory* (1945).

PETER BROOK (1925–   ). Director, born London.

Peter Brook is primarily a distinguished theatrical producer/director, but his forays into the cinema have been fruitful, if infrequent. His first film, *The Beggar's Opera* (1952), suffered during its passage and reached the screen in an emasculated version which was nonetheless pretty to look at. His 1963 version of William Golding's novel *Lord of the Flies* offered a vision of civilization suspended on a thread, as in a different sense did *Tell Me Lies* (1967), his screenplay of the Aldwych Theatre production of *US*, a polemical theatrical experience. His *Marat/Sade* was a useful record of his stage production.

Films. *The Beggar's Opera* (1952), *Moderato Cantabile* (1960), *Lord of the Flies* (1963), *Marat/Sade*, *Ride of the Valkyrie* (1966), *Tell Me Lies* (1967), *King Lear* (1971).

ADRIAN BRUNEL (1892–1958). Director, screenwriter, born Brighton. Brunel was an eminent director in the twenties, and co-founded Minerva Films with Leslie Howard (q.v.). His best-known films include *Blighty* (1927), *The Constant Nymph* and *The Vortex* (1928) and *While Parents Sleep* (1935). He faded from view after the start of the Second World War. He was a founder of the London Film Society, a body formed to evade the stringent pre-war censorship which prohibited many classic Russian films from being seen on British screens.

Films. Silent: *The Cost of a Kiss* (1917), *A Temporary Lady* (1921), *The Man Without Desire* (1923), *Lovers in Araby* (1924), *Land of Hope and Glory* (screenplay only), *Blighty* (1927), *The Constant Nymph*, *The Vortex*, *A Light Woman* (1928), *The Crooked Billet* (1929). Sound: *Elstree Calling* (co-directed) (1930), *Taxi to Paradise*, *I'm an Explosive*, *Follow the Lady*, *Little Napoleon*, *Two Wives for Henry*, *The Laughter of Fools* (1933), *Important People*, *Badger's Green* (1934), *Cross Currents*, *Vanity*, *Variety*, *The City of Beautiful Nonsense*, *While Parents Sleep* (1935), *Prison Breaker*, *Sabotage*, *Love at Sea*, *The Invader* (1936), *The Return of the Scarlet Pimpernel* (screenplay only) (1937), *The Girl Who Forgot*, *The Lion Has Wings* (co-directed) (1939). Shorts (silent): *The Bump*, *£5 Reward*, *Bookworms*, *Twice Two* (1920), *Sheer Trickery*, *Moors and Minarets*, *The Shimmy Sheik*, *Two-Chinned Chow*, *Yes We Have No* — (1923), *Crossing the Great Sagrada*, *The Pathetic Gazette* (1924), *Battling Bruisers*, *So This is Jollygood*, *Cut it Out*, *The Blunderland of Big Game*, *A Typical Budget*, *Bonzo* (screenplay only) (1925); (Sound): *Food for Thought*, *Salvage with a Smile* (1940).

RICHARD BURTON (Richard Jenkins) (1925–). Actor, born Pontrhydfen, Wales.
Originally a stage actor Burton served a long apprenticeship in films from his debut in Emlyn Williams's (q.v.) *The Last Days of Dolwyn* (1948). His career reached fruition in Hollywood in the fifties, and his fame and earning power soared after his romance and marriage to Elizabeth Taylor. Dark and rugged in physique, Burton is nevertheless a voice actor of considerable skill.

Films. *The Last Days of Dolwyn* (1948), *Now Barabbas Was a Robber* (1949), *Waterfront*, *The Woman with No Name* (1950), *Green Grow the Rushes* (1951), *My Cousin Rachel* (U.S.A.), *The Robe* (U.S.A.), *The Desert Rats* (U.S.A.) (1953), *Prince of Players* (U.S.A.) (1954), *The Rains of Ranchipur* (U.S.A.), *Alexander the Great* (U.S.A.) (1955), *Seawife*, *Bitter Victory* (1957), *Look Back in Anger* (1959), *The Bramble*

Bush (U.S.A.), *The Ice Palace* (U.S.A.) (1960), *Cleopatra* (U.S.A.), *The V.I.P.s* (1963), *Becket*, *The Night of the Iguana* (U.S.A.) (1964), *The Spy Who Came in from the Cold*, *The Sandpiper* (U.S.A.) (1965), *Who's Afraid of Virginia Woolf* (U.S.A.) (1966), *The Taming of the Shrew*, *Dr Faustus* (also co-directed), *The Comedians* (U.S.A.) (1967), *Boom!*, *Where Eagles Dare* (U.S.A.), *Candy* (U.S.A.) (1968), *Staircase* (1969), *Anne of the Thousand Days*, *Villain* (1970), *Under Milk Wood*, *Raid on Rommel* (U.S.A.) (1971), *Hammersmith is Out* (U.S.A.), *The Assassination of Trotsky*, *Bluebeard* (1972), *Divorce His*, *Divorce Hers* (1973), *The Journey* (Italy) (1974).

ALBERTO CAVALCANTI (1897–). Director, born Rio de Janeiro, Brazil.

Cavalcanti initially studied architecture, and then became a set-designer in the French cinema of the twenties, graduating to directing. His reputation was made with the documentary *Rien Que Les Heures*. In 1933 he came to Britain and joined the Post Office Film Unit to make documentaries, some of which, such as *North Sea*, *Coalface* and *Men of the Lightship*, were landmarks in the use of sound and picture to create a realistic image. During the war he joined Ealing Studios as a feature director and after the war returned to Brazil, his native country, where he made films, also in Europe.

Films. *Le Train Sans Yeux* (France), *Rien Que Les Heures* (France) (1926), *En Rade*, *Yvette*, *La P'tite Lilie*, *La Jalousie du Barbouille* (1927), *Le Captaine Fracasse* (1928), *Le Petit Chaperon Rouge*, *Vous Verrez la Semaine Prochaine* (1929), *Toute Sa Vie*, *Chemin du Ciel*, *Les Vancances du Diable* (1930), *Dans Une Ile Perdue* (1931), *Le Truc du Bresilien*, *Le Mari Garcon* (1932), *Coralie et Cie*, *Tour de Chant* (1933). IN BRITAIN 30 films produced and/or directed for G.P.O. Film Unit (1934–40). *The Foreman Went to France* (produced only), *The Big Blockade* (produced only) (1941), *Film and Reality*, *Went the Day Well?*, *Greek Testament* (1942), *The Halfway House* (1943), *Champagne Charlie* (1944), *Dead of Night* (ventriloquist and Christmas party sequences) (1945), *Nicholas Nickleby* (1946), *They Made Me a Fugitive*, *The First Gentleman* (1947), *For Them that Trespass* (1948), to Brazil *Caicara* (1950), *Terra Sempere Terra*, *Painel* (1951), *Volta Redonda*, *Simao O Coalha* (1952), *O Canto do Mar*, *Mulher de Verdade* (1954), *Herr Puntila und Seir Knecht Matti* (Austria) (1955), *Die Windrose* (E. Germany) (1956), *La Prima Notte* (Italy) (1958), *The Monster of Highgate Ponds* (1960).

JACK CLAYTON (1921–). Director, born London.

Clayton entered the film industry in the mid-thirties, and made his way slowly through the ranks, directing his first film, *The Bespoke Overcoat*, twenty years later. It received an award at Cannes. His first full-length film was *Room at the Top* (1958), which allegedly broke new ground in its treatment of its subject matter, but which followed the path of all anti-hero films. His stylish *The Innocents* (1961) offered a chillingly literal interpretation of Henry James's *The Turn of the Screw*, and his film version of Penelope Mortimer's *The Pumpkin Eater* a sad view of a collapsing middle-class marriage. Clayton's work is careful, polished, precise and well thought out; it is unfortunate that there is so little of it over the years.

Films. *The Bespoke Overcoat* (also produced) (1955), *Three Men in a Boat* (produced only) (1956), *Room at the Top* (1958), *The Innocents* (1961), *The Pumpkin Eater* (1964), *Our Mother's House* (1967), *The Great Gatsby* (1974).

SEAN CONNERY (1930–). Actor, born Edinburgh.

Inseparably linked with the image of James Bond, Connery has nevertheless fought hard to overcome the inevitable typecasting that accrued. A rugged Scot, he was in turn chorus boy, male model and bit part player before his performance in *Dr No* elevated him to international stardom. After *You Only Live Twice* (1967) he dropped out of the Bond pictures, handing the field over to George Lazenby who was unable to exert the same magnetic appeal in *On Her Majesty's Secret Service*. Connery was persuaded to return for what proved to be the most profitable of all, *Diamonds Are Forever* (1971).

Films. *No Road Back* (1955), *Action of the Tiger*, *Time Lock* (1956), *Hell Drivers* (1957), *Another Time Another Place*, *Darby O'Gill and the Little People* (U.S.A.) (1958), *Tarzan's Greatest Adventure* (1959), *The Frightened City* (1960), *On the Fiddle* (1961), *The Longest Day* (U.S.A.), *Dr No* (1962), *From Russia With Love* (1963), *Woman of Straw*, *Marnie* (U.S.A.), *Goldfinger* (1964), *The Hill*, *Thunderball* (1965), *A Fine Madness* (U.S.A.) (1966), *You Only Live Twice* (1967), *Shalako* (1968), *The Red Tent* (Italian/Russian) (1969), *The Molly Maguires* (U.S.A.) (1970), *The Anderson Tapes* (U.S.A.), *Diamonds Are Forever* (1971), *The Offence* (1973), *Zardoz*, *Murder on the Orient Express*, *Ransom* (1974), *The Wind and the Lion* (U.S.A.) (1975).

HENRY CORNELIUS (1913–58). Director, born South Africa.

One of Michael Balcon's (q.v.) Ealing protégés, Cornelius was an editor turned director, whose first film, *Passport to Pimlico* (1949), was one of the studios' most spectacular successes. Later he made the even more successful comedy *Genevieve* (1953) but the rest of his work never came near either film.

Films. *It Always Rains on Sunday* (screenplay only) (1947), *Passport to Pimlico* (1949), *The Galloping Major* (1951), *Genevieve* (1953), *I Am a Camera* (1955), *Next to No Time, Law and Disorder* (co-directed) (1958).

NOEL COWARD (1899–1973). Director, actor, composer, writer etc., born Teddington, Middlesex.

A legendary figure in the world of entertainment, Coward made a sizeable contribution to the British cinema, particularly with *In Which We Serve* (1942) and *Brief Encounter* (1945) for which his screenplay was directed by his co-director on the former film, David Lean (q.v.). Many of his plays have been filmed, some more than once. They include *The Vortex, Cavalcade, Bitter Sweet, Private Lives, Design for Living, This Happy Breed* and *Blithe Spirit*. He was played by Daniel Massey in the expensive Hollywood biography of Gertrude Lawrence, *Star!* (*Those Were the Happy Times*).

Films. *Hearts of the World* (acted) (1918), *The Queen Was in the Parlour, Easy Virtue, The Vortex* (all screenplays) (1927). Sound: *Bitter Sweet* (screenplay) (1933), *The Scoundrel* (U.S.A. – acted) (1934), *In Which We Serve* (acted, produced, directed, wrote) (1942), *This Happy Breed* (produced and wrote) (1944), *Blithe Spirit* (produced and wrote), *Brief Encounter* (produced and wrote) (1945), *The Astonished Heart* (acted and wrote) (1950), *Meet Me Tonight* (screenplay) (1952), *Around the World in Eighty Days* (U.S.A.) (1955), *Our Man in Havana* (acted) (1959), *Surprise Package* (acted) (1960), *Paris When It Sizzles* (U.S.A. – acted) (1963), *Bunny Lake is Missing* (acted) (1965), *Pretty Polly* (screenplay) (1967), *Boom* (acted) (1968), *The Italian Job* (acted) (1969).

CHARLES CRICHTON (1910–). Director, born Wallasey, Cheshire. Another member of the Ealing school, Crichton was formerly a film editor. His Ealing comedies include *The Lavender Hill Mob* and *The Titfield Thunderbolt*, both of which celebrate the English love of amateurism. Since Ealing days his output has not been spectacular, although he has directed many episodes of television series.

Films. *For Those in Peril* (1944), *Dead of Night* (part), *Painted Boats* (1945), *Hue and Cry* (1947), *Against the Wind*, *Another Shore* (1948), *Train of Events* (part) (1949), *Dance Hall* (1950), *The Lavender Hill Mob* (1951), *Hunted* (1952), *The Titfield Thunderbolt* (1953), *The Love Lottery*, *The Divided Heart* (1954), *The Man in the Sky* (1956), *Law and Disorder* (co-directed), *Floods of Fear* (also screenplay) (1958), *The Battle of the Sexes* (1959), *The Boy Who Stole a Million* (1960), *The Third Secret* (1964), *He Who Rides a Tiger* (1965).

BASIL DEAN (1888–). Producer, director, born Croydon, Surrey. A West End stage producer, lured into films, Dean founded Associated Talking Pictures in the early thirties, the company that was later to become Ealing Studios. Among stars he built up were Gracie Fields and George Formby (qq.v.) both of whom were to top the box-office popularity ratings. Dean left films when the war started and became head of ENSA (Entertainments National Service Association), the government-sponsored body responsible for bringing live performances to the armed services. For this work he was awarded the OBE

Films. Produced: *Escape* (also directed), *Birds of Prey* (also directed) (1930), *Sally in our Alley*, *A Honeymoon Adventure* (1931), *The Water Gipsies*, *Nine Till Six* (also directed), *The Sign of Four*, *The Impassive Footman* (also directed), *Love on the Spot*, *Looking on the Bright Side* (also directed) (1932), *Loyalties* (also directed), *Three Men in a Boat*, *The Constant Nymph* (directed and wrote only) (1933), *Autumn Crocus* (also directed) (1934), *Lorna Doone* (also directed), *Midshipman Easy*, *No Limit* (1935), *Queen of Hearts*, *Whom the Gods Love* (also directed), *Laburnum Grove*, *The Lonely Road*, *Keep Your Seats Please* (1936), *Feather Your Nest*, *The Show Goes On* (also directed), *Twenty-One Days* (directed only), *Keep Fit* (1937), *I See Ice*, *Penny Paradise* (also wrote), *It's in the Air* (1938).

BASIL DEARDEN (1911–71). Director, born Westcliff-on-Sea, Essex. After early experience as an actor Dearden became assistant to Basil Dean (q.v.) at Ealing, working on some of the comedy films of George Formby and Will Hay (qq.v.). Later he was to co-direct Hay's last three films. At Ealing he developed a naturalistic approach for his serious subjects such as *The Bells Go Down*, *Frieda* and *The Blue Lamp*. After 1955 he worked in conjunction with Michael Relph, often alternating the producer–director role. He was killed in a motorway car crash in 1971.

Films. *The Black Sheep of Whitehall* (co-directed) (1941), *The Goose Steps Out* (co-directed) (1942), *My Learned Friend* (co-directed), *The Bells Go Down* (1943), *Halfway House, They Came to a City* (1944), *Dead of Night* (co-directed) (1945), *The Captive Heart* (1946), *Frieda* (1947), *Saraband for Dead Lovers* (1948), *Train of Events* (co-directed), *The Blue Lamp* (1949), *Cage of Gold* (1950), *Pool of London* (1951), *I Believe in You, The Gentle Gunman* (1952), *The Square Ring* (1953), *The Rainbow Jacket* (1954), *Out of the Clouds, The Ship that Died of Shame* (1955), *Who Done It?* (1956), *The Smallest Show on Earth* (1957), *Violent Playground* (1958), *Sapphire* (1959), *The League of Gentlemen, Man in the Moon* (1960), *The Secret Partner, Victim* (1961), *All Night Long, Life for Ruth* (1962), *The Mind Benders, A Place to Go, Woman of Straw* (1963), *Masquerade* (1964), *Khartoum* (1966), *Only When I Larf, The Assassination Bureau* (1968), *The Man who Haunted Himself* (1970).

THOROLD DICKINSON (1903–   ). Director, born Bristol.
Although he entered films in 1925 and directed his first feature in 1937 Dickinson's output was lamentably small. Of his few films the most oustanding is the stylistically exciting and intensely acted *Queen of Spades* (1949), although his version of the Patrick Hamilton play, *Gaslight* (1940), was one of the cinema's most disturbing incursions into psychopathology, and considerably more effective than the subsequent Hollywood remake which caused the film to be withdrawn. Dickinson later became Professor of Film at the Slade School, University of London.

Films. *The High Command* (1937), *Spanish ABC* (documentary) (1938), *The Arsenal Stadium Mystery* (1939), *Gaslight* (1940), *The Prime Minister* (1941), *Next of Kin* (1942), *Men of Two Worlds* (1946), *Queen of Spades* (1949), *The Secret People* (1952), *Hill 24 Doesn't Answer* (Israel) (1955).

ROBERT DONAT (1905–58). Actor, born Manchester.
Blessed with a fine, if fragile voice, cursed with the agony of asthma, which hastened his early death, Donat was unfulfilled as an actor in films, and could easily have been the outstanding figure of his generation if left unblighted. A distinguished stage actor, he entered films in the early thirties. Time and again opportunities were missed because of recurring illness, or productions were held up to allow him to recover.

In spite of the handicaps he is remembered for a handful of unequalled performances – Richard Hannay in Hitchcock's *The Thirty-Nine Steps*, Chipping in Sam Wood's *Goodbye Mr Chips*, the advocate in Asquith's *The Winslow Boy*.

Films. *Men of Tomorrow, That Night in London, Cash* (1932), *The Private Life of Henry VIII* (1933), *The Count of Monte Cristo* (U.S.A.) (1934), *The Thirty-Nine Steps* (1935), *The Ghost Goes West* (1936), *Knight Without Armour* (1937), *The Citadel* (1938), *Goodbye Mr Chips* (1939), *The Young Mr Pitt* (1942), *The Adventures of Tartu* (1943), *Perfect Strangers* (1945), *Captain Boycott* (1947), *The Winslow Boy* (1948), *The Cure for Love* (also directed) (1949), *The Magic Box* (1951), *Lease of Life* (1955), *The Inn of the Sixth Happiness* (1958).

CLIVE DONNER (1926–   ). Director, born London.
Entering films as a youth, Donner graduated to direction via the cutting room and it is in the fluidity of his editing that his talents are most apparent. There is a vein of sentimentality, particularly in his early work, which seemed over-concerned with the problems of childhood and adolescence, but present also in some of the more abrasive films of the mid-sixties, such as *Nothing but the Best* and *Here We Go Round the Mulberry Bush*. Donner is adept at catching the voguishness of the time, consequently his films only a few years later seem dated, but will no doubt totally regenerate themselves in a decade or two when they will appear as an accurate mirror of their period.

Films. *The Secret Place* (1957), *Heart of a Child* (1958), *A Marriage of Convenience* (1960), *The Sinister Man* (1961), *Some People* (1962), *The Caretaker, Nothing but the Best* (1963), *What's New Pussycat?* (U.S.A.) (1965), *Luv* (U.S.A.), *Here We Go Round the Mulberry Bush* (1967), *Alfred the Great* (1969), *Vampira* (1974).

DIANA DORS (Diana Fluck) (1931–   ). Actress, born Swindon, Wiltshire.
The British cinema has always been resistant to the creation of sex symbols; Diana Dors is probably the only British actress who can be even remotely compared with Marilyn Monroe or Brigitte Bardot. As a chubby adolescent she became typecast in a series of goodtime roles, usually coming to a bad end under the puritanical pressures of the day. Only in the mid-fifties was it accepted that she could also act, and while her cavortings on the beach at Cannes in mink bikinis and the

excessive behaviour of her first husband attracted newspaper headlines, her performance in *Yield to the Night*, vaguely based on the Ruth Ellis murder case, was both effective and moving. In recent years she has become a character actress, playing blousy middle-aged parts with both relish and a well-developed sense of humour.

Films. *The Shop at Sly Corner* (1946), *Holiday Camp, Dancing with Crime* (1947), *Good Time Girl, The Calendar, My Sister and I, Oliver Twist, Penny and the Pownall Case, Here Come the Huggetts* (1948), *Vote for Huggett, It's Not Cricket, A Boy, a Girl, a Bike, Diamond City* (1949), *Dance Hall* (1950), *Worm's Eye View, Lady Godiva Rides Again* (1951), *The Last Page, My Wife's Lodger* (1952), *The Great Game, Is Your Honeymoon Really Necessary? The Weak and the Wicked, It's a Grand Life* (1953), *The Saint's Return, As Long as They're Happy* (1954), *A Kid for Two Farthings, Miss Tulip Stays the Night, Value for Money, An Alligator Named Daisy* (1955), *Yield to the Night, I Married a Woman* (U.S.A.), *The Unholy Wife* (U.S.A.) (1956), *The Long Haul, The Love Specialist* (Italy) (1957), *Tread Softly Stranger* (1958), *Passport to Shame* (1959), *Scent of Mystery* (U.S.A.), *On the Double* (U.S.A.) (1960), *The Big Bankroll* (U.S.A.), *Mrs Gibbon's Boys* (1962), *West 11* (1963), *Allez France* (1964), *The Sandwich Man* (1966), *Berserk, Danger Route* (1967), *Hammerhead* (1968), *Baby Love* (1969), *Deep End* (Germany), *There's a Girl in My Soup* (1970), *Hannie Caulder* (U.S.A.), *The Pied Piper* (France) (1971), *Every Afternoon* (Sweden), *Nothing But the Night, The Amazing Mr Blunden, Theatre of Blood* (1972), *Steptoe and Son Ride Again, Craze* (1973), *Rosie, The Amorous Milkman* (1974).

MAURICE ELVEY (William Folkard) (1887–1967). Director, born Darlington, County Durham.

Maurice Elvey was a feature director for forty-five years, during which time he made well over 300 films. His output was prolific but not prodigious and while he had the occasional box-office high flier, most of his work was acceptable but unremarkable. Many of the early films are now lost, such is the transience of the film medium. Elvey also worked in Hollywood and Europe.

British films. Silent: *The Great Gold Robbery, Maria Marten* (1913), *The Cup Final Mystery, Black-Eyed Susan, The Suicide Club, The Loss of the Birkenhead, Beautiful Jim, The Bells of Rheims, Her Luck in London, It's a Long Way to Tipperary, The Idol of Paris* (1914), *A Honeymoon for Three, Midshipman Easy, London's Yellow Peril,*

*Florence Nightingale, From Shopgirl to Duchess, Her Nameless Child,
Grip, Home, A Will of Her Own, Charity Ann, Fine Feathers, Love in
a Wood* (1915), *Meg the Lady, Esther, Driven, Vice Versa, Motherlove,
When Knights Were Bold, The Princess of Happy Chance, The King's
Daughter* (1916), *Smith, The Grit of a Jew, The Woman Who Was
Nothing, Flames, Mary Girl, Goodbye, Justice, The Gay Lord Quex,
Dombey and Son* (1917), *Hindle Wakes, Adam Bede, Nelson, The Life
Story of David Lloyd George* (1918), *Bleak House, Comradeship, Keeper
of the Door, The Rocks of Valpre, The Victory Leaders, God's Good
Man, Mr Wu, The Swindler* (1919), *The Elusive Pimpernel, The Amateur
Gentleman, At the Villa Rose, The Hundredth Chance, A Question of
Trust, The Tavern Knight* (1920), *Innocent, A Gentleman of France,
The Hound of the Baskervilles, The Fruitful Vine, A Romance of Wast-
dale, Man and his Kingdom, The Adventures of Sherlock Holmes* series
(1921), *The Passionate Friends, Debt of Honour, Dick Turpin's Ride to
York, Running Water* (1922), *The Sign of Four, The Wandering Jew,
Guy Fawkes, Royal Oak, Sally Bishop, Don Quixote* (1923), *Henry
King of Navarre, Slaves of Destiny, The Love Story of Ailette Brunton*
(1924), *Woman Tempted, Human Law, The Flag Lieutenant, Made-
moiselle from Armentieres* (1926), *Hindle Wakes, Roses of Picardy, The
Glad Eye, The Flight Commander, Quinneys* (1927), *Mademoiselle
Parley Voo, Palais de Danse, You Know What Sailors Are* (1928).
Sound: *High Treason* (1929), *The School for Scandal, Balaclava* (co-
directed) (1930), *Sally in our Alley, Honeymoon Adventure, Potiphar's
Wife, The Water Gipsies, Diamond Cut Diamond* (co-directed), *Frail
Women, In a Monastery Garden* (1931), *The Marriage Bond, The
Lodger* (1932), *The Lost Chord, I Lived With You, This Week of Grace,
The Wandering Jew, Soldiers of the King* (1933), *Princess Charming,
My Song for You, Road House, Love Life and Laughter, Lily of Kil-
larney* (1934), *Heat Wave, Clairvoyant, The Tunnel* (1935), *Spy of
Napoleon, The Man in the Mirror* (1936), *Change for a Sovereign,
Who Killed John Savage?, A Romance in Flanders, Melody and Romance*
(1937), *Who Goes Next?, The Return of the Frog, Lightning Conductor*
(1938), *Sword of Honour, The Spider, Sons of the Sea* (1939), *Room for
Two, Under Your Hat, For Freedom* (1940), *Salute John Citizen* (1942),
The Lamp Still Burns, The Gentle Sex (co-directed) (1943), *Medal for
the General* (1944), *Strawberry Roan* (1945), *Beware of Pity* (1946),
The Late Edwina Black, The Third Visitor (1951), *My Wife's Lodger*
(1952), *House of Blackmail, The Great Game, Is Your Honeymoon
Really Necessary?* (1953), *What Every Woman Wants, The Happiness*

299

of Three Women, The Harassed Hero, The Gay Dog (1954), *You Lucky People, Room in the House* (1955), *Fun at St Fanny's, Stars in Your Eyes, Dry Rot* (1956), *Second Fiddle* (1957).

DAME EDITH EVANS (1888–). Actress, born London.
Grande dame of the British theatre, Dame Edith has occasionally performed for the screen, investing her roles with a dignity rarely present on the screen. Her performance as Lady Bracknell in Anthony Asquith's (q.v.) *The Importance of Being Earnest* (1952) is a superb record of a great actress in what is probably the definitive rendering of the part. Among her original screen interpretations must be counted *Queen of Spades* (1949) and Ma Tanner (who does not appear in the stage play) in *Look Back in Anger* (1959).

Films. Silent: *A Welsh Singer* (1915), *East is East* (1916). Sound: *Queen of Spades, The Last Days of Dolwyn* (1949), *The Importance of Being Earnest* (1952), *Look Back in Anger, The Nun's Story* (U.S.A.) (1959), *Tom Jones* (1963), *The Chalk Garden* (1964), *Young Cassidy* (1965), *The Whisperers* (1967), *Fitzwilly* (U.S.A.), *Prudence and the Pill* (1968), *Crooks and Coronets, David Copperfield, The Madwoman of Chaillot* (1969), *Scrooge* (1970), *A Doll's House, Craze* (1973).

GRACIE FIELDS (Grace Stansfield) (1898–). Actress, born Rochdale, Lancs.
A stage singer and comedienne, Gracie Fields was launched into films by Basil Dean (q.v.) in 1931 and quickly established herself as the highest paid British film star. Her *jolie laide* features and warm-hearted good humour endeared her to audiences through the depression years. Her popularity received a severe buffeting when war came and she was exiled in Hollywood, although she spent much time entertaining the troops. Her contribution to the British cinema was nevertheless unique and she did much to break the persistent preoccupation with the middle classes that affected the pre-war film scene.

Films. *Sally in Our Alley* (1931), *Looking on the Bright Side* (1932), *This Week of Grace, Love Life and Laughter* (1933), *Sing as We Go* (1934), *Look up and Laugh* (1935), *Queen of Hearts* (1936), *The Show Goes On* (1937), *We're Going to be Rich, Keep Smiling* (1938), *He Was Her Man, Shipyard Sally* (1939), *Holy Matrimony* (U.S.A.) (1943), *Stage Door Canteen* (U.S.A.), *Molly and Me* (U.S.A.) (1944), *Madame Pimpernel* (U.S.A.) (1945).

PETER FINCH (William Mitchell) (1916–   ). Actor, born London. Raised in Australia, Finch went on the stage there at the age of twenty, and came to Britain after the war. Originally a romantic lead, usually in virile roles, he has latterly become an actor of depth and introspection, as in, for example, two films directed by John Schlesinger (q.v.), *Far From the Madding Crowd* (1967) and *Sunday, Bloody Sunday* (1971).

Films. *Mr Chedworth Steps Out* (Australia) (1938), *Rats of Tobruk* (Australia) (1944), *Eureka Stockade* (Britain/Australia) (1947), *Train of Events* (1949), *The Wooden Horse, The Miniver Story* (1950), *The Story of Robin Hood* (1951), *The Story of Gilbert and Sullivan, The Heart of the Matter, Elephant Walk* (U.S.A.) (1953), *Father Brown* (1954), *Make Me An Offer, The Dark Avenger, Passage Home, Simon and Laura, Josephine and Men* (1955), *The Battle of the River Plate, A Town Like Alice* (1956), *The Shiralee, Robbery Under Arms, Windom's Way* (1957), *The Nun's Story* (U.S.A.), *Operation Amsterdam* (1958), *Kidnapped, The Sins of Rachel Cade* (U.S.A.), *The Trials of Oscar Wilde* (1960), *No Love for Johnnie* (1961), *I Thank a Fool* (1962), *In the Cool of the Day* (1963), *Girl with Green Eyes, The First Men in the Moon, The Pumpkin Eater* (1964), *Judith* (U.S.A.), *The Flight of the Phoenix* (U.S.A.) (1965), *Far From the Madding Crowd, 10.30 p.m. Summer* (U.S.A.) (1967), *The Legend of Lylah Clare* (U.S.A.) (1968), *Sunday, Bloody Sunday* (1971), *The Red Tent* (Italian/Russian) (1972), *Lost Horizon* (U.S.A.), *Bequest to the Nation, Something to Hide, England Made Me* (1973), *The Abdication* (U.S.A.) (1974).

ALBERT FINNEY (1936–   ). Actor, born Salford, Lancs. A stage actor from the British theatrical renaissance in the second half of the fifties, Albert Finney has contributed a forceful integrity to films, both in his performances in such works as *Saturday Night and Sunday Morning* and *Tom Jones*, and in production, being an associate of Memorial Films. His attempt at direction, *Charlie Bubbles*, became something of a cause célèbre owing to the intractability of the system which prevented a wider distribution.

Films. *The Entertainer* (1959), *Saturday Night and Sunday Morning* (1960), *Tom Jones, The Victors* (1963), *Night Must Fall* (1964), *Two for the Road, The Picasso Summer, Charlie Bubbles* (also directed) (1967), *Scrooge* (1970), *Gumshoe* (1971), *Murder on the Orient Express* (1974).

TERENCE FISHER (1904–   ). Director, born London.

In films since the early thirties, Fisher was formerly an editor. His early directorial work was concerned mainly with romantic themes, but during the fifties he turned to horror, being responsible for some of the best-known Hammer pictures in this genre.

Films. *A Song for Tomorrow, Colonel Bogey, To the Public Danger, Portrait from Life* (1948), *Marry Me* (1949), *The Astonished Heart, So Long at the Fair, Home to Danger* (1950), *A Distant Trumpet, The Last Page, Stolen Face, Wings of Danger* (1952), *Mantrap, The Four-Sided Triangle, Spaceways, Blood Orange* (1953), *Face the Music, Mask of Dust, The Stranger Came Home, Final Appointment, Children Galore* (1954), *Murder by Proxy, The Flaw, Stolen Assignment* (1955), *The Last Man to Hang* (1956), *Kill Me Tomorrow, The Curse of Franken-stein* (1957), *Dracula, The Revenge of Frankenstein* (1958), *The Hound of the Baskervilles, The Man Who Could Cheat Death, The Mummy, The Stranglers of Bombay* (1959), *The Bridges of Dracula, The Two Faces of Dr Jekyll, Sword of Sherwood Forest* (1960), *The Curse of the Werewolf* (1961), *The Phantom of the Opera* (1962), *The Horror of it All, The Earth Dies Screaming, The Gorgon* (1964), *Dracula Prince of Darkness* (1965), *Island of Terror* (1966), *Frankenstein Created Woman, Night of the Big Heat* (1967), *The Devil Rides Out* (1968), *Frankenstein Must Be Destroyed* (1969), *Frankenstein and the Monster from Hell* (1973).

BRYAN FORBES (Brian Clarke). Director, producer, writer, actor, born London.

Youthful precocity developed into an all-round talent which has occasionally moved the cinema forward. As an actor Forbes was usually cast in baby-faced service roles, although when auditioning for *The Cruel Sea* he was told that he was not officer material. His short tenure of office as Head of Production at Elstree gave momentary hope that an indigenous British film industry could become properly established, but regrettably the tycoons had the last word.

Films. Acted: *The Small Back Room, All Over the Town* (1948), *Dear Mr Prohack* (1949), *The Wooden Horse* (1950), *Green Grow the Rushes* (1951), *Appointment in London, The World in his Arms* (U.S.A.) (1952), *Sea Devils, Wheel of Fate, The Million Pound Note* (1953), *An Inspector Calls, Up to the Neck, The Colditz Story* (1954), *Passage Home, Now and Forever, The Quatermass Xperiment, The Last Man to Hang* (1955), *The Extra Day, It's Great to be Young, The Baby and the*

Battleship, Satellite in the Sky (1956), *Quatermass II* (1957), *The Key,
I Was Monty's Double* (1958), *Yesterday's Enemy* (1959), *The League of
Gentlemen* (1960), *The Guns of Navarone* (1961), *A Shot in the Dark*
(1964). Wrote: *Cockleshell Heroes* (1955), *The Baby and the Battleship,
The Black Tent, House of Secrets* (1956), *I Was Monty's Double* (1958),
The Captain's Table (1959), *The Angry Silence, The League of Gentlemen, Man in the Moon* (1960), *Only Two Can Play, Station Six Sahara*
(1962), *Of Human Bondage, The High Bright Sun* (1964). Directed:
Whistle Down the Wind (1961), *The L-Shaped Room* (also wrote)
(1962), *Seance on a Wet Afternoon* (also wrote) (1964), *King Rat*
(also wrote) (U.S.A.) (1965), *The Wrong Box* (also produced) (1966),
The Whisperers (also wrote), *Deadfall* (also wrote) (1967), *The Madwoman of Chaillot* (1969), *The Raging Moon* (also wrote) (1971).

WALTER FORDE (Tom Seymour) (1896–   ). Director, born Bradford,
Yorks.
A graduate to films from the music hall, Forde was a silent slapstick
comedian of note, making many appearances in shorts and a handful of
features. During the twenties he worked for a spell in Hollywood;
later he returned to become an excellent comedy director through the
thirties, occasionally lapsing into thrillers and uninspired melodramas.
   British feature films. Silent: *Wait and See, What Next?* (1928),
Would You Believe It?, The Silent House (1929). Sound: *Red Pearls,
You'd be Surprised, The Last Hour, Lord Richard in the Pantry, Bed and
Breakfast* (1930), *The Ringer, Splinters in the Navy, Third Time Lucky,
The Ghost Train* (1931), *Lord Babs, Jack's the Boy, Rome Express,
Condemned to Death* (1932), *Orders is Orders* (1933), *Chu Chin Chow,
Jack Ahoy* (1934), *Bulldog Jack, Forever England* (1935), *King of the
Damned, Land Without Music* (1936), *Kicking the Moon Around, The
Gaunt Stranger* (1938), *Inspector Hornleigh on Holiday, Let's Be
Famous, The Four Just Men, Cheer Boys Cheer* (1939), *Saloon Bar,
Sailors Three, Charley's Big-Hearted Aunt, Neutral Port, Gasbags*
(1940), *The Ghost Train, Inspector Hornleigh Goes to It, Atlantic Ferry*
(1941), *Flying Fortress, The Peterville Diamond, It's That Man Again*
(1942), *Time Flies* (1944), *Master of Bankdam* (also produced) (1947),
Cardboard Cavalier (1949).

GEORGE FORMBY (1904–61). Actor, born Wigan, Lancs.
Son of a famous music-hall artist, George Formby seemed destined to
follow a career on the variety stage. Toothy and gormless, clutching

his 'ukelele' (actually a banjo) and dispensing risqué lyrics with casual innocence, Formby became a music-hall favourite. His film debut was in Manchester, and his initial appeal was to the working-class audiences of the North. Basil Dean (q.v.) built him into a star for Associated Talking Pictures, and by the end of the thirties he was the top male performer at the box-office. Comedy styles changed and his last film failed even to get a circuit release.

Films. *Boots Boots* (1934), *Off the Dole*, *No Limit* (1935), *Keep Your Seats Please* (1936), *Feather Your Nest*, *Keep Fit* (1937), *I See Ice*, *It's in the Air* (1938), *Trouble Brewing*, *Come on George* (1939), *Let George Do It*, *Spare a Copper* (1940), *Turned Out Nice Again* (1941), *South American George*, *Much Too Shy* (1942), *Get Cracking*, *Bell Bottom George* (1943), *He Snoops to Conquer* (1944), *I Didn't Do It* (1945), *George in Civvy Street* (1946).

CHARLES FREND (1909–). Director, born Pulborough, Sussex.
Frend joined BIP in 1931 in the cutting room, and moved to Gaumont-British two years later. When the war started he was given an opportunity to direct by Michael Balcon (q.v.) at Ealing, and his first film was the quasi-documentary propaganda film, *The Big Blockade*. He went on to make *The Foreman Went to France* and *San Demetrio London*. Heroism seemed to be his forte and among his successful post-war films were *Scott of the Antarctic* and *The Cruel Sea*.

Films. *The Big Blockade* (1941), *The Foreman Went to France* (1942), *San Demetrio London* (1943), *Johnny Frenchman* (1945), *The Loves of Joanna Godden* (1947), *Scott of the Antarctic* (1948), *A Run for Your Money*, *The Magnet* (1949), *The Cruel Sea* (1953), *Lease of Life* (1954), *The Long Arm* (1956), *Barnacle Bill* (1957), *Cone of Silence* (1960), *Torpedo Bay* (Italy), *Girl on Approval* (1962), *The Sky Bike* (1967).

LEWIS GILBERT (1920–). Director, born London.
Initially a child actor, Gilbert served during the Second World War in the RAF Film Unit, later making a number of short documentaries. The best known of his features are the war subjects, such as *Reach for the Sky*, *Carve Her Name with Pride* and *Sink the Bismarck!* and the lavish James Bond adventure *You Only Live Twice*. He is a reliable but emotionally cool director, at his best with action and adventure.

Films. *The Little Ballerina* (1947), *Once a Sinner* (1950), *There is Another Sun, Scarlet Thread* (1951), *Emergency Call, Time Gentlemen Please* (1952), *Cosh Boy, Johnny on the Run, Albert R.N.* (1953), *The Sea Shall Not Have Them, The Good Die Young* (1954), *Cast a Dark Shadow* (1955), *Reach for the Sky* (1956), *The Admirable Crichton* (1957), *Carve Her Name With Pride, A Cry from the Streets* (1958), *Ferry to Hong Kong* (1959), *Sink the Bismarck!, Light up the Sky* (1960), *The Greengage Summer* (1961), *H.M.S. Defiant* (1962), *The Seventh Dawn* (1964), *Alfie* (1966), *You Only Live Twice* (1967), *The Adventurers* (1969), *Friends* (France) (1971), *Paul and Michelle* (1974), *Seven Men at Daybreak* (1975).

SIDNEY GILLIAT (1908–). Writer, producer, director, born Edgeley, Warwicks.
Gilliat entered the industry in 1927 and ten years later began his long partnership with Frank Launder (q.v.) as screenwriters. They set up their own production company, Individual Pictures, in 1945, after writing a stream of excellent films including *A Yank at Oxford*, *The Lady Vanishes* and *The Young Mr Pitt*. There has always been a strong element of jokiness in Gilliat's work, scarcely rich enough to be called satire, but not broad enough for slapstick either. The style is exemplified in *Left Right and Centre* (1959), *Only Two Can Play* (1961) and the St Trinian's films.
   Films. Writing: *Rome Express* (1932), *Facing the Music, Falling for You, Orders is Orders, Friday the Thirteenth* (1933), *Jack Ahoy, Chu Chin Chow, Mr Heart is Calling* (1934), *Bulldog Jack* (1935), *King of the Damned, Twelve Good Men, Where There's a Will, Seven Sinners, The Man Who Changed His Mind* (1936), *Take My Tip* (1937), *A Yank at Oxford, Strange Boarders, The Lady Vanishes, The Gaunt Stranger* (1938), *Jamaica Inn, Ask a Policeman, Inspector Hornleigh on Holiday* (1939), *They Came by Night, Night Train to Munich, Girl in the News* (1940), *Kipps* (1941), *The Young Mr Pitt* (1942), *The Pure Hell of St Trinian's* (1960). Writer and director: *Millions Like Us* (co-directed) (1943), *Waterloo Road* (1944), *The Rake's Progress* (1945), *Green for Danger* (1946), *London Belongs to Me* (1948), *State Secret* (1950), *The Story of Gilbert and Sullivan* (1953), *The Constant Husband* (1955), *Fortune Is a Woman* (1957), *Left Right and Centre* (1959), *Only Two Can Play* (1961), *The Great St Trinian's Train Robbery* (co-directed) (1966), *Endless Night* (1972).

GRAHAM GREENE (1904–   ). Writer, born London.

Few major British novelists have shown a sustained interest in the cinema, but Graham Greene is a happy exception. Not only have most of his novels formed the basis of films, but he himself has been responsible for several screenplays. During the mid-thirties he was film critic of the *Spectator* and then moved to *Night and Day* where an inadvertent libel in his column forced the closure of the magazine. Many of his film collaborations were with Carol Reed (q.v.) and it was for him that he wrote his original screenplay for *The Third Man* (1949).

Works filmed: *Orient Express* (*Stamboul Train*) (1934), *Went the Day Well?* (screenplay), *This Gun for Hire* (*A Gun for Sale*) (U.S.A.) (1942), *The Ministry of Fear* (U.S.A.) (1943), *Confidential Agent* (1945), *The Man Within, Brighton Rock* (1947), *The Fugitive* (*The Power and the Glory* (U.S.A.), *The Fallen Idol* (screenplay) (1948), *The Third Man* (screenplay) (1949), *The Heart of the Matter* (1953), *The Stranger's Hand* (1954), *The End of the Affair* (1955), *Short Cut to Hell, Across the Bridge* (1957), *The Quiet American* (U.S.A.) (1958), *Our Man in Havana* (screenplay) (1959), *The Power and the Glory* (1962), *The Comedians* (U.S.A.) (1967), *England Made Me, Travels with My Aunt* (1973).

JOHN GRIERSON (1898–1972). Producer, born Deanstown, Scotland.

Grierson was the founder of the British documentary movement of the thirties and the coiner of the word. He started the Empire Marketing Board Film Unit, and in 1933 the GPO Film Unit, gathering together such diverse and exciting talents as Humphrey Jennings, Paul Rotha and Cavalcanti (qq.v.). Under his aegis such classic films as *Drifters* (1929), *Industrial Britain, Song of Ceylon* and *Night Mail* emerged. At the start of the war Grierson was appointed Canadian Film Commissioner and founded the National Film Board of Canada. In 1951 he became Executive Producer of Group Three, a production unit that was designed to make quality programme fillers. From 1957 he ran a successful weekly television programme on Scottish TV, *This Wonderful World*, which showed excerpts from outstanding documentaries. Grierson's academic background was responsible for the evangelistic fervour with which he pursued the cause of film as an instrument of education and enlightenment. The cinema has had no more devoted propagandist.

VAL GUEST (1911–   ). Writer, director, producer, born London.
A former film journalist and for a brief spell actor, Val Guest learned
the film business as a scriptwriter on comedies for Will Hay (q.v.) and
the Crazy Gang. His first feature as a director was *Miss London Limited*
(1943). Most of his films have been comedies, although he has occasionally attempted suspense thrillers with varying success.

Films. Writer: *No Monkey Business* (1935), *Public Nuisance Number
One*, *A Star Fell from Heaven*, *All In*, *Windbag the Sailor* (1936),
Good Morning Boys, *Okay for Sound*, *Oh Mr Porter* (1937), *Convict 99*,
Alf's Button Afloat, *Hey Hey U.S.A.*, *Old Bones of the River* (1938),
Ask a Policeman, *Where's That Fire*, *Frozen Limits* (1939), *Band Wag-
gon*, *Charley's Big-Hearted Aunt*, *Gasbags* (1940), *The Ghost Train*,
Inspector Hornleigh Goes To It, *I Thank You*, *Hi Gang!* (1941), *Back-
room Boy* (1942), *London Town* (1946), *Paper Orchid* (1948), *Happy Go
Lovely*, *Another Man's Poison* (1950), *Men Without Women* (1956),
Dentist in the Chair (1960). Writer and director: *Miss London Limited*
(1943), *Bees in Paradise*, *Give Us the Moon* (1944), *I'll Be Your Sweetheart* (1945), *Just William's Luck* (1947), *William Comes to Town*
(1948), *Murder at the Windmill* (1949), *Miss Pilgrim's Progress*, *The
Body Said No* (1950), *Mr Drake's Duck* (1951), *Penny Princess* (also
produced) (1952), *Life with the Lyons* (1953), *The Runaway Bus* (also
produced), *Men of Sherwood Forest*, *Dance Little Lady* (1954), *They
Can't Hang Me*, *The Lyons in Paris*, *Break in the Circle*, *The Quatermass Xperiment* (1955), *It's a Wonderful World*, *The Weapon* (1956),
Carry On Admiral, *Quatermass II*, *The Abominable Snowman* (1957),
The Camp on Blood Island, *Up the Creek*, *Further up the Creek* (1958),
Life is a Circus, *Yesterday's Enemy*, *Expresso Bongo* (also produced)
(1959), *Hell is a City*, *The Full Treatment* (also produced) (1960), *The
Day the Earth Caught Fire* (also produced) (1961), *Jigsaw* (also pro-
duced) (1962), *80,000 Suspects* (also produced) (1963), *The Beauty
Jungle* (also produced) (1964), *Where the Spies Are* (also produced)
(1965), *Casino Royale* (co-directed only) (1966), *Assignment K* (1967),
When Dinosaurs Ruled the Earth (1969), *Tomorrow* (1970), *Confessions
of a Window Cleaner* (1974).

SIR ALEC GUINNESS (1914–   ). Actor, born in London.
A distinguished stage actor who began his theatrical career in 1933,
Guinness made a striking debut in films as Herbert Pocket in David
Lean's (q.v.) *Great Expectations* (1946). In the early part of his film
career he was much admired for the virtuosity of his characterizations,

particularly as Fagin in Lean's *Oliver Twist* and in the multiple parts played in Robert Hamer's (q.v.) *Kind Hearts and Coronets* (1949). Precise and polished in performance, Sir Alec's distinctive voice and dignified bearing have provided a substantial presence in many films.

Films. *Great Expectations* (1946), *Oliver Twist* (1948), *Kind Hearts and Coronets*, *A Run for Your Money* (1949), *Last Holiday*, *The Mudlark* (1950), *The Lavender Hill Mob*, *The Man in the White Suit* (1951), *The Card* (1952), *The Malta Story*, *The Captain's Paradise* (1953), *Father Brown*, *To Paris With Love* (1954), *The Prisoner*, *The Ladykillers* (1955), *The Swan* (U.S.A.) (1956), *The Bridge on the River Kwai* (1957), *Barnacle Bill*, *The Scapegoat*, *The Horse's Mouth* (1958), *Our Man in Havana* (1959), *Tunes of Glory* (1960), *A Majority of One* (U.S.A.) (1961), *H.M.S. Defiant*, *Lawrence of Arabia* (1962), *The Fall of the Roman Empire* (U.S.A.) (1964), *Situation Hopeless But Not Serious* (1965), *Dr Zhivago* (U.S.A.), *Hotel Paradiso*, *The Quiller Memorandum* (1966), *The Comedians* (U.S.A.) (1967), *Cromwell* (1970), *Scrooge* (1971), *Brother Sun Sister Moon* (Italy), *Hitler: The Last Ten Days* (1973).

ROBERT HAMER (1911–63). Director, writer, born Kidderminster, Warwicks.

Another Ealing graduate from the cutting room, Hamer was the most polished of all Balcon's (q.v.) Ealing stable of young film-makers. There was a marked Gallic influence in his work and a rare stylishness. *Kind Hearts and Coronets* is one of the most perfect comedies to emerge from a British studio, and it is disappointing that so little in the Hamer cannon comes near it, although several films, notably *Father Brown* and *It Always Rains on Sunday*, have momentary flashes that disclose an unfulfilled talent of considerable magnitude.

Films. *San Demetrio London* (wrote only) (1943), *Dead of Night* (co-directed), *Pink String and Sealing Wax* (1945), *It Always Rains on Sunday* (also wrote) (1947), *Kind Hearts and Coronets* (also wrote), *The Spider and the Fly* (1949), *His Excellency* (also wrote) (1952), *The Long Memory* (also wrote) (1953), *Father Brown* (1954), *To Paris With Love* (1955), *The Scapegoat* (1959), *School for Scoundrels* (1960), *A Jolly Bad Fellow* (wrote only) (1963).

GUY HAMILTON (1922–). Director, born Paris.

Guy Hamilton has mostly directed thrillers of an elaborate and modish kind, such as *Funeral in Berlin* and three James Bond films. When he has strayed from this territory the results have not always been satisfactory. His film *The Party's Over* (1963) ran into serious censorship problems, preventing it from being seen by a wide audience. His *The Battle of Britain* (1969) was his costliest work to date, but by no means the best, which one hopes is still to come.

Films. *The Ringer* (1952), *The Intruder* (1953), *An Inspector Calls* (1954), *The Colditz Story* (1955), *Charley Moon* (1956), *Manuela* (1957), *The Devil's Disciple* (1958), *A Touch of Larceny* (1959), *The Party's Over*, *The Man in the Middle* (1963), *Goldfinger* (1964), *Funeral in Berlin* (1966), *The Battle of Britain* (1969), *Diamonds are Forever* (1971), *Live and Let Die* (1973), *The Man with the Golden Gun* (1974).

REX HARRISON (Reginald Carey) (1908–   ). Actor, born Huyton, Lancashire.

On the stage since 1924, Rex Harrison played debonair young men with a hint of caddishness until quite late in his career, the archetypal screen role in this area being *The Rake's Progress*. In more recent years he became closely associated with the role of Professor Higgins in the musical *My Fair Lady*, a part specially written to encompass his narrow singing range, with immensely effective results.

Films. *The Great Game, The School for Scandal* (1930), *Get Your Man, Leave it to Blanche, All at Sea* (1934), *Man Are Not Gods* (1936), *Storm in a Teacup, School for Husbands* (1937), *St Martin's Lane, The Citadel* (1938), *Over the Moon, The Silent Battle* (1939), *Ten Days in Paris, Night Train to Munich* (1940), *Major Barbara* (1941), *I Live in Grosvenor Square, Blithe Spirit* (1945), *The Rake's Progress, Anna and the King of Siam* (U.S.A.) (1946), *The Ghost and Mrs Muir* (U.S.A.), *The Foxes of Harrow* (U.S.A.) (1947), *Unfaithfully Yours* (U.S.A.), *Escape* (1948), *The Long Dark Hall* (1951), *The Fourposter* (U.S.A.) (1952), *King Richard and the Crusaders* (U.S.A.) (1954), *The Constant Husband* (1955), *The Reluctant Debutante* (U.S.A.) (1958), *Midnight Lace* (U.S.A.) (1960), *The Happy Thieves* (U.S.A.), *Cleopatra* (U.S.A.) (1963), *My Fair Lady* (U.S.A.), *The Yellow Rolls-Royce* (1964), *The Agony and the Ecstasy* (U.S.A.) (1965), *The Honey Pot* (U.S.A.), *Dr Doolittle* (U.S.A.) (1967), *A Flea in Her Ear* (U.S.A./France) (1968), *Staircase* (U.S.A./France) (1969).

WILL HAY (1888–1949). Actor, born Stockton-on-Tees.

After twenty-five years in the music halls Will Hay reached the screen in 1934 and soon built up his seedy, scoundrelish, incompetent school-master characterization which found its way into other walks of life, such as prison governing, station-mastering and even spying. A master of comic timing, Hay's skill was such that he was able to capture the sympathy of the audience in spite of the unappealing nature of the guise in which he performed. *Oh Mr Porter!* (1937) endures as one of the comic masterpieces of the British cinema.

Films. *Those Were the Days, Radio Parade of 1933* (1934), *Dandy Dick, Boys Will be Boys* (1935), *Where There's a Will, Windbag the Sailor* (1936), *Good Morning Boys, Oh Mr Porter!* (1937), *Convict 99, Old Bones of the River, Hey Hey U.S.A.* (1938), *Ask a Policeman, Where's That Fire?* (1940), *The Ghost of St Michael's, The Black Sheep of Whitehall* (also co-directed) (1941), *The Big Blockade, The Goose Steps Out* (1942), *My Learned Friend* (also co-directed) (1944).

CECIL HEPWORTH (1874–1953). Director, producer, born London. A major pioneer of the British cinema, Hepworth invented a type of arc lamp for Robert Paul in 1895, assisted Birt Acres in the following year and in 1897 wrote the first book on the cinema, *Animated Photography*. He began making shorts in the following year, and later established his own company at Walton-on-Thames, which by the turn of the century was producing over a hundred short subjects a year. Among them was the most famous early British film, *Rescued by Rover* (1905). After the British industry slumped around 1910 Hepworth led its resurgence, introducing the star system to Britain, and directing many full-length features himself, which, although old-fashioned in style, attracted considerable prestige. But he could not escape eventual bankruptcy, and many of his films were lost after 1923 when his company was liquidated.

Feature films: *The Basilisk, Time the Great Healer, The Deadly Drug, The Canker of Jealousy, Courtmartialled, The Battle, The Man Who Stayed at Home, The Outrage, Sweet Lavender, Iris, The Baby on the Barge* (1915), *Trelawny of the Wells, Annie Laurie, Sowing the Wind, Comin' Thro' the Rye, The Marriage of William Ashe, Molly Bawn, The Cobweb* (1916), *The American Heiress, Nearer My God to Thee* (1917), *The Blindness of Fortune, The Touch of a Child, Boundary House* (1918), *The Nature of the Beast, Sunken Rocks, Sheba, The Forest on the Hill* (1919), *Anna the Adventuress, Alf's Button, Helen of Four Gates, Mrs Erricker's Reputation* (1920), *Tinted Venus, Narrow Valley, Wild Heather, Tansy* (1921), *The Pipes of Pan, Mist in the*

Valley, Strangking Threads, Comin' Thro' the Rye (1922), *The House of Marney* (1927).

ALFRED HITCHCOCK (1899–   ). Director, born London.
The most substantial film-maker to emerge from the British studios, it is sad for the native industry that the bulk of his work since 1940 has been made in America. The famous Hitchcock trademarks, the sinister editing, the red herrings, the distress of heroines, were already recognizable in his third film, *The Lodger* (1926). He pioneered the use of sound in Britain and was responsible for the first full-length talkie, *Blackmail*. During the thirties the stream of thrillers he made for Gaumont-British, beginning with *The Man Who Knew Too Much*, not only consolidated his international reputation, but provided a rare lustre for the unhappy British industry of the time. His removal to Hollywood was inevitable.

Films. Silent: *The Pleasure Garden* (1925), *The Mountain Eagle*, *The Lodger* (1926), *Downhill, Easy Virtue, The Ring* (1927), *The Farmer's Wife, Champagne* (1928), *The Manxman* (1929). Sound: *Blackmail* (1929), *Juno and the Paycock, Murder* (1930), *The Skin Game* (1931), *Rich and Strange, Number Seventeen* (1932), *Waltzes from Vienna* (1933), *The Man Who Knew Too Much* (1934), *The Thirty-Nine Steps* (1935), *The Secret Agent, Sabotage* (1936), *Young and Innocent* (1937), *The Lady Vanishes* (1938), *Jamaica Inn* (1939), *Rebecca* (U.S.A.), *Foreign Correspondent* (U.S.A.) (1940), *Mr and Mrs Smith* (U.S.A.), *Suspicion* (U.S.A.) (1941), *Saboteur* (U.S.A.) (1942), *Shadow of a Doubt* (U.S.A.) (1943), *Lifeboat* (U.S.A.) (1944), *Spellbound* (U.S.A.) (1945), *Notorious* (U.S.A.) (1946), *The Paradine Case* (U.S.A.) (1947), *Rope* (U.S.A.) (1948), *Under Capricorn* (1949), *Stage Fright* (1950), *Strangers on a Train* (U.S.A.) (1951), *I Confess* (U.S.A.) (1953), *Dial M for Murder* (U.S.A.), *Rear Window* (U.S.A.) (1954), *To Catch a Thief* (U.S.A.) (1955), *The Trouble with Harry* (U.S.A.), *The Man Who Knew Too Much* (U.S.A.) (1956), *The Wrong Man* (U.S.A.) (1957), *Vertigo* (U.S.A.) (1958), *North by Northwest* (U.S.A.) (1959), *Psycho* (U.S.A.) (1960), *The Birds* (U.S.A.) (1963), *Marnie* (U.S.A.) (1964), *Torn Curtain* (U.S.A.) (1966), *Topaz* (U.S.A.) (1969), *Frenzy* (1972).

SETH HOLT (1923–71). Director, born Palestine.
A former Ealing editor, Seth Holt's first feature film was the thriller, *Nowhere to Go*. He established a reputation for tautly conceived, quirky

thriller subjects such as *Station Six Sahara* and *The Nanny*, but his promise went unrealized because of his early death.

Films. *Nowhere to Go* (1958), *Taste of Fear* (1961), *Station Six Sahara* (1962), *The Nanny* (1965), *Danger Route* (1967), *Monsieur Lecoq* (1968), *Blood from the Mummy's Tomb* (1971).

LESLIE HOWARD (Leslie Stainer) (1893–1943). Actor, director, born London.

In spite of Hungarian antecedents Leslie Howard was a quintessentially English performer, usually appearing as a gentle, pipe-smoking man of reason, often troubled by the madness of the world around him. He was widely revered and greatly mourned after his death in a plane crash in the middle of the war. Originally a bank clerk, he went on the stage in 1918 and appeared in a number of short films during the twenties. He was one of the founders of Minerva Films. In the thirties he became established as a romantic star in Hollywood, his culminating role being that of Ashley Wilkes in *Gone With the Wind* (1939). He returned home to act and direct, notably *Pimpernel Smith* and the biography of Mitchell, the Spitfire designer, *The First of the Few*.

Films. *Outward Bound* (U.S.A.) (1930), *Never the Twain Shall Meet* (U.S.A.), *A Free Soul* (U.S.A.), *Five and Ten* (U.S.A.), *Devotion* (U.S.A.) (1931), *Smiling Through* (U.S.A.), *The Animal Kingdom* (U.S.A.) *Service for Ladies* (1932), *Secrets* (U.S.A.), *Captured* (U.S.A.), *Berkeley Square* (U.S.A.) (1933), *The Lady is Willing*, *Of Human Bondage* (U.S.A.), *British Agent* (U.S.A.) (1934), *The Scarlet Pimpernel* (1935), *The Petrified Forest* (U.S.A.), *Romeo and Juliet* (U.S.A.) (1936), *It's Love I'm After* (U.S.A.), *Stand In* (U.S.A.) (1937), *Pygmalion* (also co-directed) (1937), *Gone With the Wind* (U.S.A.), *Intermezzo* (*Escape to Happiness*) (U.S.A.) (1939), *Pimpernel Smith* (also produced and directed), *Forty-Ninth Parallel* (1941), *The First of the Few* (also directed) (1942), *The Gentle Sex* (produced only), *The Lamp Still Burns* (produced only) (1943).

TREVOR HOWARD (1916–). Actor, born Cliftonville, Kent.

Gruff-voiced and impressive, Trevor Howard's presence has strengthened many films. His first memorable role was in *Brief Encounter*, since when he has passed from romantic parts to character performances, often of a seedy and corrupted kind. His Captain Bligh in the remake of *Mutiny on the Bounty*, overshadowed by Laughton's earlier portrayal, was consequently under-rated, but more recently he was excellent as the priest in David Lean's *Ryan's Daughter*, renewing an association with the director of his first great success.

Films. *The Way Ahead* (1944), *The Way to the Stars* (1945), *Brief Encounter*, *I See a Dark Stranger*, *Green for Danger* (1946), *So Well Remembered*, *They Made Me a Fugitive* (1947), *The Passionate Friends* (1948), *The Third Man*, *The Golden Salamander* (1949), *Odette*, *The Clouded Yellow* (1950), *An Outcast of the Islands* (1951), *The Gift Horse* (1952), *The Heart of the Matter* (1953), *The Lovers of Lisbon* (France), *The Stranger's Hand* (1954), *Cockleshell Heroes* (1955), *Around the World in Eighty Days* (U.S.A.), *Run for the Sun* (U.S.A.) (1956), *Interpol*, *Manuela* (1957), *The Key* (1958), *The Roots of Heaven* (U.S.A.), *Moment of Danger* (1959), *Sons and Lovers* (1960), *Mutiny on the Bounty* (U.S.A.), *The Lion* (1962), *The Man in the Middle*, *Father Goose* (U.S.A.) (1964), *Von Ryan's Express* (U.S.A.), *Morituri* (U.S.A.), *Operation Crossbow*, *The Liquidator* (1965), *The Poppy Is Also a Flower*, *Triple Cross* (1966), *The Long Duel*, *Pretty Polly* (1967), *The Charge of the Light Brigade* (1968), *The Battle of Britain* (1968), *Twinky*, *Ryan's Daughter* (1970), *The Night Visitor* (1971) *Mary Queen of Scots*, *Catch Me a Spy*, *Kidnapped* (1972), *Pope Joan*, *The Offence*, *Craze* (1973), *Persecution* (1974), *Hennessy. Conduct Unbecoming* (1975).

KEN HUGHES (1922–   ). Director, born Liverpool.
Associated with the film industry for over thirty years Hughes has also been a television playwright and a novelist. Most of his films have been crime thrillers, including a bizarre version of *Macbeth* transposed to American gangland, *Joe Macbeth* (1955). His most ambitious work to date was *Cromwell* (1970), in which the dictator of the Commonwealth was seen as a seventeenth-century Castro, leading his freedom fighters.

Films. *Wide Boy* (1952), *The Brain Machine*, *Little Red Monkey*, *Confession*, *Timeslip*, *Black Thirteen* (1953), *The House Across the Lake* (1954), *Joe Macbeth*, *Confession* (1955), *Wicked as They Come* (1956), *The Long Haul* (1957), *Jazzboat*, *In the Nick*, *The Trials of Oscar Wilde* (1960), *The Small World of Sammy Lee* (1963), *Of Human Bondage* (1964), *Drop Dead Darling* (1966), *Casino Royale* (co-directed) (1967), *Chitty Chitty Bang Bang* (1968), *Cromwell* (1970), *Ten Days that Shook the World* (1972), *The Internecine Project* (1974), *Alfie Darling* (1975).

HUMPHREY JENNINGS (1907–50). Director, born Walberswick, Suffolk.
Formerly a painter, Jennings joined the GPO Film Unit at the be-

hest of John Grierson (q.v.) in 1934, and was responsible for the most poetic of films made under his aegis there and at Crown. His wartime documentaries are a brilliantly evocative record of their time, their persuasive atmosphere constructed by a careful synthesizing of sound and image. After the war Jennings's work seems diminished as though there was little left for him to say, and his last film, *Family Portrait*, is disappointing. He met his death on a Greek island, where he fell from a cliff while prospecting for locations. He was without doubt the foremost British documentarist, an artist who brought a personal, idiosyncratic vision to the cinema.

Films. *Birth of a Robot* (co-directed) (1936), *The First Days* (co-directed), *Spare Time*, *An Unrecorded Victory*, *Speaking from America*, *Her Last Trip* (1939), *London Can Take It* (co-directed), *Welfare of the Workers* (1940), *Words for Battle*, *Heart of Britain*, *Listen to Britain* (1941), *The Silent Village*, *Fires Were Started* (1943), *The True Story of Lilli Marlene* (1944), *A Diary for Timothy* (1945), *A Defeated People* (1946), *The Cumberland Story* (1947), *Dim Little Island* (1949), *Family Portrait* (1950).

ANTHONY KIMMINS (1901–63). Writer, director, producer, born Harrow, Middlesex.

After professional naval service Kimmins became an actor in quota quickies, and then adaptor of his own celebrated farces such as *While Parents Sleep*. He wrote and directed some of George Formby's (q.v.) best comedies, and then returned to the Royal Navy for the war. Afterwards his output was variable, from the intricate psychological thriller *Mine Own Executioner* to the disastrous *Bonnie Prince Charlie*. His last film was in a sense a return to the beginning of his cinema career, an adaptation of his West End farce *The Amorous Prawn*.

Films. Acted: *The Golden Cage* (1933), *White Ensign* (1934). Directed: *Bypass to Happiness*, *How's Chances?*, *Designing Women* (script only) (1934), *Once in a New Moon*, *His Majesty and Co*, *All at Sea*, *Midshipman Easy* (script only), *While Parents Sleep* (script only) (1935), *Laburnum Grove* (script only), *The Lonely Road* (script only), *Keep Your Seats Please* (script only), *Talk of the Devil* (script only) (1936), *Feather Your Nest* (script only), *The Show Goes On* (script only), *Who's Your Lady Friend?* (script only), *Keep Fit* (also wrote) (1937), *I See Ice* (also wrote), *It's in the Air* (also wrote) (1938), *Come on George* (also wrote), *Trouble Brewing* (also wrote) (1939), *Under Your Hat* (script only) (1940), *Mine Own Executioner* (1947),

Bonnie Prince Charlie (1948), *Flesh and Blood* (1950), *Mr Denning Drives North* (1951), *Who Goes There?* (1952), *The Captain's Paradise* (also wrote) (1943), *Aunt Clara* (1954), *Smiley* (also wrote) (1956), *Smiley Gets a Gun* (1958), *The Amorous Prawn* (also wrote) (1962).

SIR ALEXANDER KORDA (1893–1956). Producer, director, born Turkeye, Hungary.

One of the most colourful figures in British films, Korda was also the most ambitious and at one time appeared to be singlehandedly saving the industry. A man of persuasive charm and excellent taste, he arrived in the early thirties by way of Paris and Hollywood and instantly began making quota quickies. In 1933 he produced and directed *The Private Life of Henry VIII* which was a resounding success on both sides of the Atlantic, and inspired the grandiose plans for his London Films in the years following. The vast Denham Studios were built by Korda on money borrowed from the Prudential Insurance company. Among the films he produced in the pre-war period were *The Scarlet Pimpernel*, *Sanders of the River*, *Things to Come*, *The Ghost Goes West*, *Rembrandt*, *Knight Without Armour*, *Elephant Boy*, *The Drum*, *The Thief of Bagdad* and many more. The bubble burst and the studios were sold up, but after the war Korda renewed his energies, producing such post-war successes as *The Fallen Idol*, *The Third Man*, *Seven Days to Noon*, *The Sound Barrier* and *Richard III*. His brother Zoltan was an able director in his own right of such films as *The Four Feathers*, and another brother, Vincent, an excellent art director.

Films as director: *The Stolen Bride* (U.S.A.), *The Private Life of Helen of Troy* (U.S.A.) (1927), *The Yellow Lily* (U.S.A.), *Night Watch* (U.S.A.) (1928), *Love and the Devil* (U.S.A.), *The Squall* (U.S.A.), *Her Private Life* (U.S.A.) (1929), *Women Everywhere* (U.S.A.), *The Princess and the Plumber* (U.S.A.) (1930), *River Gauche* (France), *Marius* (France), *Service for Ladies* (1931), *Women Who Play*, *Wedding Rehearsal* (1932), *The Girl from Maxim's* (France), *The Private Life of Henry VIII* (1933), *The Private Life of Don Juan* (1934), *Rembrandt* (1936), *Lady Hamilton* (U.S.A.) (1941), *Perfect Strangers* (1945), *Ideal Husband* (1947).

STANLEY KUBRICK (1928–). Director, writer, producer, born New York.

Formerly a photo-journalist, Kubrick is one of the most careful and stylish of film-makers, presenting a despairing picture of the world we shall soon know with the polish and gloss of a *Life* picture story. For more than a decade he has based himself in England, during which time he has made four compelling films – *Lolita*, *Dr Strangelove*, the breathtaking *2001* and *A Clockwork Orange*.

Films. *Fear and Desire* (U.S.A.) (1953), *Killer's Kiss* (U.S.A.) (1955), *The Killing* (U.S.A.) (1956), *Paths of Glory* (U.S.A.) (1957), *Spartacus* (U.S.A.) (1960), *Lolita* (1962), *Dr Strangelove or How I Learned to Stop Worrying and Love the Bomb* (1963), *2001 – A Space Odyssey* (1969), *A Clockwork Orange* (1971), *Barry Lyndon* (1975).

CHARLES LAUGHTON (1899–1962). Actor, born Scarborough, Yorkshire.

A character actor of great distinction, Laughton went on to the stage in 1926 after a spell at RADA. His rotund appearance ruled him out for romantic leads, but he quickly established a reputation for brilliant characterization, essaying even at a comparatively youthful age roles far in advance of his own years. Most of his work was in the American cinema, but he enhanced British films with his portrayals of Henry VIII and Rembrandt, both for Korda.

Films. *Piccadilly* (1929), *Comets, Wolves* (1930), *Down River* (1931), *The Old Dark House* (U.S.A.), *The Devil and the Deep* (U.S.A.), *The Sign of the Cross* (U.S.A.), *Island of Lost Souls* (U.S.A.), *Payment Deferred* (U.S.A.), *If I Had a Million* (U.S.A.) (1932), *The Private Life of Henry VIII*, *White Woman* (U.S.A.) (1933), *The Barretts of Wimpole Street* (U.S.A.) (1934), *Les Misérables* (U.S.A.), *Ruggles of Red Gap* (U.S.A.), *Mutiny on the Bounty* (U.S.A.) (1935), *Rembrandt* (1936), *Vessel of Wrath* (1937), *St Martin's Lane* (1938), *Jamaica Inn*, *The Hunchback of Notre Dame* (U.S.A.) (1939), *They Knew What They Wanted* (U.S.A.) (1940), *It Started with Eve* (U.S.A.), *The Tuttles of Tahiti* (U.S.A.) (1941), *Tales of Manhattan* (U.S.A.), *Cargo of Innocents* (U.S.A.) (1942), *Forever and a Day* (U.S.A.), *This Land Is Mine* (U.S.A.), *The Man from Down Under* (U.S.A.) (1943), *The Canterville Ghost* (U.S.A.), *The Suspect* (U.S.A.) (1944), *Captain Kidd* (U.S.A.) (1945), *Because of Him* (U.S.A.) (1946), *The Paradine Case* (U.S.A.), *The Big Clock* (U.S.A.) (1947), *The Girl from Manhattan* (U.S.A.), *Arch of Triumph* (U.S.A.), *The Bribe* (U.S.A.) (1948), *The Man on the Eiffel Tower* (France) (1950), *The Blue Veil* (U.S.A.) (1951), *The Strange Door* (U.S.A.), *Abbott and Costello Meet Captain Kidd* (U.S.A.) (1952), *Full House* (U.S.A.), *Young Bess* (U.S.A.), *Salome* (U.S.A.) (1953), *Hobson's Choice* (1954), *The Night of the Hunter* (directed only) (U.S.A.) (1955), *Witness for the Prosecution* (U.S.A.) (1957), *Spartacus* (U.S.A.), *Under Ten Flags* (U.S.A.) (1960), *Advise and Consent* (U.S.A.) (1962).

FRANK LAUNDER (1907–). Director, writer, born Hitchin, Herts. In partnership with Sidney Gilliatt (q.v.) for many years Frank Launder was one half of Individual Films, taking it in turns to direct. He initially joined the story department of BIP in 1928 and during the thirties wrote such outstanding films as *The Lady Vanishes*, *Oh Mr Porter!* and *Night Train to Munich*. It is hard to differentiate his style from that of his partner, but in recent years the tendency has been towards broad comedy rather than the thrillers of the *I See a Dark Stranger*, *Green for Danger* mould.

Films. Writing: *Under the Greenwood Tree* (1929), *Song of Soho*, *The W. Plan*, *The Middle Watch*, *Children of Chance* (1930), *How He Lied to Her Husband*, *Keepers of Youth*, *Hobson's Choice* (1931), *After Office Hours*, *The Last Coupon*, *Josser in the Army*, *For the Love of Mike* (1932), *Hawleys of High Street*, *Facing the Music*, *You Made Me Love You*, *A Southern Maid* (1933), *Happy*, *Those Were the Days* (1934), *Emil and the Detectives*, *So You Won't Talk*, *Mr What's His Name*, *Get Off My Foot*, *I Give My Heart*, *The Black Mask* (1935), *Twelve Good Men*, *Where's Sally?*, *Seven Sinners*, *Educated Evans* (1936), *Don't Get Me Wrong*, *Oh Mr Porter!* (1937), *The Lady Vanishes* (1938), *A Girl Must Live*, *Inspector Hornleigh on Holiday* (1939), *They Came by Night*, *Night Train to Munich* (1940), *Inspector Hornleigh Goes to It*, *Kipps* (1941), *The Young Mr Pitt* (1942). Directed: *Millions Like Us* (co-directed), *2000 Women* (1943), *I See a Dark Stranger* (1946), *Captain Boycott* (1947), *The Blue Lagoon* (1949), *The Happiest Days of Your Life* (1950), *Lady Godiva Rides Again* (1951), *Folly to Be Wise* (1952), *The Belles of St Trinian's* (1954), *Geordie* (1955), *Blue Murder at St Trinian's* (1957), *The Bridal Path* (1959), *The Pure Hell of St Trinian's* (1960), *Joey Boy* (1965), *The Great St Trinian's Train Robbery* (co-directed) (1966).

DAVID LEAN (1908–). Director, born Croydon, Surrey. David Lean entered the film industry in 1928, graduating from clapper-boy to editor. He co-directed *In Which We Serve* (1942) with Noël Coward (q.v.) and went on to direct three of Coward's screenplays, *This Happy Breed*, *Blithe Spirit* and *Brief Encounter*, with considerable success. Two Dickens films followed, *Great Expectations* and *Oliver*

Twist. From then on Lean's work became glossier but less inspired. Since *The Bridge on the River Kwai* (1957) he has worked exclusively on international epics of an expensive kind, in collaboration with his screenwriter Robert Bolt.

Films. *In Which We Serve* (1942), *This Happy Breed* (1944), *Blithe Spirit*, *Brief Encounter* (1945), *Great Expectations* (1946), *Oliver Twist* (1948), *The Passionate Friends* (1949), *Madeleine* (1950), *The Sound Barrier* (1952), *Hobson's Choice* (1954), *Summer Madness* (1955), *The Bridge on the River Kwai* (1957), *Lawrence of Arabia* (1962), *Dr Zhivago* (U.S.A.) (1966), *Ryan's Daughter* (1970).

VIVIEN LEIGH (Vivien Hartley) (1913–67). Actress, born Darjeeling, India.

After a number of routine films in the thirties, culminating with the second female lead in *A Yank at Oxford* (1938), Vivien Leigh became internationally famous when she was selected to play Scarlett O'Hara in *Gone With the Wind*, amidst much controversy generated by disgruntled American actresses. Her performance vindicated criticism and she remained in Hollywood, making *Lady Hamilton* for Korda with her husband Laurence Olivier (qq.v.). Later in the war she played the Egyptian queen in *Caesar and Cleopatra*. Poor health kept her from making a large number of films, but her screen performances reveal her as an actress compensating in beauty and personality for what she lacked in depth.

Films. *Things are Looking Up* (1934), *The Village Squire, Gentleman's Agreement, Look Up and Laugh* (1935), *Fire Over England* (1936), *Dark Journey, Storm in a Teacup, Twenty-One Days* (1937), *St Martin's Lane, A Yank at Oxford* (1938), *Gone With the Wind* (U.S.A.) (1939), *Waterloo Bridge* (U.S.A.) (1940), *Lady Hamilton* (U.S.A.) (1941), *Caesar and Cleopatra* (1945), *Anna Karenina* (1948), *A Streetcar Named Desire* (U.S.A.) (1951), *The Deep Blue Sea* (1955), *The Roman Spring of Mrs Stone* (1961), *Ship of Fools* (U.S.A.) (1965).

DICK LESTER (1932–   ). Director, born Philadelphia, U.S.A.

Since the fifties Dick Lester has been domiciled in England, and sprang to attention in the early days of ITV with his work in connection with the Goons (Peter Sellers (q.v.), Spike Milligan, Harry Secombe). His first cinema film was a rapidly made short, *The Running Jumping and Standing Still Film* (1960) which encapsulated his humorous approach. His two films with the Beatles and *The Knack* displayed a trendy originality which was later dissipated in *How I Won the War* and the disastrous *The Bed-Sitting Room*. His most satisfactory film to date is *Petulia*, made in America.

Films. *The Running Jumping and Standing Still Film* (short) (1960), *It's Trad Dad* (1962), *The Mouse on the Moon* (1963), *A Hard Day's Night* (1964), *The Knack, Help!* (1965), *A Funny Thing Happened on the Way to the Forum* (1966), *How I Won the War, Petulia* (U.S.A.) (1967), *The Bed-Sitting Room* (1969), *The Three Musketeers*, (1974). *The Four Musketeers, Juggernaut, Royal Flash* (1975).

KEN LOACH (1936–). Director.

Ken Loach emerged as a film-maker from television where he excited considerable attention for his work with fictionalized documentaries, the most famous of which was *Cathy Come Home*. One of the few genuinely radical voices in the British cinema Loach's films to date have all shown the plight of the individual on the bottom rung of society fighting the machinery's inexorable weight. *Family Life* (1971) is the most disturbing statement yet made on film to explode the myth of the family as a protective and supportive unit.

Films. *Poor Cow* (1967), *Kes* (1969), *Family Life* (1971).

MARGARET LOCKWOOD (Margaret Day) (1916–). Actress, born Karachi, India.

Margaret Lockwood's early film roles were usually as haughty but nubile girls, eventually won over by irresistible heroes, e.g. *The Lady Vanishes*. As she matured she became typecast as wicked heroines in Gainsborough costume melodramas. In the mid-forties she was Britain's leading female star in terms of box-office popularity. She retired from films during the fifties, but has since appeared frequently on the stage and in television series.

Films. *Lorna Doone* (1934), *The Case of Gabriel Perry, Some Day, Honours Easy, Man of the Moment, Midshipman Easy* (1935), *Jury's Evidence, The Amateur Gentleman, Beloved Vagabond, Irish for Luck* (1936), *The Street Singer, Who's Your Lady Friend, Dr Syn, Melody and Romance* (1937), *Owd Bob, Bank Holiday, The Lady Vanishes* (1938), *A Girl Must Live, Susannah of the Mounties* (U.S.A.), *Rulers of the Sea* (U.S.A.) (1939), *The Stars Look Down, Night Train to Munich, Girl in the News* (1948), *Quiet Wedding* (1941), *Alibi* (1942), *The Man in Grey, Dear Octopus* (1943), *Give Us the Moon, Love Story* (1944), *A Place of One's Own, I'll be Your Sweetheart, The Wicked Lady* (1945), *Bedelia, Hungry Hill* (1946), *Jassy, The White Unicorn*

(1947), *Look Before You Love* (1948), *Cardboard Cavalier, Madness of the Heart* (1949), *Highly Dangerous* (1950), *Trent's Last Case* (1952), *Laughing Anne* (1953), *Trouble in the Glen* (1954), *Cast a Dark Shadow* (1955).

JOSEPH LOSEY (1909–   ). Director, born Lacrosse, Wisconsin, U.S.A. Losey has worked in Britain since the early fifties when he left Hollywood as a result of the witch-hunting of the McCarthy era. His first British films were directed under pseudonyms. Losey's preoccupation with class and social order are discernible as far back as *The Gypsy and the Gentleman* (1958) and recur in *Eve* (1962), *The Servant* (1963), *King and Country* (1964), *Accident* (1967), *The Secret Ceremony* (1968), *Figures in a Landscape* (1970) and *The Go-Between* (1971). Constantly demonstrating the limitations that beset his heroes Losey traps them in a struggle they cannot win. His visual sense is acute, his poetic awareness intense. He is currently one of the most exciting forces in the British cinema.

Films. *The Boy With Green Hair* (U.S.A.) (1948), *The Lawless (The Dividing Line* in U.K.) (U.S.A.) (1949), *The Prowler* (U.S.A.) (1950), *M* (U.S.A.), *The Big Night* (U.S.A.), *Stranger on the Prowl* (Italy) (alias Andrea Forzano) (1951), *The Sleeping Tiger* (alias Victor Hanbury) (1954), *The Intimate Stranger* (alias Joseph Walton) (1956), *Time Without Pity* (1957), *The Gypsy and the Gentleman* (1958), *Blind Date* (1959), *The Criminal* (1960), *The Damned* (1961), *Eve* (Italy) (1962), *The Servant* (1963), *King and Country* (1964), *Modesty Blaise* (1966), *Accident* (1967), *Boom, The Secret Ceremony* (1968), *Figures in a Landscape* (1970), *The Go-Between* (1971), *The Assassination of Trotsky* (1972), *A Doll's House* (1973), *Galileo, The Romantic English Woman* (1975).

ALEXANDER MACKENDRICK (1912–   ). Director, born Boston, Mass.
Mackendrick worked in advertising before entering films as a screen-writer. He was one of the many talented figures working at Ealing under Michael Balcon (q.v.) and scripted such films as *Saraband for Dead Lovers, The Blue Lamp* and *Dance Hall*. His first two films, which he also wrote, were the excellent Ealing comedies *Whisky Galore* and *The Man in the White Suit*. When the steam ran out at Ealing he went to Hollywood, where he made the most effective film of his career, the under-rated *Sweet Smell of Success*.

Films. *Whisky Galore* (1949), *The Man in the White Suit* (1951), *Mandy* (1952), *The Maggie* (1953), *The Ladykillers* (1955), *Sweet Smell of Success* (U.S.A.) (1957), *Sammy Going South* (1962), *A High Wind in Jamaica* (1965), *Don't Make Waves* (1967).

JAMES MASON (1909–). Actor, born Huddersfield, Yorks.
Trained as an architect, and a graduate of Cambridge University, James Mason went on the stage in 1931. He entered films in 1935 and established himself as an attractive juvenile lead, distinguished by saturnine looks and a silky speaking voice. By the forties he had become renowned for introspective and semi-sadistic parts, a development that reached its peak with *The Seventh Veil* (1945) and *The Wicked Lady* of the same year. After a brilliant performance in Carol Reed's (q.v.) *Odd Man Out* and a lesser one in *The Upturned Glass* he denounced British films in general and Lord Rank in particular and went to Hollywood. Mellowed, he is now a character actor of distinction.
Films. *Late Extra* (1935), *Twice Branded, Troubled Waters, Prison Breakers, Blind Man's Bluff* (1936), *Secret of Stamboul, The Mill on the Floss, The High Command, Fire Over England, Catch as Catch Can* (1937), *The Return of the Scarlet Pimpernel* (1938), *I Met a Murderer* (1939), *This Man is Dangerous (The Patient Vanishes)* (1941), *Hatter's Castle, The Night Has Eyes, Alibi, Secret Mission* (1942), *Thunder Rock, The Bells Go Down, The Man in Grey, They Met in the Dark* (1943), *Candlelight in Algeria, Fanny by Gaslight, Hotel Reserve* (1944), *They Were Sisters, A Place of One's Own, The Seventh Veil, The Wicked Lady* (1945), *Odd Man Out, The Upturned Glass* (1947), *Caught* (U.S.A.), *Madame Bovary* (U.S.A.), *The Reckless Moment* (U.S.A.) (1949), *East Side West Side* (U.S.A.), *One Way Street* (U.S.A.) (1950), *Pandora and the Flying Dutchman, Rommel – Desert Fox* (U.S.A.) (1951), *Lady Possessed* (U.S.A.), *Five Fingers* (U.S.A.), *The Prisoner of Zenda* (U.S.A.), *Face to Face* (U.S.A.) (1952), *The Desert Rats* (U.S.A.), *Julius Caesar* (U.S.A.), *The Story of Three Loves* (U.S.A.), *Botany Bay* (U.S.A.), *The Man Between, Charade* (1953), *Prince Valiant* (U.S.A.), *A Star is Born* (U.S.A.), *Twenty Thousand Leagues Under the Sea* (U.S.A.) (1954), *Forever Darling* (U.S.A.) (1955), *Bigger than Life* (U.S.A.) (1956), *Island in the Sun* (U.S.A.) (1957), *Cry Terror!* (U.S.A.), *The Decks Ran Red* (U.S.A.) (1958), *North by Northwest* (U.S.A.), *Journey to the Centre of the Earth* (1959), *A Touch of Larceny, The Trials of Oscar Wilde* (1960), *The Marriage-go-round* (U.S.A.) 1961, *The Land We Love* (U.S.A.), *Escape from Zahrein*

(U.S.A.), *Tiara Tahiti*, *Lolita* (1962), *The Fall of the Roman Empire* (U.S.A.), *Finche Dura La Tempesta* (Italy), *The Pumpkin Eater* (1964), *Lord Jim* (U.S.A.), *Les Pianos Mecaniques* (France/Spain), *Genghis Khan* (U.S.A.), *The Blue Max*, *Georgy Girl* (1966), *The Deadly Affair*, *Stranger in the House* (1967), *Duffy*, *Mayerling* (1968), *Age of Consent* (Australia), *The Sea Gull* (1969), *Spring and Port Wine* (1970), *Bad Man's River* (U.S.A.) (1972), *The Last of Sheila*, *Dr Frankenstein* (1973), *11 Harrowhouse*, *The Marseille Contract* (1974), *Great Expectations* (1975).

RICHARD MASSINGHAM (1898–1953). Actor, director, writer, born London.

Massingham was originally a doctor who began making amateur films in the thirties. His well-observed portrayal of the agonies of dentistry (*Tell Me If It Hurts*, 1935) and the frustrations of boarding-house life (*And So to Work*, 1936) brought him into John Grierson's (q.v.) orbit and he began making short films for the Post Office. When the war came Massingham became a familiar and endearing figure to cinemagoers, being featured in many propaganda shorts exhorting citizens to use less bathwater, gather salvage and avoid careless talk. He appeared as a bald, flustered and bewildered member of the public, put upon by bureaucrats but somehow struggling through. He was the embodiment of the wartime civilian. It is a matter of regret that his unique talent was never revealed in a full-length feature.

JESSIE MATTHEWS (1907–). Actress, born London.

During the thirties Jessie Matthews was the leading British musical star. An energetic, high-kicking dancer and a careful, fluting singer she had a brittle, fragile personality that endeared her to the audience of the day. Born in Soho and on the stage from the age of ten she seemed to embody the essence of British show business and starred in a number of hit musical films, several directed by Victor Saville (q.v.). Perhaps wisely she withdrew from films during the war, making only one appearance after it. In recent years she became the leading character in a long running daily radio serial, *The Dales*.

Films. Silent: *Beloved Vagabond* (1923), *Straws in the Wind* (1924). Sound: *Out of the Blue* (1931), *There goes the Bride*, *The Midshipmaid* (1932), *The Man from Toronto*, *The Good Companions*, *Friday the Thirteenth*, *Waltzes from Vienna* (1933), *Evergreen* (1934), *First a Girl* (1935) *It's Love Again* (1936), *Head over Heels*, *Gangway* (1937),

Sailing Along (1938), *Climbing High* (1939), *Forever and a Day* (U.S.A.), *Candles at Nine* (1943), *Tom Thumb* (1958).

JOHN MILLS (1908–   ). Actor, born North Elmham, Norfolk.
A graduate from light comedies and musicals John Mills made his film debut in 1932, coming into his own during the war when he was frequently called upon to brandish a stiff upper lip. In later years he has become a character actor, winning great respect for performances in *Tunes of Glory* (1960), *Ryan's Daughter* (1970). His daughters Juliet and Hayley also have film careers.

Films. *The Midshipmaid* (1932), *Britannia of Billingsgate, The Ghost Camera* (1933), *River Wolves, A Political Party, Those Were the Days, The Lash, Blind Justice, Doctor's Orders* (1934), *Royal Cavalcade, Forever England, Charing Cross Road, Car of Dreams* (1935), *First Offence, Tudor Rose* (1936), *O.H.M.S., The Green Cockatoo* (1937), *Goodbye Mr Chips* (1939), *Old Bill and Son* (1940), *Cottage to Let, The Black Sheep of Whitehall* (1941), *The Big Blockade, The Young Mr Pitt, In Which We Serve* (1942), *We Dive at Dawn* (1943), *This Happy Breed, Waterloo Road* (1944), *The Way to the Stars* (1945), *Great Expectations* (1946), *So Well Remembered, The October Man* (1947), *Scott of the Antarctic* (1948), *The History of Mr Polly, The Rocking Horse Winner* (1949), *Morning Departure* (1950), *Mr Denning Drives North* (1951), *The Gentle Gunman, The Long Memory* (1952), *The Colditz Story* (1953), *Hobson's Choice, The End of the Affair* (1954), *Above Us the Waves, Escapade* (1955), *It's Great to be Young, The Baby and the Battleship, Around the World in Eighty Days* (U.S.A.) (1956), *Town on Trial, Vicious Circle* (1957), *Dunkirk, Ice Cold in Alex, I Was Monty's Double* (1958), *Tiger Bay* (1959), *Summer of the Seventeenth Doll, Swiss Family Robinson* (U.S.A.), *Tunes of Glory* (1960), *The Singer not the Song, Flame in the Streets* (1961), *Tiara Tahiti, The Valiant* (1962), *The Chalk Garden* (1964), *The Truth About Spring, Operation Crossbow, King Rat* (U.S.A.) (1965), *Sky West and Crooked* (directed only), *The Wrong Box, The Family Way* (1966), *Africa Texas Style, Chuka* (U.S.A.) (1967), *Lady Hamilton* (Germany) (1968), *Oh! What a Lovely War, Run Wild Run Free* (1969), *Adam's Woman* (Australia), *Return of the Boomerang, Ryan's Daughter* (1970), *Dulcima, Young Winston, Lady Caroline Lamb* (1972), *Oklahoma Crude* (U.S.A.) (1973).

DAME ANNA NEAGLE (Marjorie Robertson) (1904–   ). Actress, born Forest Gate, London.

Originally a dancer and Cochrane Young Lady, Anna Neagle became celebrated for her historical portrayals in films directed by her husband, Herbert Wilcox (q.v.), such as Nell Gwyn, Edith Cavell, Amy Johnson, Florence Nightingale and Queen Victoria. In the late-forties she partnered Michael Wilding in a series of frothy comedies (*Spring in Park Lane, Maytime in Mayfair*, etc.) which were favourably received at the box-office. In more recent years she has been confined to the stage in the long-running musical, *Charlie Girl* and subsequently *No No Nanette*.

Films. *Should a Doctor Tell?, The Chinese Bungalow* (1930), *Goodnight Vienna, The Flag Lieutenant* (1932), *The Little Damozel, Bitter Sweet* (1933), *The Queen's Affair, Nell Gwyn* (1934), *Peg of Old Drury* (1935), *Limelight, The Three Maxims* (1936), *London Melody, Victoria the Great* (1937), *Sixty Glorious Years* (1938), *Nurse Edith Cavell* (U.S.A.) (1939), *Irene* (U.S.A.), *No No Nanette* (U.S.A.) (1940), *Sunny* (U.S.A.) (1941), *They Flew Alone* (1942), *Forever and a Day, The Yellow Canary* (1943), *I Live in Grosvenor Square* (1945), *Piccadilly Incident* (1946), *The Courtneys of Curzon Street* (1947), *Spring in Park Lane* (1948), *Elizabeth of Ladymead, Maytime in Mayfair* (1949), *Odette* (1950), *The Lady With a Lamp* (1951), *Derby Day* (1952), *Lilacs in the Spring* (1955), *King's Rhapsody, My Teenage Daughter* (1956), *No Time for Tears* (1957), *The Man Who Wouldn't Talk, The Lady is a Square* (1958).

RONALD NEAME (1911–   ). Director, born London.
Neame's mother was the actress Ivy Close and his progression to films in 1928 was a matter of course. He worked as an assistant on Hitchcock's (q.v.) *Blackmail*, and in 1934 became a lighting cameraman, shooting such films as *Major Barbara, In Which We Serve* and *Blithe Spirit*. He produced several outstanding films of the forties, including *Great Expectations* and *Oliver Twist*, and turned to directing in 1947. His films have always been polished but are occasionally disappointing in content.

Films. *Take My Life* (1947), *The Golden Salamander* (1950), *The Card* (1952), *The Million Pound Note* (1953), *The Man Who Never Was* (1956), *Windom's Way* (1958), *The Horse's Mouth* (1959), *Tunes of Glory* (1960), *Escape from Zahrein* (U.S.A.) (1962), *I Could Go On Singing* (1963), *The Chalk Garden* (1964), *Mister Moses* (1965), *A Man Could Get Killed* (co-directed) (U.S.A.), *Gambit* (U.S.A.) (1966), *The Prime of Miss Jean Brodie* (1969), *Scrooge* (1970), *Isabelle of Spain*

(1972), *The Poseidon Adventure* (U.S.A.) (1973), *The Odessa File* (1974).

ROBERT NEWTON (1905–56). Actor, born Shaftesbury, Dorset.
Renowned for his menacing rolling eyes and snarling voice Newton tended to be stereotyped in roles calling for bravura villainy, such as Bill Sykes in Lean's (q.v.) *Oliver Twist*. That he could engage sympathetic roles was apparent in *They Flew Alone*, *This Happy Breed* and *Temptation Harbour*. He will best be remembered, however, as Long John Silver in Disney's *Treasure Island*, a performance that led later to a television series.

Films. *Reunion* (1932), *Fire Over England* (1936), *Dark Journey*, *Farewell Again*, *The Squeaker*, *Twenty-One Days*, *The Green Cockatoo* (1937), *Vessel of Wrath*, *Yellow Sands* (1938), *Dead Men are Dangerous*, *Jamaica Inn*, *Poison Pen*, *Hell's Cargo* (1939), *Bulldog Sees it Through*, *Gaslight*, *Busman's Honeymoon* (1940), *Major Barbara*, *Hatter's Castle* (1941), *They Flew Alone* (1942), *This Happy Breed* (1944), *Henry V* (1945), *Night Boat to Dublin* (1946), *Odd Man Out*, *Temptation Harbour* (1947), *Snowbound*, *Oliver Twist* (1948), *Obsession* (1949), *Treasure Island*, *Waterfront* (1950), *Tom Brown's Schooldays* (1951), *Les Miserables* (U.S.A.) (1952), *Androcles and the Lion* (U.S.A.) (1953), *The Beachcomber* (1954), *Around the World in Eighty Days* (U.S.A.) (1955).

IVOR NOVELLO (Ivor Davies) (1893–1951). Actor, composer, writer, born Cardiff.
Matinée idol of the pre-war stage, Ivor Novello's intense good looks were prominent in the cinema during the twenties in Britain, France and Hollywood. A versatile figure, he composed the popular 'Keep the Home Fires Burning' song of the First World War and wrote many musicals for the West End stage, many of which such as *Glamorous Night*, *The Dancing Years*, *Kings Rhapsody* were filmed. He was not happy with the talkies and appearances in them were rare.

British films. Silent: *Carnival* (1921), *The Bohemian Girl* (1922), *Bonnie Prince Charlie*, *The Man Without Desire* (1923), *The Rat* (also wrote) (1925), *The Triumph of the Rat*, *The Lodger* (1926), *Downhill*, *The Vortex* (1927), *The Constant Nymph*, *The South Sea Bubble* (1928), *The Return of the Rat* (1929). Sound: *Symphony in Two Flats* (1930), *The Lodger* (1932), *Sleeping Car*, *I Lived With You* (also wrote) (1933), *Autumn Crocus* (1934).

SIR LAURENCE OLIVIER (Lord Olivier) (1907–   ). Actor, director, born Dorking, Surrey.

The film debut of Laurence Olivier was in 1930 after eight years of acting in the theatre. He moved from early romantic parts to more serious characterizations, notably Heathcliff in William Wyler's *Wuthering Heights* and Nelson in Korda's (q.v.) *Lady Hamilton*. Both these films were made in America. On his return to England he made *Forty-Ninth Parallel* and *The Demi-Paradise*, in which he played a Russian engineer working in an English shipyard. He then embarked on his ambitious *Henry V* project which he produced and directed as well as playing the lead, the first of a trio of notable Shakespearean films (the others were *Hamlet* and *Richard III*), all of which are important milestones in the British cinema. Sir Laurence's superb diction and overpowering presence have sometimes been too much for the cinema, although appropriate on the stage.

Films. *Too Many Crooks, The Temporary Widow* (1930), *Potiphar's Wife, The Yellow Ticket, Friends and Lovers, Westward Passage* (1931), *Perfect Understanding* (U.S.A.), *No Funny Business* (1932), *Conquest of the Air, Moscow Nights* (1935), *As You Like It, Fire Over England* (1936), *Twenty-One Days* (1937), *The Divorce of Lady X* (1938), *Q Planes, Wuthering Heights* (U.S.A.) (1939), *Rebecca* (U.S.A.), *Pride and Prejudice* (1940), *Lady Hamilton* (U.S.A.) (1941), *Forty-Ninth Parallel* (1942), *The Demi-Paradise* (1943), *Henry V* (also directed) (1945), *Hamlet* (also directed) (1948), *The Magic Box* (1951), *Carrie* (U.S.A.) (1952), *The Beggar's Opera* (1953), *Richard III* (also directed) (1956), *The Prince and the Showgirl* (also directed) (1957), *The Devil's Disciple* (1959), *Spartacus* (U.S.A.), *The Entertainer* (1960), *Term of Trial* (1962), *Bunny Lake is Missing, Othello* (1965), *Khartoum* (1966), *The Shoes of the Fisherman* (U.S.A.) (1968), *Oh! What a Lovely War, The Dance of Death, The Battle of Britain* (1969), *David Copperfield, Three Sisters* (also directed) (1970), *Nicholas and Alexandra* (1971), *Lady Caroline Lamb* (1972), *Sleuth* (U.S.A.) (1973).

GABRIEL PASCAL (1894–1954). Producer, director, born Arad, Hungary.

Somehow Gabriel Pascal, who like Korda (q.v.) was possessed of a peculiarly effective Hungarian charm, managed to persuade Bernard Shaw to allow him to transform his plays into films. To be fair, the first, *Pygmalion* with Leslie Howard as Professor Higgins, was a creditable transposition which did well at the box-office as well. Pascal's downfall came during the middle of the war when he embarked on the extravagant and time-consuming production of *Caesar and Cleopatra*, spending a great deal of the J. Arthur Rank (q.v.) fortunes. The critics savaged the film perhaps rather too strongly, and Pascal left for America, where he could only achieve one further Shavian film.

Films. *Pygmalion* (produced only) (1938), *Major Barbara* (1940), *Caesar and Cleopatra* (1945), *Androcles and the Lion* (U.S.A.) (1953).

GEORGE PEARSON (1875–1973). Director, producer, writer, born London.

A pioneering figure of amazing longevity, George Pearson did not turn to films until he was thirty-seven, having already advanced to a headmastership in his former profession of teaching. His peak period was between 1915 and 1925 and he was responsible for the *Ultus* series, inspired by Feuillade's *Judex*, and the *Squibs* series, starring Betty Balfour. When talkies came he faltered into the area of quota quickies, and ended his film career doing documentaries for the Colonial Film Unit.

Films. Silent: *The Fool, Sentence of Death, A Lighter Burden, Mr Henpeck's Dilemma, Heroes of the Mine, The Live Wire, A Fisher Girl's Folly* (1913), *A Study in Scarlet, Cinema Girl's Romance, Great European War, Christmas Day in the Workhouse, A Son of France, The Life of Lord Roberts, The Man of Mystery* (1914), *Buttons, The True Story of the Lyons Mail, John Halifax, Gentleman, Ultus the Man from the Dead, Ultus and the Grey Lady* (1915), *Ultus and the Secret of the Night, Sally Bishop, Ultus and the Three Button Mystery* (1916), *Canadian Officer's Story* (1917), *The Better 'Ole, The Kiddies in the Ruins* (1918), *Garryowen, Hughie and the Victory Derby* (1919), *Nothing Else Matters, Mary Find the Gold* (1920), *Squibs, Mord Em'ly* (1921), *Wee Macgregor's Sweetheart, Squibs Wins the Calcutta Sweep* (1922), *Love Life and Laughter, Squibs M.P., Squibs' Honeymoon* (1923), *Reveille* (1924), *Satan's Sister, Mr Preedy and the Countess, The Little People* (1925), *Blinkeyes* (1926), *Huntingtower* (1927), *Love's Option, Auld Lang Syne* (1929). Sound: *Harry Lauder's Songs, East Lynne on the Western Front, The Third String* (1930), *A Shot in the Dark, River Wolves, The Pointing Finger, Ace of Spades, Four Masked Men, Whispering Tongues, Open All Night* (1934), *Jubilee Window, Gentleman's Agreement, Once a Thief, That's My Uncle* (1935), *Checkmate, The Secret Voice, Wednesday's Luck, Murder by Rope* (1936), *The Fatal Hour* (1937).

ROMAN POLANSKI (1933–   ). Director, born Paris.

Polanski's interest in the macabre undertones of existence, so superbly realized in such films as *Repulsion*, *Cul de Sac* and the American-made *Rosemary's Baby*, was tragically echoed in reality when his wife was murdered by hippie cultists in California. The most exciting film-maker to emerge from Eastern Europe into the West, Polanski has happily chosen Britain as his main base.

Films. *Knife in the Water* (Poland) (1961), *Repulsion* (1965), *Cul de Sac* (1966), *Dance of the Vampires* (1967), *Rosemary's Baby* (U.S.A.) (1969), *Macbeth* (1972), *What?*, *Chinatown* (U.S.A.) (1974).

MICHAEL POWELL (1905–   ). Director, producer, writer, born Canterbury, Kent.

Michael Powell began his career in Nice in the mid-twenties when Rex Ingram was working there. His early directorial assignments were quota quickies, but in 1937 he achieved acclaim with a film set in the Western Isles, *The Edge of the World*. He later established a partner-ship with Emeric Pressburger as The Archers, which lasted from 1942 to 1957. Powell's style has always been glossy on the surface with a hard edge beneath, often using allegory in ways regarded with suspicion by critics. Some outstanding films emerged from the partner-ship, including *The Life and Death of Colonel Blimp* and *A Matter of Life and Death*.

Films. *Two Crowded Hours*, *My Friend the King*, *Rynox*, *The Rasp*, *The Star Reporter* (1931), *Hotel Splendide*, *Born Lucky*, *C.O.D.*, *His Lordship* (1932), *Perfect Understanding* (scripted only), *The Fire Raisers* (1933), *Night of the Party*, *Red Ensign*, *Something Always Happens*, *The Girl in the Crowd* (1934), *Some Day*, *Lazybones*, *Her Last Affaire*, *The Love Test*, *The Price of a Song*, *The Phantom Light* (1935), *The Brown Wallet*, *Crown v. Stevens*, *The Man Behind the Mask* (1936), *The Edge of the World* (1937), *The Spy in Black* (co-directed), *The Lion Has Wings* (co-directed) (1939), *The Thief of Bagdad* (co-directed), *Contraband* (1940), *Forty-Ninth Parallel* (1941), *One of Our Aircraft is Missing* (1942), *The Volunteer*, *The Life and Death of Colonel Blimp* (1943), *A Canterbury Tale* (1944), *I Know Where I'm Going* (1945), *A Matter of Life and Death* (1947), *Black Narcissus* (1947), *The Red Shoes*, *The Small Back Room* (1948), *Gone to Earth*, *The Elusive Pim-pernel* (1950), *Tales of Hoffman* (1951), *Oh Rosalinda!!* (1955), *The Battle of the River Plate* (1956), *Ill Met by Moonlight* (1957), *Peeping*

Tom (1960), *The Queen's Guards* (1961), *They're a Weird Mob* (Australia) (1966), *Age of Consent* (Australia) (1969).

LORD RANK (1888–1972). Magnate, born Hull, Yorkshire.
J. Arthur Rank, a member of a Yorkshire flour-milling family, entered films in the mid-thirties, apparently seeing them as a means of propagating his Methodist faith. Having failed to secure proper distribution for a quasi-religious film, *The Turn of the Tide*, he set about acquiring the means of not only production, but distribution and exhibition as well. Within a few years Rank owned two of three major circuits, studios, laboratories and equipment-manufacturers. To many he appeared as an arch-monopolist and ogre, to others the salvation of the British industry. To his credit he encouraged much independent film-making, allowing such talents as Carol Reed, David Lean, Launder and Gilliatt, Michael Powell (qq.v.) and many others to develop. But his ambitions to establish Britain as a rival to Hollywood toppled the delicate balance of the industry, his ventures one by one faded away as did the directing talent which had given temporary lustre to films in the mid-forties. Rescued by the firm accountancy of John Davis, the Rank Organization survived, but with films a secondary interest behind hotels, real estate, ballrooms, bingo and – most profitable of all – copying machines.

SIR MICHAEL REDGRAVE (1908–   ). Actor, born Bristol.
After a spell of schoolmastering Redgrave went on to the stage in 1934 and made his film debut four years later in Hitchcock's (q.v.) *The Lady Vanishes*. A tall, craggy figure with a reedy and distinctive speaking voice he has in recent years become a major character actor. Married to Rachel Kempson, he is the father of an impressive acting family, his children Vanessa, Corin and Lynn all establishing themselves in the profession.
  Films. *The Lady Vanishes, Climbing High* (1938), *A Window in London, A Stolen Life* (1939), *The Stars Look Down* (1940), *Kipps, Atlantic Ferry, Jeannie* (1941), *The Big Blockade, Thunder Rock* (1942), *The Way to the Stars, Dead of Night* (1945), *The Captive Heart, The Years Between* (1946), *The Man Within, Fame is the Spur, Mourning Becomes Electra* (U.S.A.) (1947), *The Secret Beyond the Door* (U.S.A.) (1948), *The Browning Version* (1951), *The Magic Box, The Importance of Being Earnest* (1952), *The Green Scarf, The Sea Shall Not Have Them* (1954), *The Night My Number Came Up, The Dambusters,*

Confidential Report (U.S.A.), *Oh Rosalinda!!* (1955), *Nineteen Eighty Four* (1956), *Time Without Pity* (1957), *Law and Disorder, Behind the Mask, The Quiet American* (U.S.A.) (1958), *Shake Hands With the Devil* (1959), *No My Darling Daughter* (1960), *The Innocents* (1961), *The Loneliness of the Long-Distance Runner* (1962), *Young Cassidy* (1964), *The Hill, The Heroes of Telemark* (1965), *Assignment K* (1967), *Oh! What a Lovely War, Goodbye Mr Chips, The Battle of Britain* (1969), *David Copperfield, Goodbye Gemini* (1970), *Connecting Rooms, Nicholas and Alexandra* (1972).

SIR CAROL REED (1906–   ). Director, born Putney, London.
During the forties Carol Reed was the most distinguished director working in British films, responsible for such works as *The Way Ahead* (1944), *Odd Man Out* (1947), *The Fallen Idol* (1948) and *The Third Man* (1949). His subject matter was broad, his attack stylish. During the fifties the steam ran out and his later work, although polished and technically sound, left a sense of emptiness. In 1968 he scored a resounding international success with the musical *Oliver!*

Films. *Midshipman Easy, It Happened in Paris* (co-directed) (1934), *Talk of the Devil, Laburnum Grove* (1936), *Who's Your Lady Friend?* (1937), *Bank Holiday, Penny Paradise, Climbing High* (1938), *A Girl Must Live* (1939), *The Stars Look Down, Night Train to Munich, The Girl in the News* (1940), *Kipps* (1941), *The Young Mr Pitt* (1942), *The Way Ahead* (1944), *The True Glory* (co-directed) (1945), *Odd Man Out* (1947), *The Fallen Idol* (1948), *The Third Man* (1949), *An Outcast of the Islands* (1951), *The Man Between* (1953), *A Kid for Two Farthings* (1955), *Trapeze* (U.S.A.) (1956), *The Key* (1958), *Our Man in Havana* (1959), *The Running Man* (1963), *The Agony and the Ecstasy* (U.S.A.) (1965), *Oliver!* (1968), *The Last Warrior* (U.S.A.) (1970), *Follow Me* (1972).

KAREL REISZ (1926–   ). Director, born Ostava, Czechoslovakia.
Domiciled in Britain since childhood, Karel Reisz was one of the leading figures in the Free Cinema movement of the mid-fifties, and was a critic for *Sequence* and other publications. He produced and directed a number of shorts during this period, and worked in conjunction with Lindsay Anderson and Tony Richardson (qq.v.). His first feature film, *Saturday Night and Sunday Morning*, was one of the most acceptable products of the British new wave. Later work by Reisz failed to live up

to the promise of this first film, although *Morgan – a Suitable Case for Treatment* had occasional fine flashes.

Films. Shorts: *Momma Don't Allow* (co-directed) (1955), *Every Day Except Christmas* (produced only) (1957), *We are the Lambeth Boys* (1958), *March to Aldermaston* (associate producer) (1959). *Features: Saturday Night and Sunday Morning* (1960), *Night Must Fall, This Sporting Life* (produced only) (1963), *Morgan – a Suitable Case for Treatment* (1966), *Isadora* (1967), *The Gambler* (U.S.A.) (1974).

SIR RALPH RICHARDSON (1902–). Actor, born Cheltenham, Gloucestershire.

Entering on a long theatrical career in 1921, Sir Ralph is one of the most eminent figures of the British stage. He has also appeared in many films, although sometimes his excessively theatrical style has caused problems. There are however a number of memorable and extraordinary performances: the boss in *Things to Come*, the butler in *The Fallen Idol*, the oppressive father in *The Heiress*.

Films. *The Ghoul, Friday the Thirteenth* (1933), *The Return of Bulldog Drummond, Java Head, The King of Paris* (1934), *Bulldog Jack* (1935), *Things to Come, The Man Who Could Work Miracles* (1936), *Thunder in the City* (1937), *South Riding, The Divorce of Lady X, The Citadel* (1938), *Q Planes, The Four Feathers, The Lion Has Wings, On the Night of the Fire* (1939), *The Day Will Dawn, The Silver Fleet* (1942), *The Volunteer* (1943), *School for Secrets* (1946), *Anna Karenina, The Fallen Idol* (1948), *The Heiress* (U.S.A.) (1949), *An Outcast of the Islands* (1951), *Home at Seven* (also directed), *The Sound Barrier, The Holly and the Ivy* (1952), *Richard III, Smiley, The Passionate Stranger* (1956), *Our Man in Havana* (1959), *Exodus* (U.S.A.), *Oscar Wilde* (1960), *The 300 Spartans* (U.S.A.), *Long Day's Journey into Night* (U.S.A.) (1962), *Woman of Straw* (1964), *Dr Zhivago* (U.S.A.), *The Wrong Box, Khartoum* (1966), *Oh! What a Lovely War, The Midas Run, The Bed-Sitting Room, The Battle of Britain, The Looking Glass War* (1969), *David Copperfield* (1970), *Lady Caroline Lamb* (1972), *O Lucky Man, Dr Frankenstein, A Doll's House* (1973), *Rollerball* (1975).

TONY RICHARDSON (1928–). Director, born Shipley, Yorkshire.
A primary figure of the British new wave, Tony Richardson became engaged in films via Free Cinema and the Royal Court Theatre. Where his cinema is concerned there is a conscious striving for effect which

has sometimes dissipated the strength of his work. His subjects have always been interesting, if often based on tried stage plays such as *Look Back in Anger* and *A Taste of Honey*, but occasionally a literary classic has been filmed, sometimes successfully (*Tom Jones*), sometimes disastrously (*The Loved One*). His near-epic *The Charge of the Light Brigade* was a vidid, glorious mess, no less so than the event it commemorated.

Films. *Momma Don't Allow* (short) (co-directed) (1955), *Look Back in Anger* (1959), *The Entertainer* (1960), *A Taste of Honey*, *Sanctuary* (U.S.A.) (1961), *The Loneliness of the Long-Distance Runner* (1962), *Tom Jones* (1963), *The Loved One* (U.S.A.) (1965), *Mademoiselle* (1966), *The Sailor from Gibraltar*, *Red and Blue* (1967), *The Charge of the Light Brigade* (1968), *Laughter in the Dark* (1969), *Hamlet*, *Ned Kelly* (1970), *A Delicate Balance* (1973), *Dead Cert* (1974).

PAUL ROTHA (1907–). Director, writer, born London.
A leading documentarist who joined Grierson back in the days of the Empire Marketing Board Paul Rotha also wrote a number of basic film books, including *The Film Till Now* and *Documentary Film*. His documentaries often contained a slightly more astringent note than those of his contemporaries, but his attempt at a fiction feature, *No Resting Place*, was a failure.

Films. *Contact*, *The Rising Tide* (1933), *Shipyard*, *The Face of Britain* (1934), *Death on the Road* (1935), *The Future's in the Air* (1936), *New Worlds for Old* (1938), *The Fourth Estate* (1940), *World of Plenty* (1942), *Land of Promise* (1945), *Total War in Britain* (1946), *A City Speaks* (1947), *The World is Rich* (1948), *No Resting Place* (1951), *World Without End* (1952), *Cat and Mouse* (1957), *Cradle of Genius* (1961), *The Life of Adolf Hitler*, *The Silent Raid* (1962).

KEN RUSSELL (1927–). Director, born Southampton, Hampshire.
The ageing *enfant terrible* of the British cinema, Ken Russell has done more than any other director to open up controversy and anger among those who rarely go near their local screen. In *Women in Love* he introduced a nude wrestling scene, *The Music Lovers* over-reached itself in portraying bizarre and impossible events in Tchaikovsky's life, *The Devils* had every excess that has yet found its way to the screen. In spite of his propensity to shock Russell is a serious director of distinction and promise, whose grounding in television, where he made a number of excellent, imaginative biographies of composers (Elgar, Sibelius,

Strauss, etc.), has given him a command of cinematic language of astonishing fluency.

Films. *French Dressing* (1964), *Billion Dollar Brain* (1967), *Women in Love* (1969), *The Music Lovers* (1970), *The Devils* (1971), *The Boy Friend*, *Savage Messiah* (1972), *Mahler* (1974), *Tommy*, *Liszt* (1975).

VICTOR SAVILLE (1897–). Director, producer, born Birmingham. In partnership with Michael Balcon (q.v.) Victor Saville set up a production company in 1923 and later became an important British director. His films were stylish and glossy, made in the manner of the better Hollywood product, and it is ironic that after his departure for the West Coast his work, while lush, was curiously empty.

Films. *Conquest of Oil* (documentary) (directed) (1921), *The Arcadians* (directed), *Hindle Wakes* (produced), *Roses of Picardy* (produced), *The Glad Eye* (produced), *A Sister to Assist 'Er* (produced), *The Flight Commander* (produced), *A Woman in Pawn* (produced) (1927), *Iesha* (produced, directed) (1928), *Kitty* (produced, directed), *Woman to Woman* (directed) (1929), *The W Plan* (produced, directed), *A Warm Corner* (directed) (1930), *The Sport of Kings* (directed), *Michael and Mary* (directed), *Sunshine Susie* (directed), *Hindle Wakes* (directed) (1931), *The Faithful Heart* (directed), *Love on Wheels* (directed) (1932), *The Good Companions* (directed), *Friday the Thirteenth* (directed), *I Was a Spy* (directed) (1933), *Evergreen* (directed), *Evensong* (directed) (1934), *The Iron Duke* (directed), *The Love Affair of the Dictator* (directed), *Me and Marlborough* (directed), *The Dictator* (directed), *First a Girl* (directed) (1935), *It's Love Again* (directed) (1936), *Dark Journey* (produced, directed), *Storm in a Teacup* (produced, directed), *Action for Slander* (produced, directed) (1937), *South Riding* (produced, directed), *The Citadel* (produced) (1938), *Goodbye Mr Chips* (produced) (1939), *Bitter Sweet* (U.S.A.) (produced) (1940), *The Earl of Chicago* (U.S.A.) (produced), *Dr Jekyll and Mr Hyde* (U.S.A.) (produced) (1941), *White Cargo* (U.S.A.) (produced) (1942), *Above Suspicion* (U.S.A.) (produced) (1943), *The Mortal Storm* (U.S.A.) (produced), *A Woman's Face* (U.S.A.) (produced), *Smilin' Through* (U.S.A.) (produced), *The Chocolate Soldier* (U.S.A.) (produced), *Keeper of the Flame* (U.S.A.) (produced), *Tonight and Every Night* (U.S.A.) (produced, directed) (1944), *The Green Years* (U.S.A.) (produced, directed) (1946), *Green Dolphin Street* (U.S.A.) (directed), *If Winter Comes* (U.S.A.) (directed) (1947), *Conspirator* (directed) (1949), *Kim* (U.S.A.) (produced), *Calling Bulldog Drum-*

mond (directed) (1951), *Twenty-Four Hours of a Woman's Life* (directed) (1952), *I the Jury* (U.S.A.) (1953), *The Long Wait* (U.S.A.) (produced, directed) (1954), *The Silver Chalice* (U.S.A.) (produced, directed), *Kiss Me Deadly* (U.S.A.) (produced) (1955), *The Greengage Summer* (produced) (1961).

JOHN SCHLESINGER (1926–). Director, born London.
After Oxford Schlesinger worked as an actor, playing the occasional bit part in British films in the fifties. Encouraged and supported by the BBC he made a number of short arts subjects for the Monitor programme, but eventually achieved public prominence with a documentary about Waterloo station, *Terminus*. Skilled at observing contemporary life, Schlesinger's films have always been imbued with a cynical quality of the moment, a trap that leads to premature dating. In 1969 he achieved considerable success with his first American picture, *Midnight Cowboy*, and consolidated it a couple of years later with *Sunday, Bloody Sunday*.

Films. *Terminus* (documentary) (1960), *A Kind of Loving* (1962), *Billy Liar* (1963), *Darling* (1965), *Far From the Madding Crowd* (1967), *Midnight Cowboy* (U.S.A.) (1969), *Sunday, Bloody Sunday* (1971), *The Day of the Locust* (U.S.A.) (1974).

PETER SELLERS (1925–). Actor, born Southsea, Hampshire.
Following the Second World War Sellers became a radio comedian, renowned for impersonations and odd voices. Eventually his comedy crystallized into the Goon Show, with Spike Milligan, Harry Secombe and Michael Bentine. During the late fifties he developed into a character actor of comic distinction, creating such immortals as Mr Kite in *I'm All Right Jack* and the Indian doctor in *The Millionairess*, as well as *Dr Strangelove* himself. Over-exposure has tended to reveal Sellers' limitations as a serious actor, and he has yet to find a role that will satisfy this demand.

Films. *Penny Points to Paradise* (1951), *Down Among the Z Men* (1952), *Orders are Orders* (1954), *John and Julie*, *The Ladykillers* (1955), *The Smallest Show on Earth* (1957), *The Naked Truth*, *Tom Thumb*, *Up the Creek* (1958), *Carlton-Browne of the F.O.*, *The Mouse that Roared*, *I'm All Right Jack* (1959), *The Battle of the Sexes*, *Two Way Stretch* (1960), *Never Let Go*, *The Millionairess*, *Mr Topaze* (also directed), *Only Two Can Play*, *Waltz of the Toreadors*, *Lolita* (1961), *The Dock Brief*, *The Wrong Arm of the Law* (1962), *The Pink Panther*

(U.S.A.), *Heavens Above, Dr Strangelove* (1963), *The World of Henry Orient* (U.S.A.), *A Shot in the Dark* (U.S.A.) (1964), *What's New Pussycat?* (U.S.A.) (1965), *After the Fox* (U.S.A.), *The Wrong Box, Casino Royale* (1966), *The Bobo, Woman Times Seven* (U.S.A.) (1967), *The Party* (U.S.A.), *I Love You Alice B. Toklas* (U.S.A.) (1968), *The Magic Christian* (U.S.A.) (1969), *Hoffman, A Day at the Beach* (1970), *There's a Girl in My Soup* (1971), *Where Does It Hurt* (U.S.A.) *Alice's Adventures in Wonderland* (1972), *The Optimists of Nine Elms, Soft Beds, Hard Battles* (1973), *Ghost in the Noonday Sun* (1974), *The Blockhouse, The Great McGonagle, The Return of the Pink Panther* (1975).

PENROSE TENNYSON (1921–41). Director, born London.
Pen Tennyson's career was tragically unfulfilled for he was killed in an air crash shortly after joining the Navy in the Second World War. In spite of an illustrious ancestry (Macaulay and Tennyson) and a background of Eton and Oxford he revealed an interest in social problems that comes through in the first two of his three films. The last, *Convoy*, was in some senses a prototype for the typical British war film, but *There Ain't No Justice* with its low-life background of the world of the boxing ring, and *The Proud Valley* set in a Welsh mining district, showed a concern for humanity so rarely present in the British film of the day. He was unquestionably a director of promise.

Films. *There Ain't No Justice* (1939), *The Proud Valley* (1940), *Convoy* (1941).

PETER USTINOV (1921–   ). Actor, director, writer, born London.
Originally a prodigy, Peter Ustinov's contribution to the cinema has, on the whole, been rather less exciting than that to the theatre or to television talk shows. The handful of films that he himself directed have been flawed by occasional pretentious overtones, with the exception of his first, *School for Secrets*, which is an above-average war adventure.

Films. *Hello Fame, Mein Kampf My Crimes* (1940), *One of Our Aircraft Is Missing. The Goose Steps Out* (1942), *The Way Ahead* (also wrote) (1944), *Carnival* (wrote) (1945), *School for Secrets* (directed and wrote) (1946), *Vice Versa* (directed and wrote) (1947), *Private Angelo* (directed and wrote) (1949), *Odette* (1950), *Quo Vadis?* (U.S.A.), *The Magic Box, Hotel Sahara* (1952), *Beau Brummell* (1954), *School for Scoundrels* (wrote), *The Sundowners* (1960), *Romanoff and Juliet* (U.S.A.) (also directed and wrote)(1961), *Billy Budd* (also directed and wrote) (1962), *Topkapi* (U.S.A.), *John Goldfarb Please Come Home* (U.S.A.) (1964), *Lady L* (U.S.A.) (also directed and wrote) (1965), *Hot Millions* (1968), *Blackbeard's Ghost* (U.S.A.) (1969), *Viva Max* (U.S.A.) (wrote and directed) (1970), *Hammersmith is Out* (U.S.A.) (also directed), (1972), *One of Our Dinosaurs is Missing* (1975).

MARCEL VARNEL (1894–1947). Director, born Paris.
Astonishingly the most accomplished director of British comedies in the thirties was French. Marcel Varnel began his film career in Hollywood in 1924 and came to Britain in the mid-thirties, working with Will Hay, George Formby (qq.v.) and the Crazy Gang. His skill lay in keeping his films moving, and not allowing the comic temperature to drop. *Oh Mr Porter!* is his masterpiece, and one of the funniest films in the history of cinema.

British films. *Freedom of the Seas, Girls Will Be Boys* (1934), *Dance Band, I Give My Heart, No Monkey Business* (1935), *All In, Public Nuisance Number One* (1936), *Good Morning Boys, Okay for Sound, Oh Mr Porter!* (1937), *Convict 99, Alf's Button Afloat, Hey Hey U.S.A. Old Bones of the River* (1938), *Ask a Policeman, Frozen Limits, Where's that Fire?* (1939), *Band Waggon, Neutral Port, Gasbags, Let George Do It* (1940), *I Thank You, Hi Gang!, The Ghost of St Michael's, South American George, Turned Out Nice Again* (1941), *Much Too Shy, King Arthur Was a Gentleman* (1942), *Get Cracking, Bell Bottom George* (1943), *He Snoops to Conquer* (1944), *I Didn't Do It* (1945), *George in Civvy Street, This Man is Mine* (1946).

HERBERT WILCOX (1892–). Director, producer, born Cork, Ireland.
Entering the film industry, after service in the Royal Flying Corps, as a renter in 1919 Herbert Wilcox established a name for himself in the twenties by importing stars from Hollywood and the Continent. In 1926 he co-founded Elstree Studios and two years later became head of production at British and Dominions. During the thirties he developed Anna Neagle (q.v.) into a star, directing her in a number of historical roles, the most prominent of which was Queen Victoria. Eventually he married her. After the war he teamed her with Michael Wilding in a number of frothy comedies acclaimed at the box-office, but when the tide turned against the Wilcox-type of film he went bankrupt. An energetic and tireless man of the cinema, he fought through difficult years to keep the industry buoyant.

Films. Silent: *The Wonderful Story* (1920), *The Dawn of the World* (1921), *Chu Chin Chow* (1923), *Southern Love, Decameron Nights* (1924),

The Only Way (1925), *Nell Gwyn, Dawn* (1926), *London, Tiptoe, Mumsie* (1927), *The Bondman, Wolves* (1928), *The Woman in White* (1929). Sound: *Rookery Nook* (produced only), *The Loves of Robert Burns* (1930), *Chance of a Night-Time* (co-directed), *Carnival* (1931), *The Blue Danube, Goodnight Vienna* (1932), *Yes Mr Brown, The King's Cup, Bitter Sweet, The Little Damozel* (1933), *The Queen's Affair, Nell Gwyn* (1934), *Peg of Old Drury* (1935), *Limelight, The Three Maxims, This'll Make You Whistle* (1936), *London Melody, Victoria the Great* (1937), *The Frog* (produced only), *Our Fighting Navy* (produced only), *Sixty Glorious Years* (1938), *Nurse Edith Cavell* (U.S.A.), *Sunny* (U.S.A.) (1939), *No No Nanette* (U.S.A.) (1940), *Irene* (U.S.A.) (1941), *They Flew Alone* (1942), *The Yellow Canary* (1943), *I Live in Grosvenor Square* (1945), *Piccadilly Incident* (1946), *The Courtneys of Curzon Street* (1947), *Spring in Park Lane* (1948), *Elizabeth of Lady-mead, Maytime in Mayfair* (1949), *Odette* (1950), *Into the Blue, The Lady With the Lamp* (1951), *Derby Day, Trent's Last Case* (1952), *Laughing Anne* (1953), *Trouble in the Glen, Lilacs in the Spring* (1954), *King's Rhapsody* (1955), *My Teenage Daughter* (1956), *These Dangerous Years* (1957), *The Man Who Wouldn't Talk, Wonderful Things* (1958), *The Lady Is a Square, Heart of a Man* (1959).

EMLYN WILLIAMS (1905–). Actor, playwright, born Mostyn, Flintshire.

A stage actor since 1927, Emlyn Williams made a great point of projecting his Welshness, using his melodious and distinctive voice. In his early days in films he tended to be stereotyped in psychopathic roles, and one of his most successful stage plays in this genre, *Night Must Fall*, was filmed twice. Another play, also successfully filmed, *The Corn is Green*, was partly autobiographical.

Films. *The Frightened Lady, Men of Tomorrow, Sally Bishop, Friday the Thirteenth* (also wrote) (1932), *Evergreen* (wrote), *My Song for You, Evensong, Roadhouse, The Man Who Knew Too Much* (wrote) (1933), *The Iron Duke, The Love Affair of the Dictator, City of Beautiful Nonsense, The Divine Spark* (wrote) (1935), *Broken Blossoms* (also wrote) (1936), *Dead Men Tell No Tales* (also wrote), *A Night Alone, The Citadel* (also wrote), *They Drive by Night* (1938), *Jamaica Inn* (1939), *The Stars Look Down, Girl in the News, You Will Remember* (1940), *This England* (also wrote), *Major Barbara, Hatter's Castle* (1941), *The Last Days of Dolwyn* (also wrote and directed) (1949), *Three Husbands* (U.S.A.) (1950), *Another Man's Poison, The Magic*

Box (1951), *Ivanhoe* (1952), *The Deep Blue Sea* (1955), *I Accuse* (1957), *Beyond This Place* (1959), *The L-Shaped Room* (1962), *Eye of the Devil* (1966), *The Walking Stick*, *David Copperfield* (1970).

MICHAEL WINNER (1936–). Director, born London.
Noted for his ebullience, Michael Winner is an energetic and per-severing figure who has managed to master the system. After Cambridge he was for a short time a journalist and entered the film industry in programme-filling documentaries, graduating to his first serious film, *The System*, via skin-flicks and pop pictures. His pace is fast, his style trendily professional and of the moment, and he knows his cinema.

Films. *Climb up the Wall* (also wrote), *Shoot to Kill* (also wrote) (1960), *Old Mac*, *Some Like It Cool* (also wrote), *Out of the Shadow* (also wrote), *Haunted England* (also wrote) (1961), *Play It Cool* (1962), *The Cool Mikado* (also wrote), *West Eleven* (1963), *The System* (1964), *You Must Be Joking* (also wrote) (1965), *The Jokers* (also wrote) (1966), *I'll Never Forget What's 'is Name* (1967), *Hannibal Brooks* (1969), *The Games* (1970), *Lawman* (U.S.A.) (1971), *The Nightcomers*, *Chato's Land* (U.S.A.), *The Mechanic* (1972), *Scorpio*, *The Stone Killer* (U.S.A.) (1973), *Death Wish* (1974).

PETER YATES (1929–). Director, born Aldershot, Hampshire.
After directing a Cliff Richard musical and an adaptation of an N. F. Simpson play Peter Yates scored an international success with an American thriller, *Bullitt*, the highpoint of which was a car chase stunningly filmed in San Francisco. The prototype of the chase appears in an earlier British film, *Robbery*, which was based on the celebrated Great Train Robbery. He is a careful director with actors, and at his best in the spectacular and the visual tour-de-force.

Films. *Summer Holiday* (1963), *One Way Pendulum* (1964), *Robbery* (also wrote) (1967), *Bullitt* (U.S.A.) (1968), *John and Mary* (U.S.A.) (1969), *Murphy's War* (1971), *How to Steal a Diamond in Four Uneasy Lessons* (*The Hot Rock*) (U.S.A.) (1972), *The Friends of Eddie Gale* (U.S.A.) (1973), *For Pete's Sake* (U.S.A.) (1974).

TERENCE YOUNG (1915–). Director, born Shanghai, China.
Originally a screenwriter, whose credits included *On the Night of the Fire* (1939), *Dangerous Moonlight* (1941), *Secret Mission* (1942), *On Approval* (1944), *Hungry Hill* and *Theirs Is the Glory* (both 1946), Terence Young's chief directorial contribution to the cinema has been

338

in the shape of three James Bond films, including the first, *Dr No*. He was also responsible for the war films, *They Were Not Divided* and *The Red Beret*. Many of his films have been popular at the box-office, but his style is hardly electrifying.

Films. *Corridor of Mirrors, One Night With You, Woman Hater* (1948), *They Were Not Divided* (1950), *Valley of the Eagles* (1951), *The Tall Headlines* (1952), *The Red Beret* (1953), *That Lady* (1954), *Storm over the Nile* (co-directed) (1955), *Safari, Zarak* (1956), *Action of the Tiger, No Time to Die* (1957), *Serious Charge* (1959), *Too Hot to Handle* (1960), *Dr No* (1962), *From Russia With Love* (1963), *The Amorous Adventures of Moll Flanders, Thunderball* (1965), *Guerre Secret* (France), *Danger Grows Wild, Triple Cross* (1966), *Wait Until Dark* (U.S.A.) (1967), *Mayerling* (1968), *The Christmas Tree* (France) (1969), *From the Boys, Night Visitors, Soleil Rouge* (France) (1971). *The Valachi Papers* (U.S.A.) (1972), *The Amazons*, (Italy/France) (1974).

Bibliography

General History, Technique, Criticism and Reference

ANDERSON, LINDSAY, *Making a Film* plus script of *The Secret People*, Allen and Unwin, 1952.

ANON, *The Elstree Story: Twenty-one years of film making*, Clerke and Cockeran, 1948.

ANSTEY, EDGAR; HARDY, FORSYTH; LINDGREN, ERNEST; MANVELL, ROGER (eds), *Shots in the Dark* (critical anthology), Allan Wingate, 1951.

THE ARTS ENQUIRY, *The Factual Film*, Oxford, 1947.

BALCON, MICHAEL; LINDGREN, ERNEST; HARDY, FORSYTH; BAXTER, R. K. NEILSON; MANVELL, ROGER; WOLLEN-BERG, H. H., *The Penguin Film Review* 1–9, Penguin, 1946–9.

BETTS, ERNEST, *The Film Business: a history of British Cinema 1896–1972*, George Allen and Unwin, 1973.

BETTS, ERNEST, *Inside Pictures*, Cresset Press, 1960.

BLAKESTON, OSWELL (ed.), *Working for the Films*, Focal Press, 1947.

BOARD OF TRADE, *Report of a Committee of Enquiry on The Distribution and Exhibition of Cinematograph Films*, H.M.S.O., 1949.

BOARD OF TRADE, *Report of the Film Studio Committee*, H.M.S.O., 1948.

BOARD OF TRADE, *Report of the Working Party on Film Production Costs*, H.M.S.O., 1949.

BOARD OF TRADE, *Tendencies to Monopoly in the Cinematograph Film Industry*, H.M.S.O., 1944.

BROWNLOW, KEVIN, *How it Happened Here*, Secker and Warburg, 1968.

BRUNEL, ADRIAN, *Filmcraft: The Art of Picture Production*, George Newnes, 1933.

BUTLER, IVAN, *Cinema in Britain: an illustrated Survey*, Tantivy, 1973; U.S.A.: Barnes.

BUTLER, IVAN, *To Encourage the Art of the Film* (The story of the British Film Institute), Robert Hale, 1971.

CAMERON, A. C., *The Film in National Life:* Being the Report of an Enquiry conducted by the Commission on Educational and Cultural

Films into the Service which the Cinematograph may render to Education and Social Progress, Allen and Unwin, 1932.

CARRICK, EDWARD, *Art and Design in the British Film*, Dobson, 1948; U.S.A.: Arno, 1972 reprint.

CERAM, C. W., *The Archaeology of the Cinema*, Thames and Hudson, 1965; U.S.A.: Harcourt Brace Jovanovich, 1965.

COLLIER, JOHN W., *A Film in the Making* featuring *It Always Rains on Sunday*, World Film Publications, 1947.

CROSS, BRENDA (ed.), *The Film Hamlet*, Saturn Press, 1948.

DAVY, CHARLES (ed.), *Footnotes to the Film*, Lovat Dickson, 1938; U.S.A.: Arno.

DEANS, MARJORIE, *Meeting at the Sphinx* – Gabriel Pascal's production of Bernard Shaw's *Caesar and Cleopatra*, Macdonald, 1945.

DURDEN, J. V.; FIELD, MARY; SMITH, PERCY, *Cine-Biology*, 1941, *See How They Grow*, 1953, Penguin.

DURGNAT, RAYMOND, *A Mirror for England*, Faber, 1970; U.S.A.: Praeger, 1971.

FIELD, MARY, and SMITH, PERCY, *Secrets of Nature*, Faber, 1934.

FIELD, MARY, *Good Company*, Longmans Green, 1952.

GIBBON, MARK, *The Red Shoes Ballet: A Critical Study*, Saturn Press, 1968.

GIFFORD, DENNIS, *British Cinema: An Illustrated Guide and Index to 5000 Films*, Zwemmer, 1968; U.S.A.: Barnes.

GIFFORD, DENIS, *The British Film Catalogue 1895–1970*, David and Charles, 1973.

GREENE, GRAHAM *The Pleasure Dome: The Collected Film Criticism 1935–1940*, Secker and Warburg, 1972.

HALLIWELL, LESLIE, *The Filmgoer's Companion*, Paladin, 1972; U.S.A.: Hill & Wang, 1970.

HARDY, FORSYTH (ed.), *Grierson on Documentary*, Collins, 1946; U.S.A.: Praeger, 1972.

HENRY, ROBERT, *A Film Star in Belgrave Square*, Peter Davies, 1948.

HOME OFFICE AND MINISTRY OF EDUCATION, *Report of the Departmental Committee on Children and the Cinema*, H.M.S.O., 1950.

HOUSTON, PENELOPE, *The Contemporary Cinema*, Penguin, 1963.

HUNNINGS, NEVILLE MARCH, *Film Censors and the Law*, Allen and Unwin, 1967; U.S.A.: Fernhill.

HUNTLEY, JOHN, *British Film Music*, Skelton Robinson, 1947; U.S.A.: Arno, 1972 reprint.

HUNTLEY, JOHN, *British Technicolor Films*, Skelton Robinson, 1948.

JAMES, DAVID, *Scott of the Antarctic*, Convoy Publications, 1948.

KELLY, TERENCE; NORTON, GRAHAM; PERRY, GEORGE, *A Competitive Cinema*, Institute of Economic Affairs, 1966; U.S.A.: International Publications Service, 1966.

KNIGHT, DERRICK and PORTER, VINCENT, *A Long Look at Short Films*, ACTT Report, Pergamon Press, 1967.

LEE, NORMAN, *A Film is Born: Choose from Forty Careers in Film-Making*, Jordan, 1945.

LEE, NORMAN, *Log of a Film Director*, Quality, 1949.

LEJEUNE, C. A., *Chestnuts in Her Lap*, Phoenix House, 1947.

LINDGREN, ERNEST, *The Art of the Film*, Allen and Unwin, 1948; U.S.A.: Macmillan, 1963, revised edn.

LOVELL, ALAN and HILLIER, JIM, *Studies in Documentary*, Secker and Warburg, 1972; U.S.A.: Viking.

LOW, RACHEL, *The History of the British Film*:

  Vol. 1, *1896–1906*, Allen and Unwin, 1948 (with Roger Manvell).

  Vol. 2, *1906–1914*, Allen and Unwin, 1949.

  Vol. 3, *1914–1918*, Allen and Unwin, 1950.

  Vol. 4, *1918–1929*, Allen and Unwin, 1971.

MANVELL, ROGER, *The Animated Film*, Sylvan Press, 1954.

MANVELL, ROGER (ed.), *The Cinema 1950–1952*, Penguin.

MANVELL, ROGER, *Film*, Penguin, 1944, revised 1946.

MANVELL, ROGER, *The Film and the Public*, Penguin, 1955.

MANVELL, ROGER, *New Cinema in Britain*, Studio Vista, 1969; U.S.A.: Dutton.

MANVELL, ROGER, *Twenty Years of British Films 1925–1945*, Falcon Press, 1947; U.S.A.: Arno, 1972 reprint.

MAYER, J. P., *British Cinemas and Their Audiences* (Sociological Studies), Dennis Dobson, 1948.

MAYER, J. P., *Sociology of the Film*, Faber, 1946; U.S.A.: Arno, 1972 reprint.

MINNEY, R. J., *Talking of Films*, Home and Van Thal, 1947.

MONTAGU, IVOR, *Film World*, Penguin, 1964.

MOSLEY, LEONARD, *The Battle of Britain: The Making of the Film*, Weidenfeld and Nicolson, 1969; U.S.A.: Stein and Day.

MULLALLY, FREDERIC, *Films: an Alternative to Rank*, an analysis of power and policy in the British Film Industry, Socialist Book Centre, 1946.

NOBLE, PETER, *British Film Yearbook, 1945–6*, and *1947–8*, British Yearbooks.

OAKLEY, CHARLES, *Where We Came In*, George Allen and Unwin, 1964.

PEP, *The British Film Industry*, report on its history and present organization, with special reference to the economic problems of British feature film production, Political and Economical Planning, 1952.

POWELL, DILYS, *Films Since 1939*, The British Council, 1947.

POWELL, MICHAEL, *Two Hundred Thousand Feet on Foula*, Faber, 1938.

REISZ, KAREL, *The Technique of Film Editing*, Focal Press, revised edition 1968; U.S.A.: Amphoto.

RICHARDS, JEFFREY, *Visions of Yesterday*, Routledge & Kegan Paul, 1973.

RILLA, WOLF, *A–Z of Movie Making*, Studio Vista, 1970; U.S.A.: Viking.

342

ROBINSON, DAVID, *The Great Funnies: A History of Film Comedy*, Studio Vista, 1969; U.S.A.: Dutton.

ROTHA, PAUL, *Documentary Film* (3rd edition), Faber, 1952; U.S.A.: Hastings, 1964.

ROTHA, PAUL, *The Film Till Now*, Jonathan Cape, 1930, revised Vision Press, 1949.

ROTHA, PAUL. *Rotha on the Film: A selection of Writings about the Cinema*, Faber, 1958.

SADOUL, GEORGES, *British Creators of Film Technique*, British Film Institute, 1948.

SHARP, DENNIS, *The Picture Palace and Other Buildings for the Movies*, Hugh Evelyn, 1969; U.S.A.: Praeger.

SHIPMAN, DAVID, *The Great Movie Stars: The Golden Years*, Hamlyn, 1970; *The International Years*, Angus and Robertson, 1972; U.S.A.: Crown.

SPEED, F. MAURICE, *Film Review 1944*, continued annually Macdonald 1944–1965, W. H. Allen, 1966; U.S.A.: A. S. Barnes.

SPOTTISWOODE, RAYMOND, *Film and its Techniques*, Faber, 1951; U.S.A.: University of California Press.

SPRAOS, JOHN, *The Decline of the Cinema* (*An Economist's Report*), George Allen and Unwin, 1962.

THOMAS, D. B., *The First Colour Motion Pictures*, A Science Museum Monograph, H.M.S.O., 1969.

THOMAS, D. B., *The Origins of the Motion Picture*, A Science Museum Booklet, H.M.S.O., 1964.

TREVELYAN, JOHN, *What the Censor Saw*, Michael Joseph, 1973.

WALKER, ALEXANDER, *Hollywood, England*, Michael Joseph, 1974.

WINNGTON, RICHARD, *Drawn and Quartered*, Saturn Press, 1948.

WOOD, LESLIE, *The Miracle of the Movies*, Burke, 1947.

WRIGHT, BASIL, *The Uses of the Film*, Bodley Head, 1948; U.S.A.: Arno, 1972 reprint.

WRIGHT, BASIL, *The Long View*, Secker and Warburg, 1974.

Biography and Individual Studies

ACKLAND, RODNEY and GRANT, ELSPETH, *The Celluloid Mistress or The Custard Pie of Dr Caligari*, Allan Wingate, 1954.

ALLISTER, RAY, *Friese-Greene: Close-up of an Inventor*, Marsland Publications, 1948; U.S.A.: Arno, 1972 reprint.

BALCON, MICHAEL, *Michael Balcon Presents . . . A Lifetime of Films*, Hutchinson, 1969.

BARKER, FELIX, *The Oliviers: Biography*, Hamish Hamilton, 1953.

BARKER, FELIX, *The House that Stoll Built*, Frederick Muller, 1957.

BAXTER, JOHN, *An Appalling Talent*, (Ken Russell), Michael Joseph, 1974.

BRUNEL, ADRIAN, *Nice Work: Thirty Years in British Films*, Forbes Robertson, 1949.

BUTLER, IVAN, *The Cinema of Roman Polanski*, Zwemmer, 1970; U.S.A.; Barnes.

DALRYMPLE, IAN, *Sir Alexander Korda*, British Film Academy, 1956.

DANISCHEWSKY, M. (ed.), *Michael Balcon's 25 Years in Films*, World Film Publications, 1947.

DURGNAT, RAYMOND *The Strange Case of Alfred Hitchcock*, Faber, 1974.

FORBES, BRYAN, *Notes for a Life*, Collins, 1974.

HEPWORTH, CECIL M., *Came the Dawn: Memories of a Film Pioneer*, Phoenix House, 1951.

HINXMAN, MARGARET and D'ARCY, SUSAN, *The Films of Dirk Bogarde*, Literary Services, 1974.

LEAHY, JAMES, *The Cinema of Joseph Losey*, Zwemmer, 1967; U.S.A.; Barnes.

MILNE, TOM (ed.), *Losey on Losey*, Secker and Warburg, 1967.

NATIONAL FILM ARCHIVE, *Victor Saville*, booklet, British Film Institute, 1972.

NOBLE, PETER, *Anthony Asquith* (Index), British Film Institute, 1951.

NOBLE, PETER, *Hitchcock* (Index), British Film Institute, 1949.

PEARSON, GEORGE, *Flashback: Autobiography of a British Film-maker*, Allen and Unwin, 1957.

PERRY, GEORGE, *The Films of Alfred Hitchcock*, Studio Vista, 1965; U.S.A.: Dutton.

PERRY, GEORGE, *Hitchcock*, Macmillan, 1975; U.S.A. Doubleday.

PRATLEY, GERALD, *The Cinema of David Lean*, Tantivy, 1974.

SINGER, KURT, *The Charles Laughton Story*, Robert Hale, 1954.

SUSSEX, ELIZABETH, *Lindsay Anderson*, Studio Vista, 1969.

TABORI, PAUL, *Alexander Korda: A Biography*, Living Books (New York), 1966.

TENNYSON, CHARLES, *Penrose Tennyson*, privately published, 1943.

TREWIN, J. C., *Robert Donat: A Biography*, Heinemann, 1968.

TRUFFAUT, FRANCOIS, *Hitchcock*, Secker and Warburg, 1968; U.S.A.: Simon & Schuster.

TYNAN, KENNETH, *Alec Guinness*, Rockcliff, 1953.

WILCOX, HERBERT, *Twenty-five Thousand Sunsets* (Autobiography), The Bodley Head, 1967; U.S.A.: Barnes, 1969.

WOOD, ALAN, *Mr Rank: A Study of J. Arthur Rank and British Films*, Hodder and Stoughton, 1952.

Index

346

347

350

355